MW01252936

Reading Aristotle

Philosophia Antiqua

A SERIES OF STUDIES ON ANCIENT PHILOSOPHY

VOLUME 146

The titles published in this series are listed at *brill.com/pha*

Reading Aristotle

Argument and Exposition

Edited by

William Wians
Ron Polansky

BRILL

LEIDEN | BOSTON

Library of Congress Cataloging-in-Publication Data

Names: Wians, William Robert, editor. | Polansky, Ronald M., 1948- editor.
Title: Reading Aristotle : argument and exposition / edited by William Wians, Ron
      Polansky.
Description: Boston : Brill, 2017. | Series: Philosophia antiqua ; Volume 146 |
      Includes bibliographical references and index.
Identifiers: LCCN 2017023189 (print) | LCCN 2017024266 (ebook) |
      ISBN 9789004340084 (e-book) | ISBN 9789004329584 (hardback : alk. paper)
Classification: LCC B485 (ebook) | LCC B485 .R36 2017 (print) | DDC 185–dc23
LC record available at https://lccn.loc.gov/2017023189

Typeface for the Latin, Greek, and Cyrillic scripts: "Brill". See and download: brill.com/brill-typeface.

ISSN 0079-1687
ISBN 978-90-04-32958-4 (hardback)
ISBN 978-90-04-34008-4 (e-book)

Helen S. Lang
1947–2016

∴

Contents

Abbreviations

Cat.	*Categories*
Int.	*On Interpretation*
APr.	*Prior Analytics*
APo.	*Posterior Analytics*
Top.	*Topics*
Soph. El.	*Sophistical Refutations*
Phys.	*Physics*
Cael.	*On the Heavens*
GC	*On Generation and Corruption*
Mete.	*Meteorology*
An.	*On the Soul*
PN	*Parva Naturalia*
Sens.	*On the Senses*
Mem.	*On Memory*
Som.	*On Sleep*
Insom.	*On Dreams*
Div. Som.	*On Divination in Sleep*
Long. Vit.	*On Length and Shortness of Life*
Resp.	*On Breath*
HA	*History of Animals*
PA	*Parts of Animals*
MA	*Movement of Animals*
IA	*Progression of Animals*
GA	*Generation of Animals*
Probl.	*Problems*
Metaph.	*Metaphysics*
NE	*Nicomachean Ethics*
MM	*Magna Moralia*
EE	*Eudemian Ethics*
Pol.	*Politics*
Rhet.	*Rhetoric*
Poet.	*Poetics*

About the Contributors

Andrea Falcon

is Associate Professor of Philosophy at Concordia University, Montreal. He is the author of *Corpi e Movimenti: Il "De caelo" di Aristotele e la sua tradizione nel mondo antico* (Naples, 2001), *Aristotle and the Science of Nature: Unity without Uniformity* (Cambridge, 2005), and *Xenarchus of Seleucia and Aristotelianism in the First Century BCE* (Cambridge, 2011). He is especially interested in how Aristotle integrates a plurality of investigations—as in the different physical writings—into a single explanatory project.

Edward C. Halper

is Distinguished Research Professor of Philosophy at the University of Georgia. He has published two books on the problem of the one and the many in Aristotle's *Metaphysics* and is now completing a third volume on its final books. His textbook for students on Aristotle's *Metaphysics* has recently appeared. Halper has also published another book and some fifty papers in academic journals and books, many on Aristotle, others on a wide variety of philosophers and philosophical issues.

Malcolm Heath

is Professor of Greek Language and Literature at Leeds University. He works in many areas of Greek poetry and rhetoric, and ancient and modern literary theory. He is author of seven books as well as numerous articles, including a translation of Aristotle's *Poetics* (Penguin Classics, 1996) and *Ancient Philosophical Poetics* (Cambridge, 2013). He has recently completed *Poetical Animals: Aristotle, Anthropology and Poetry*, and is working on a theoretical commentary on Aristotle's *Poetics*.

Helen S. Lang

received her Ph.D. from the University of Toronto and was until her death Professor of Philosophy at Villanova University. She was a Senior Fellow at the Dibner Institute for the History of Science and Technology, MIT and a Fellow at the Institute for Advanced Study, Princeton. In addition to numerous articles, she published *Aristotle's Physics and its Medieval Varieties* (Albany, 1992), *The Order of Nature in Aristotle's Physics* (Cambridge, 1998), and (with A.D. Macro) *Proclus: de Aeternitate Mundi* (Berkeley, 2001).

Mariska Leunissen

is Associate Professor at the University of North Carolina at Chapel Hill. She is the author of *Explanation and Teleology in Aristotle's Science of Nature* (Cambridge, 2010) and several articles on Aristotle's theory of demonstration, natural science, and the relationship between his natural science and political science. In 2010–2011, she was a fellow at Harvard University's Center for Hellenic Studies in Washington, D.C.

Thornton C. Lockwood

is Associate Professor of Philosophy at Quinnipiac University. He has published articles on Aristotle's *Nicomachean Ethics* and *Politics* in *Phronesis, Journal of the History of Philosophy, History of Political Thought, Archiv für Geschichte der Philosophie, Ancient Philosophy*, and *Oxford Bibliographies Online*. He is Associate Editor at *POLIS: The Journal of Ancient Greek Political Thought*.

Ron Polansky

is Chair of the Department of Philosophy at Duquesne University. He has been editor of the journal *Ancient Philosophy* for thirty-six years. He is the author of *Aristotle's "De anima": A Commentary* (Cambridge, 2007) and *Philosophy and Knowledge: A Commentary on Plato's Theaetetus* (Bucknell, 1992), and has edited the *Cambridge Companion to Aristotle's Nicomachean Ethics* (Cambridge, 2014). He has published numerous articles and reviews on ancient philosophy. He has co-edited with Mark Kuczewski *Bioethics: Ancient Themes in Contemporary Issues* (MIT, 2000).

Vasilis Politis

studied in Oxford and has taught at Trinity College Dublin since 1992, where he is a Fellow of the College and Director of the Plato Centre. His main project in recent years has been the place of *aporia* in philosophical inquiry, especially in Plato but also in Aristotle. His book *The Structure of Inquiry in Plato's Early Dialogues* has been published by Cambridge.

Diana Quarantotto

is Lecturer in History of Ancient Philosophy at the University of Rome "La Sapienza". Many of her publications seek to uncover dimensions of Aristotelian textuality: *Causa finale sostanza essenza in Aristotele. Saggio sulla struttura dei processi teleologici naturali e sulla funzione del* telos (Naples, 2005); "Dalla diversità per specie alle condizioni di possibilità dell'essenza: Aristotele, *Metaphysica* X 8, 9,10" (2004); "*Metaphysica* Iota 8–9: le cose diverse per specie e lo status dei principi" (2005), "Il dialogo dell'anima (di Aristotele) con se stessa. *Problemata* l'indagine e l'opera" (2014).

Jun Su

received his Ph.D. from Trinity College Dublin. He is a lecturer in the Department of Philosophy, Faculty of Humanities, at China University of Political Science and Law. His main areas of research interest are Platonic and Aristotelian
metaphysics and epistemology. He was an Irish Research Council Scholar
(2014–2016). In 2012/13, He was a Newman Fellow at the Trinity Plato Centre.
He has published several articles both in English and in Chinese. He is currently
working on the argumentative structure of Aristotle's *Metaphysics* Theta.

Philip van der Eijk

is Alexander von Humboldt Professor of Classics and History of Science at
the Humboldt University Berlin. He has published widely on ancient philosophy (especially Aristotelian philosophy), medicine and science, patristics and
comparative literature, including work on the formal and rhetorical aspects
of ancient scientific texts. Publications include *Aristoteles. De insomniis. De
divinatione per somnum* (Berlin, 1994), "Towards a rhetoric of ancient scientific discourse: Some formal characteristics of Greek medical and philosophical
texts" (1997), and "Galen and the scientific treatise" (2013).

William Wians

is Professor Philosophy at Merrimack College and adjunct professor at Boston
College. He has edited *Aristotle's Philosophical Development: Problems and Prospects* (Rowman and Littlefield, 1996), and *Logos and Muthos: Philosophical
Essays in Greek Literature* (SUNY Press, 2009; a second volume is in preparation)
and is co-editor of the *Proceedings of the Boston Area Colloquium in Ancient Philosophy*. His approach to exposition in Aristotle is developed in articles including "The Beginnings of the *Metaphysics*" (2012); "The Philosopher's Knowledge
of Non-Contradiction" (2006); and "Aristotle, Demonstration, and Teaching"
(1989).

Marco Zingano

is Professor of Ancient Philosophy at the University of São Paulo, Brazil; from
1984 to 2001 he was Professor of Ancient Philosophy at the University of Rio
Grande do Sul. Major publications are *Estudos de Ética Antiga* (São Paulo, 2007)
and a translation, with introduction and commentary, of Books I 13–III 8 of
Nicomachean Ethics (2008). He has also published several papers and articles
related to Aristotelian ethics, psychology, metaphysics, and logic.

Introduction

William Wians and Ron Polansky

Growing numbers of scholars have in recent years begun to approach an Aristotelian treatise not as a disconnected compilation of often tentative and exploratory arguments, but as a progressive unfolding of a unified position that may extend over one of its books, the entire treatise, or even across several works. *Reading Aristotle: Argument and Exposition* seeks to build on and focus this trend. The twelve original essays commissioned for this collection demonstrate that the key to understanding many major Aristotelian doctrines and writings lies in the recognition that Aristotle employs not just explanatory principles in composing his works, but expository principles as well.

Explanatory principles include familiar Aristotelian doctrines such as the four causes, the priority of actuality over potentiality, and the principle that nature does nothing in vain. We are convinced that equally pervasive—though much less appreciated—are what we call expository principles. These derive from Aristotle's convictions about such matters as proper sequence and pedagogical method, the equivocity of key explanatory terms, and the need scrupulously to observe distinctions between the different sciences.

Expository principles carry direct implications for the way in which both individual arguments and whole treatises should be read. Rather than displaying a tentative working out of issues, compiled by Aristotle or later editors with little if any regard for a larger unity, Aristotle's works should be read (at least in most cases) as being designed by Aristotle to present material in what he took to be the most epistemologically compelling and pedagogically useful order, including at each stage of the exposition the considered choice of the form of argument to employ and cognizance of the degree to which an initial problem was resolved. We contend that Aristotle's philosophical positions and supporting arguments require attending to expository principles for their full comprehension. This, we believe, gives compelling significance to the familiar assertion that Aristotle moves from what is more intelligible to us to what is more intelligible by nature. Rather than presuming that his considered view is disclosed in any single passage, early or late in a treatise, we instead suggest that it must be sought in the progressive unfolding of the investigation over which it extends. Because of the care Aristotle takes in crafting the presentation of his views, one must attend to both argument and exposition in reading his works. "Argument and Exposition", as our subtitle implies, must be read together, and crucially with the former in light of the latter.

© KONINKLIJKE BRILL NV, LEIDEN, 2017 | DOI: 10.1163/9789004340084_002

Attending to the larger expository context of Aristotelian arguments avoids a tendency—and we would say shortcoming—shared by the two dominant methods of interpreting Aristotle during the twentieth century. Especially in the first half of the century, many scholars viewed the treatises and their parts as products of different and often conflicting stages of Aristotle's philosophical development, assembled in many cases after Aristotle's death by sometimes incompetent or overly pious editors. From this perspective, apparent contradictions in the corpus could be explained as the result of different developmental stages. This is a familiar story not in need of retelling.[1] In reaction to the excesses of chronological and developmental treatments, other scholars focused on the rigorous analysis of individual arguments, free of developmental assumptions. Nevertheless, these interpreters also identified many tensions and inconsistencies between arguments from different treatises or different parts of a single treatise, just as those emphasizing development had. And as many developmentalists had done, analytic interpreters often regarded the treatises as being shaped or compiled by later editors—only in this case of what originally had been working drafts and tentative explorations rather than dogmatic products from different stages of Aristotle's development.[2]

At stake between the two approaches was the way that Aristotle can and should be read: as a dogmatic thinker passing through distinct phases and positions, or as an anti-dogmatist dedicated to open-ended philosophizing, who tolerates multiple senses of terms, conditional explorations, and a studied lack of closure. Yet while allowing for their differences, the two approaches shared a crucial tendency. Despite—or perhaps because of—the close attention each party paid to individual arguments (and readers of Aristotle have learned much from their efforts), both displayed a corresponding neglect of the larger context. Both approaches, we would charge, tended to concentrate on small argumentative units and to rule out of court any appeal to the larger context of an exposition. Indeed, both might be said to deny, though for different reasons, the reality of a larger context at all.[3]

---

1 A summary of developmental approaches and reactions to them can be found in Wians ed. 1996.

2 Allegations of meddling and malfeasance by Aristotle's editors are common in the literature. A useful tonic with regard to one work can be found in Menn 1995.

3 This is not to deny the importance of the well-known cruxes that gave rise to developmentalist interpretations in the first place, nor is it to suggest that hard details of specific arguments may be skimmed over while focusing on a larger expository picture: textual unitarians face temptations of their own in approaching Aristotle's works, a point noted in Wians 2012.

There is surely an alternative. Guided by the hermeneutical caution that differences in perspective or position should not be attributed too readily (not to say reflexively) to developmental shifts, logical inconsistency, or editorial intervention, the contributors to this collection may collectively be regarded as maintaining that in reading the *corpus Aristotelicum*, the interpreter should attend as carefully to the unfolding stages of an Aristotelian exposition as to the structure of its arguments. Each science, for Aristotle, has its own "causes and principles and elements" (*aitiai kai archai kai stoicheia*). While always sensitive to the distinctions between the sciences and their different sorts of principles, Aristotle does not typically start from principles—and certainly not principles in a fully stated form—in a particular investigation. Rather, he works toward their establishment, moving (broadly speaking) from what is more intelligible initially to what is truly more intelligible as such. Revealing an appreciation that one must move judiciously in this difficult terrain, the progress toward principles often proceeds through what predecessors have said, through *aporiai* (perplexities), and through clarifying complex and ambiguous notions by closely attending to the many ways in which a thing is spoken. What contributors to this volume emphasize is the extent to which the organized pursuit of principles is carefully and deliberately structured both at the level of fine detail and across the unfolding exposition. A carefully crafted pursuit of principles can occupy a significant portion of a treatise, giving a work and its particular arguments their distinctive character. Arguments offered in the course of the larger exposition must be judged in relation to the context within which they are placed and with the reasons why they are being treated in the manner that they are where they are.

Put in a more Aristotelian way, "argument" can be spoken of in many ways, so that argument in Aristotle can range from the frustratingly telegraphic and enthymematic to the broad sense in which one may speak of the "argument" of an entire work, such as the argument of the *De Anima* or the *Nicomachean Ethics*. We would contend that even at the smallest unit of argument what we are calling expository principles have implications for interpretation, and generally argument in Aristotle cannot be properly understood without sensitivity to the deployment of the full range of expository principles that shape the argument of a treatise and the arguments within it. At no level of analysis can expository principles be ignored.

A prominent feature of our approach is to take very seriously the idea of the treatises as pedagogical, though in a way quite different from the formulation by Barnes 1975 in his classic article about the logical treatises. Barnes argued that demonstration provided a formal model for imparting achieved knowledge. But because the treatises contained few if any demonstrations, he continued to regard the works of the corpus as tentative and unsystematic. We, in contrast, find in the treatises a steady concern with teaching—in particular, with imparting the knowledge in the most epistemologically compelling order needed to transform the student into an expert.[4] Just as much as the treatises investigate principles, they aim to bring the student into possession of the science by inducing a grasp of those principles and the recognition of them *as* principles. As Aristotle puts it in *Posterior Analytics* I 2, one who has scientific understanding must recognize the cause *as* the cause. In this way the treatises lead the learner along the route to understanding. At the same time (though very seldom appreciated), that which is most familiar is also an obstacle to gaining understanding, as *Metaphysics* II 3 points out.[5] Therefore, in their functioning as pedagogical instruments, the treatises seem designed to be challenging. They are contrived to force the student—and the reader—to unpack their concentrated thought. The effort required fully to enter into the way Aristotle sets out a field is meant to lead to the reader's secure assimilation of the principles and what follows from them.

A more particular way to signal what is distinctive about our approach is to draw attention—as we have just done in the previous sentences—to the demands placed on the reader. Contrary to the old saw that the corpus consists of lecture notes, the treatises as we encounter them are so compressed and requiring of commentary that it appears unlikely that they were meant for oral presentation. Rather it seems more plausible that they were school materials, which would be copied, read, and discussed. Given the challenging approach taken by Aristotle in his writing, constant attention must be extended to his manner of composition as well as to the content of what he is saying. The clues offered by Aristotle to the structure of a treatise are usually very succinct, which is perhaps why their full import has often not been properly appreciated. Yet only by way of such attention do the treatises illuminate their fields as Aristotle intended.[6]

Our approach is not without its precedents, of course.[7] Our contributors take such earlier work as their foundation, extending previous insights over a

---

4   Barnes's position was criticized from this very perspective by Burnyeat 1981 and Wians 1989.

5   A point emphasized in the final section of Wians 2012.

6   Polansky 2007 emphasizes the careful arrangement and placement within natural philosophy of the *De Anima*.

7   Kahn 1963, 16, with notes 45 and 46, for example, offered trenchant observations about what he termed the progressive exposition of the *De Anima* and *Parva Naturalia*, along with a few highly suggestive remarks about the motivations behind Aristotle's general expository methods. Owen's influential paper on *phainomena* in Aristotle has given rise to a whole

wider range of texts than has been common. Thus, the collection covers most of the main works in the Aristotelian corpus, while also shedding light on some obscure and neglected texts.[8] In some cases there emerge ways to read an entire treatise or series of treatises;[9] in other cases there is the working out of the way to read one or more sections of a treatise in relation to the entire work of which it forms a part.[10] A treatment of issues raised earlier in a treatise may be preliminary or deliberately incomplete, left in need of later elaboration and supplementation. The argument of a later section may follow from explanatory principles guiding the exposition as a whole, but will at the same time develop and articulate those principles and key terms and concepts beyond what had been stated or even implied by the arguments at earlier stages of the inquiry.[11] In other cases, contributors concentrate not on a single work, but on a major

---

area of scholarship devoted to the question of dialectic in Aristotle. In a "map" that is both focused in its attention and broad in its implications, Burnyeat 2001 provides a guide to the exposition of the work by utilizing textual signposts to follow what seems a most tortuous line of argument in *Metaphysics* VII. A second example dealing with the *Metaphysics* is the comprehensive reading of the treatise as a unified text in Menn 2015a. Finally, contributor Helen Lang, to whom the collection is dedicated, took just this approach in her book devoted to the unfolding and unified exposition of the *Physics* and *De Caelo*.

8   Among less frequently discussed treatises, Quarantotto uses a careful reading of the *Problemata* as the basis for deeper insights into the construction of the *De Caelo* and biological works, while van der Eijk concentrates on the structure and argument of several of the works making up the *Parva Naturalia*. Falcon reinforces his conclusions about the *De Motu Animalium* with an extended discussion of the *Progression of Animals*.

9   Thus Lang, in her contribution to the collection, is able to conclude that body is a "special attribute" that functions at a generic level in physics through her analysis of the structure of the *Physics* and *De Caelo*.

10   Leunissen argues that Aristotle's puzzling tendency, as in *De Caelo* II, to posit principles while postponing their proof—propositions she terms "surrogate principles"—reflects his desire to preserve the proper order of exposition, even when it would seem to leave an explanation at a particular point in the treatise wanting. Politis and Su argue that the concept of *ousia* advanced in *Metaphysics* IV 1–2 must be understood in light of *aporiai* in book III that prepare for it, puzzles that themselves arise out of the unanalyzed concept of *ousia* used in book I.

11   Wians's paper takes just this approach to the question of parental resemblance in *Generation of Animals* I and IV. Lockwood places Aristotle's apparently negative evaluation of history in *Poetics* 9 in the context of an exposition extending across several chapters meant to clarify the nature of poetic mimesis rather than to denigrate historical studies. Heath, seeking to determine Aristotle's answer to the question of the best kind of tragedy, counters a familiar conclusion regarding *Poetics* 13 by identifying the argument as a stage in a larger sequence concluded only in *Poetics* 14.

Aristotelian theme relevant to several works. Other contributors pay particular attention to the type and nature of the argument employed. At a minimum (and subject to much attention in the literature), one must ask whether the argument aspires to meet the strictures of demonstration, and therefore (a question asked less often) whether it should be judged by these standards. If not, then rather than being formally inadequate or otherwise inferior, the argument may be a *logikos* proof or one of the other non-demonstrative forms that Aristotle frequently employs. But if so, why, and why at that point in the treatise?[12] And because an Aristotelian demonstration depends on principles that define its science and scope, one must ask what sort of principles does an argument invoke or rely on—physical, ethical, or theoretical? For Aristotle insists that properly scientific arguments cannot cross between sciences demarcated by essentially different principles, except in some relatively minor cases.[13] In these different but complementary ways the papers presented here emphasize what one contributor terms the "large-scale architecture" of a treatise,[14] while also attending to the order, nature, and interaction between argument and exposition.

In combination, we believe that the different treatments offered here will show why paying attention to the expository principles Aristotle employs is as important for illuminating the texts of the corpus as is concentrating on arguments and doctrines. Indeed, it is our conviction that no proper interpretation can ignore them. *Reading Aristotle: Argument and Exposition* aims to offer exemplary instances of an appreciation of Aristotle's often subtle and significant manner of setting out his thought. In doing so we hope it will inspire readings of Aristotle's texts that open new lines of interpretation of the corpus.

---

12   Zingano's contribution opens the collection with a painstaking delineation of *logikos* argument in comparison to other non-demonstrative argument forms, examining how such forms are employed in and serve to shape the *Posterior Analytics*, *De Caelo*, *Physics*, and especially *Metaphysics*, among other works. Halper draws the *Physics* close to the *Posterior Analytics* by arguing that the former—and by extension Aristotle's other scientific works—are inquiries in line with the search for causes described in *Posterior Analytics* II.

13   Polansky argues that the *Nicomachean Ethics* is throughout designed to be a practical treatise relying entirely on practical arguments and principles rather than theoretical arguments or principles, as often contended. In considering the most important and controversial-seeming exception to Aristotle's prohibition against kind-crossing, Falcon uses the opening lines of *De Motu Animalium* in combination with the curriculum map at the start of the *Meteorology* to place *De Motu* firmly within the sequence of Aristotle's natural science and to show by this means what can be learned about Aristotle's multi-leveled explanatory project as a whole.

14   The phrase comes from Heath, in this volume.

CHAPTER 1

Ways of Proving in Aristotle*

Marco Zingano

Abstract

Aristotle usually contrasts proving φυσικῶς with proving λογικῶς. In many cases, the former carries the real burden of the proof, with the latter being a kind of introduction or preparatory argument to it. And as arguing λογικῶς is sometimes assimilated to proving dialectically and in a vacuous way, there is a tendency to look at λογικοί arguments with some diffidence. But Aristotle has a much more complex use for these expressions, and marking λογικοί arguments with the negative note of dialecticity or vacuity will surely lead to serious misunderstanding of key passages in Aristotle's treatises. For instance, Aristotle also contrasts ἀναλυτικοί arguments with λογικοί arguments in his logical works, and taking the latter as *dialectical* arguments will certainly miss the point, for they are considered good arguments, and no dialectical argument is adequate for a logical treatise. But more interestingly, there are also cases in which proving λογικῶς gets the point perfectly well and is only to be complemented by a φυσικός argument. These cases of λογικός argument are particularly salient in metaphysics. As a matter of fact, we find in Aristotle a variety of ways of proving a point: proving it in a geometrical fashion, or mathematically, or medically, and so on. The λογικοί and φυσικοί arguments are the best known (and to a certain extent disputable) cases of a much larger family of ways of proving a point. I examine these different ways of proving, and attempt a general account of the relationships among them.

We find in Aristotle a variety of terms to designate appropriate ways of proving a point. He mentions proving μαθηματικῶς in mathematics, and φυσικῶς in physics.[1] But we also find in the *Analytics* an ἀναλυτικῶς way of proving. More-

---

* An ancestor of this paper was published in the *Festschrift* to María Isabel Santa Cruz, *Eunoia—estudios de filosofía antigua* (Colombia 2009, 439–470), under the title of "Provar *logikôs, phusikôs, analytikôs* em Aristóteles". The present study contains a broader survey of the topic, and revises some of the claims made in that first version.

1 For the sake of clarity, I shall generally refer adverbially to these ways of proving. By "λογικῶς argument" one is required to read something like "an argument that proceeds λογικῶς". The

---

over, the *Topics* explicates dialectic as a way of persuasion based on reputable opinions, and provides parallel διαλεκτικῶς proofs of points demonstrated ἀναλυτικῶς in the *Analytics*. More importantly, Aristotle often refers to proving λογικῶς in his treatises, and some of those proofs seem to bear the main burden of the demonstration, most notably in the *Metaphysics*. In some passages, however, λογικῶς arguments are deemed bad and void arguments. Platonic dialectic is characterized as unsound, and dismissed as useless. To complicate matters further, the *Metaphysics* argues ἐλεγκτικῶς as a way of proving the principle of non-contradiction. Proving ἐλεγκτικῶς cannot but remind us of dialectical procedure. Is it a special case of proving διαλεκτικῶς brought forward in the *Topics*? And how is it to be related to the λογικῶς proofs one finds in the *Metaphysics*?

Aristotle is not only at pains to distinguish different types of argument, but he is also deeply concerned about problems that arise when one mixes these different types of proof. Besides being invalid, or being valid but leading to an irrelevant conclusion, he is concerned about an argument that:

> Comes to a conclusion relevant to what was proposed, but yet not in accordance with the appropriate study (and this is when it appears to be medical though it is not medical, or geometrical though it is not geometrical, or dialectical though it is not dialectical [ὅταν μὴ ὢν ἰατρικὸς δοκῇ ἰατρικὸς εἶναι, ἢ γεωμετρικὸς μὴ ὢν γεωμετρικός, ἢ διαλεκτικὸς μὴ ὢν διαλεκτικός]), whether what follows is false or true.
>
> *Topics* VIII 12.162b7–11, SMITH trans.

These are bad arguments, which are to be banned from a well-formed discourse. I examine the ways of proving in accordance with the appropriate study, and attempt a general account of the relationships among them. I focus on the most controversial one: proving λογικῶς.

Most of the papers in this collection deal with explanatory arguments, attempting to show that Aristotle progressively unfolds his positions by various strategies, so that explanation emerges as different pieces fit into a large expository stratagem. The papers typically work with larger contexts, in order to deploy the whole series of steps in the arguments. They thus avoid developmental interpretations that explain away apparent conflicting passages, or that merely focus on very short arguments, so that conflicts do not arise. The

---

same is true for the other types of arguments: φυσικῶς, ἀναλυτικῶς, μαθηματικῶς, διαλεκτικῶς, and ἐλεγκτικῶς arguments.

approach I use here is complementary. I try to show that for scientific explanation Aristotle may tackle the issue either in a broader and more general way, or in precise and minute detail. His choice depends on what data are available, how the discipline is to be construed, and which theories he is targeting. My approach is also context sensitive. Yet the contrast between arguing λογικῶς and a proof that is specific to its domain, on which I focus, is rather a methodological tool of Aristotle. This methodological tool may be apprehended independently of any context, but the way it is to be applied in a given explanation will be shown to be crucially context dependent. It takes on the color of its subject matter, while remaining the same general tool. Moreover, a clear understanding of the way arguing λογικῶς operates in metaphysics requires—or so will I argue—a developmental perspective, given that metaphysics undergoes a major change in Aristotle's thought, and this change has direct consequences for the way this methodological tool is to be applied. But as a whole the contrast between λογικῶς and proper arguments remains complementary to explanatory arguments, with no developmental agenda, as it is a methodological tool for scientific explanations.

I

Some of the arguments Aristotle employs in his texts are characterized as proving a point λογικῶς. Different translations have been proposed for this term: in a dialectical manner,[2] in a logical manner,[3] in a general way,[4] in a formal way,[5] or in a verbal manner,[6] to mention the most common. Those terms are not synonyms, to say the least; and the variety of translations is a clear sign

---

2   E.g., Ross 1924, 168; 1936, 540; Kirwan 1993, 88–89.

3   E.g., Williams 1982, 65–66; Ferejohn 1994, 292; Bostock 1994, 86; Smith 1997, 91–92; Peramatzis 2010, 124.

4   E.g., Barnes 1993, 173.

5   E.g., Frede and Patzig 1988. They translate it at *Metaphysics* z 4.1029b13 by "rein formale Bermerkungen", taking it to refer to an enquiry devoted to the way we speak, the concepts we employ, in contrast with investigations that focus on the contents of a given scientific field. They distinguish the "rein formal" enquiry from a "bloss formal" one, the latter taking on a pejorative sense, and comment: "jedoch bestreitet Aristoteles keineswegs die Wichtigkeit solcher formalen Analysen; man muss sich darüber in klaren sein, dass sie durch inhaltliche Überlegungen ergänzt werden müssen und vor allem nicht anderen Stellen treten können" (II 59).

6   E.g., Woods 1982, 69–70.

of a problem of interpretation.[7] Yet arguing λογικῶς enters passages that are crucial to setting out some of Aristotle's main metaphysical tenets. What are such arguments? When does he resort to them, and what distinguishes them from other types of argument?

Often λογικῶς arguments are accompanied by other sorts of argument; these other arguments may be said to be φυσικῶς arguments. We should distinguish the λογικῶς arguments that thus come alongside other types of argument from λογικῶς arguments that come just on their own. When alone they are seen as dialectical in a negative sense, that is, as empty of content, and this has led to supposing that they are always vacuous, even when accompanied by the other sorts of arguments. But these different situations of arguing λογικῶς are not to be conflated, for there is a positive use of arguing λογικῶς. We should be sensitive to the different arrangements: arguing λογικῶς apart from other sorts of arguments is empty, whereas such argumentation alongside other types of arguments carries weight. Whether λογικῶς arguments carry the point within the set of arguments or only give support to the other arguments, λογικῶς arguments in conjunction with other arguments will perform some positive task, in sharp contrast to those λογικῶς arguments appearing apart from other sorts of reasoning.

The λογικῶς arguments in their positive usage are still to be contrasted with arguments based on premises proper to the fields in which they occur. Λογικῶς arguments go alongside arguments that are appropriate to the subject matter of the proof. Since for the most part the arguments to which λογικῶς arguments are contrasted are φυσικῶς arguments, one may be tempted to say that φυσικῶς arguments are scientific arguments.[8] But this ignores the fact that physics is

---

7   As Lewis 2013, 29 puts it, "the use of the term λογικῶς by Aristotle, not to mention his commentators, is complex, and invites controversy". Worthwhile discussions are found in Mosquera 1998, Burnyeat 2001, 19–24, Chiba 2011, Peramatzis 2010, and Lemaire 2015. Chiba 2011, 204 summarizes his analyses of this notion carried out in his book *Aristotle on the Possibility of Metaphysics: Complementary Development between Dialectic and Natural Philosophy* (Keiso Shobo 2002), of which I was unable to get a copy.

8   As in Charles 2000, 286, who is representative of a widespread position: "I construe '*logikos*' as referring to a manner of proceeding which is based on considerations of a general kind, not based on principles particular to a given science or subject matter (cf. *APo.* I 21.82b35 with Barnes's note). By contrast, considerations are '*phusikos*' if they are specific to a given subject matter". There are some unexpected consequences for this position; for instance, the λογικῶς considerations with which *Metaphsyics* VII 4 opens the discussion of the essence have a φυσικῶς counterpart in VII 7–9, but these chapters only seem to be inserted artificially into the discussion of essence, though from this perspective they should be doing the main

not the only theoretical science. Besides physics, there are also mathematics and first philosophy, and each of them may have its proper argument, against which λογικῶς arguments are to be weighed. If one translates φυσικῶς simply as *scientific*, and takes it for granted that a φυσικῶς argument is a scientific argument, one does away with other sciences considered genuine by Aristotle.

There is a philosophical discipline that investigates being as such—first philosophy (or metaphysics)—and this discipline provides arguments that are valid for every specific science of being. Its arguments necessarily go further than the limits of each of those sciences. Physics, for instance, studies that which has within itself a principle of motion and rest. Metaphysical arguments apply to physics, but not as proper physical arguments. One may thus think that metaphysical arguments, when applied to other fields, play the role of λογικῶς arguments, and that λογικῶς arguments have their origin in metaphysics. Actually, arguments will be λογικῶς whenever there are distinct epistemological levels among its premises. Such different levels may occur within specific sciences; for example, biology may seek support from a premise from general physics, as explaining the falling of leaves by appeal to the general principle that heavy bodies fall. Hence λογικῶς arguments are not necessarily metaphysical arguments applied to other fields.[9] However, there remains the question whether metaphysics operates at such a general level that it will unavoidably be pervaded by λογικῶς arguments, such that being a metaphysical argument would be a sufficient condition for being a λογικῶς argument.

II

Let us illustrate the negative side of a λογικῶς argument. In a well-known passage of the *Eudemian Ethics*, Aristotle criticizes the Platonic Form of Good. After having presented what he takes to be the Form of Good—the Form of Good is the first of goods and is by its presence the cause of the other goods' being good—he bids farewell not only to it, but to any Form whatsoever, dismissing them because "the existence of any Form not only of good but of anything else is affirmed λογικῶς καὶ κενῶς" (*EE* I 8.1217b20–21). This is surely not

scientific investigation of essence. See Ferejohn 1994, for whom the final answer in VII 10–11 gathers together the λογικῶς and the φυσικῶς trends.

9 See Mosquera 1998. According to him, λογικῶς arguments are those arguments (a) whose universality exceeds the genus at issue, and (b) as such belong to metaphysics as the science of contraries. Thesis (a) is uncontroversial, but (b) does not seem to be a necessary condition for an argument to be λογικῶς, and neither is it a sufficient condition.

a positive assessment: κενῶς means *in an empty way*, and this negative meaning is carried over into λογικῶς, which cannot adequately be rendered by *logical*, for it is negatively characterized. And it is so characterized because something went astray, and so terribly astray that, in *Posterior Analytics*, Aristotle, as he also bids farewell to the Forms, declares them to be *mere babbling* (*APo*. 83a33: τερετίσματα).

But what went wrong? Aristotle distinguishes between two groups of predecessors. On the one side are the *physiologoi*, for whom the principles of the universe are the material elements from which everything else is composed. On the other side stand those for whom formal principles have more explanatory power than the material elements. The second group are also referred to as "the thinkers of the present day", whereas the philosophers of the first group are referred to as "the old philosophers". To present day thinkers notably belong Plato and his companions. In *Metaphysics* XII 1.1069a25–30, Aristotle introduces them in an apparently favorable light. The old philosophers sought the principles and causes of substance, as do the philosophers of the present day. However, the old philosophers ranked particular things as substances, whereas the thinkers of the present day posit universals as substances. The same contrast is made in *Metaphysics* VII 2.1028b16–27. There Aristotle says that the philosophers of the present day think that the limits of the body—surface, line, point, and unit—are more substances than body or the solid. Plato takes the Form as principle and cause of the particular sensible substances which imitate it. Plato ranked the Form of x as the first x and that by the presence of which the other xs are x. Aristotle explains that the Platonists rank universals as substances and the principles and causes of the sensible substances because they think that *genera*—what is common to particular substances—are substances more than the particular sensible things. And they proceeded in this way owing to their arguing λογικῶς (XII 1.1069a28).

For Aristotelian metaphysics does also look for what is common to particular things, their form. However, Aristotelian forms are close to the individuals of which they are the forms. Beneath a form there is no other common predicate that characterizes a thing as what it is, but only individuals; above it there are genera and even wider universals that can be applied to various forms.[10]

---

10 Universal is defined in VII 13 as that which naturally belongs to more than one thing. Accidents are in this sense typically universal; even if a specific shade of color happens to occur only in Socrates, it can always also belong to another body—it is only by accident that it belongs only to one individual. Form, however, is what is peculiar to a certain set of objects (VII 13.1038b10, ἡ ἴδιος ἑκάστῳ, following Aᵇ and taking ἕκαστον as referring not necessarily to a token, but more likely to a type). Such a set cannot be null, if there is a

Plato seemed to go in the other direction: the more universal a term is, the more substantial it is. The most universal terms are *being* and *one*, so these are the most genuine substance (see, e.g., *Metaph.* III 6.1003a5–12; V 3.1014b9–14; VII 16.1040b21–27; X 2.1053b16–21). Aristotle has a double diagnosis; Plato was right to search for something above individuals as their cause and principle, but he went too far in taking as cause and principle what is most universal. Since the substance of something is proper to it and distinguishes it from all the rest, *being* and *one* cannot be substances, for they are common to everything.

One must keep to some sort of universality, shunning any excess, for being is knowable, and one can only know what is universal. But universality can be spelled out in many ways. We must draw a line between a sound universal, with counterpart in the world, and a universal with no real counterpart. Are there horses, or Appaloosas, or are there animals, living beings, or rather Being? No response comes from the concepts themselves; one has to scrutinize nature itself, and see that horses graze and breed together, Appaloosas and Norfolk Trotters alike, but not with cattle or baboons.

A passage in *De Generatione et Corruptione* may help us determine how not to go astray. In I 2, after having praised Democritus for being the only philosopher who applied himself to examine the conditions under which alteration or growth is attributed to things, Aristotle asks himself whether the primary things are divisible or indivisible magnitudes, and, if they are indivisible magnitudes, as one would expect, whether they are bodies, as Democritus maintained, or planes, as is asserted in the *Timaeus* (315b30). According to Aristotle, the response Plato gave leads to many absurdities, for those who divide bodies as if they were planes are in many respects in contradiction with mathematics, and, more importantly, there are many attributes necessarily present in physical bodies that are necessarily absent from those indivisibles. For instance, as it is argued in *De Caelo* III 1, planes are composed of lines, and lines of points. Now, point has no weight, and so neither do lines; if the lines have none, neither have the planes. Therefore, no body has weight (299a30); but this is an absurdity. Hence it is better to assert that there are indivisible bodies. For it is

---

form at all, but it can have only one element—as in the case of sun or moon. Or it may have many and even uncountable members, as in the case of human. The language of form is non-committal about the extension of the set it constitutes, except that the set cannot be null. The point seems thus to be that form is not universal in the sense that universals naturally belong to more than one thing (either a token or a type); by its own nature forms can belong to only one individual, as in the case of sun or moon. Yet a form can be predicated of a thing, thereby sharing with the universal, which naturally belongs to more than one thing, being predicated of something. See on this Zingano 2005.

possible to construe alteration and coming-to-be in terms of dissociation and association of those indivisible bodies, by means of turning and contact, and through the varieties of the figures, as Democritus did. Yet these indivisible bodies involve much that is unreasonable as well, according to Aristotle. Still, they allow for construing alteration and coming-to-be in terms of association and dissociation, whereas those who divide bodies into planes no longer have such a possibility. Aristotle envisages Plato's treatment of the issue as being unable to explain the facts; as a matter of fact, it simply tries to explain them away. The atomists have a much better explanation for the phenomena of alteration and coming-to-be. And their better power of explanation derives from their dwelling in intimate association with nature, so that they are more able to lay down principles in accordance with the facts, keeping themselves closer to observation, while those who have no comprehensive view of the facts by lack of experience (GC I 2.316a6: ἡ ἀπειρία) go on too hastily to assert things on the basis of numberless reasons (316a8: ἐκ τῶν πολλῶν λόγων), as happens with Plato and his companions, standing unconcerned with the established facts (316a8–9: ἀθεώρητοι τῶν ὑπαρχόντων ὄντες). As Aristotle says, those rival treatments of the same subject illustrate pretty well "how great is the difference between those who investigate φυσικῶς and those who investigate λογικῶς" (316a9–10).[11]

What does λογικῶς mean here? Aristotle thinks the atomists are wrong in positing indivisible bodies. Still, they are better off than the Platonists. Platonists praise above all coherence of reasoning, devoting themselves especially to scrutinizing reasons. That attitude is not by itself negative, but as long as they remain unconcerned with the established facts, they easily go astray. Aristotle highlights the danger involved in ignoring the observable data right at the beginning of the *De Anima*, for, as he says there, one has to recognize not only that knowledge of the essence is useful for the discovery of the properties of an object, but conversely also that knowledge of the nature of an object is largely promoted (I 1.402b22 μέγα μέρος) by acquaintance with its properties. And the

---

11   Joachim's translation, reprinted and revised by Barnes in the *Revised Oxford Translation*, reads: "the rival treatments of the subject now before us will serve to illustrate how great is the difference between a scientific (φυσικῶς) and a dialectical (λογικῶς) method of inquiry". This seems an unfortunate rendering for φυσικῶς and λογικῶς. Φυσικῶς is a significant part of scientific research, and may well have the lion's share, but it is not to be identified with science in totality. On the other side, λογικῶς here has in effect something to do with what Plato thinks a dialectical method is, but this is not what is brought forward in that passage. Moreover, the reader may possibly take *dialectical* in its Aristotelian sense, and so be totally misled by the translation, for no appeal is made here to reputable opinions.

acquaintance with its properties requires being concerned with what experience shows us about them. Otherwise our propositions will remain *dialectical and empty* (403a2 διαλεκτικῶς ... καὶ κενῶς).

Διαλεκτικῶς is smeared here with κενῶς, and seems to bear the same negative sense as λογικῶς in the *Eudemian Ethics* passage quoted above. If we keep to dialectic as it is presented in Plato's *Republic*, it seems to have two main features. Dialectic has the power of grasping the truth in its entirety, but will be thus revealing only to someone with experience (*Rep.* VII 533a8). Experience, though, is only a necessary condition for having it, and experience does not capture the very idea of arguing dialectically. Whereas mathematics uses sensible images and is forced to use hypotheses in making their demonstrations, dialectic does not consider any hypotheses as principles, but seeks to do away with them on the way to the first principle itself, the unhypothetical first principle of everything (VI 511b4–6; see also VII 533c9). In so doing, dialectic makes no use at all of anything visible (VI 511c1: αἰσθητῷ παντάπασιν οὐδενὶ προσχρώμενος). The *Republic* warns us that learning to proceed dialectically will take many years, but leaves it unclear how exactly it proceeds. At least dialectic seems to reach the unhypothetical by means solely of considering Forms in relation one another, as it simultaneously turns its back on visible things. It is these two features that help us understand why διαλεκτικῶς can substitute for λογικῶς in the negative phrase λογικῶς καὶ κενῶς: Platonic dialectic is a method remaining unconcerned with the facts and paying attention basically to the coherence of reasons.[12]

---

12   In *De Anima* I 1, immediately after having said that definitions that disregard empirical facts are all διαλεκτικῶς καὶ κενῶς (402b19–403a2), Aristotle examines how to define the passions of the soul (403a3–b19). He dismisses two opponents, one who defines natural items in terms solely of their material components, and one who defines them only by their form. Aristotle wants definitions of natural items to involve both matter and form. The one who assigns only form is dubbed "dialectician" (I 1.403a29). Since this passage immediately follows the passage about speaking διαλεκτικῶς καὶ κενῶς, one might think that dialecticians express themselves in this same way. However, the passage on how to define the affections of soul is a separate piece from the passage concluding negatively about speaking in a dialectical and useless way. In this new *aporia* solely material and solely formal definitions are both dismissed as inadequate for physics. Those definitions are then contrasted, on the one hand, with mathematical definitions, where forms exist only in matter but are separable from bodies by abstraction, and on the other, with metaphysical definitions, where forms are themselves separate (403b14–16). This is clearly the Aristotelian and positive tripartite scheme: physics, mathematics, first philosophy, each one requiring its own object and its own way of formulating its subject matter. The conclusion of the preceding passage, in contrast, is purely negative.

III

This is not to say that any dialectical argument will bear such a negative bias. Platonic dialectic goes astray, but there are also good Aristotelian dialectical arguments. They carry out their own function: their premises are ἔνδοξα, reputable opinions, and as such they are useful for intellectual training, casual encounters, and also for philosophical sciences, given that the ability to examine both sides is very useful to detect truth and error about the problem at issue. Moreover, inasmuch as it is impossible to discuss within the sciences their own principles, and Aristotelian dialectic is so conceived as to be able to speak about anything, it will also involve a process of criticism and discussion of first principles. There is still a heated debate over whether dialectic so conceived is only able to say something about those principles, or whether it discharges a much stronger function: that of holding the key to, or paving the way to the first principles. Such discussion does not concern us here. My point is that Aristotle distinguishes dialectical from scientific arguments. The latter have as premises propositions that are true, primitive, immediate, more familiar than, prior to, and explanatory of the conclusions (*APo.* I 2.71b20–22). The former have as premises reputable opinions. Reputable opinions may be true, but need not be true: they are assumed as premises of an argument not because they are true, but because they are accepted by everyone or by the majority or by the wise—and of them, either by all, by the majority or by the most reputable ones. In this sense, they are not necessarily true, as is the case for the premises of a scientific demonstration. There is a gap between being a reputable opinion, which may be true, and a scientific proposition, which cannot but be true. This is why Aristotle writes, in *Posterior Analytics*, that "those people are silly who think they get their principles correctly if the proposition is reputable *and true*" (I 6.74b21–23, my italics). In the same vein, he notes that those who are (in an Aristotelian sense) deducing dialectically need only consider whether their deduction comes about from reputable propositions, even though there is in fact no middle term of the syllogism, but only appears to be (I 19.81b18–22). But, he adds, "with regard to truth one must inquire on the basis of what actually holds" (b22–23).

Aristotle thus keeps separate these two ways of reasoning, each one with its own purposes and outcomes. The *Topics* works with the same division of labor. In *Top.* I 14, Aristotle observes that "for purposes of philosophy we must treat of these things [*sc.* ethical, physical, and λογικαί problems] according to their truth, but for dialectic only with an eye to opinion" (105b30–31). There are thus two ways of dealing with theoretical problems, one leading to conviction, in accordance with the restrictive rules deployed in *Posterior Analytics*, the outcome of which is (scientific) truth; the other results in persuasion, in accordance with dialectical rules, and the upshot is agreement based on reputable opinions. Aristotle even offers double proofs of the same subject matter, one dialectical, the other scientific, provided that their purposes do not become confused. Concerning the problem of begging the question, Aristotle gives a dialectical proof of it in *Top.* VIII 13, declaring in that very spot having already demonstrated it according to truth in the *Analytics* (162b32: κατ' ἀλήθειαν μὲν ἐν τοῖς Ἀναλυτικοῖς εἴρηται). In effect, one finds in *Prior Analytics* II 16 a scientific proof of begging a point. In the conclusion of his scientific proof, one reads this: "in scientific demonstrations the point at issue is begged when the terms are so related in regard to truth, in dialectical arguments when they are so related in regard to opinion" (65a36–37). No embarrassment comes about when one proposes merely a dialectical proof, provided its purposes are not mixed up with those of a scientific proof. Both proofs can coexist peacefully, each fulfilling its own function, one for persuading, the other for convincing. Aristotelian dialectical proofs are not empty, but neither are they scientific; Platonic dialectic pretends to be scientific, but becomes empty and useless due to its very peculiar (and wrong) way of chasing for what is more universal.[13]

IV

Therefore, in the Aristotelian sense, there are good dialectical proofs, which are not empty or useless; they correctly discharge their function of persuading the opponent in accordance with reputable opinions. The problem is this, that Aristotelian dialectic is a world apart from truth, since it is restricted to reputability. Platonic dialectic, instead, aims at discovering the truth, putting aside the realm of opinion, however reputable it is. But because it dispenses with experience, it becomes empty and useless.

However, a positive use of λογικῶς in Aristotle comes alongside proving φυσικῶς. In order to understand this positive role of arguing λογικῶς, we need to clarify what arguing φυσικῶς is. To do this, though, we must first understand the contrast between arguing ἀναλυτικῶς and λογικῶς. This analysis will show that arguing λογικῶς plays a similar role vis-à-vis the other two, arguing φυσικῶς and ἀναλυτικῶς, these other two carrying out the tasks of specificity and appropriateness of the proof, respectively, in the physical and logical domains.

---

13 Διαλεκτικῶς, thus, in this negative sense of λογικῶς, characterizes Platonic dialectic; see also Lemaire 2015, 211–212. But there are λογικῶς cases in this negative sense as well that do not refer to Platonic doctrines; see, e.g., *Metaph.* VII 4.1030a35.

In the *Posterior Analytics*, Aristotle provides a proof according to which it is not possible for the terms used in a demonstration to be indefinitely many, given that the predications come to a stop either toward the universal, or toward the particular. This result is valid for negative and positive demonstrations alike, and Aristotle demonstrates the point showing that the terms do come to a stop in the affirmative demonstrations. Now, in the case of affirmative demonstrations, the point at issue "becomes evident if we consider it λογικῶς, as follows" (I 21.82b35–36). Then follows I 22, where it is said, right at the beginning, that the coming to a stop is evident in the case of essential predication, for definitions are possible and knowable, and they could not be both if they went through indefinitely many terms. Two proofs are provided, both presented as καθόλου, proceeding from a general point of view (83a1), which is synonymous with λογικῶς, for both proofs are so called at the end of the whole passage (84a7: λογικῶς). The first proof is given in lines 83a1 to 83b21 and has four steps. In the first step, which goes from 83a1 to 83a23, Aristotle brings in the distinction between proper and improper predication, as illustrated, respectively, by "the log is white" and "the white thing is a log". The second step (83a24–35) builds on the distinction between essential and accidental predication, so important for Aristotelian philosophy. In the third step (83a36–83b17), the impossibility of a counter-predication in the case of a proper predication is shown. For if x belongs to y according to a proper predication, for instance in the case of x being a quality of the substance y, then it is not possible for the substance y to be predicated of the quality x. They can be counter-predicated in case of an improper predication, e.g. when white is predicated of musical, and musical is predicated of white, because both are qualities of an underlying substance. But improper predications are to be eliminated by means of being rephrased in terms of proper predications, and proper predications do not allow counter-predication. In the fourth and last step (83b17–31), the outcome obtained in the previous step is applied to proper predications, essential and accidental predications alike. In both the series of terms are limited, for they would be indefinitely many only under the condition of counter-predication, but such a condition has already been ruled out. Aristotle then provides a second proof λογικῶς, displayed in lines 83b32–84a6. This proof makes an appeal to the supposition of having knowledge of something: if we know c as derived from premises P_1 ... P_n, we cannot know c unless the number of the premises employed is finite. But it was supposed that we know c, therefore the number of premises is finite, and if so, the number of terms in the premises is also finite.

A third proof is then brought in (84a7–28), but this time the proof is called ἀναλυτικῶς (84a8). The gist of that proof lies in the fact that a demonstration operates with *per se* predicates, either as that which belongs in the what-it-is (the first sense of *per se* according to *Posterior Analytics* I 4), or as the things that have what they themselves belong to belonging in their what-it-is (the second sense of *per se*, illustrated by odd to number or female to animal). It is not possible for either of these two sorts of term to be indefinitely many. For, in the second sense of *per se*, like odd to number, there would again be something else belonging to odd in which odd inhered, like prime, but such a case cannot be indefinitely many, for it is necessary that everything belongs to a primitive term, in the present case to number. Nor yet can the terms be indefinitely many in the case of the first sense of *per se*, for then there would be no definition whatsoever.

At the end of the chapter, it is said again that it has been proved at first λογικῶς and then ἀναλυτικῶς (84b2) that the terms come to a stop and are not indefinitely many. Nothing is said about the difference between these two sorts of proof. How do they differ? The ἀναλυτικῶς proof is said to be more concise (84a8: συντομώτερον), but this does not seem to be of much relevance. The ἀναλυτικῶς proof calls on the distinction of *per se* predication, which is a topic expressly examined in *Posterior Analytics* I 4, belonging thus to the official analytic topics, whereas the first λογικῶς proof resorts to the general structure of predication, assumed throughout the *Analytics*, but not expressly discussed in them. In effect, the general construal of an assertion that was examined in the *De interpretatione* is taken for granted in the *Analytics*. The second λογικῶς proof builds on the general idea that knowing something requires a limited number of premises, with no hint of what is the nature of such premises; in contrast, the *Analytics* examine very precisely the nature of a scientific premise. The relevant difference between the two sorts of proof seems to be this. On the one hand, we have premises grounded on the general construal of an assertion (but not on assertion as playing a role in a demonstration), or on the general idea of knowing something; on the other hand, everything hinges upon the way assertions are used as pieces of reasoning, and not as propositions by themselves. That seems to be sufficient to demarcate ἀναλυτικῶς proofs from λογικῶς proofs: an ἀναλυτικῶς proof takes propositions as premises (which is the main topic of the *Analytics*), whereas a λογικῶς proof treats the premises as propositions (which is a topic examined in the *De interpretatione* and taken for granted in the *Analytics*). There is no ἀναλυτικῶς counterpart to the second λογικῶς argument, but one may guess that it would build on the nature of scientific premises to explain knowledge in contrast to an argument based on the idea that one uses a limited number of premises to know something, whatever the nature of these propositions.

However, such a demarcation is quite thin. For even though λογικῶς proofs resort to the analysis of assertion and predication as such (and not to assertion as playing the role of a premise in a deduction), or to the general idea of having knowledge of something (but not of having scientific knowledge), while ἀναλυτικῶς proofs depend on the sort of role judgments perform as premises in a deduction, both types of proof nonetheless crucially depend upon the analysis of judgment as a way either of referring to things, or of reasoning about things. The demarcating line becomes sometimes difficult to draw, as judgments are always at issue. Yet one should notice that judgments are taken differently as long as they operate as pieces of information about the world or as premises, and thus as parts within demonstrations. The former may thus characterize a λογικῶς deduction in the *Analytics*, while the latter operates as proof proper to the *Analytics*. Something similar would distinguish both types of proof regarding the argument about knowing an object: knowing a thing in a general way, and knowing it in a scientific way.

There is another passage in the *Analytics* in which a λογικῶς proof is followed by an ἀναλυτικῶς proof. This passage furnishes another example useful in formulating the same outcome. Aristotle devotes *Posterior Analytics* I 32 to demonstrating that it is impossible for deductions to have all the same principles. He endeavors first to prove his point λογικῶς (88a19). The proof is divided into two parts. In the first part, it is shown that one can reach a true conclusion based on false premises. If one wants to demonstrate one of those premises (by hypothesis false), one needs to resort to another false premise, for from true premises the conclusion cannot but be also true. But if one proves that first conclusion by means of true premises, those premises will be different from the false premises upon which was based the first deduction. Therefore, it is impossible that the principles are the same for all deductions. In the second part, it is shown that falsehoods can also be of different sorts, based either on a contrariety, or only on distinct things, as saying, e.g., that justice is injustice, or that it is cowardice, or that human is not human, or that it is a horse or a cow. Therefore, the premises must be different for all deductions, even if they are all false. To this is added another proof, from 88a30 to 88b29, which is not expressly called ἀναλυτικῶς, but is said to derive from what has been established (88a30: ἐκ δὲ τῶν κειμένων). Ἀναλυτικῶς proofs are proofs based on topics proper to the *Analytics*, so that it looks reasonable to take a proof based on what has been previously established in the work as proving ἀναλυτικῶς.

The ἀναλυτικῶς proof is this. There are two sorts of principles: the common principles, *with* which the proof is made, and the proper principles, *from* which the proof is made. In some cases, common principles, like the principle of noncontradiction, can function as the premise for a deduction, but this happens rarely, for common principles are rather rules governing the obtaining of a proof, not that which constitutes the very matter of the proof. Proper principles, therefore, carry the main burden for a proof, for they are the very matter of the proof. Now, proper principles belong to different genera. And as it has already been shown in the *Analytics* that proper principles for different genera are different from one another, it is therefore impossible for all deductions to have the same proper principles. In effect, it has been shown in *Posterior Analytics* I 7 that proper principles for different genera are different from one another. Again, the difference between a λογικῶς and an ἀναλυτικῶς proof looks very thin at first sight. In particular, in the first part of the λογικῶς proof, one resorts to types of premise, namely true and false premises, and calls on the fact that from true premises one cannot but derive a true conclusion. This looks to be a lesson from the *Analytics*, for it deals with deductions and the role played by propositions as premises in a deduction, such that the difference from the ἀναλυτικῶς proof becomes even thinner. Nonetheless they do seem to differ, as the λογικῶς proof operates with the general idea of being a true or false proposition, while the ἀναλυτικῶς proof refers to a precise topic in the *Analytics*, to wit, common and proper principles as they discharge different functions within a deduction. However thin such a difference may be, it is nonetheless a significant difference in the nature of proofs within the *Analytics*.

Both proofs, the ἀναλυτικῶς and the λογικῶς alike, are seen in *Posterior Analytics* I 22 as succeeding well in proving the problem at hand. One proof is not superseding the other, nor is one proof seen to be in need of support from the other. In what regards the proof that the terms come to a stop and cannot be indefinitely many, this is successfully proved either by the λογικῶς proofs, or by the ἀναλυτικῶς proof, with no idea of one proof having priority over the other or being more apt than the other. The demonstration that it is impossible for all deductions to have the same principles, given at *Posterior Analytics* I 32, has the same upshot. One type of proof does not supersede the other type, but both seem to have equal force in establishing the point at issue.

V

Equipped with these outcomes, it is time now to investigate the φυσικῶς proof in contrast to a λογικῶς proof. The result will be that proving λογικῶς calls on general features, while proving φυσικῶς remains closer to its subject matter, natural objects, being so to say tailor-made to the treatment of those natural items. However, it is important to keep in mind the two results we have already obtained. First, a λογικῶς proof as contrasted with a φυσικῶς proof is surely not useless or empty. Emptiness characterized διαλεκτικῶς proving whenever that proof dispensed with empirical data. But this need not be the case with λογικῶς proofs. Second, one should not take it for granted that φυσικῶς proofs will supersede λογικῶς proofs, or that the former are to be taken as the proper proofs, the latter being only preparatory to them. We have seen that this is not the case when λογικῶς proofs come alongside ἀναλυτικῶς proofs. We still have to see whether φυσικῶς proofs bring about stronger requirements such that they may substitute for, or render λογικῶς proofs only introductory steps to them, or whether they may coexist in an equal claim with λογικῶς proving, as is the case for λογικῶς proofs alongside ἀναλυτικῶς proofs, or else (as we are about to see) the λογικῶς proofs are the only available proofs in the province of physics, but they are genuine proofs indeed.

An interesting case is found in the first book of the *De Caelo*. There Aristotle endeavors to show that the heaven cannot be both generated and indestructible, contrary to what Plato maintained in the *Timaeus*. According to Aristotle, the heaven cannot but be ungenerated and indestructible, the pair generated and indestructible being a conceptual impossibility. But how does he demonstrate his point? At the end of I 10, he tells us that there is clear evidence, from a φυσικῶς point of view, that it is not possible for the heaven to be generated and indestructible. One of these signs is something we observe ordinarily: generated things are always seen to be destroyed; given that the heaven cannot pass away or be destroyed, being indestructible, it evidently cannot be generated. But how strong is this φυσικῶς evidence? It is a reasonable induction, but is not an exhaustive induction. It thus cannot be conclusive. To be conclusive, Aristotle has to appeal to a καθόλου argument, a more general proof, which examines everything that is and shows thereby that the only possible conceptual pairs are either generated and destructible, or ungenerated and indestructible. Hence, given that the heaven is indestructible, it is also ungenerated.

This way of proving is said to be καθόλου. The *De Caelo* never uses the word λογικῶς. However, it looks clear that καθόλου is to be taken in the *De Caelo* as a synonym of λογικῶς.[14] The καθόλου–λογικῶς proof in *De Caelo* I 11–12 is quite

---

14   Καθόλου occurs also in I 7.274a20 and a29, to characterize a more general proof that there is no infinite body, in contrast with a detailed consideration (κατὰ μέρος). Aristotle refers there to the discussion in *Physics* III 4–8 about the existence of the infinite, qualified in the *De Caelo* as καθόλου (274a22), whereas, in *Phys.* III 5.204b4 the discussion to determine whether there is a body that would be infinite in the direction of increase is brought forward as a λογικῶς argument (translated by Hardie and Gaye in the ROT, to my mind wrongly, as "a dialectical argument"). The proof that there can be no more than one heaven is also presented as a καθόλου argument (*Cael.* I 8 276a19). The first proof that the heavens are of necessity spherical is also said to be a καθόλου proof, since it is based on

complex, notably due to the role played by the modalities in it, and one may wonder whether or not it requires the principle of plenitude. Fortunately, we do not need to examine the proof itself, but only to indicate that it qualifies as a λογικῶς argument. That it so qualifies, or at least that it is very plausible that it so qualifies can be seen from the concluding remarks of the whole proof. As Aristotle writes, "to those who investigate φυσικῶς, that is, not καθόλου, it is also impossible that what was formerly eternal should later be destroyed, or that what formerly was not should later be eternal" (I 12.283b17–19). In the realm of physics, what is contrasted to a φυσικῶς proof is a λογικῶς proof, and thus it seems plausible here to equate καθόλου with λογικῶς.

It is worth noticing that, in the present case, the φυσικῶς proof neither replaces, nor is only introduced by the καθόλου–λογικῶς proof, but instead the former is made perfect and certain only by means of the latter. The impasse the φυσικῶς proof cannot get rid of is this: the observed facts point to assuming that whatever is generated is destructible, for we constantly see generated things being destroyed. But this is an inductive proof, and it will remain inconclusive, as long as it does not list exhaustively all items involved. But producing all items involved does not seem to be humanly possible—or simply impossible, in the case of the universe as a whole. The only way to get out of that impasse is to come up with a different sort of argument, which can range over anything generated or ungenerated. To attain certainty, it is necessary to produce what *De caelo* calls a καθόλου argument about any generated thing, including any particular material object and the whole universe (I 10.280a33–34: καθόλου δὲ περὶ ἅπαντος σκεψαμένοις ἔσται καὶ περὶ τούτου δῆλον). Such an argument will be a λογικῶς argument, according to which the disputed concepts come necessarily in the following pairs: either generated and destructible, or indestructible and ungenerated, excluding as invalid such pairs as generated and indestructible, or ungenerated and destructible. As it is agreed that the heaven is indestructible, it will follow that the heaven cannot be generated, given that no other option is available—*q.e.d.*

Another significant example is the discussion on *Physics* III 5 about the possibility of the infinite existing in actuality. After dismissing as absurd the Pythagorean manner of treating the infinite as a substance divided into parts, Aristotle remarks that such a discussion involves a more general (καθόλου) question, for it has to deal with the possibility of the infinite being present in mathematical objects and in the intelligible realm alike, both of which

---

the properties of every shape among planes and solids (II 4.286b12), and this is typically a λογικῶς proof as opposed to a φυσικῶς proof.

have no extension, not being thus restricted to the subject matter of physical bodies. From such an enlarged vantage point, two arguments are produced to show that there is no infinite in actuality. The first one occupies 204b4–10. The argument is said to be λογικῶς (204b4) and proceeds as follows.[15] If body is defined as what is bounded by a surface, there cannot be an infinite body either intelligible or sensible. Nor can number or any mathematical object be infinite in actuality, for, although the numerable extends forever, each numerable in actuality is numbered, and as such it cannot be infinite, given that it is necessarily determinate. The second argument is φυσικῶς and is deployed through 204b10–205a6. The infinite can be either complex or simple. If it is complex, either (a) it is composed of many elements, one of which at least is infinite, or (b) all of them are infinite. But it cannot be (a), for, in that case, the infinite element would obviously prevail over the finite ones, and would thus destroy them, creating an imbalance inside the physical compound. Nor can it be (b), for each element would be infinite, but body was defined as what has extension in all directions, so that each element would be boundlessly extended in all directions. But if it is simple, neither can it exist in actuality, for either (c) it would be another element over and above the so-called elements (from which they would be generated), or (d) it would be one of them, into which the others would resolve themselves. But it cannot be (c), because there is no such sensible body alongside the so-called elements, given that everything else can be resolved into the elements they are composed of, but there is no observed sign of things resolving into such an element (204b35: φαίνεται δ' οὐδέν). Neither can (d) be the case. For everything changes from contrary to contrary, e.g., from cold to hot, so that if there were only one element motion and change would be annihilated, independently of a body being finite or infinite.

The difference between these arguments is evident. The first one, the λογικῶς deduction, assumes as a premise something common to intelligible and sensible bodies, while the φυσικῶς argument restricts itself to physical bodies. Moreover, the φυσικῶς argument makes appeal to observable facts, as the fact that no one has ever seen composed bodies resolving themselves into an ele-

---

15   The ROT translation renders λογικῶς as "dialectical argument". Two elements may plead for this translation. In 204b23 Anaximander is referred to by a general λέγουσί τινες, "some say", and in 205a3 the opinion according to which all things become eventually one single element, i.e., fire, is attributed to Heraclitus. Both are reputable opinions or ἔνδοξα, and thus one may think that the argument is typically dialectical. However, both opinions occur outside the λογικῶς argument; actually, they both belong to the φυσικῶς argument begun at 204b10. It thus seems misleading to translate λογικῶς at 204b4 by "dialectical".

ment over and above the four so-called basic elements. A λογικῶς argument does not appeal to observable facts. It is also worth noting that both deductions are seen as complementary to each other. One proof does not supersede the other, or is merely introduced by the other. The conclusion can be reached by either of them. In the present case, one may choose to argue by means of a λογικῶς or a φυσικῶς argument.

A similar case of complementarity is found in *Physics* VIII 8, when Aristotle goes on to show that an infinite motion may be single and continuous. Aristotle shows first, from 261b27 to 263a3, that, given that all motions are either rotatory, rectilinear, or a compound of the two, whereas the rectilinear motion cannot be single and continuous, the rotatory motion may satisfy both conditions. This is a φυσικῶς proof, based on premises argued for in other passages of *Physics*. Now, after an excursion into Zeno's arguments against motion (263a4–264a6), Aristotle says that the very same result (that there is an infinite motion that is single and continuous) may also be obtained in a λογικῶς manner (264a8). The proof is this (264a8–21). Suppose a rectilinear motion from A to C such that, when it arrives at C, it goes back to A with no interruption. In this case, then, when it goes from A to C, the same motion is taken simultaneously to be going to A from C. This is obviously contradictory, for it should be either going to A from C, or to C from A. Therefore, no rectilinear motion can be infinite, single and continuous, for one must establish a stop such that the motions from A to C and from C to A become distinct. Its λογικῶς nature seems to derive from the fact that the proof proceeds on a very general and abstract level concerning locomotion as motion.

Another argument is then produced, still more general about every change (264a21: καθόλου μᾶλλον περὶ πάσης κινήσεως). As a matter of fact, it is basically the same argument, only that it involves now all types of change (alteration, generation, growing, and locomotion), and not only locomotion, which was the sole motion taken into account in the previous argument. We have thus every reason to treat it as a λογικῶς argument as was already the case for the first argument, and even more so, because it is still more general, expanding the first argument to all kinds of change. From 264b1, a third argument is added, and this new argument is said to be "more appropriate than its predecessors" (264b2: μᾶλλον οἰκεῖος τῶν εἰρημένων). This argument deals only with one type of change, alteration, by means of the example of becoming white. The fourth argument is given from 264b9 on, followed by a fifth one, which begins at 264b21, and a sixth one, which begins at 264b28. Finally, at 265a2–5, is presented the corollary from all those proofs: all physicists who assert that all sensible things are always in motion are wrong, for only the rotatory locomotion can satisfy the requirements of singleness and continuity. The last four arguments were introduced as being more appropriate, and this may lead one to think that they are all φυσι-κῶς arguments, in contrast with the preceding ones. However, in the conclusion of the whole series of arguments (265a7–12), it is again expressly asserted that all considerations were made καθόλου concerning all kinds of change (265a8), and this points again to a whole λογικῶς argument. The lesson to be drawn from this case is twofold. Firstly, within a λογικῶς argument there may be degrees of generality, parts of it being more distant, and other parts being closer to the subject matter. Second, proofs following the λογικῶς patttern can prove a point on their own, with no help from a φυσικῶς, although they are compatible with such arguments, and may consequently occur alongside them.

One may object that there were some special conditions that gave the λογι-κῶς arguments some precedence over the φυσικῶς proofs, or put the former at an equal level regarding the latter. In effect, in the *De Caelo* case, the rarity and difficulty of getting data about celestial objects forces one to produce λογικῶς proofs, since there are no available data, or only minimal data. In the case of the proof against the infinite being a thing in itself, as there is no such thing, no datum will ever be available, and thus one cannot but resort to abstract and general arguments to disprove its claims to existence. In the case of the single, continuous, and infinite motion the situation is more complex. On the one hand, there are very abstract accounts regarding a single, continuous, and infinite motion. On the other, there is physical evidence for a negative account of rectilinear motion as satisfying the conditions of singleness and continuity. This is why one finds both types of argument, φυσικῶς and λογικῶς arguments alike, to prove the same point. The objection runs thus: whenever observable facts are available, it is preferable to produce appropriate arguments that take those data into account; therefore, φυσικῶς arguments are to be preferred, unless absence or rarity of data forces us to resort to more abstract reasoning.

The objector is right. In natural philosophy, more appropriate arguments are those that take into account observable data. However, the point was to show that λογικῶς arguments are not to be mechanically replaced, or always to be complemented or concluded by φυσικῶς arguments. Λογικῶς arguments are not mere placeholders for φυσικῶς proofs, but have also a place in physical discussions, even though their place is rather restricted, for they are superseded whenever more data are available. We may illustrate this point through a discussion in the *De Generatione Animalium*. There, in II 8, Aristotle investigates the fact that sterility occurs sporadically in humans and in other kinds, whereas the whole kind of mule is sterile. Democritus and Empedocles provided different φυσικῶς explanations for this fact, but Aristotle prefers a λογικῶς argument in place of them. According to Democritus, the genital passages of mules are spoiled in the female's uterus because the offspring does not come from parents of the same kind, for the mule is born of horse and ass. However, this happens also with other animals, and they are nonetheless able to procreate, remarks Aristotle, and if this were the reason of sterility, all others that unite in the same manner ought to be sterile. According to Empedocles, the mixture of the seeds becomes dense, while the two seminal fluids are originally soft, because the hollows in each fit into the densities of the other, and in such cases a hard substance is formed out of soft one, like copper mixed with tin. Aristotle replies that this is false regarding the mixture of copper and tin. Moreover, Empedocles's explanation is a far cry from clear—for how do the hollows and solids fit into one another? There is also no clue as to why the mixture of spermatic fluids when ass and horse procreate becomes dense, but not when a female horse procreates with a male horse, or a male ass with a female ass.

A λογικῶς demonstration (747b28: ἀπόδειξις λογική) looks more promising than these two φυσικῶς explanations. It runs as follows. From parents of the same species, the offspring is of the same species, but from parents of different species, the offspring is different in species from both parents. Mules are produced of both sexes and are of the same species, but as they come from different species, namely horse and ass, it is impossible that anything be produced from mules. In effect, they cannot have an offspring of another species, for both the female mule and the male mule are of the same species; but they cannot generate a young one of the same species, because they come from parents of different species, and from animals of different species is born an animal different in species from both parents. But parents can procreate individuals only either of the same species, or of different species. Therefore mules cannot procreate.

Compared to the theories of Democritus and Empedocles, such a λογικῶς explanation is better off. However, it still is "too general and empty" (748a8: καθόλου λίαν καὶ κενός).[16] Actually, to account for this case of infertility, one ought to examine more carefully the facts peculiar to the two kinds concerned, horse and ass. First, each of them bears only one young one; and infertility is more common when only one offspring is generated. Second, the females are not always able to conceive from the male. Both animals are not especially fertile; quite the contrary, they tend naturally toward sterility. Indeed, the mare is deficient in menstrual flow, and the female ass ejects the semen with her urine. Again the ass is an animal of cold nature, and so must its semen be also,

---

16 "Too general" (καθόλου λίαν) emphasizes its inappropriateness: in *EE* VII 1 it is said that those who think that like is friend to like come even to argue that in all of nature like goes to like, "whence Empedocles said that the dog sat on the tile because it was most like it" (*EE* VII 1.1235a11–12; λίαν καθόλου is employed at 1235a30).

whereas the horse is of hot nature, and its semen is likewise. When they unite
with each other, the generative elements are preserved by the heat of the horse,
although in the ass the semen and the menstrual material are cold. The result is
that the embryo arising from heat and cold is preserved, and these animals are
fertile when crossed with one another, but the young one is no longer fertile.

The latter counts as a good φυσικῶς explanation, compared to which that
λογικῶς proof previously given is to be dismissed, however more interesting
than Democritus's or Empedocles's it may be. The chapter on the infertility
of mules provides significant clues to understanding the relationship between
φυσικῶς and λογικῶς proofs in the field of natural sciences, when data are
already available or cognizable, not being concealed from us by any circumstances. "I call it λογική because the more general (καθόλου) it is, the further is
it removed from the appropriate principles" (747b28–30). This clearly pleads
for φυσικῶς proofs, as they are based on principles appropriate to the subject
matter. We shall be more likely to find the causes of the infertility of mules by
considering the facts peculiar to the horse and the ass, ἐκ δὲ τῶν ὑπαρχόντων τῷ
γένει τῷ τῶν ἵππων καὶ τῷ τῶν ὄνων (748a14–15). This is what Aristotle does, and
in so doing he substitutes the latter physical explanation for the other proofs,
including the logical proof evaluated as better off than the physical proofs provided by Democritus and Empedocles.

VI

Let us pause and take stock. When contrasted to ἀναλυτικῶς deductions, a λογικῶς argument operates with basic notions of the nature of a proposition taken
by itself, without considering it as a piece of reasoning, that is, as a premise in a
deduction or demonstration, as ἀναλυτικῶς proofs do. This is a distinct abstract
level from the level ἀναλυτικῶς reasoning dwells on, and its characterization
as λογικῶς marks it off as a special kind of consideration within logical analyses. This kind of consideration is not to be conflated with dialectical reasoning,
either in the Aristotelian, or in the Platonic sense of dialectic. For both ways of
reasoning depart from scientific inquiry, the former due to its being rooted in
reputable opinions, the latter because it does not stop at the appropriate levels in which proper principles are to be established, but instead searches for
the most universal. On the other hand, when contrasted with φυσικῶς explanations, a λογικῶς argument may or may not count as an adequate proof. To
those physical subject matters in which observable facts are scanty, λογικῶς
arguments may have a proper place as adequate proofs. However, whenever
empirical data are available, λογικῶς arguments are to be superseded by φυσι-

κῶς arguments that account for the peculiar facts involved—albeit, when the latter fail to do so, and provide obscure explanations or simply come up with false reasons, λογικῶς proofs may be preferable to them.

Equipped with these considerations, we can now tackle a more difficult problem, to determine whether metaphysical arguments tend naturally to be λογικῶς arguments, or whether they may be superseded or substituted by (an)other type(s) of proving. Λογικῶς arguments do pervade metaphysical enquiries due to their very abstract level of reasoning, but are they the appropriate arguments in metaphysics? It may be hard to imagine what sort of reasoning is to be contrasted with them such that there would be a distinct or appropriate mode of reasoning in the domain of metaphysics, but we have already seen that very subtle distinctions can be made in this respect, such as the distinction between ἀναλυτικῶς and λογικῶς arguments. Given the very general level at which metaphysical arguments seem to operate, will it be the case that λογικῶς arguments are not only pervasive in metaphysics, but also being a metaphysical argument is a sufficient condition for being a λογικῶς argument?

There is no simple answer to this question. And the reason seems to be that metaphysics underwent an important change in Aristotle's thinking. *Metaphysics* IV testifies to the crucial move. There Aristotle asserts the possibility of a unified science of being *qua* being by means of his notion of focal meaning. Thanks to this notion the theory of substance substitutes for the vainly sought-after doctrine of being, and it does so as substance becomes not the whole being, but first being, such that all other genera of being—the categories—refer to it in their own definitions, even though they are not reduced or assimilated to it. This is a portentous moment for Aristotelian metaphysics, rescued from the rubble as soon as Aristotle refused the Platonic notion of degrees of being, and adopted the view of being as a πολλαχῶς λεγόμενον, an item said in many ways, with no other way of connecting one to another than the existential dependence of all items on the primary substances of *Categories*, the particular substances (everything else being either said of them, or inhering in them). I am following in broad lines Owen's proposal of two main moments in Aristotle's way of tackling the problem of being.[17] Such a reading is of course controversial. I will take it for granted and will try to show that our discussion about λογικῶς arguments may lend supplementary support for it.

Aristotle does not yet have the conceptual tools to mitigate the original dispersal of being in the categories, as in *Eudemian Ethics* I 8, when he is discussing the Platonic Form of Good. He says that, because good has as many

---

17   Cf. Owen 1986, 180–199.

senses as those of being, there is not one and the same good or one and the same being over and above all of them, for they are all scattered in those very senses. This is not to say that there is no way of connecting all them together— the primary substances of the *Categories* play this role as they are the existential condition for there being all other items, and, in ethics, the rational agent is the ultimate bearer of all ethical categories. And this is also not to say that there is no way of discussing and examining those supreme kinds of being at a very abstract level. Only that such a discussion belongs necessarily to a "much more λογική inquiry, for arguments that are at the same time destructive and common belong to no other science" (1217b17–19).[18] Two questions come immediately to the mind. First: what kind of inquiry is this? Second: what does λογική mean here?

To answer the first question, it is helpful to mention two passages in the *Posterior Analytics*. In *APo*. I 9, Aristotle shows that, since one cannot demonstrate anything except from its own principles, an argument proving in virtue of a common feature that also belongs to something else will not be an adequate proof. For we will then be knowing the thing only accidentally, in so far we do not know it in virtue of that to which it belongs. Granted this, it is also evident, says Aristotle in that chapter, that one cannot demonstrate the proper principles of anything, for, he argues, "those will be principles of everything, and the science of them will dominate all sciences" (76a17–18). If there were such a demonstration, there would thus be a super-science, from which all other sciences would be derived. But such a super-science is nowhere to be found.

Sciences are not disconnected from one another, however, for they use common principles. Two chapters later, in I 11, Aristotle says that all sciences associate with one another in respect of those common principles or axioms, like the principle of non-contradiction. But, in the terms of the *Analytics*, there is no science to which those common principles belong. Nonetheless, as dialectic is not concerned with any determined set of things (as is the case for the well-established sciences), but, quite the contrary, can discuss any topic of the proper sciences, dialectic is useful in relation to the principles employed in the several sciences, either the principles proper to each domain, or the principles common to all domains. For as dialectic is a process of criticism of everything (*Top*. I 2.101b3–4: ἐξεταστικὴ γὰρ οὖσα) dialectic, as long as it can

---

18   One may take the phrase κατ' οὐδεμίαν ἄλλην ἐπιστήμην as saying that those arguments
      belong to no other science *than* dialectic (thus implying it to be a science), or that those
      arguments belong to no science at all, for there is no *other science* that deals with them,
      but dialectic. I adopt the second reading.

discuss, by means of reputable opinions, the proper principles of any science and the common principles of all of them as well, it associates with all the sciences, and somehow provides a discursive link between them all. This is why dialectic comes in at *Posterior Analytics* I 11: as it is not restricted to any one genus since it is not a science, it provides a way of examining the proper and common principles of any science.

The answer is thus this: dialectic does the job. But dialectic is not a science, for it is only critical, whereas science is properly cognitive of its objects. So, according to the scientific project delineated in the *Analytics*, there is no science of the common principles. This is in line with what Aristotle has said in the *Eudemian Ethics*: there is no available science of being *qua* being, but only departmental sciences, and inquiries about principles are relegated to a distinct discipline, which has a way to them, but has no scientific grasp of them. That inquiry was in the *Eudemian Ethics* characterized as much more λογική. The *Posterior Analytics* names it: it is dialectic, an inquiry that goes through all principles, but that is cognitive of none. And this is also in line with a passage in *Topics* I 14, in which Aristotle divides in broad lines dialectical propositions and problems into three groups: ethical, physical, and λογικαί. The example given of the latter is, "Is the knowledge of opposites the same or not?" (105b23–24). This is one of the questions that *Metaphysics* IV ascribes to the newly born first philosopher, who investigates being *qua* being and is thus not restricted to particular sciences, but deals with principles that are common to all particular sciences from now on in a scientific manner. But in the *Topics* it was still a λογικός problem. Λογικός means here, and this is the answer to our second question, that it is a most general, abstract problem, one that is not restricted to objects under a determinate genus. It is thus no proper science, for every science has a determinate genus as its subject matter. With the difference that, in the *Eudemian Ethics*, such an inquiry was seen as basically destructive, whereas in the *Topics* the positive role of constructing proofs comes alongside the negative role of eliminating or destroying arguments.

What now of those abstract arguments when Aristotle has already established a new science by means of the focal meaning relationship? Such a science maintains its very abstract level, but constitutes a unified scientific field as a doctrine of substance. As a science, one might think that it has its own arguments, the metaphysical arguments, in contrast with the λογικῶς arguments that occur in any other science. Does the metaphysical science have metaphysical arguments distinct from λογικῶς arguments? The analyses of essence in *Metaphysics* VII may help settle this question. In VII 3 Aristotle puts forward four candidates vying, so to say, for the notion of substance. There is the substratum, that of which other things are predicated, while it is not predicated of anything else. This candidate is examined in the remaining part of VII 3. The outcome is apparently negative, insofar as it is assimilated to matter, and matter does not satisfy the requirements of being a this and separable, the two criteria that are taken to be the most basic requirements to be substance.[19] Three other candidates are also mentioned at the beginning of VII 3: essence, genus, and universal. The universal will be dismissed in VII 13–14; according to those chapters, no universal can be a substance.[20] The genus is not expressly dismissed in VII, but VIII 1 links it directly to the notion of universal, for genus is a sort of universal, and can thus be dismissed alongside the universal. Essence remains as a candidate, and it comes out that essence is a good candidate for substance of a being, οὐσία ἑκάστου.

Essence is examined from VII 4 to 12. The discussion in those chapters is far from straightforward, for in between there is a group of chapters, 7 to 9, which deals with problems of generation in sensible substances, whose connection to the argument developed from VII 4–6 is not at first sight very clear. And there is also VII 12, which looks like a chapter apart in the treatment of essence, as it deals with the problem of the unity of the *definiens* as it is composed of a genus and a differentia, apparently more closely connected to what has been said about definition in the *Analytics* (to which it expressly refers) than to the preceding analyses in chapters 10–11 of the formula that exhibits the essence of a thing and the nature of its parts, these chapters building on the notion of essence as it was displayed in VII 4–6. We will concentrate our attention to VII 4–6 and 10–11 in order to answer our question about the nature of the metaphysical explanations that Aristotle provides within his new science of being *qua* being.

A very important clue is indeed given in these chapters: right at the beginning of VII 4,[21] the investigation about essence is said to be pursued by means of a λογικῶς argument (1029b13). This argument builds on the senses of *in virtue of itself* (examined in *Posterior Analytics* I 4), given that the essence of a thing

---

19   However, in VIII, matter will reappear as substance in potentiality, in contrast to form, already a this in actuality, both being the components out of which the particular thing is composed.

20   Such an outcome may put in jeopardy the notion of form as it is traditionally attributed to Aristotle, for form is usually seen as predicated of many things, and as such would be a universal, but if no universal can be a substance, it becomes hard to see how to make this claim compatible with another Aristotelian tenet expressly argued for in VII, namely, that form is not only substance, but substance in the primary sense.

21   I adopt the transposition of lines 1029b3–12 to the preceding chapter, as suggested by Bonitz, but my argument does not depend on such transposition.

is what it is said to be in virtue of itself. Aristotle immediately rules out the second sense of being in virtue of itself (1029b15–22), that is, what it belongs to is included in its what it is (the example in the *Metaphysics* is the surface being colored in virtue of itself). Essence is a *per se* attribute in the first sense of *per se* in *Posterior Analytics* I 4; that is, it is the predicate that exhibits what the thing is, as "rational animal" to "human". One ought to address two issues. First: why is it a λογικῶς argument? Second: where does such an argument end, for Aristotle says that he will *first* (1029b13: πρῶτον) make some observations from a λογικῶς vantage point, making us expect that later he will turn to another sort of reasoning?

The first question is not easy to answer. It may count as a λογικῶς argument because the premises it employs come from the *Analytics*, and as the analytics are taken to be a sort of tool to the other sciences, metaphysics, from now on a science, will stay in an analogous position to it, availing itself of the *Analytics* as a tool, albeit metaphysics is much more abstract that the other sciences due to its own subject matter, being *qua* being. But if this is the right answer, there must be a proper argument of metaphysics in contrast to which arguments stemming from the *Analytics* are said to be λογικῶς. One would thus expect to have λογικῶς arguments introducing, and being complemented or superseded by the appropriate metaphysical proofs. What then might count as a proper metaphysical proof?

An analogy may be helpful. Mathematics is a theoretical science, apart from physics and metaphysics. In *Metaph.* XIII 6, Aristotle says that Pythagoreans wrongly treat mathematical numbers φυσικῶς, for they construe the first mathematical unity as having magnitude. They do so in order to claim that sensible objects are made out of mathematical unities. But this is evidently wrong, for mathematical numbers have no magnitude. Other thinkers make the same sort of error. Some say of the lines, planes, and solids that not every spatial magnitude is divisible into magnitudes, speaking thus of mathematical objects, but not in a mathematical way (XIII 6.1080b27–28). They also want to explain sensible objects by means of mathematical properties, but they reason non-mathematically when the matter requires mathematical thinking. Aristotle suggests that their error stems from taking Forms and mathematical objects as the same. However, he also remarks that there are other thinkers that do not make the Forms mathematical objects, and so investigate the latter μαθηματικῶς. There is thus a mathematical way of dealing with mathematical objects; as they do not depend on matter and their definitions do not involve reference to motion, one should refrain from arguing φυσικῶς about them, for physical objects have all matter and their definitions necessarily involve reference to motion. The analogy would be this. As there are three theoretical sciences, mathematics, physics, and metaphysics, one might expect to find, respectively, μαθηματικῶς, φυσικῶς, and some sort of specific reasoning in first philosophy.

There is no mention of a specific way of dealing with metaphysical objects. One may suggest that metaphysics turns to φυσικῶς arguments whenever it has to prove a point scientifically. The idea would be this. In physics, Aristotle argues for a three-item scheme to explain motion: an underlying subject, which remains during the change, and the contrary pair of privation and form, from which and toward which, respectively, the change takes place. When applied to generation, such a scheme yields the tripartite division of matter, form, and composite. Now, whenever one has in metaphysics an argument that operates with, assumes, or requires the notions of matter and form, one is facing a φυσικῶς argument. By contrast, a λογικῶς argument makes no appeal to such notions. However interesting this reading may seem to be, I think one should resist adopting it. According to it, scientific argument is to be equated with φυσικῶς reasoning. But mathematics is a science, and arguing φυσικῶς is inappropriate for mathematics. Also, such a perspective treats as homogeneous content and formal issues. A φυσικῶς argument becomes an argument whose content has to do with the notions of matter and form. But reasoning φυσικῶς has primarily to do with the formal appropriateness of premises of a deduction with regard to the object that is studied. It may be the case that in physics any proper argument deals in one way or another with the notions of matter and form. But this only points to an extensional convergence between the contents of the arguments and their formal appropriateness to the fields of physics; intensionally speaking, content and formal perspectives are different ways of assessing what is going on in a scientific inquiry. Moreover, if scientific metaphysical arguments were φυσικῶς arguments, one should expect Aristotle to characterize the main arguments produced in the *Metaphysics* accordingly. The term φυσικῶς occurs twice in the *Metaphysics*, but never to characterize a positive metaphysical argument. It occurs once at XI 10.1066b26, but there one has a text coming from *Physics* about the infinite, against the existence of which λογικῶς as well as φυσικῶς arguments are produced. The second time it occurs is in XIV 4.1091a19, wherein Aristotle, referring to the Pythagoreans, says that they produced mathematical arguments in a φυσικῶς manner, as they attributed magnitude to numbers in order to make sensible substances out of numbers. Aristotle observes this with an eye to censuring their alleged scientific procedure. Lastly, a λογικῶς argument in the *Metaphysics*, by contrast, according to this view, would not operate with, assume, or require the notions of matter and form or essence. But then many arguments brought forward in the *Metaphysics* would not count as appropriate metaphysical arguments—most notably the well-celebrated argument against those who deny the principle of non-contradiction. Besides, a well-known λογικῶς argument, the one that opens up the investigation about essence in VII 4, assumes the very notion of essence (form) from the beginning.

If φυσικῶς arguments do not characterize arguments as appropriate in the realm of metaphysics, perhaps ἐλεγκτικῶς arguments may do the job. For, in the argument against those who deny the principle of non-contradiction spelled out in IV 4, there are two mentions of an ἐλεγκτικῶς way of proving (1006a12 and a15), and one may take it that ἐλεγκτικῶς proving would count as the proper proof for metaphysics. One would then have the triad μαθημα-τικῶς–φυσικῶς–ἐλεγκτικῶς, corresponding to the triad mathematics–physics–first philosophy. This would make the method of metaphysics rather akin to dialectic, for an ἐλεγκτικῶς argument retains close connections with dialectical reasoning. As an ἔλεγχος typically refutes an opposing argument, an ἐλεγκτικῶς method would then emphasize its destructive role concerning the principles, as has already been brought out in the *Eudemian Ethics*, when common principles were dealt with by dialectic conceived basically as a destructive activity (I 8.1217b18: ἀναιρετικοί). Such a reading is quite tempting, and part of its attractive power resides in the fact that it would reinstate the idea of dialectic as the appropriate method of metaphysics.[22]

Now, a first difficulty for such an interpretation is this. In IV 2, as metaphysics is brought into the path of a science (due to the focal meaning relationship among the categories), it is at the same time contrasted with two other disciplines, which range over the same objects, but proceed differently: sophistic, on the one side, which only appears to be philosophy, but is not; and dialectic, which is merely critical, while metaphysics claims to know (IV 2.1004b25–26). Establishing as its proper argument the ἐλεγκτικῶς proving as a sort of dialectical reasoning would put in jeopardy the drawing of a line between sophistic and dialectic, on the one side, and metaphysics, on the other. And one may even take the argument the other way round. If it is not dialectical, why does Aristotle speak of an ἐλεγκτικῶς proof at all? One likely explanation for Aristotle's use of the term ἐλεγκτικῶς at this juncture is this: λογικῶς arguments need to be strengthened whenever they concern the first, most basic principles, like the principle of non-contradiction. The principle of non-contradiction is supposed in any other deduction, including its own, if there were to be a deduction of it. To tackle such very specific types of principles one is supposed to have recourse to a strengthened λογικῶς proving under the form of an ἐλεγκτικῶς proving. What counts as significant for this explanation is the very fact that

---

22   Cf. Irwin 1988.

Aristotle avoids employing the term διαλεκτικῶς to refer to such a strengthened λογικῶς proving, preferring instead the term ἐλεγκτικῶς, thereby keeping those two ways of proving apart: λογικῶς (in its strengthened version of ἐλεγκτικῶς) and διαλεκτικῶς reasoning.

A second difficulty is this. In VII 17 Aristotle takes another starting point in the hope of getting a clear view of what it is to be a substance, and whether a substance exists apart from sensible substances. This new starting point amounts to taking substance as cause. Much is to be said about this new strategy, both in relation to the preceding chapters of VII, and what follows, notably VIII 1–6. But what interests us here is that, from this new vantage point, essence comes out to be cause, such that being a cause is being that which makes these stones and bricks a house, or that sound produced in the thunderstorm. The essence is the cause of these objects being what they are. In one case it is that for the sake of which something comes to be, illustrated by the example of a house (1041a29–30). In the other case, it is the efficient cause. Aristotle does not provide any explicit mention of thunder, but it is very likely that he is referring to it, for thunder is said to be the quenching of fire in the clouds, where the extinguishing of fire is its essence as its efficient cause. More importantly, Aristotle expressly says in VII 17 that mentioning the essence as cause amounts to mentioning it λογικῶς (1041a28). For it is still to be specified in each case—for thunder, e.g., as an efficient cause, or for a house, as its end. Such specification is to be reached in accordance with the respective special sciences, as building in one case, or meteorology in the other. He provides these two causes—the final and efficient causes—in close correspondence with the two examples provided: a house and thunder. He could also have mentioned the formal cause, and, with some restrictions, the material cause that is an object only in potentiality. Specifying each type of cause brings the argument home to a certain sort of scientific discourse. Presenting the essence simply as the cause of a thing's being what it is, is a λογικῶς argument. Λογικῶς seems here to circumscribe the type of explanation one is supposed to obtain in metaphysical inquiries. Λογικῶς cannot stand here for a refutative proof, ἐλεγκτικῶς, or broadly speaking a dialectical proof. Instead, it seems to refer to the general manner one should proceed with when arguing in such an abstract field as the science of being *qua* being. It seems thus preferable to take λογικῶς already in VII 4 as referring to this sort of argument, the kind of argument one is supposed to expect within metaphysics as it is the general science of being as being.

So the answer to the first question is—or so I surmise it to be: λογικῶς arguments are at home in the realm of metaphysics, due to its high level of abstraction, given that its subject matter is being as such, not any being in particular, but being as being. Now what of the second question: where do they finish? This looks like a reasonable question, for Aristotle has said that he was going *first* (VII 4 1029b13: πρῶτον) to say something about the essence in a λογικῶς manner. One is thus entitled to expect a moment in which the λογικῶς arguments are dropped out in favor of a more specific reasoning. Ross took λογικῶς as suggesting "plausibility rather than truth (*Top.* 162b27), dialectic or sophistic as opposed to science". It comes thus as no surprise that he was anxious to find where it finishes and where "the real as opposed to the verbal inquiry begins".[23] He thinks that the alleged "real enquiry" begins toward the end of VII 4, more precisely at 1030a27–28, where Aristotle says that "we should investigate how we should express ourselves on each point, but no more than how the facts actually stand".[24] This would be a sort of signpost announcing the scientific side of the investigation further to be developed.

It need not be so, though. On the contrary, the sentence at 1030a27–28 may only say that there must be a balance between how we speak about things, and how the facts actually stand. A disagreement between them would be fatal—but this is not to say, or not yet to say that λογικῶς arguments are to be superseded by other sort of argument, and still less to indicate what this other sort of argument would amount to. A better reading of this passage seems to require—or so I surmise—only that somewhere another sort of argument about essence is to be found, and that this other argument ought to agree with

---

23   Cf. Ross 1924, II 168.

24   The Greek text reads: δεῖ μὲν οὖν σκοπεῖν καὶ τὸ πῶς δεῖ λέγειν περὶ ἔκαστον, οὐ μὴν μᾶλλόν γε ἢ τὸ πῶς ἔχει. Ross seems to me to over-translate it, probably due to his anxiety toward verbal arguments: "now we must inquire how we should express ourselves on each point, but *still more* how the facts actually stand" (my italics). But in fact the text is just saying to look for a balance between the two arguments, as if one is to stand as complementary to the other. There are two occurrences of λογικῶς in VII 4, and perhaps they do not have the same meaning. The first one is 1029b13, opening the λογικῶς metaphysical inquiry about the nature of form. The second occurs in 1030a35 and concerns those who say λογικῶς that that which is not is, in the sense that it is non-existent. This is likely to be an eristic usage of a λογικῶς argument. The argument surrounding this second occurrence of λογικῶς proceeds by analogy, namely, that qualities and the other categories have in some sense (but not in the primary sense) a what it is or definition, as one may say λογικῶς that that which is not is because it is non-existent—that is, in a feeble and derivative manner (this is the analogy: qualities and other categories have essence only in a secondary and derivative way; but there is also a disanalogy, for to say that that which is not is goes further than this and makes a clearly very disputable claim). Ross took it that both occurrences had the same meaning, that of verbiage, and accordingly looked for another sort of argument inside VII in order to ground essence as the right candidate for substance of a thing.

the results of the λογικῶς argument. As a matter of fact, VII 5 and 6 continue the λογικῶς inquiry with no sign of having dropped it, or having superseded it by another sort of reasoning. The same sort of λογικῶς inquiry occurs in VII 10–11, this time by means of the investigation about the formula in which the essence is exhibited, i.e., the definition. And likewise in VII 12, which carries on a λογικῶς argument, even if VII 12 is apparently more connected to problems of definition stated in *Posterior Analytics* II 1–13 than to the two preceding VII chapters. For Z 12 reckons on a λογικῶς reasoning, the same sort of argument with which Aristotle had begun his examination of what it is to be the substance of a thing in VII 4.

The λογικῶς argument seems thus to run from VII 4 to 6, and to resume from VII 10 to 11 (12). But if it is pervasive within the investigation of essence, why did Aristotle say that he was going to assert first some things in a λογικῶς manner, creating in the reader the expectation that another sort of proof was to follow?[25] Now, we do find a break inserted in between this whole λογικῶς inquiry, namely VII 7–9. In this group of chapters, Aristotle endeavors to show that everything that is produced is something produced from something and by something, and that it is the same in species as that from which it is produced. This is a typically φυσικῶς inquiry, although the term is not applied in it. Very cursorily, the point is this. For something to be generated, one has to suppose as existing previously to it something of the same species that functions as the efficient cause of the generation. Aristotle even pauses to consider the case of mules, for there is a problem linked to the regularity of infertility in their generation. This may strike one as a particularly non-metaphysical topic inserted in the most metaphysical reasoning about essence—but in these chapters one deals with a φυσικῶς argument purporting to provide a supplementary proof of what has already been determined about the essence of a thing. For matter and form, which are decisive for anything to come to be, are supposed not to be themselves generated in a generation. To the contrary, they ought to be eternal, if coming to be and passing away is to be viable, since if not only a composite of matter and form is generated each time, but also matter and form,

---

25   One may also wonder why Aristotle says he is going first to make *some* observations (ἔνια) in a λογικῶς way, if λογικῶς arguments go throughout the whole stretch. But he may simply mean that one will begin making λογικῶς observations, to wit, those observations that are strictly relevant to the point, and only afterward will complement them with a φυσικῶς argument. It is worth noting that the concluding remarks at VII 11 remind one that it has been explained καθόλου (here in the sense of λογικῶς) what essence is and how it is *per se* (1037a22: καθόλου περὶ παντὸς εἴρηται), referring back from VII 4 to VII 11.1037a20 (but not to VII 7–9).

out of which the particular things are generated, there would be no stable element during the generation of a thing, and consequently no change at all. This is the outcome resulting from such a φυσικῶς inquiry, namely, the being eternal for form (the point on matter is put aside, for matter is not substance in actuality). And this is what interests Aristotle the most. For this is a φυσικῶς upshot that is in agreement with what has been proved in the λογικῶς part of the investigation about essence or form. Now, this φυσικῶς argument functions as complementary to the λογικῶς argument, but in no way is thought to substitute for, or supersede the λογικῶς argument. They are complementary. And, more importantly, the leading argument is, in the case of metaphysics, the λογικῶς inquiry about essence.[26]

Let us take stock again before moving on. It is evident that the group VII 7–9 governed by a φυσικῶς argument breaks up the leading λογικῶς argument begun at VII 4 and resumed at VII 10 to 11 (12), as it is inserted right in between.

---

26   There is another case of a φυσικῶς argument being complementary to a λογικῶς argument. It occurs in *Nicomachean Ethics* VII on *akrasia*. The solution of the problem of *akrasia* is reached through four steps. In the first step (*NE* VII 3.1146b31–35), Aristotle appeals to the distinction of the senses of someone knowing something: both the man who has knowledge but is not using it and he who is using it are said to know. In the second step (1146b35–1147a10), he distinguishes between two types of proposition: the universal and the particular. In the third step (1147a10–24), he refines one of the members of the first distinction: one may know grammar in the sense of not using it, but being able to use it at once, and not using it, and also momentarily not able to use it, as when one is asleep, mad, or drunk. Finally, at the fourth step (1147a24–b9), Aristotle brings forward side-by-side two competing syllogisms, one restricting us from tasting something, and the other bidding us to taste it. Appetite makes us put aside the knowledge of the particular proposition of the opposing syllogism so as to favor the other one. The four steps are clearly supposed to merge into a single explanation of the phenomenon of *akrasia*. It is important to note that Aristotle characterizes the fourth step as a φυσικῶς approach to the problem (1147a24). This is probably due to the appeal to desires (appetites) that it contains, whereas, in the preceding steps, there was no recourse whatsoever to physical notions. Now, what is interesting is that the explanation of *akrasia* is reached through the meshing of all four steps, one of which is φυσικῶς. Although Aristotle does not employ the word, one can characterize the first three as λογικῶς arguments, for they all operate with very abstract notions of having or not having knowledge. The whole argument, with its four steps, differs from the metaphysical argument brought forward in VII 4–11(12) because, in the *Metaphysics*, the leading argument is the λογικῶς one, supported by the φυσικῶς argument inserted in VII 7–9; here, in the *Nicomachean Ethics*, there is no leading argument to be further supported, but the explanation of *akrasia* is reached only by the four steps being perfectly complementary to one another. On the problem of *akrasia*, see Natali 2009.

However, it is not a discussion alien to the argument, as it supplements the λογικῶς proof and, moreover, the λογικῶς argument itself pointed to such a complementary thesis right at the beginning.[27] If we look afresh with no prejudice at the whole of VII 1–16, one should acknowledge that the burden of proof about form is carried out mainly by the λογικῶς argument. The λογικῶς argument in VII 4–6 and 10–11 (12) is complemented in a salutary way by the φυσικῶς reasoning inserted in VII 7–9, but does not depend on it to be a good proof of the essence as the right candidate for what it is to be the substance of a thing. Λογικῶς arguments do pervade metaphysics, and this is to be expected, as λογικῶς proofs are the main metaphysical proofs. However, being a metaphysical proof is not sufficient for being a λογικῶς argument—as we have seen, metaphysics can also make use of other sorts of proofs, and VII 7–9 exhibits a φυσικῶς proof loaded with all its infertile mules and corresponding physical objects. Nor is it necessary that a λογικῶς proof be metaphysical. Being λογικῶς is relative to the level of generality within each scientific domain, and we may find λογικῶς arguments alongside ἀναλυτικῶς or alongside φυσικῶς ones with no metaphysics intruding on those logical or physical inquiries.

---

27   That is, by saying in VII 4 that *first* some considerations about essence will be laid down λογικῶς, which makes us expect a counterpart of another sort, to begin somewhat later. There are back-references to the φυσικῶς argument carried out in VII 7–9 already in VII 15.1039b26–27, where it is said that it has been shown that the form of a composite is neither generated nor produced. Again, in VIII 3.1043b16 one finds the remark that "it has been shown, as well as exhibited elsewhere" (δέδεικται δὲ καὶ δεδήλωται ἐν ἄλλοις) that forms are neither generated nor produced, but what is produced and generated is only a new composite of matter and form. In IX 8.1049b27–28 Aristotle writes that "we have said in our treatise on substance that everything that is produced is something produced from something and by something, and is the same in species as it", referring back again to VII 7–9. Referring back three times to this same point stresses the significance it has in Aristotle's eyes—and incidentally allows us to know how Aristotle himself refers to VII or to the group VII–VIII, to which VII 7–9 belongs. Any account of the argumentative structure of VII must explain this reiterated back-reference to 7–9, and avoid simply explaining them away as a later insertion. (The phrase δέδεικται δὲ καὶ δεδήλωται ἐν ἄλλοις in VIII 3 may look surprising, for it seems to imply that such a treatment is not to be found in the preceding book, with which VIII seems to make a thematic unity, but in a separate work. However, one can take δέδεικται as referring to a proof to be found in the thematic group VII–VIII, namely to VII 7–9, the phrase saying also that the same point has been exhibited elsewhere (δεδήλωται ἐν ἄλλοις)—a likely candidate being the *De Generatione Animalium* or *Historia Animalium*, as one finds in both texts a variety of exhibitions of something being generated by something of the same species, but form and matter being supposed all along to preexist their generation).

A special mention shall be made to a recent proposal to distinguish between logical and metaphysical arguments within the province of metaphysics. Burnyeat 2001 proposes a very sophisticated reconstruction of VII in which for each topic there is first a logical investigation, followed by a properly metaphysical discussion. According to him, a first line of inquiry begins with the logical specification of substantial being as subject (VII 3.1028b36–37), followed by a metaphysical discussion of it (1029a2–28), the conclusion being that form and composite are substantial being more than matter is (1029a29–30). A second logical specification is substantial being as essence; its logical discussion is made through VII 4–6, followed by a metaphysical discussion in VII 10–11. VII 7–9 are treated as inserted in between, and are seen by him as providing a discussion of the "synonymy principle". The conclusion of the second route is given at VII 11.1037a5–6: primary substance is form. There follows, according to him, a combined recapitulation of VII 4–6 and VII 10–11 at 1037a21–b7. VII 12 is treated as an insertion of an incomplete metaphysical account of the unity of definition. The third route, substantial being as universal, begins with a preliminary definition of universal (VII 13.1038b11–12), then continues with a logical discussion on the one hand (VII 13–14), and a metaphysical discussion on the other (VII 15–16). A twofold conclusion is reached at VII 15.1039b22 (substantial being as definable is form taken generally) and VII 16.1040b5–6 and b8 (the parts of substantial beings and the elemental stuffs are only potentialities). Both theses are seen as reasserted in VII 16.1041a4–5. Then begins a fourth and distinct line of inquiry, according to which substantial being is cause to nature as form is envisaged in contrast to matter. VII 17.1041a10–32 accounts for the logical discussion of the role of essence as cause in scientific explanation, and is consequently followed by a metaphysical discussion of it (1041a32–b27). The conclusion reached at 1041b27–33 takes it that substantial being as the primary cause of a thing's being is nature as form. VIII, after a summary of the discussions in VII 2–17 (minus VII 7–9 and VII 12), is seen as setting out a didactic exposition of the metaphysical doctrine in terms of form and matter, and actuality and potentiality.

In respect to the two levels, a logical discussion corresponds to what Aristotle calls a λογικῶς presentation, whereas the metaphysical one goes along with the sense of the ancient pedagogical interpretation of "metaphysics" as "the things to be studied after the study of nature" (including prominently notions as form and matter). This is, however, a vague characterization of metaphysical discussion, and the best way to demarcate it from the logical level is to contrast it with the first level as the metaphysical level being typically Aristotelian, whereas the logical one is a non-partisan analysis of substance that could be accepted by every contender. But this requires envisioning some of the logical claims, as in VII 4 on the precise meaning of essence as a *per se* of the first sort, or in VII 17 on the essence as cause of the thing being what it is, as not committed to the Aristotelian doctrines, which seems to downplay too much their approach. Form and matter are taken to be Aristotelian concepts only present in the second level, but many of the logical arguments either operate with them, or presuppose them, as in VII 4–6. Moreover, VII 7–9 has no place in this two-level argumentation. What I am proposing here is that there is no relevant distinction between the logical and the metaphysical levels with regard to the way of proving within the province of metaphysics; they constitute the same and continuous discussion in favor of form as substantial being. VII 7–9, as I see them, are to be contrasted with this λογικῶς discussion as providing a complementary φυσικῶς proof of the ungenerated character of form and its primacy vis-à-vis the composite. If I am correct, Burnyeat's reading of VII–VIII distorts the way metaphysics handles its own arguments.[28]

To sum up: the outcome is that the proof proper to metaphysics is a λογικῶς argument, supplemented whenever possible by a φυσικῶς argument. One would then have the triad μαθηματικῶς—φυσικῶς—λογικῶς corresponding to the triad mathematics—physics—first philosophy or metaphysics. And the reason for this seems to be that metaphysics, be it a science or not, deals with such generality that there is no way of contrasting within it a more general proof (which counts in other fields as a λογικῶς argument for them) with its own appropriate argument. Metaphysics has indeed successfully distinguished itself from dialectic, as it becomes science and is thus cognitive of its objects, but keeps λογικῶς reasoning as its appropriate type of argument, given the abstract level at which it inevitably operates.[29]

VII

There remain two points to examine, in which the precise meaning of λογικῶς and its cognates is not easy to determine. The first one is the phrase λογικὸς συλλογισμός, which occurs three times in Aristotle. Already in *Posterior Analytics* it occurs in II 8.93a15, inside the phrase λογικὸς συλλογισμός τοῦ τί ἐστιν. There are two main points that cloud the issue here. First, after having established the equivalence between looking for the essence of a thing and looking

---

28   Another Burnyeat thesis worth mentioning is that each of the four routes is to be conceived independently, there being no overlapping or accumulative progress among them. This thesis has no impact on our point here.

29   For a different interpretation, see Lemaire 2015, 220–221.

for the cause of its being what it is in the two first chapters of *Posterior Analytics* II, Aristotle sets out in II 3 to investigate the relationship between definition and demonstration. II 3–7 develops the difficulties surrounding any attempt to define by means of a demonstration; Aristotle's answer to this problem is to be found in II 8–12, in which chapters he explains "how the what it is is expressed by the terms (of a deduction), and in what sense it does or does not admit of demonstration or definition" (II 13.96a20–21).[30] The discussion is convoluted as both parts mingle in one and same examination, and it is not clear what is to be revised and corrected from the aporetic section and what is to be preserved in it as one goes to the second and more positive section. Second, neither is it clear whether the phrase λογικὸς συλλογισμός refers backward, or forward, that is, whether it refers to the discussion of II 4, which attempts to show that any demonstration of the essence is doomed to fail, or points forward to a more positive usage of demonstration in the search for the essence a thing. The decision about this second issue proves crucial to determining the exact meaning to be ascribed to λογικός in the referred phrase.

If it refers forward to what will be obtained in the positive II 8–12 section, λογικὸς συλλογισμός will be given a rather positive account. For even though there is no strict demonstration of an essence, deductions will not only prove to be helpful in the search for the relevant properties that make up the essence of a thing, but also, and more importantly, they will be involved in the definition

---

30   This is how Aristotle refers back to what he has done in chapters 8 to 12. In II 13 he sets out to consider how one should hunt for the items that will appear in the definition of a thing, and rescues the method of division from the rather negative assessment given to it in II 5 (within the aporetic part). The aporetic part begins in II 3, which shows that demonstration and definition are to be kept apart, for not everything demonstrable is definable, nor is everything definable demonstrable, nothing being in fact simultaneously demonstrable and definable. It follows thus that demonstration and definition are quite distinct. Then comes II 4 showing that an essence might be obtained by demonstration only by *petitio principii*; II 5 adds that division also cannot function as deduction of the essence. II 6 examines the case of attempting to demonstrate the essence by means of a hypothesis. Then II 7 brings in induction, restates the precedent arguments, and concludes the whole aporetic section in a quite negative mood: "from these considerations it appears that definition and demonstration are not the same, and that there cannot be deductions and definitions of the same thing; and further that definitions neither demonstrate nor prove anything, and that it is not possible to know what something is either by a definition or by a demonstration" (92b35–38, Barnes trans.). The next section (II 8–12) will provide a more positive assessment, showing that in some cases there can be demonstration of the essence, to wit, whenever the middle term stands for the external cause of the item to be defined by demonstration.

of things whose causes are distinct from them. When defining items of this sort, like thunder, the middle term in a demonstration will express the efficient cause of it, such that the terms of the demonstration, when arranged otherwise, turn out to be its definition. For instance, in the syllogism "noise belongs to quenching the fire", "quenching of fire occurs in clouds", therefore "noise occurs in the clouds", one has all the pieces of a good definition, for rearranging them one obtains that thunder is "noise in the clouds caused by quenching of fire", and this is the proper definition of it. So a λογικός συλλογισμός will have much in its favor in the search for a definition of certain items, if such a phrase points forward to the more positive results obtained in II 8–12. It will still not have everything in its favor, for it remains inappropriate whenever one deals with essences whose cause is not distinct from themselves, like the classical cases of *human* or *soul*. In such cases, any demonstration will assume precisely what it is supposed to demonstrate, for the essence of the thing already appears in it as the middle term, whereas it was supposed to emerge only in the conclusion.

However, that would be an anomalously quite positive sense of λογικός συλλογισμός. It would mean something like this: it is not sound everywhere, but it is perfectly sound somewhere (namely, in cases where there is an external cause of a thing being what it is). Moreover, such a reading depends on taking the phrase as referring forward, and not backward. Fortunately, there is another passage in which λογικοί συλλογισμοί are also mentioned. This passage is not exempt from obscurities, but it may help shed some light into the issue. Right at the beginning of the *Rhetoric*, after having already alluded to the enthymeme as the appropriate way of demonstrating a point in rhetorical deductions, Aristotle says that one should also learn "what its subject matter is and in what respects it differs from the λογικούς συλλογισμούς" (I 1.1355a13–14). Waitz, who took it that, in the *APo*. II 8 passage, λογικός συλλογισμός was opposed to a true demonstration, now observes that, in this passage of the *Rhetoric*, a λογικός συλλογισμός seems to stand for true deduction, with which one has to contrast the rhetorical syllogism or enthymeme.[31] One of his reasons was that, in the following lines (1355b14), Aristotle opposes the true to what is only similar to it; as the enthymeme goes with the latter, the λογικός συλλογισμός was taken by Waitz to go with the former, since it is opposed to the enthymeme. This would suppose again a very positive meaning for λογικῶς, in the sense of "logical" or "logically true" in our modern sense.

---

31   Waitz 1844–1846, *ad* 82b35; see also Cope 1877, I 20–21, who follows Waitz, as well as Rapp 2002, II 69–77, who translates *Rhet.* I 1.1355a13–14 as "welche Unterschiede es zu den Deduktionen der Logik [πρὸς τοὺς λογικοὺς συλλογισμούς] aufweist".

But there is another way of reading this passage in the *Rhetoric*, and to my mind it is to be preferred. One should notice that, since rhetoric is the counterpart of dialectic, distinguishing the proper rhetorical deduction (the enthymeme) from the other λογικῶς deductions may amount to no more than distinguishing it from the many other deductions that occur within dialectical contexts broadly conceived. This would make the λογικοὺς συλλογισμούς in *Rhetoric* I 1 stand for the members of a set that includes enthymemes and dialectical deductions as well. Enthymeme turns out to be only a case of such a set. As rhetoric is the counterpart of dialectic, resemblance between them is to be expected, and accordingly one should distinguish enthymemes from those dialectical arguments. This explains why Aristotle says some lines further, in *Rhet.* I 1.1355a17, that those who make a good guess at truth are likely to make a good guess at what is reputable (ἔνδοξον). For truth and what is similar to truth are apprehended by the same faculty; if human beings have a natural tendency to arrive at the truth (as Aristotelian epistemology supposes), human beings are likely also to have a natural tendency to arrive at what is similar to truth, the ἔνδοξον, the reputable opinion that demarcates the whole domain of dialectic (within which enthymemes are to be found) from the field of truth.[32]

Whenever we are in a dialectical context, there is only similarity to truth, not truth itself, to speak properly, for the propositions can be true, but they become premises due to their being accepted or reputed as true. Within the domain of what is similar to truth, enthymemes discharge their function in rhetorical deduction, while endoxastic deductions carry out their function in dialectical reasoning. But such a set may have other items as well. As is said in *Topics* I 1, there is also contentious reasoning (100b24: ἐριστικὸς συλλογισμός), either if it is based on opinions that appear to be reputable but are not really so, or it merely appears to demonstrate from premises that either are reputable, or

---

32   As said in *Topics* VIII 1.155b7–16, dialectical and scientific arguments have in common the syllogistic structure of a proof, despite the fact that they differ in what concerns the nature of their premises. Dialectic has thus to know how validly to deduce a conclusion, besides correctly establishing its premises as ἔνδοξα. This is why Aristotle says that "the consideration of deductions of all kinds alike [ὁμοίως] is the business of dialectic" (*Rhet.* I 1.1155a8–9), albeit not only of dialectic (for it is the business of scientific explanations as well). The important thing to note here is that ὁμοίως expressly includes the enthymemes, which have been mentioned just before, at 1355a8, and thus become also the business of dialectic. Aristotle goes on to say that having a broader view on deductions (including not only enthymemes, but also scientific deductions) enables one to clearly distinguish within the λογικοὶ συλλογισμοί the specific kind of rhetorical enthymemes.

only appear to be so. In the former case, the argument is deductively valid, but falsely based on reputable opinions. In the latter, there is only an appearance of deduction, whether the premises are in fact reputable, or only appear to be.

Let us come back to *Posterior Analytics* II 8 with this sense of λογικὸς συλ-λογισμός in mind. Looking backward to II 4, its meaning would be this. When one attempts to know a definition by means of a demonstration, it will turn out that no valid demonstration is produced, for, according to the aporetic investigation carried out in II 4, the demonstration assumes what is to be proved, committing thus a *petitio principii*. Granted the premises "A belongs to B" and "B belongs to C", the conclusion "A belongs to C" will only follow as the definition of a thing if "A belongs to B" and "B belongs to C" already exhibit the essence of it. For to express an essential item in the conclusion, it is necessary that the premises do the same. If the premises express a simple predication, the conclusion cannot express a definition. Hence, the definition to be obtained in the conclusion ought to be already assumed in the premises. This is why, according to II 4, every demonstration of a definition will necessarily beg the question, for it will always involve a *petitio principii*. A *petitio principii* is an invalid deduction. It is not a dialectical argument, nor an enthymeme. However, it is a λογικὸς συλλογισμός, for the set of λογικοὶ συλλογισμοί includes dialectical deductions, and enthymemes as well, but not only these arguments. Contentious reasoning belongs also to it. Contentious dialectical reasoning is the case whenever it is only in appearance dialectical, either because the premises are not really reputable, or because it is an invalid deduction, independently of its premises being really reputable or only in appearance. One may thus include in this set as well those arguments that are only in appearance scientific, because they are invalid deductions, independently of their premises being false or true. They will make up for the contentious scientific reasoning.

In this sense, our λογικὸς συλλογισμός is a *useless scientific argument*. There is a variety of reasons for its being useless: it is an invalid deduction, the premises are not scientific but only reputable, or more precisely it contains a *petitio principii*. This is a strong negative sense of λογικὸς συλλογισμός, but I think it is more in line with the other meanings of λογικῶς we have already examined. It stresses the negative side of emptiness and uselessness that one encounters also in the phrase λογικῶς καὶ κενῶς. This is the reason—or so I suggest—why the syllogism of an essence is said to be a λογικὸς συλλογισμός in *APo.* II 8, for, as Aristotle there remarks, "it was said earlier that this way will not be a demonstration [of the essence], but there is a λογικός syllogism of what the thing is" (93a14–15). He is not referring forward to the more positive outcome in II 8–12, but is referring back to the aporetic investigation carried out in II 4, according to which all deductions of this sort turn out to be a *petitio principii*.[33]

A third occurrence of λογικός συλλογισμός is found in *Topics* VIII 12. In this chapter, Aristotle says that an argument is false in four ways: (i) when it is an invalid argument, (ii) when it comes to a conclusion that is not relevant to what was proposed, (iii) when the conclusion is relevant to what was proposed, but yet not in accordance with the appropriate study (we have quoted this passage right at the beginning of this chapter), and (iv) when it is concluded through falsehoods. The intrusion of truth and falsity into dialectical proceedings, in which reputability is the core notion, not truth or falsity, may come as a surprise, but two elements account for their relevance here. First, the second part of *Topics* VIII is concerned with cooperative forms of dialectical reasoning, in which questioner and answerer work together with a view to a common outcome, namely, correctly grasping the conclusion. It is now significant, in this cooperative approach, whether one is operating with true or false premises. Second, in VIII 11 and 12, arguments are envisaged in themselves, in contrast with their being envisioned in the light of a dispute between a questioner and an answerer. Clearly a poor participant impedes the common work, but so also does a poor argument. When one envisages the argument in itself, having false premises makes it a poor argument, even if one may succeed through them in winning a verbal dispute. Now, when summing up, at the end of chapter 12, the ways in which an argument is to be envisaged as a poor argument in itself, Aristotle says (among other cases) that it so happens when it has reputable, but false premises. He dubs such a poor argument as λογικός [συλλογισμός] (VIII 12.162b27). Again, what does λογικός mean here? It cannot mean "logical argument" in our modern sense of "logical".[34] I suggest that it retains the meaning of being *useless* that we have already found in the two other occurrences, only that, here, it is *useless* for that common task of setting up a good argument in itself, in accordance with the cooperative approach of dialectic carried out in these two chapters.

The second and last point concerns a λογικὴ ἀπορία, or a λογικῶς difficulty, in our vocabulary. After having produced his well-known definition of motion as the actuality of what is in potentiality as such in *Physics* III 1, and having

---

33 I thus adopt Barnes's suggestion, who notes that "much of the discussion has been vitiated by the ancient error of identifying the 'general deduction' [his translation of λογικὸς συλλογισμός] with the argument at 93a16–35" (1993, 218), that is, referring forward to II 8, and not backward to II 4.91a14–b11.

34 This is Smith's translation; Brunschwig 2007 also renders it as "un argument logique". Alexander added, however: "or rather: dialectical" (*in Top.* 577, 26).

indirectly confirmed that definition through comparison to theses of other philosophers in III 2, Aristotle has to tackle the following problem: motion being the actuality of what is in potentiality as such, that is, of what is movable as movable, and what is movable requiring a mover to be put into motion, perhaps two actualities will be required, the actuality of the agent or mover, on the one side, and the actuality of the patient or thing moved, on the other, if a motion is to occur. But in which of those two poles do those actualities take place, in case the subjects are different? Either both actualities are in what is moved and acted on or in what acts on and moves it, or else the agency is in the agent and the being moved is in the patient. Consider the former possibility. In this case, teaching and learning, for instance, will occur in the same person, the learner, or will both occur in the teacher. If both occur in the teacher, the learner will not learn—but precisely the learner is supposed to learn. It must then occur both in the learner. But, in this case, the teacher will have no actuality in teaching, which is absurd; and the learner will have simultaneously two motions, that of teaching and that of learning, which is equally absurd. So the good answer is the teaching is in the teacher, and the learning in the learner. But one may object to it that, as motion is only one thing, it seems contrary to reason to suppose two things that are different in kind, as the learner and the teacher are, while the same motion occurs in each of them. Aristotle replies to the objection remarking that, as the road from Athens to Thebes is the same as the road from Thebes to Athens, so teaching describes one direction of the same actualization, the one from the teacher to the learner, while learning is the description of the other direction, the one from the learner to the teacher.

Such difficulty is brought forward as a λογικὴ ἀπορία (III 3.202a21–22). What does λογική mean in this phrase? The *Revised Oxford Translation* renders it by "dialectical difficulty", but nothing in this context points to a dialectical discussion, at least not in an Aristotelian sense. There are no views in contention for a dialectical argument to be mounted. The French translation (Carteron's) takes it to be a "difficulté logique". However, there is no genuine logical puzzle in this difficulty, at least not in our contemporary use of logical difficulty. It looks rather like an artificial problem, which arises from some misunderstanding about how to determine one and the same actualization whenever there are two distinct poles involved, as in the case of the teacher and the learner. Actually, this is always the case in a motion: there are always two poles. When only one pole seems to exist because there is only one thing, as in the case in which a physician heals himself, he in fact does not heal himself as agent, but as patient, there being thus two poles in one and the same subject, the agent and the patient. Such *aporia* is hence not a genuine difficulty, but only appears to be a difficulty. There is thus some resemblance with the previous cases, where λογικὸς συλλογισμός conveyed the idea of something only appearing to be a scientific argument. In this instance, λογική *aporia*, not being a genuine difficulty, is solved simply by means of an observation on how the language of motion is to be conceived, whereas genuine *aporiai* require much more reasoning to be solved.[35]

VIII

To sum up, as conclusion: to the three Aristotelian theoretical sciences correspond three leading ways of proving: μαθηματικῶς for mathematics; φυσικῶς for physics; λογικῶς for metaphysics. Other disciplines also have their own methods. The *Analytics* have an ἀναλυτικῶς way of proving; the *Topics* develops (Aristotelian) dialectic as a way of persuasion based on reputable opinions. Platonic dialectic and its chase for the more universal is taken as an unsound method. Sometimes the proper way of proving can be supplemented by another sort of argument; sometimes it requires this other sort of argument, as when data are not available in physical inquiries, thus requiring a λογικῶς explanation. But proving scientifically tends to conform to the pattern of proof in accordance with the subject matter. This may not be an exciting metaphysical tenet, but looks like a sound epistemological procedure.

---

35   The same result is to be applied to the phrase λογικαὶ δυσχερείαι ("logical" difficulties), which occurs twice in the *Metaphysics* (IV 4.1005b22 and XIV 1.1087b20). In both cases one is confronted with verbal and vacuous objections, to be dismissed with no further ado (for a more detailed examination, see Lemaire 2015, 215–217).

CHAPTER 2

Aristotle's Scientific Method[*]

Edward C. Halper

Abstract

It is often said that Aristotle's works rarely follow the deductive method he expounds in the *Posterior Analytics* but that, instead, they often use a dialectical method that cannot produce the necessary, eternal truths required to deduce certain conclusions. This latter method involves setting out contrary common opinions and exploring ways of reconciling them so as to "save the phenomena". This paper challenges this interpretation. First, I argue that the *Posterior Analytics* describes not deductions, but demonstrations—contemporary readers have not appreciated the difference, possibly because of a lack of mathematical sophistication—and that it sketches a method of inquiry (*zetēsis*) that seeks not to deduce a conclusion but to discover the cause, that is, to discover the middle term of a demonstrative syllogism. Aristotle insists that to know is to grasp the cause: this middle term is the cause he is talking about. The paper goes on to explain how *Posterior Analytics* II briefly describes a way to use common opinions to locate an intermediate middle term and to use this latter to find the cause. The rest of the paper tests this account of Aristotelian inquiry by examining the first two books and part of the third book of the *Physics*. It argues that in *Physics* I Aristotle, in effect, posits the motion of substances as the conclusion of a demonstrative syllogism and systematically examines common opinions about the number of principles of motion in order to argue for an intermediate middle term. This term expresses, collectively, the necessary conditions of any motion. Then, the paper argues that in *Physics* II, Aristotle uses this intermediate middle term to argue for a properly causal middle term, form. Initially, form is a refinement of the intermediate middle, but he spends the entirety of book II—which can now be seen to be nicely coherent—showing why a determinate motion must necessarily result from a particular form. In this way, the *Physics* uses common opinions to arrive at a cause that serves both as the middle term of a scientific syllogism and as a constituent of necessary, eternal truths that are the premises of this syllogism. Finally, the paper argues that Aristotle expands this account of the cause of motion to apply to all motions and, thereby, advances a definition of motion in *Physics* III. In short, this paper shows that the first books of the *Physics* constitute

---

[*]   Comments from Bill Wians and an anonymous reader helped me improve this paper.

ARISTOTLE'S SCIENTIFIC METHOD

an inquiry into the cause of motion that follows closely the scientific method that Aristotle sketches in *Posterior Analytics* II. These books are not exploratory probes but a carefully constructed path toward a cause. My claim is that the best way to read the *Physics* is to inquire into the cause of motion along with Aristotle. We can follow his moves by reflecting on the cause his method seeks and thinking through what is at issue in attaining this cause, though we must recognize that he rarely supplies us with the signposts that mark the progress of the inquiry. To read Aristotle in this way is to reflect philosophically on the subject of his inquiry. The same method can be used to read all the works in the corpus. In sum, what have come down to us as Aristotle's works are *inquiries* that are best read and understood as instances of the (properly interpreted) scientific method he sketches in the *Posterior Analytics*.

Aristotle's works often begin by surveying the opinions of others, usually other philosophers. These examinations of opinions are supposed to lead to necessary truths about the world, truths that can serve as the premises of syllogisms through which he can demonstrate essential attributes of inalterable natures. How Aristotle can derive, or can imagine that he can derive, necessary truths from common opinions is a central mystery for readers.

This problem is one version of a more general problem that has exercised contemporary philosophers: the relation of language to the world. Concerned with this issue, a number of scholars looked to Aristotle to see both how he addresses it and whether his work could contribute to contemporary investigations. What they noticed is the sharp difference between Aristotle's examinations of common opinions and what they take to be the model of logical deductions of scientific truths that he expounds in the *Analytics*. Thus, they distinguished between his "dialectic" and his "syllogistic".

This is, I propose, the context in which we should understand the work of G.E.L. Owen and his students and the context that generates a way of reading Aristotle that remains so influential that alternative ways are often simply not on the table. In a widely praised article, Owen argues that many parts of Aristotle's *Physics* come under dialectic rather than syllogistic.[1] He shows that the Greek term φαινόμενα signifies both the facts of experience and the common opinions (ἔνδοξα) or things said (λεγόμενα) about those facts. Aristotle did not always appreciate the difference between establishing the facts as the premises of a science and working with what is commonly said; the *Prior Analytics* (I 30.46a28–30), for example, refers to the *Topics*'s claim that

---

1   Owen 1968, 167–177.

the first principles of a science can be established from common opinions (1 2.101a36–b4).[2] Although some portions of Aristotle's scientific works focus on determining the facts of experience, the *Physics* often seeks to resolve conceptual puzzles that arise from the way we speak about the facts. Thus, Owen sees, on one side, Aristotelian empirical sciences that aim to establish facts that can serve as the premises of the necessary syllogisms envisioned in the *Analytics* and, on the other, sciences, wholly or partly dialectical, that explore conflicting common opinions with the aim of "saving the phenomena", that is, of establishing which are the best and most authoritative common opinions. The dialectical investigations are probing explorations of ordinary language usage and thus remain of interest, in contrast with Aristotle's outmoded science.

Whereas Owen sees a gap between facts in the world and what we say about them, Terence Irwin and Martha Nussbaum hold that dialectic can indeed describe the world. Irwin argues that, in the *Metaphysics*, Aristotle discovered a "strong dialectic" through which he could prove necessary truths that ground the science, in contrast with other uses of dialectic that produce only consistency.[3] Moving in the opposite direction, Nussbaum argues that because it is impossible to speak of an empirical fact without expressing how that fact appears to us, dialectic pervades empirical science.[4] Both see Aristotle's dialectic as a tool for exploring the world. Although Irwin thinks it can sometimes achieve the certainty necessary for knowledge, it can do so in only limited instances, all in metaphysics; namely, in respect of the principle of non-contradiction and in a conception of substance that "we use to guide empirical inquiry".[5] Even strong dialectic cannot produce the truths about the world that Aristotle requires for the premises of scientific syllogism, nor does it generally arrive at truths grasped by the intellect (*nous*). Likewise, although Nussbaum

---

2   Owen 1968, 176–177.

3   Irwin 1988, 19–20.

4   Nussbaum 1982, 273–274, laments Owen's "uncharacteristically conservative" preservation of two senses of φαινόμενα. She argues that this term always refers to common opinions (ἔνδοξα) by explaining how Aristotle uses the latter to argue for the principle of non-contradiction. She rejects both logical truths and "Baconian facts". Rather, all logical and physical principles are things said and, thus, common opinions. So are syllogisms, she presumably holds. Although this approach seems to expand Owen's position, it would saddle him with including Aristotle's (outmoded) empirical science as part of dialectic. The former, however, holds little interest for Owen because he thinks empirical facts should be the province of science rather than philosophy.

5   Irwin 1988, 276.

claims that dialectic is about the world, she does not see it as arriving at the necessary truths that Aristotle's sciences need for syllogisms.

In short, Owen and his followers see dialectic to be primarily an examination of linguistic usage. One job of philosophical scholarship is to make past work accessible to the present generation. Not only did Owen do this; he inspired a generation of scholars and a wide range of philosophers not trained in ancient philosophy, a remarkable achievement. Aristotle's empirical sciences have long been outmoded. But Owen showed how to read large portions of his work, even portions hitherto supposed to be empirical, as dialectical explorations of linguistic usage. He cut off, as it were, dialectic from empirical science and syllogistic, and treated it by itself. He made what might have seemed obstacles to this reading to be points in its favor. Aristotle was taken to embody the best philosophical trait, the willingness to inquire non-dogmatically into ordinary usage, to test hypotheses that might account for distinctions, and to recognize that it was often not possible to bring the rich variety of usage under firm headings.

Owen has, I think, cleverly forestalled some objections. If one complains that he has overlooked the approach that Aristotle himself takes to his sciences, Owen can say that he is focusing on a single strand of his philosophy that he finds of continuing interest and ignoring Aristotle's own way of conceiving the method of science. If one complains further that the dialectical elements Owen focuses on should be understood in the context of Aristotle's entire method, within which they play an important role, Owen can cite passages in the *Physics* where Aristotle seems to rely only on linguistic usage. In other words, Owen seems to me *both* to distinguish dialectic from the scientific method described in the *Analytics* and to suggest that dialectic *is* truly Aristotle's approach to science.

It is this latter position that subsequent readers have adopted or, at least, emphasized. As I said, they are concerned with the question of how Aristotle conceives dialectic to advance his sciences. They repeatedly quote the passages where Aristotle speaks of preserving "common opinions" (e.g., *EN* VII 1.1145b2–6), that is, consistency; and they take the *aporiai* to catalogue puzzles with which Aristotle himself struggles, puzzles that arise from the implications of divergent locutions. Thus, they need to address the problem of how Aristotle's discussions of language can justify claims about the world or, often, how he could ever have imagined that such discussions would lead to concrete necessary truths about natures.

The three positions I have sketched here have been widely discussed and, of course, widely criticized. However, even the critics accept the basic framework; in particular, that dialectic is a discussion of linguistic usage and that the task for scholars is to determine the extent to which linguistic usage truly describes the world and so contributes to or, even, constitutes empirical science.[6] Whatever the framework's appeal, it does not fit Aristotle's texts very well. Yet, the problem that these scholars pursue, namely, how our thoughts and opinions could possibly be the basis for firm knowledge about the world, is a central and perennial philosophical problem, a problem with which all philosophical movements must wrestle. If we are to understand how Aristotle treats it, we must take another approach. Or, better, we must look to the texts to see how he approaches it, instead of coming to these texts with our own framework. The foregoing discussion makes clear the apparent tension between three elements of Aristotle's philosophy: dialectic, syllogistic, and empirical science. We must look to the texts to see how he examines common opinions, what role he

---

6   One person who rejects the role of dialectic while accepting this understanding of it is Robert Bolton 1991, 11. He argues that both the *Posterior Analytics* and *Physics* I use an empirical method, rather than dialectic. He contends that *Physics* I justifies first principles through an induction of the sort described at *APo.* II 19; he thinks these principles are hypotheses that are inductively confirmed by an empirical review of cases (*APo.* II 16, 28). Bolton denies that the principles proposed in *Physics* I are definitions, and he does not think syllogisms play a role in justifying them (22).

Another version of the framework is apparent in David Charles's discussion of how scientific inquiry begins with the "meaning of natural-kind terms" and arrives by stages at the essence of the kind, 2000, 1, 19. However, Charles is arguing that, unlike contemporary essentialists, Aristotle does not make essences intelligible by elucidating the meanings of the terms signifying them. In the second part of his book, he examines how Aristotle arrives at definitions of essences without referring to meanings.

Among scholars who have challenged the framework is Helen S. Lang (Lang 1998). Surprisingly, she does not mention Owen's "*Tithenai*" paper. However, she probably has it in mind when she speaks of the "acontextual method", the evaluation of individual arguments independently of their context. Lang argues that Aristotle's arguments cannot be judged on their "formal" validity because they are mostly "substantive", that is, they depend on the peculiar features of the particular topics that are under consideration (16–18). Since, moreover, these arguments are not usually intelligible independently of the topics they elucidate, considering them without their context requires substantive assumptions and these assumptions, separated from context, can only be arbitrary. Hence, Lang proposes what she calls the "method of subordination", the consideration of arguments as subordinate to the topics they elucidate (18–19). In particular, she aims to consider place and void as subordinate to the central topics of the *Physics*, nature and motion. (She examines these latter [39–65] as a kind of preamble to her central concerns, whereas my concern here is with how Aristotle arrives at and justifies his notions of nature and motion.) In short, she denies that the study of language can be separated from the things that language is about, but, unlike Nussbaum, focuses on the things.

assigns the syllogism in scientific inquiry, and what sorts of truths about the world he arrives at. Again, we owe Owen and his students a debt for raising and pursuing the question of how Aristotle uses language to arrive at truths about the world, but they came to the texts with preconceived notions of dialectic and of how language could signify the world, and they found that Aristotle does not fit these notions well. My remedy is to set aside the notion of dialectic as an examination of language along with the range of standard answers to the question of whether it is words, sentences, or language as a whole that can signify things and to consider how Aristotle pursues inquiries into nature.

My first aim is to explain Aristotle's method of conducting scientific investigations. I begin with his account of scientific method in the *Posterior Analytics* and then turn to the first two books and the first two chapters of the third book of the *Physics* to show how Aristotle puts his method into practice. My first claim is that Aristotle explains and uses a method of inquiry through which philosophers examining common opinions can arrive at scientific knowledge. Through this method, language can come to express universal and necessary truths about the world.

My other aim is to explain how to read an Aristotelian text. My second claim is that to understand how Aristotle conducts a philosophical inquiry is to understand how to read Aristotle. In other words, by working though Aristotle's inquiry into nature, we come not only to understand his philosophical method but to see how to read one of his texts. Understanding how to read one text, we are prepared to read and appreciate Aristotle's other texts. Moreover, in reading the text as it is intended to be read, we will be working through an inquiry into the subject the text examines.

It may seem bizarre to speak of how Aristotle "intends" the texts to be read, given the state of the texts we have. These texts have very few of the signposts that let readers know what has been done, what remains to be done, or how an individual passage contributes to the overall aims of the work. Lacking these signposts, readers have doubted the coherence of what has come down to us as individual works. In my view, they have not appreciated that Aristotle's works belong to the characteristically Greek philosophical genre of "inquiry" or, more literally, a "seeking" (ζήτησις). Plato often speaks of seeking a form or something else (*Cratylus* 406a, *Apology* 29c, *Timaeus* 47a, *Phaedo* 66d), and Hellenistic philosophers such as Sextus Empiricus speak of the act of inquiring into philosophical truth as the preeminent activity of the best life. Some later philosophers have also conducted inquiries. Descartes conducts a "search for truth", and Hume includes "inquiry" in the titles of his two major philosophical works. Inquiry has, though, fallen out of philosophical fashion. Most contemporary philosophers set out their conclusions as theses to be proven. Whereas

ancient thinkers construct their texts so that astute readers *arrive at* a conclusion, contemporary philosophers aim to *justify* their conclusions without
necessarily explaining how they arrived at them.

Before we can determine whether or not Aristotle's method in the *Analytics*
is the method he employs in the *Physics*, we need to appreciate what his
method is. Section I is devoted to this task. Section II shows that *Physics* I argues
for an intermediate middle term of the sort Aristotle illustrates in the *Posterior
Analytics*. Section III shows how *Physics* II uses this intermediate middle to
arrive at a cause that is known immediately to be necessarily true, exactly
the sort of cause that the *Posterior Analytics* requires for a scientific syllogism.
It reiterates the understanding of language and the world that has emerged
from the analysis. Section IV uses this cause to account for the definition of
motion that *Physics* III 1–2 advances, arguing that the definition depends on
an analogy. Section V explains how the entire analysis serves as a method for
reading Aristotle's *Physics* and his other works as philosophical inquiries.

I

It is well-known that Aristotle sets out his account of the syllogism in the
Prior Analytics and that he explains how to use the syllogism scientifically
in the *Posterior Analytics*. The latter opens with the claim that all teaching
(διδασκαλία) and all learning (μάθησις) begin from pre-existing knowledge. The
first of the *Posterior Analytics*'s two books is devoted principally to teaching,
the second clearly to learning, specifically, to the learning of what is not already
known, that is, to inquiry.[7] We will see that the difference lies in the syllogism's
role or, rather, its direction.

---

7   Richard McKeon taught me this point along with the general understanding of how to read
    Aristotle as conducting an inquiry. He is not directly responsible for the details that I present
    here. McKeon was an extraordinary philosopher whose work is too little appreciated, perhaps
    because he was more interested in the forms inquiry could take than in any particular inquiry.
    For an account of the *Physics* inspired by McKeon, see Buckley 1971, 15–43, esp. 28.
        Barnes 1975, 84 thinks the idea that Aristotle uses syllogisms for inquiry is "clearly mis-
    taken". His argument is that the form of the syllogism of the "that" is the same as the form of
    the syllogism of the "why" and that we must, therefore, rely on something outside the syllo-
    gism to gain knowledge of the cause. It is true that Aristotle uses other faculties to arrive at
    the cause, but it does not follow that syllogism is not used in inquiry. Barnes assumes that the
    syllogism would be used in inquiry only if it demonstrated or, rather, deduced the cause. This
    assumption is not warranted, as we will see.

ARISTOTLE'S SCIENTIFIC METHOD   57

This second book opens by distinguishing four things that are sought through inquiry (τὰ ζητούμενα): (1) the that (τὸ ὅτι), (2) the why (τὸ διότι), (3) if it is (εἰ ἔστι), and (4) what it is (τί ἐστιν). Aristotle's examples make clear that the first two of these involve a connection between two terms; such as moon and eclipse. Thus, we seek to know *that* the moon is eclipsed and, after this, *why* the moon is eclipsed. The remaining two concern a single term; for example, whether a man exists and, if so, what a man is. In the first two questions, the thing sought is a link between the two terms. Thus, in inquiring "is the moon eclipsed?" we ask whether there is some thing or nature that would cause the moon's light to be diminished. In inquiring "why is the moon eclipsed" we seek to know what this cause is. The cause, call it x, is the middle term of the following syllogism: the moon is x; whatever is x is eclipsed; therefore, the moon is eclipsed. Thus, question (1) asks whether there is a middle term; question (2) asks what it is. The middle term is the cause of the conclusion, in which it does not appear.

In these two cases, it is obvious that there are two terms and that their connection through a middle term is sought. Surprisingly, though, Aristotle argues (in II 2) that all four questions seek a middle term. Although the second pair, "is it?" and "what is it?", mention only a single term, he claims that even here a middle is sought to link two terms. His argument is that someone who inquires "what is an eclipse?" seeks the same thing as one who inquires "why is the moon eclipsed?"; for each inquiry assumes the existence of the eclipse (II 2.89b37–90a23).

What are the two terms in this example? There are, perhaps, four possible answers, three of which can be eliminated. The most obvious answer is that although "eclipse" is a single term, it signifies a conjunction: it is the moon (or the moon's light) that is hidden. Hence, when someone inquires whether an eclipse exists, he is really asking whether there is some cause in respect of which the moon's light is hidden. In this case, Aristotle's argument for questions (3) and (4) seeking middle terms would be that question (4) presupposes the existence of the eclipse, just as question (2) presupposes an answer to question (1).

This interpretation cannot be correct because (a) question (2) presupposes an existence of a middle, not an end term and because (b) it would limit questions (3) and (4) to attributes. However, Aristotle's examples of these last two questions are subjects: a man or a god (89b34–35).

Aiming to explain why to inquire into the existence of substances is to seek a middle term, Ross refers us to *Metaphysics* VII 17 where Aristotle says that even in an inquiry into the nature of a single thing, we seek to know why something is said of something else—why, for example, these bricks and boards are a house—and we answer this question by finding the essence of the house.[8] However, this example is problematic. First, it requires taking a plurality, bricks and boards, as a single subject, but these materials only become one through the form they acquire. Second, it is peculiar to the *Metaphysics*: Aristotle claims that other sciences assume their subject genus, whose instances are often apparent to perception, and demonstrate essential attributes of it (VI 1.1025b7–18). Thus, a science of houses would take the house as its subject—rather than a predicate, as per Ross—and the boards and bricks as possible attributes, just as a science of human beings would take legs to be attributes, rather than the subject of the science. Further, VII 17's mode of inquiry cannot proceed if the subject is, like a god (one of Aristotle's examples here), indivisible and without matter. Yet, Aristotle argues for the existence of such beings in *Metaphysics* XII 6–7. So there must be another way to understand inquiring into the being or nature of a god. Hence, Ross's interpretation cannot be what Aristotle has in mind when he claims that "is it?" and "what is it?" questions seek a middle term.

A third unsuccessful answer is suggested by Aristotle's claim here that the questions "whether or not the moon is" and "whether or not night is" are instances of an inquiry into "being simply" (ἁπλῶς) (II 2.90a4–6). Moon and night look to be subjects and being their predicate. The middle term would, then, be the essence of the subject. Supporting this interpretation is that Aristotle thinks that something exists if it has an essential nature (7.92b4–5), for to be is to be some sort of being, an instance of a category (*Metaph.* V 7.1017a19–30).[9] To answer an "is it?" question is, thus, to show that it has a nature, and to answer a "what is it?" question to show what this nature is. Further, the reason neither a centaur nor a goat-stag (*APo.* 92b5–8) exists is that neither has a single essence; each is an imagined unity of parts that exist elsewhere. However, despite its appeal, this understanding of questions (3) and (4) cannot

---

8 Ross 1965, 612. The definition is the cause of the predication of "house" of the matter, but Ross complains that (1) Aristotle does not "remain faithful to this view" because most often he defines by the genus and differentia method and that (2) Aristotle loses sight of definitions of substances and focuses instead on definitions of attributes. Barnes 1975, 196, cf. 194, rejects (2) claiming that 90a6–14 provides the principal evidence for understanding the "is it?" and "what is it?" questions as inquiries into substances. However, this passage is about the eclipse, and the eclipse is an attribute of the moon. Barnes should have referred to 90a4–5.

9 In Halper 2009, 458, cf. 505, I argue that Aristotle's treatment of the principle of non-contradiction shows that each being must have an essential nature of some sort. Both this book and its sister volume, Halper 2005, show in detail how to read a complicated Aristotelian work as an inquiry.

be Aristotle's because it requires that being be a predicate. Being cannot be a predicate because it signifies nothing besides a thing's essence (*Metaph.* IV 2.1003b22–33).

There is, I propose, a better way to understand inquiry into whether some single thing exists. We come to know a thing through its attributes. Hence, to ask whether something exists is to ask whether there is some one thing responsible for a set of attributes, that is, whether all these attributes belong to some single thing in respect of its nature. The goat-stag does not exist because there is no nature with the pertinent attributes of a goat and of a stag. To ask "is it?" of an eclipse is to ask whether the observed diminution of light is due to some nature. Is it a recurring phenomenon regularly experienced or an accidental conjunction of events? Aristotle's argument (*APo.* II 2.89b37–90a23) is that just as the question "why is the moon eclipsed?" presupposes an answer to the *that* question, "is the moon eclipsed?", so, too, the question "what is the eclipse?" presupposes an answer to "is there an eclipse?" If the former pair requires a middle term, so does the latter. These questions concern an attribute, but they are rooted in the nature of the subject, the moon. To ask "is it?" of a god, the moon, or some other subject is to ask whether there is some one nature to which some known attribute belongs. The essence of the moon is, presumably, to be a body that does not emit its own light located in the heavenly sphere that is between the earth and the sphere of the sun (cf. *Metaph.* VII 15.1040a27–b2). That it exists follows from its being the cause of the observed phases. Since the moon reflects the light of the sun, only the surface opposite the sun is illuminated. Since the moon revolves around the earth, progressively larger and smaller portions of its illuminated surface are visible from earth, which is to say, the moon appears to wax (αὔξεται) and to wane. The middle term is the nature of the moon, rather than the nature of the waxing.[10] To ask whether the moon exists is, thus, to ask whether there is some nature that causes the apparent waxing and waning (90a2–4). In my view, to inquire whether some subject is is to ask whether it has a nature, and this nature is the middle term, the cause, in respect of which some essential attribute belongs to it.

It follows that questions (1) and (3) both ask whether there is some essential nature. Likewise, Aristotle claims that to know *what* a thing is (4) is to know *why* it is (2) (90b31–34). Thus, all four questions are answered by finding the middle term, the essence that defines a nature. However, Aristotle insists that answering the former set is prior to answering the latter:

---

10   St. Thomas Aquinas, 1970, 167–168.

After knowing "that it is", we seek "what it is"; for the cause of its being not this or that but being simply (ἁπλῶς) substance or of its not being simply but being some essential or accidental attribute is the middle. By "what is simply" I mean the subject, such as moon, earth, sun, or triangle; by its "being something", the eclipse, equal, unequal, whether it is in the middle or not.

90a8–14

Here being simply is being a substance and not-being simply is being an attribute. In both cases, the *Posterior Analytics* claims, we first show that there is a middle and then inquire into what it is.

This sequence of inquiry seems to be at odds with *Metaphysics* VI's claim that both the "is it?" and the "what is it?" are answered together by finding the middle term (1.1025b7–16). Later in the *Posterior Analytics*, Aristotle explains how both can be true:

To inquire whether or not the moon is eclipsed is to inquire whether or not some middle term is, and this is not different from inquiring whether there is some reason for it. ... When we discover [the answer] we know the that and the why at the same time, provided that the premises are immediate; if they are not immediate, we know the that without the why.

II 8.93a31–37; also 93a16–20

The premises are immediate when there is no other middle term between the subject and its predicate as, for instance, when the predicate is the essential definition of the subject. The premises are not immediate when there is some other middle term. Thus, if we discover a subject's essential definition, we know that the subject is and what it is at once; whereas if we find a middle term that produces a syllogism even though it is not immediate, we will not have a definition of the subject. In this case, we know *that* the subject is without knowing *what* it is. The *Posterior Analytics* tacitly assumes that inquiry discovers a non-immediate middle term before discovering an essential definition. The *Metaphysics*, on the other hand, refers to the subject's essential definition, the middle term through which a subject's attributes are known scientifically. That *this* middle exists is known by grasping what it is. However, other middle terms are generally necessary to arrive at this middle, as we will see.

Another seeming discrepancy between the *Posterior Analytics* and *Metaphysics* VI is that the latter claims that the essence is apparent to perception or simply assumed, that is, posited, by a particular science (1025b11–12), whereas the former identifies the thing sought by a science with the middle term, the essence. The *Posterior Analytics* takes finding the essence to be a goal of a science; *Metaphysics* VI claims that a science begins with an essence and demonstrates its essential attributes. I do not think these texts are at odds, for our *Metaphysics* passage quickly adds that there is no demonstration of an essence from induction but that essence is made clear in some other manner (1025b14–16). Aristotle is acknowledging that a science must somehow make clear the essential nature of its subject; if the science does not do this by sensation, it must do so in some other manner.

Just how does a science make clear the essential nature of its subject matter? Aristotle notes that if we were on the moon, we could simply *see* the cause of the eclipse (2.90a24–30). Lacking the ability to perceive the pertinent causal nature, we must resort to some other method. As I have already suggested, we cannot determine whether the moon exists by perceiving it. Of course, we can see images, but they differ nightly. Whether the moon exists turns on whether there is one cause of all these images.

How, then, can we find whether there is such a cause? We have seen that all inquiry seeks a middle term. How can we find this term? Answering this question is, I think, the central concern in most of *Posterior Analytics* II, but Aristotle does not ask it explicitly. Instead, without providing us any signposts, he launches into a lengthy treatment of whether the same thing can be known through a definition and a demonstration (II 3–10). If a definition could be demonstrated, then we would have a way to arrive at the all-important middle term and, thus, a method of proving that something is a cause. We would also have a vicious circle. The definition is the middle term of a syllogism, part of the latter's premises. If it can be demonstrated, then what was supposed to be the first principle of knowledge is not a first principle, but demonstrated from prior claims that must themselves, in turn, be demonstrated from the "first principle". This circle would undermine the opening claim of the *Posterior Analytics* that all teaching and learning start from pre-existing knowledge. Indeed, it would undermine the possibility of any knowledge at all. Surely, then, a definition cannot be demonstrated. However, this cannot be right either. The terms in a scientific syllogism are what G.R.G. Mure in his "Oxford translation" of the *Posterior Analytics* calls "commensurately universal": they belong *'per se'* (καθ' αὑτό) and "as such" (ᾗ αὑτό) to every instance of the subject genus (I 4.73b26–27).[11] In other words, all the terms in a scientific syllogism are extensionally identical. That means that it

---

11   Mure 1928. The Greek could be rendered simply as "universal" (καθόλου).

is possible to rearrange the terms so that the definition becomes a conclusion of a valid syllogism. So it *is* possible to demonstrate a definition, at least formally. Aristotle denies that such a syllogism is properly scientific. Indeed, one point at issue here is how to distinguish the essential definition from the other terms in a syllogism and so ensure that the definition is prior to the predicate.

Before continuing, we need to consider Aristotle's account of the scientific syllogism (συλλογισμὸν ἐπιστημονικόν) in *Posterior Analytics* I. The canonical form for a scientific syllogism has traditionally been called "Barbara" because its three propositions are all universal (I 14.79a17–32; *An. Pr.* I 23):[12]

> All M is P.
> All s is M.
> ∴ All s is P.

The syllogism is scientific when (a) the conclusion cannot be otherwise and (b) the premises are "true, primary, immediate, and more known than, prior to, and causes of the conclusion" (2.71b19–22). Lacking either of these features, the syllogism will not produce scientific knowledge (71b22–25). The syllogism whose conclusion is that the moon is eclipsed is a special case of the Barbara syllogism because s, though universal, has a single instance. We have seen that the middle term, M, is the cause through which the conclusion is known to be true, and this holds of every scientific syllogism. If M is the definition of the essential nature of s, then the second premise meets the requirement of immediacy, truth, and primacy (72a14–24). As noted, it is immediate in the sense that it is not known through anything else: there is no M* through which s could be shown to be M. The proper subject, s, of a scientific syllogism is a genus (I 28.87a38–39). M expresses the essential nature of the genus, and the syllogism demonstrates that an essential attribute belongs to each instance of

---

12   Syllogisms in the other two figures can be reduced to syllogisms in the first figure, and the other syllogisms with positive conclusions in the first figure can be reduced to this one. Another reason Aristotle mentions (in 79a17–32) for the primacy of the first figure is that mathematics uses it.

    Wians 1996, 143–144, denies that Greek mathematics uses syllogisms. He argues that in the *Posterior Analytics* "mathematics, despite being the preferred source of example, is handled carelessly and inaccurately" (149). Although the *Posterior Analytics* mentions most examples in passing, the one example that it does develop at length to show how the syllogism serves as a tool of inquiry, the eclipse, belongs to astronomy, and this latter is, as Wians notes (136), a mathematical science.

the genus because of this essential nature. The essential nature is prior to the attribute, and the attribute is known through it.

As I said, the definition M cannot be demonstrated through a prior term, but it can be demonstrated in another way. Because all three terms of a scientific syllogism are extensionally identical, they can be interchanged to produce the following valid syllogism:

All P is M.
All S is P.
∴ All S is M.

The definition is, thus, "demonstrated" formally, but it does not serve as a cause in this syllogism (I 13). Aristotle illustrates this point with a syllogism for the moon's being spherical:

What waxes in a particular way is spherical.
The moon waxes in this particular way.
Hence, the moon is spherical.

78b4–11

But the moon is not spherical because it waxes; it waxes because it is spherical. Hence, a more properly scientific syllogism is:

The moon is spherical.
What is spherical waxes in a particular way.
Hence, the moon waxes in a particular way.

In this chapter (I 13) Aristotle refers to the former as a syllogism of the "that" (τοῦ ὅτι) and the latter as a syllogism of the "why" (τοῦ διότι) (78a22–23, a36–38; 78b32–34). The former places what is "more known", the manner of the moon's waxing, in the middle position, rather than what is prior in nature, its sphericity (78a28–30). Or, to use Aristotle's regular distinction, the manner of the moon's waxing is more knowable for us, whereas its being a sphere is more knowable in nature.

Clearly, then, although a definition can be demonstrated, it cannot be known *through* the middle term of this syllogism because the definition is prior to this term (cf. II 8.93a14–15). But, as noted, the premises of a scientific syllogism are prior to the conclusion. Hence, when Aristotle denies that there is demonstration of a definition, he means that there is no *scientific* demonstration. Of course, it might turn out that a formula thought to be definition can be demonstrated, but in that case it would be in the conclusion of a syllogism whose middle term is another definition. This latter would have a better claim to being the definition of the subject than the supposed definition in the conclusion.

If it cannot be demonstrated, how can we arrive at the essential definition? Aristotle explains that it can be "made clear" from a demonstration (8.93b15–18). We know from the first line of the *Posterior Analytics* that all inquiry begins from pre-existing knowledge, and we know from the opening of book II that all inquiry seeks the middle term of a syllogism. It follows that inquiry begins from the *conclusion* of a syllogism. This latter is the assertion that s is P. Inquiry seeks the middle term or middle terms that link s and P. Although there may be multiple middle terms and, thus, multiple causes, the first cause is the essential definition of s. This is the M that inquiry ultimately seeks. Once we have this cause, it may be possible to construct syllogisms that lead downward to conclusions, but these mostly serve for teaching. Inquiry proceeds in the opposite direction, from conclusions upward to causes.[13]

On this account the syllogism does not prove the conclusion but, at best, shows us where to look for the cause and confirms that we have found it, when we do find it. Yet, we might wonder whether it does even that, for multiple terms could, in principle, serve as middle terms that demonstrate a single conclusion. Could there be multiple essential definitions of the same subject?

Aristotle addresses this problem and illustrates how to use the syllogism as a tool of inquiry by means of the same recurring example, the eclipse. What he says is so cryptic that many readers have had difficulty understanding it.[14] Yet, it is important to appreciate it if we are to see how the syllogism guides inquiry in the *Physics* and elsewhere. That the moon suffers eclipse is a matter of observation. That is to say, on certain occasions the moon is deprived of its light. This fact stands as the conclusion of an implicit syllogism: s is the moon, and P is being deprived of light (that is, having diminished light reflected to earth). Scientific inquiry seeks to know why this happens. Thus it seeks the middle term, the cause of the eclipse. This cause is, of course, the interposition

---

13   This point is well argued by Landor 1985, 123–124. Goldin 1996, 128 and Harari 2004, 137–138, arrive at the same conclusion. Charles 2000, 200–203, speaks of the close connection between defining and explaining. We can find the essential definition by finding a term that, by being the middle term of a syllogism, explains the presence of an attribute: "what is definitionally prior (viz. the essence) is determined by what is causally prior". Although Charles discusses non-causal syllogisms, he does not see them as a step in the process of arriving at an essence.

14   Goldin 1996 has a very helpful treatment of the example.

of the earth between the moon and the source of the light it reflects, the sun. Interposition is, thus, the middle term of a syllogism in which it stands as a kind of attribute of the moon. The syllogism would go something like this:

> Interposition of the earth between the moon and the sun diminishes the light it reflects to earth.
> The moon suffers interposition of the earth between it and the sun.
> Hence, the moon suffers the diminishment of the light it reflects to earth.

This syllogism is valid, and the middle term is the (formal) cause and the definition of the eclipse. By itself, however, it does not make clear that other causes do not produce an eclipse. Hence, it does not count as scientific knowledge.

Aristotle's key move to arrive at scientific knowledge is the introduction of a kind of intermediate syllogism that is constructed from an alternative middle term that is not a definition.[15] His characterization of the middle term is particularly difficult to understand: "the shadow of the full moon's not being able to be made when there is nothing between us [earth and moon]" (93a37–39; 93a39–b1).[16] It is usually supposed that Aristotle is talking about the full

---

15   Ross 1965, 631–632, claims that although Aristotle seeks an immediate sequence of causes that would demonstrate the existence of the eclipse, he relies instead on this non-causal premise as an intermediate step on the way to discovering the cause, namely, the interposition of the earth. He thinks that this cause enables Aristotle to define the eclipse by merely rearranging the syllogism's terms. His definition is "a lunar eclipse is loss of light by the moon in consequence of the earth's interposition between it and the sun". Ross does not explain how "the moon's inability to produce a shadow" (as he understands this passage) helps us arrive at the middle term. Further, although Aristotle sometimes speaks, as Ross does, as if the definition of the eclipse includes all three terms (e.g., II 2.90a16–18; 10.94a5), the definition expresses an essential nature, and this must be *one* (7.92b9–10). I consider Aristotle's multiple definitions later.

    McKirahan 1992, 199–200, distinguishes between the "superficial essence" in contrast with the "deep essence" to be discovered. The former phrase could well designate 93a37–39, but McKirahan uses it instead to refer to "a privation of light" at 93a23, a description that I take to be equivalent to "eclipse". He claims that 93a37 mentions a sign of the eclipse that is not part of the eclipse's essence (p. 207).

16   τὸ πανσελήνου σκιὰν μὴ δύνασθαι ποιεῖν μηδενὸς ἡμῶν μεταξὺ ὄντος. Aristotle's second statement of the phrase omits "full moon". The phrase is usually understood as the moon's inability to cast shadows on earth when it is full; see Mure's note on this passage in his 1928 translation. An alternative understanding is "the inability of the full moon to reflect light when nothing is between earth and moon", but this requires taking σκιάν as "reflec-

moon's not being bright enough to cast shadows on earth, but this fact is not helpful for understanding the nature of the eclipse and is, thus, not likely to be what Aristotle means. I think his point is, rather, that the full moon comes to be in a shadow. The syllogism is:

> A full moon that is shadowed without there being anything between it and earth is eclipsed.
> The moon is sometimes, when full, shadowed without there being anything between it and earth.
> _____
> Therefore, the moon is eclipsed.

That the moon can appear to be in a shadow is known by observation. This syllogism makes clear the that of the eclipse, but not the why (93b2). To appreciate the syllogism, we need to understand the geometry, a detail that Aristotle probably regards as too well known to need any explanation. What is important here is that the eclipse occurs only when the moon is full. The moon goes through phases because it does not produce its own light and only the side that faces the sun is illuminated. When the moon is at right angles with the earth relative to the sun, it appears to us to be only half illuminated. Accordingly, when the moon appears to us fully illuminated, it is in a direct line with the earth and the sun. Only in this position can the earth block the sun's light from reaching the moon, though it does not do so if it is higher or lower than the line between sun and moon. If, then, the full moon is shadowed when there is nothing between the earth and the moon, it can only be the earth that is interposed between it and the sun.

The "only" is important here. How can we know that something else will not succeed as a middle just as well as "the interposition of the earth between the moon and sun" does? Aristotle's discussion in II 8 goes some way toward answering this question. After introducing what I am calling an intermediate middle term, the full moon's being in a shadow that cannot be caused by anything between it and us, Aristotle asks why the eclipse occurs and proposes three possibilities: (a) interposition, (b) rotation of the moon, and (c) an extinguishing [of sunlight in the moon] (93b4–6). Without explanation, he imme-

_____

tion" instead of the more likely "shadow". Goldin 1996, 122n, appreciates this difficulty but, nonetheless, cites Aristotle's "artificial" example. Bolton 1987, 134–136, seems to accept the usual view but he adds that the moon's inability to make things on earth cast shadows even when it is full would be noticed by a hunter who relies on the full moon to stalk his prey. The idea would be that during an eclipse, the brightness of the moon is so diminished that it is unable to cause objects on earth to cast shadows.

diately says that it is the interposition of the earth (93b6–7). Indeed, (a) looks to be all that remains when the other cases are excluded: (b) since the moon reflects the sun's light, its rotating would not cause a shadow unless some surface were non-reflective, but this would be apparent whenever the moon is full; (c) there would have to be some change in the moon for it to extinguish light during an eclipse, but heavenly bodies change only their positions and, anyway, there is no cause of this change that could be conceived to operate only during some full moons, but not during all full moons. Aristotle does not give these arguments, but they help to explain the implicit process of elimination that is suggested by Aristotle's mentioning alternative causes and quickly settling on one. Interposition of the earth has to be the cause because there is nothing else that could cause the moon to be shadowed when it is full.

Someone might, of course, want to hold out the abstract possibility that the moon's shadow comes from some unrecognized cause, but interposition is such an obvious and adequate cause that other contenders are silenced, as it were. Moreover, any alternative cause would need to account for the eclipse's occurring only during a full moon. This latter is the intermediate middle term that Aristotle uses to come to see that interposition is the cause. It is not properly causal; but we can now see that it provides an additional term that must itself, in turn, be caused by whatever causes the eclipse. In this way, the intermediate middle term plays not only an epistemic role in arriving at the cause, but an ontological role in justifying the cause.

This understanding of Aristotle's procedure tightens the noose around the cause, but not completely. Interposition, as Aristotle explains it, is the definition of the eclipse and the cause of its occurring only when the moon is full.[17]

---

17 Barnes 1975, 210, rejects interposition as a definition on the grounds that (a) it is incomplete and (b) the syllogism in which it occurs is a preliminary sketch for the syllogism in which the moon's not producing a shadow is the middle term. Neither objection can stand; (a) the more complete definition that Aristotle gives in II 10 cannot be a middle term because it includes the subject to which it belongs, and (b) the syllogism Barnes has in mind does not have a cause for a middle term and is, thus, the intermediate step toward interposition. Barnes thinks that his own rejection of the middle term's containing the definition shows that Aristotle intends the syllogism to demonstrate a definition. Indeed, he claims the bulk of II 8 "tries to show in what way it is possible to demonstrate what a thing is" (208). Barnes's conclusions that Aristotle's argument in this chapter is "tortuous" and entirely unsuccessful (not to say, redundant) should have suggested to him that he had mischaracterized that argument as well as Aristotle's aim here. In any case, Barnes thinks that Aristotle ultimately shows that it is not possible to demonstrate a nature, but that it can sometimes be revealed in a syllogism (though Barnes dismisses the value of exhibiting essences this way [211]). In his second edition, Barnes 1993, 220 acknowledges

It is a definition whose formula includes its subject, the moon, within it and, as such, defines an essential attribute of the moon (I 4.73a37–b3). So, even though it is not strictly a definition of the subject term of the syllogism as envisioned earlier, it tacitly includes the definition of the moon and belongs to the moon because of the moon's nature.[18] Moreover, the definition of the eclipse belongs to the moon immediately in the sense that nothing else is needed or even possible to cause it to belong to the moon, in contrast with the shadow of the full moon that is itself caused to belong by our definition.[19]

However, the question remains whether there is not another, altogether different definition of the eclipse that is also an immediate essential attribute of the moon. There would be no problem if such a definition defined a distinct attribute that either caused interposition or was caused by it. However, if there are two distinct definitions of the *same* attribute, the eclipse, then in finding only the one, we would not have attained that necessary and certain knowledge of the cause that Aristotle's sciences seek. In fact, there are multiple definitions of the eclipse, but they are not distinct. In II 10, Aristotle distinguishes (a) the definition that is an indemonstrable formula from (b) the definition that is the syllogism of the "*that*" and (c) the definition that is the conclusion of the syllogism (94a11–14). The first of these is the essential formula that serves as the middle term alone. Both alternatives contain all three terms. They add a completeness and intelligibility to our understanding of the eclipse: (b) the moon's having earth interposed between it and the sun because

---

that "screening by the earth" is a definition of eclipse, and he concedes (p. 221) that showing the definition as the middle term could be a "peculiar way" of revealing it through a syllogism. Finally, he thinks the syllogism whose middle term is the moon's not producing a shadow (as he interprets it) illustrates "unfavorable searches" for middle terms, and that is all he has to say about it. Apparently, Barnes has come to reject all his earlier conclusions but does not advance a positive account of II 8 or of the role the syllogism plays in scientific inquiry.

18   Goldin, 1996, 127–130, argues at length that Aristotle uses the syllogism to make a definition clear much as I have argued here, but he confines this result to definitions of predicates and insists that definitions of subjects cannot be demonstrated in any sense. He aims to preserve Aristotle's claim in *Posterior Analytics* I 3 that definitions are not demonstrated by confining it to substances (3–4), and he understands the definition of the attribute to include the subject and, thus, as more complex than would do for a middle. However, a definition of a subject that serves as a *premise* in a demonstration of its essential attribute would not demonstrate the definition. We will see why this is important when we consider the *Physics*.

19   Ross 1965, 77–78, claims that there is a sorites of syllogisms that leads to the definition of the eclipse.

of its being seen to be in a shadow; (c) the moon's experience of diminution of the light it reflects from the sun caused by the interposition of the earth between it and the sun is the eclipse. However, this very completeness prevents these definitions from serving as the middle term of the syllogism and, thereby, obscures the reasoning through which this term is found.[20] This type of multiplicity of definitions does not, though, challenge the definition's being the cause.

Aristotle considers such a challenge near the end of II 13. There he raises the question of how to decide between two definitions of the same thing (97b13–25). This is tantamount to the question of two distinct causes, each of which is grasped with an immediate noetic act. He suggests considering whether the definitions have something in common that would allow them to be two species of a single genus. Excluding this, he says that we would have to declare the things being defined as distinct. In the former case, the things share a partial definition because they are not fully distinct, in the latter the definitions are distinct because what they define is distinct. Evidently, Aristotle simply rejects there being distinct essential definitions of the same thing, either of which could serve as the middle term. Perhaps he is motivated by the thought that the thing would both be one essence and not be it, a contradiction.

How, then, can we be assured that the definition of the nature of the eclipse counts as necessary and certain? That the definition is able to serve as the middle term of a syllogism shows it to be a cause. Since this definition accounts for the fact that the eclipse occurs only when the moon is full, and no other conceivable cause can do so, it is necessary. Since there is no prior cause, that is, no middle between the definition and the moon, the definition is immediate. This immediacy is prior in nature; we arrive at it from what is prior for us, namely, the conclusion of the syllogism and the intermediate characterization.[21] Inasmuch as there can only be a single definition of a single

---

20 See notes 15 and 17. Drawing on II 10, McKirahan 1992, 205–206, argues that Aristotle is chiefly thinking of the complex expressions as definitions, but he also acknowledges that they cannot be definitions in the sense Aristotle means in II 1–2. In my view, the seeming discrepancy vanishes once we realize that the most proper definition of the eclipse is the nature (a) that functions as the middle term of the syllogism. This is the definition that we come to see as immediate.

21 Using the terminology of Irwin 1988, 19–20, we could call the procedure described in this paragraph "strong dialectic" because it establishes definitively the truth of a sentence that serves as a premise of a scientific syllogism, in contrast with the dialectic that can establish only the coherence of beliefs. Irwin himself does not designate the defining of the eclipse as "strong dialectic". He thinks this latter procedure applies only to logical

thing, the definition is certain. In short, seeing that the definition is adequate and having eliminated the possibility of any contending middle terms, we see through a noetic act that interposition must define the eclipse.

Aristotle has not, of course, given us a method or a fixed procedure for arriving at the causal middle term in other cases. Since each definition is peculiar to what it defines, there is no way to lay down a method that will apply to all the sciences. Some of what we find in the remainder of *Posterior Analytics* II consists of tips that might help someone arrive at the middle term of a scientific syllogism. Insofar as the middle term is a definition, Aristotle seems to be speaking about procedure when he asks, at the beginning of II 13, how to arrive at the predicates in a definition (96a20–23). He has much to say about conjoining predicates so that they designate just one nature, but none of this is particularly helpful for discovering the cause of an eclipse. Conjunctions and divisions can help to identify attributes of an eclipse, but they do not show which attribute can cause the others—the feature crucial for a definition, as we now see. Indeed, he says as much: "as for the manner of their [*sc.* the definitions'] being proved, it has been said earlier" (96b25–27). He is, I think, referring to the discussion in II 8 that we just examined. The syllogism makes clear what we are looking for, and discovering essential attributes makes the syllogism more effective. Ultimately, though, we just need to see that some character is a cause of and prior to another. Our minds simply have this noetic capacity, and Aristotle thinks we can rely on it.

The eclipse serves as a good example for the *Posterior Analytics* because it turns on a scientific syllogism that requires knowing very little about the subject term. Aristotle's account of the eclipse presupposes understanding that the moon is the heavenly body occupying the sphere closest to the earth, its reflecting the sun's light, and its having phases. In coming to explain the eclipse, we come to understand something about the nature of the moon. The eclipse is an essential attribute of the moon, not because it is always present to the moon, but because, by virtue of the moon's nature, the moon has the capacity to suffer eclipse.

One more point remains to complete this discussion of the *Posterior Analytics*. It emerges most clearly in the difficult and controversial final chapter, II 19. There, Aristotle considers how we come to grasp universals from experience. We need not be concerned with the details of the process, and, anyway, Aristotle does not devote much attention to them. What is crucial for us is

---

premises, like the principle of non-contradiction, that Aristotle is able to justify because they are required even to discuss their own truth.

that we somehow have the ability to extract universals from experience; for if we extract them from experience, then we do not deduce them from a syllogism. Aristotle's syllogism is in this respect quite different from a contemporary axiomatic deduction. For Aristotle, a science works with universals that have been extracted from experience, and it aims to organize them in such a way that it can discover the one term that stands between the other two and, thereby, causes these others to be connected with each other. In other words, science aims to discover the connection between universal terms it has already grasped, and this connection is a third, causal term. Contrast this perspective with an axiomatic system where the terms are given initially along with any rules of inference in the system. The task is then to deduce all that follows from the initial axioms and inferential rules. The axioms, rules, and what is deduced from them all belong to a single system. The idea that mathematics or science is such a deductive system is not in Aristotle. Indeed, it does not appear before the seventeenth century. Contrary to deductive sciences, Aristotelian science assumes that terms already known will be discovered to be causal or that we will be led to discover causal terms not already in the system. Hence, it is an anachronism to speak of a syllogism as a "deduction". It is more appropriate to call it a "demonstration". The demonstration is achieved when a middle is found.

If we think of the syllogism as a deduction, it is hard or even impossible to understand how the middle term could be the end of inquiry, for we cannot even talk about a conclusion until we have the premises from which it follows. If, though, the syllogism is an arrangement of terms, there is nothing impossible or even surprising about starting with the conclusion and working backward to discover the premises or the middle term through which the conclusion is demonstrated. As we saw, this conclusion is prior for us in that it is perceived through the senses. Inquiry seeks to find a cause for the observation, and the syllogism helps us to see that this cause is indeed the reason for the observed conclusion. There is no mechanical way to discover this cause. However, knowing the end sought is crucial for pursuing a science and, equally, for studying Aristotle's pursuit of a science; for Aristotle's works should be read, I claim, as inquiries into sciences, not as expositions of doctrine.

II

If the *Physics* uses the method sketched in the *Posterior Analytics*, we would expect it to inquire into the causes of its subject matter, nature. Indeed, the *Physics*'s very first sentence announces that "it is necessary to try to define first what concerns the principles" (πειρατέον διορίσασθαι πρῶτον τὰ περὶ τὰς ἀρχάς) because "to know and to have scientific knowledge (τὸ ἐπίστασθαι) in all investigations (μεθόδους)" is to know "the first causes and first principles, even down to the elements" (184a10–16). Whereas the *Posterior Analytics* speaks of knowing the cause, this passage is more general. It speaks of knowing principles and elements along with causes; Aristotle regards causes and elements as principles (*Metaph.* v 1.1013a17, a20). Given this qualification, he could hardly be clearer that inquiry into nature must seek its first principles, that is, the causes through which nature itself is known and through which its attributes can be shown to belong to it; that is, demonstrated of it.

Moreover, the *Physics* immediately specifies that we begin from what is more known to us and proceed by a path (ὁδός) toward what is more knowable and clearer by nature, that which is knowable simply (184a16–21). We saw that the *Posterior Analytics* assumes that inquiry starts from what is more known to us, the conclusion of a syllogism, and seeks the middle term, the cause, through which the conclusion could be demonstrated. With what, then, does the *Physics* begin? The answer comes in the next chapter, and is apparent through the rest of the first book: "For us, let it be assumed that what is by nature, either all or some, are in motion, and this is clear from induction (τῆς ἐπαγωγῆς)" (*Phys.* I 2.185a12–14). Nature is in motion, and we know that immediately from sensation in much the way we grasp that the moon suffers eclipse. This is where *Physics* starts. What it seeks to find is the principle, that is, the cause of motion. If the *Physics* uses the method of the *Posterior Analytics*— we will see that it does—this cause will be the middle term of a syllogism whose conclusion is that nature is in motion. In respect of what character is nature in motion?

One minor reason to think that the *Physics* is following the method of the *Posterior Analytics* is that it nicely explains its first chapter. Aristotle says there that our science begins with a subject that is "universal" (καθόλου) but more knowable to sense and proceeds to the particulars (καθ' ἕκαστα), somewhat in the way children begin by calling all men "father" and later come to distinguish between individuals (184a21–b14). This passage is difficult because Aristotle speaks later in *Physics* I, as he usually does elsewhere, of beginning with sensible individuals, which are prior for us, and working toward universals, which are prior in nature (*Phys.* I 5.189a5–8; *Metaph.* I 1.981a4–16; VII 3.1029a33–b3). Despite appearances, these two passages are consistent. Here in *Physics* I 1 Aristotle is speaking about something that is universal because it is a whole whose parts have been "jumbled together" (συγκεχυμένα); this whole comes to be known by separating its elements and principles (184a21–23; cf. *Metaph.* v 26.1023b29–32). Since these latter are also universals (as we will see), Aristotle is speaking of dividing a comprehensive universal into universals of lesser scope. The claim in the other passages that we start with particular individuals refers to investigations that occur before we arrive at any universal. So the passages are consistent, but why does *Physics* I 1 speak of beginning with a "jumbled" whole and just what is this universal? Since the *Physics* starts from motion and, indeed, since the entire first book is dedicated to finding its principles, Aristotle must be referring to motion here. The sense in which motion is a jumbled whole becomes clear in *Physics* II and especially at the beginning of *Physics* III where we discover that different natures move in characteristic ways and that there are different types of motion in different genera of being. *Physics* I seeks the principles of undifferentiated motion in general. Yet, there is no universal motion. Because neither being nor one is a genus (*Metaph.* III 3.998b22–27), there is no nature common to all beings. Neither then can there be a single motion common to all beings or even to multiple genera of being. Hence, to speak of motion as one thing, as Aristotle does throughout *Physics* I, is to jumble together what is properly distinct. The *Physics* starts with this jumbled universal, but it comes eventually to distinguish the principles of the "individual" (also καθ' ἕκαστα) genera of motion, that is, the different principles of the distinct kinds of motion in distinct genera of being.[22]

The philosophers whose opinions *Physics* I canvases also treat motion as one thing. It makes sense for Aristotle to follow their lead, but it is puzzling how the *Physics* can study something that does not belong to one genus; for we saw that according to the *Posterior Analytics* one science knows one genus, and this genus is the subject of the science, that is, the s of the science's demonstrative syllogisms. How one science can treat motion is parallel to a central metaphysical problem: how can there be science of being when being is not a genus? An answer to the former question will emerge as we work through the text of the *Physics*, but it is well to note that it is not the same as the answer the *Metaphysics* gives to the parallel question about being. The *Metaphysics*

---

22   Alternative interpretations: Wieland 1975, 139 argues that *Physics* I begins with *all* of what is said about principles and comes to distinguish the empirical components of all assertions. Charlton 1983, 52 thinks that Aristotle is treating physical objects without distinguishing products of nature and products of art. Irwin 1988, 496n62 thinks that the *Physics* "begins with a fairly undifferentiated notion" of a principle and proceeds to distinguish types of principles. *Physics* I does come to distinguish three (or two) types of principle, but Aristotle distinguishes types of principles in the *Metaphysics*. His aim here in the *Physics* is to come to a more refined knowledge of nature and motion.

treats being as a kind of genus;[23] we will see that motion is an analogy.[24] Like the child who initially calls all men "father" and only later distinguishes his own father from other men, *Physics* I passes over large and significant differences in treating all motions together.

How, then, does Aristotle inquire into the principles of motion? He considers whether those principles are one or many (*Phys.* I 2.184b15), and this inquiry occupies most of *Physics* I. This approach to the issue is, Aristotle explains, similar to that of those who inquire into how many beings there are; "for in seeking to discover whether the primary constituents of all beings are one or many (and if many, whether they are finite or infinite), they inquire into whether the principles and elements are one or many" (184b22–25). Aristotle is clearly talking about the Pre-Socratics' inquiries into the problem of the one and the many, an inquiry that he pursues in *Metaphysics* I 3–7 in order to consider the number of causes. This inquiry into the number of causes is, in turn, a way for Aristotle to delimit the general types of causes. So, too, *Physics* I inquires into the number of causes of motion in order to determine what those causes are. Moreover, just as the treatment in *Metaphysics* I draws in large measure on the views of other philosophers, so too *Physics* I expounds principles of motion advanced by other philosophers. That is to say, here as in the *Metaphysics*, Aristotle is presenting and wrestling with "common opinions". These are not the opinions of the many but of the wise. So *Physics* I is a prime example of dialectic. However, by arranging the common opinions carefully and eliminating them systematically, Aristotle is able to arrive at a necessary truth that he uses as the middle term of a syllogism. This middle term proves temporary, like the full moon's being in a shadow, yet it too is an essential heuristic device for the proper cause that emerges in *Physics* II. If this account is on the right track, logic and dialectic are not separate, as many scholars suppose, but closely interwoven.[25] Just how will emerge from Aristotle's text.

---

23   See Halper 2009, section 5.1.2. Aristotle distinguishes between a genus in the strict sense, that is, a *kath' hen* genus, and a genus in an extended sense, *a pros hen* genus (*Metaph.* IV 2.1003b12–15, b19–20).

24   That the principles of motion that emerge from *Physics* I are distinct in each genus, but analogous is clear from *Metaphysics* XII 2–5.

25   In contrast, Irwin 1988, 43–44 distinguishes (a) the "dialectical discovery" of the *Physics* that proceeds from universal to particular from (b) the "empirical discovery" (in other works) that proceeds from particular to universal. He claims that "beliefs that all sides hold in common ... allow the dialectician to begin with a point that is not in dispute ... and ... to argue from premises that are unaffected by puzzles" (p. 44). We will see that the principles of motion depend on more than consensus.

Are the principles of motion one or many, and if many, just how many? Aristotle considers the possibilities in turn. *Physics* I 2–3 consider whether there is one principle and argues that there cannot be one. I 4–6 consider different accounts that make the principles two and argues against them. I 7 explains why the principles must be three. I 8–9 show that the three-principle account can answer the concerns that led other philosophers to propose one or two causes. These last two chapters also make clear, tacitly, why Aristotle needs to make a fresh start in *Physics* II. We cannot explore the details of Aristotle's arguments here, but we need to see the way his inquiry progresses from step to step to arrive at a conclusion that is more than mere opinion.

The first answer Aristotle examines is that there is one principle. He identifies two variations: either the principle is immobile or it is moving (184b15–16); the former, the view of Parmenides and Melissus, is explored in I 2–3. It gradually emerges that if there were one immobile principle, then there could be no change nor any way to distinguish one thing from another or even to distinguish the principle from that of which it is the principle. The first option Aristotle considers is that *being* is one and immobile (184b25–185a1). If being were strictly one, there *could* be no motion, contrary to the initial assumption of the *Physics* that there is motion. Hence, consideration of this option does not properly belong to physics; it should be treated in metaphysics. Nonetheless, Aristotle devotes a good bit of attention to it here and, as we will see, it helps to explain the other possibilities.

Since "being" and "one" are each "said in many ways", the claim "being is one" is multiply ambiguous. (1) Which sort of being is the subject of this claim? Is it a substance, quality, quantity, or something else? Since quality, quantity, and each of the other categorial beings only exist *in* some substance, being could not be any of them without there also being substance; but, in that case, being is a plurality. Yet if being were substance alone, it could not be infinite, as Melissus claims, without also being a quantity and, so, many. Nor could it have a limit, as Parmenides claims, for that would be a magnitude, and magnitude is quantity (185a20–b5).

(2) Which sort of unity do Parmenides and Melissus intend to assert of being? Is being one because being is: (a) continuous, (b) indivisible, or (c) that of which the formula and essence is one and the same? (a) What is continuous is a magnitude, but a magnitude is infinitely divisible and, therefore, many. (b) What is indivisible cannot have quantity or quality and, therefore, cannot be infinite or limited as Melissus and Parmenides claim. (c) If all things have the same formula and essence, then one thing will be the same as its contradictory, and the principle of non-contradiction will not hold. In this case, a being could no more be said to be one than to be many (185b–186a3).

In general, to say that being is one is to predicate something of being or to predicate being of some substrate. However, there cannot be predication unless there is a plurality, namely, subject and predicate. Hence, Parmenides must mean that being is the very thing that is or, in other words, that being is neither a predicate nor a subject. It would follow that nothing else could be predicated of being without also making it many (186a32–b14). Nor could one being be distinguished from another, for each would need some additional character to define it. However, the defining characters would either be attributes or substances themselves. In the former case, the attributes would make the substances to which they belong many (namely, substance and attribute); in the latter case, there would be a plurality of distinct substances, and, again, being would be many (186b14–35). Still, Aristotle continues, even if each being is an indivisible substance that has no defining character, nothing prevents there being many of them, for "who understands being itself unless it is some thing that is" (186b35–187a10). Apparently, Aristotle means to say that the Eleatics, who claim that being is one, still speak of a plurality of individual beings, even though there is no way to distinguish one being from another.

Aristotle's conclusion is definitive: "It is clear that it is impossible for being to be one in this way" (187a10–11). There is every reason to think he means to refute the Eleatic position. To be sure, claims that "being" and "one" are said in many ways and that substances have essences have a meaning and a significance in Aristotle's philosophy that the Eleatics would scarcely grant. But Aristotle's arguments do not depend on their doing so.[26] His point is rather that the Eleatics cannot give any sense to their claim that being is one, because to do so would require that they identify some nature that being or one has and any such nature would either differ from other beings, in which case being is many, or include all beings under a single nature. In the former case, the Eleatics contradict themselves. In the latter, the Eleatics would violate the principle of non-contradiction and, thereby, undermine their own ability to make scientific assertions.

Just as the person who denies the principle of non-contradiction finds himself unable to say anything determinate about any being because all predicates will belong to it equally,[27] the person who asserts that all is one cannot say any-

---

26   For an alternative interpretation, see Irwin 1988, 59–60. Irwin contrasts the dialectic in the *Physics* with the "strong" dialectical arguments for the principle of non-contradiction in the *Metaphysics*. As I indicated earlier, I think the *Physics*'s dialectic could equally well be called "strong".

27   For a discussion of arguments for the principle of non-contradiction, see: Halper 2009, 429–432. Ostensibly, the *Metaphysics* argues against denials of the principle of non-

ARISTOTLE'S SCIENTIFIC METHOD

thing more determinate without making being a plurality. The real problem with Aristotle's arguments is not that they rely on his own assumption but that they rely too heavily on the particular accounts of Parmenides and Melissus, when Aristotle needs to defeat *all* possible versions of the one principle thesis. However, as I said, the arguments show the difficulty of interpreting the claim that being is one as well as the need to do so in order to assert it. This is a powerful argument against the one-principle view.

Even so, Aristotle's account of the Eleatics here does not address their central argument, namely, that since nothing can come from nothing, and since every change is a generation from nothing, there can be no change. Aristotle does address the argument in I 8, and he acknowledges there that there is something to it, even if it does not justify the conclusion that the Eleatics draw.

There is another group of philosophers who propose a single principle of motion, the "physicists"; they think air, water, or some other element is the sole principle (184b16–18). However, unlike the Eleatics, they think the principle is in motion. In *Metaphysics* I (3.983b20–27; 984a5–7), Aristotle argues that if matter is in motion, it requires, in addition to its nature, a second principle, a mover (984a16–27). (As noted, the *Metaphysics*'s inquiry into the number of principles of *being* is an inquiry into the number and kind of principles there are, whereas the *Physics* is concerned to find the principles of motion.) Here in the *Physics*, Aristotle understands these philosophers to posit a one from which everything else is generated by condensation and rarefaction (187a12–16). These contraries, condensation and rarefaction, are the movers. Other philosophers, such as Anaxagoras and Empedocles, posit a one in which the contraries are mixed and from which they are separated (187a20–23). For them, change occurs when one of the contraries comes to predominate over the other.

Whereas the former group of philosophers use contraries as efficient causes that act on a single matter, Anaxagoras and Empedocles make the contraries material constituents of a composite whole. Aristotle has much to say against this latter view. However, the real point of his discussion is to show that these thinkers use contraries as principles of motion. Aristotle claims that *all* thinkers make contraries principles, even those who said that all is one (5.188a19–24). But he also argues the point: in order for something to come to be white, musical, or anything else, it must initially not have been what it comes to be. But things do not come to be randomly, as the white that comes to be musical.

---

contradiction, but Aristotle requires the deniers to grant that at least one term means a single thing. This thing is, I argue, an essential nature. Since, though, the principle of non-contradiction is presupposed by any knowledge and since there is knowledge, Aristotle is really showing that there must be essential natures.

Something comes to be white from having been not-white. Not anything not-white, for that would include musical and many other things that could come to be white only randomly. Rather, something comes to be white from having been black or some other color. A complete privation *in a genus* is a contrariety (*Metaph.* X 4.1055a29–33). Contraries are principles of change because change is a move from one contrary toward the other (*Phys.* I 5.188a30–b26; *Metaph.* X 7.1057b23–34). In other words, because a change is transition from not being some thing to being that thing, and because these two, the something, and its privation are contraries, change is between contraries. Hence, contraries are the principles of change. Moreover, in order that something change to what it is not, there must be a cause that moves it to this contrary and, obviously, a cause that opposes this movement. These two efficient causes are contrary principles of change.

It is obvious now why Aristotle begins with the Eleatics. If there is only one principle, there is nothing that anything could come to be. Motion requires two poles. It is equally obvious that the principles of motion cannot be infinite because the infinite is unknowable, and we already know that motion and being can be known (to some extent, at least) by the contraries in a genus (6.189a11–14). The issue is whether two principles are sufficient to account for motion. They are not, Aristotle argues, because one contrary cannot act on the other (189a21–27). What is not-white can become white, but not-white cannot become white. Furthermore, substances are not contraries. Instead, the contraries belong to some substrate. Hence, there would have to be a principle upon which the contraries depend and that is, thus, prior to the contraries. Then, contraries would not be the first principles (189a27–34).

Aristotle resolves these puzzles by positing a third principle, a substrate upon which the contraries act (189a34–b2). He explains these three principles in I 7. A man becomes musical after having been not-musical. Musical and not-musical are contraries; man is the substrate. In one sense, it is the substrate that changes, whereas musical and not-musical remain whatever they are. In another sense, the substrate, man, persists through the change in attributes.

Physics I concludes with two chapters showing how Aristotle's three-principle account avoids the conclusions drawn by Parmenides and Plato while acknowledging the impetus to their doctrines. Parmenides argues that any change would require something to come to be from what is not, that is, from not-being, which is impossible. I 8 counters that a thing does not come to be from absolute not-being; rather, it comes to be something from not-being what it becomes. This latter not-being is a qualified not-being, a not-being of some form that it can come to be. Qualified not-being is possible because the substrate persists in its nature and there are forms that a substrate could have or not have. That is to say, the substrate becomes white insofar as it is not-white, not insofar as it is not-being. Alternatively, something comes to be white from having been potentially white. These two, actuality and potentiality, can serve as the principles of motion. In short, Parmenides is right to reject coming to be from nothing but wrong to think that every change requires such a coming to be.

Plato and the Academy recognize the need for a matter on which the form can act, but they identify that matter as the great and the small, though they treat it as a non-being. I 9 argues that this Platonic matter is not a substrate and privation, but, despite its name, a single thing; hence, the Academy has only two principles, (a) the one and (b) the great and the small. The Academy takes them to be contraries and takes (b) to be matter. It errs by making principle (a) act upon (b) and destroy it. If they are contraries, the one cannot act on the other, let alone destroy it. Further, if matter really were destroyed, no further change would be possible; if matter came to be again, it would require some other matter that would underlie this change. The Academy thinks the substrate must be destroyed when it is actualized because they assume that what is numerically one is one in potentiality (192a1–2). Aristotle agrees that the specific potentiality for the actualized form is destroyed, but he maintains that when actualized, matter has the potentiality to revert to its prior state. In short, I 8–9 incorporate the truths that motivate Parmenides and Plato into Aristotle's own account even while these chapters reject the details of their accounts.

The three-principle account applies plausibly to Socrates's becoming musical or white, that is, to accidental changes. It is a challenge to explain substantial change. Aristotle claims that the account applies to substances because a substance comes to be from a seed that is initially deprived of the substantial form but comes to possess it (190b1–5). This requires that the seed persist in the substance as its matter. However, if the seed undergoes a substantial change and its nature is indeed transformed, then it would not persist as matter. On the other hand, the seed does not initially possess the form that comes to be its nature: how could a nature that the seed does not yet have cause the seed to acquire its nature? Recognizing that more needs to be said about substantial change, Aristotle says in I 7: "whether the form or the matter is substance is not yet clear" (191a19–20).

This issue may be what motivates Aristotle to conclude *Physics* I with the announcement that it is necessary to make a fresh start (192b4). Indeed, *Physics* II does consider whether substance is form or matter (1.193a9–b21). However, it is more likely that the need for a fresh start stems from an inadequacy in book I's account of the principles, an inadequacy that our discussion of the

Posterior Analytics helps us recognize. *Physics* I's penultimate sentence recalls the *Posterior Analytics*: "Let this be sufficient to show *that* there are principles, *what* they are, and how many is their number" (192b2–3). The that and the what depend on finding a middle term for a syllogism whose conclusion is that some subject moves. The issue throughout *Physics* I is how many principles are necessary for motion, and Aristotle arrives at three, a pair of contraries (that is, a form and its privation) and a substrate. It would seem that these three serve together as the middle term of an implicit syllogism:

> What consists of a substrate that persists and one or the other of a pair of contraries is capable of motion.
> A sensible being consists of a substrate that persists and one or the other of a pair of contraries.
> Therefore, a sensible being is capable of motion.

However, the first premise is not true. Sometimes a substrate that has as an attribute one of a pair of contraries can lose this attribute and acquire its contrary; but when the attribute is essential to the substrate, it cannot be lost without destroying the substrate's nature. What is true is that the three principles are *necessary* for motion. Although Aristotle does not do so, we can express this point in a syllogism of the "that" (cf. *APo.* I 13.78a31–38):

> What is capable of motion consists of a substrate and one or the other of two contraries.
> A sensible being is capable of motion.
> Therefore, a sensible being consists of a substrate and one or the other of two contraries.

This syllogism is sound, but the middle term is not a cause. Thus, *Physics* I has not arrived at scientific knowledge. Perhaps the most perspicuous way to understand what is missing is to see that the three principles are a necessary condition for motion, but not a sufficient condition. A being with these three principles is capable of motion, but the principles do not tell when, why, or how it does move. The three principles are always present in what can move, but this latter is not always in motion. In this respect these principles are like "the shadow of the full moon that is not caused by anything between moon and the earth". Just as the latter does not indicate when the moon will be eclipsed, the three principles do not determine when a thing will move. It is easy to miss this comparison, though, because, whereas the cause of the eclipse turns out to be quite different from the shadowed moon, the cause of motion is a refinement of the three principles; it is, namely, one of them understood in a different way. Nonetheless, the three principles elucidated in *Physics* I amount collectively to an intermediate middle term in the inquiry into the cause of motion in much the way that the shadow of the full moon is an intermediary middle. Just as the cause of the eclipse is its essential definition, a definition that, in turn, depends on the essential nature of the moon, motion should be shown to be a consequence of its essential nature and the latter, in turn, a consequence of the essential nature of what moves. The three principles go some way toward defining motion as an essential attribute of sensible beings. Aristotle continues on this path when he inquires whether substance is form or matter (191a19–20); we will see that this determination contributes to finding a middle term that is a necessary and sufficient cause. It is for the sake of such a cause, I propose, that Aristotle makes a fresh start in *Physics* II.

Before turning to this book, it is important to emphasize that the dialectic at work in *Physics* I is directed toward finding a middle term, that it argues against alternative accounts to make a decisive case for a particular middle term, and that the middle term it discovers marks a real advance over the positions of other philosophers. Aristotle does sort through common opinions and chooses those that are most compatible with most others and that preserve the truth as most people or, at least, most philosophers understand it. But this is not merely a matter of coherent opinions. This dialectic is a compelling argument for a truth that is certain. Nor do we see in *Physics* I an Aristotle "at work" exploring various options as they occur to him, testing and rejecting hypotheses that are suggested by ordinary language. Rather, we have here a highly structured inquiry that aims to arrive at a causal middle term. Finally, that Aristotle makes a fresh start in the next book is not due to the inquiry's failure, but its progress.

III

Physics II opens with the assertion that "some beings are by nature, and others from other causes" (192b5–6). After giving examples of natures, Aristotle explains that what is by nature has an internal principle of motion and rest, in contrast with the products of art. He concludes that nature is a principle and cause of motion and rest in that to which it belongs primarily and *per se* (192b20–23).

There are three changes from *Physics* I. First, Aristotle takes nature to account for motion. He is substituting it for the three principles. Second, he refers to nature as a "cause". Evidently, we are to understand that nature occupies the middle position in a syllogism whose conclusion is that something moves and that nature is the cause of the conclusion. To be sure, all causes are principles (*Metaph.* V 1.1013a17), but the three principles are not properly causal because they are not sufficient for motion. Nature, we will see, is sufficient. Third, Aristotle limits the inquiry to what has an *internal* principle of motion in contrast with art, which has an *external* principle of motion. Aristotle explains that a thing that has a nature is a substance because a substance is a *substrate*, and nature lies in a substrate (192b32–34). Thus, it is substance that is a nature, and Aristotle has limited the scope of his inquiry from all motion (cf. 184a23– b14, as explained earlier) to the motions of substances.

Different substances have different characteristic motions, and these motions are "according to nature". One example that Aristotle suggests here is: fire moves upward because of its nature (193a35–36). Nature functions here as the middle term of an implicit syllogism: a substance has a nature, something with a nature moves by itself in a characteristic way (= motion occurs "in respect of a nature"); hence, a substance moves by itself in a characteristic way. For example: (s) fire has (M) a nature; (M) what has this nature, (P) moves upward; hence, (s) fire (P) moves upward. We do not know what the nature of fire is, but we do know that it differs from the nature of earth because this latter causes earth to move downward. Again, a substance has an essential nature in respect of which it has characteristic motions. Nature is an internal cause of the substance's essential motions, and one nature must differ from another insofar as the motions they cause differ.

In a passage that clearly invokes *Posterior Analytics* II 1–2, Aristotle announces "*what* nature is has been stated and what is 'by nature' and 'in accordance with nature', but *that* nature is would be absurd to prove because it is clear that there are many such beings" (193a1–4). Aristotle has stated "what nature is" only in a very general way. We know it only as the inner cause of a thing's motion. To have such knowledge is not yet to understand how nature causes motion or what character a nature has that enables it to cause motion, nor is it to link a particular nature with the motion peculiar to it. In short, it remains to explain fully what nature is.

Why, though, does Aristotle say here that it would be absurd to prove *that* there are natures? We might suppose that if it really were absurd, he would not have needed to argue in *Physics* I against the notion that there is one principle and, thus, that motion does exist. However, even there Aristotle assumes that what is by nature can be in motion (*Phys.* I 2.185a12–14). His point here in *Physics* II is that it would be absurd to prove that there are *many* natures. It is obvious that different things move differently when they are in motion according to their natures. There have to be many natures because there are many different sorts of motion in accordance with nature. Thus, the nature of fire must differ from the nature of earth because the former rises by nature, the latter falls. Plants and animals, have their own distinctive motions and, therefore, distinct natures. In short, since the *nature* of each substance accounts for its motion, it is obvious *that* there are distinct *natures*.

It remains to examine more fully *what* these natures are. Aristotle does not announce that he is addressing this issue, but he devotes the rest of II 1 to it. *Physics* I had discovered a collective middle term to explain motion: the three principles. II 1 advances nature as the cause of motion. These texts are compatible unless nature is one or more of the principles. Indeed, Aristotle must be drawing upon *Physics* I when he inquires in II 1 (193a9–b21) whether nature is form or matter; for the three principles are form, privation, and matter, and privation is simply the absence of form (I 7.191a5–7).[28]

Aristotle begins with arguments for identifying a nature with matter, and his examples here are those that book I had also used to speak about matter; namely, the wood of the bed and the bronze of the statue (193a8–12). Antiphon had argued that if a bed were planted and could somehow regenerate, what would come out would be wood, not a bed. Hence, it seems that a thing's nature is its matter (193a12–17). Since, though, the wood has its own matter, it would seem on this same reasoning that earth, air, fire, and water, the matter of all things, are also the natures of all things because they persist eternally (193a17–28).

Taking the other side, Aristotle argues that it is not the wood but the bed that is the work of an artisan, inasmuch as the artisan imposes a form on the wood to fashion the bed. Since what has a nature resembles a work of art, nature is a shape or form (193a32–b5). Another argument, one that is decisive, is a reinterpretation of Antiphon's argument.[29] Since a bed that would be planted would sprout wood, if it sprouted anything, it is wood that has a nature, Antiphon is supposed to have reasoned. But a bed is an object fashioned by art; unlike natures, art objects do not reproduce. Man is born from man. For man and all such cases, it is the fully formed nature, the man, that has the power to generate, not the material from which the man comes. If, then, it is the capacity for generation that marks a nature, as Antiphon reasons, the nature of something is its form (193b6–12). Still another argument is that something comes to be a nature through a process of growth. The path growth takes is also called "nature", but its steps are in accordance with the end it realizes, that is,

---

28   "The privation is, in a way, a form" (193b19–20). "The formula that makes clear the thing also makes clear its privation" (*Metaph.* IX 2.1046b8–9).

29   Sachs 1995, 56–57 notes that Aristotle's conflicting claims about Antiphon's argument illustrate why his claims should not be "plucked out of context".

the nature it comes to be. Since it is the thing's form that comes to be present in its matter, and since what is posterior in time is prior in nature, this form is the thing's nature (193b12–18).

If, then, nature is form, and the physicist is concerned with nature, it might seem that he could confine his attention to form. This is what the mathematician does, and mathematics and physics are often concerned with the same forms. It is, thus, appropriate for Aristotle to distinguish between mathematics and physics. He does this in the first part of II 2, though, as is typical, he does not explain why (II 2.193b22–194a12).[30] The mathematician treats shapes and numbers as if they were separate from matter even though they cannot exist apart from matter. He is able to do so because nothing in his treatment of mathematicals depends on their matter. Although physicists also consider mathematical shapes, they do not separate them from matter. Instead, they consider the objects of physics as they consider the snub—a composite; for the snub is neither without matter nor an attribute of matter (194a12–15).

Since the physicist is concerned with motion, and we know that motion requires both a form and a matter that is its substrate, it is obvious that the physicist must consider both form and matter, unlike the mathematician. So, it seems inappropriate for Aristotle to ask again in II 2 whether the physicist is concerned with form or matter (194a15–18), as if he had forgotten what he just argued. However, the real issue here is whether the same science *can know* both form and matter (194a18). Inasmuch as one science treats one genus of being, and form is a different sort of being from matter (as the mathematician's treating it separately implies), form and matter would seem to belong to distinct sciences. Indeed, the early physicists confined themselves to matter (194a18–21).

To show that matter can be treated together with form, Aristotle again invokes the analogy between art and nature. Just as an art is concerned not only with a form, but with imposing the form on a matter and, thus, with whether the matter is capable of receiving the form, so too the physicist must be concerned with both the form and the matter in which it comes to exist, as well as the way that form comes to be in the matter. To be sure, sometimes the art that makes an artifact is distinct from the art that uses it, as for example the carpenter's art of making a ship's rudder and the sailor's art of using it. However, the art of using is "architectonic": it directs the art of making to produce the

---

30   This passage resembles *Metaphysics* VII 11, but there Aristotle compares mathematicals and the forms of natures in order to delimit the latter. In general, mathematical forms are more formal because they are not connected with matter, whereas the forms of natures belong to things in motion. See Halper 2009, 106–110.

artifact so that it can be used. So, too, a human being cannot come to be in any matter; human functioning requires particular types of bones, sinews, heart, etc.; that is, organs that are so structured as to be capable of supporting the proper human functioning. It follows that matter is relative to form: to each form there is a matter that is capable of the use—that is, the functioning— that is the form (194b8–9). It follows, too, that the science that knows the form must know what sort of matter can take on the form, for the matter and the process by which the form comes to be in it are relative to the form.

With this conclusion, it is clear to the reader that the three principles that serve in *Physics* I as the middle term to account for motion have been whittled down to one, the form. Aristotle does not state this conclusion, but he rarely provides the signposts and status updates that would make it easy for his readers to follow the inquiry. The crucial arguments are in the text, even if he leaves it up to the reader to think them through and to come to understand how they further the inquiry. From this point (II 2) forward, nature is form. What has yet to be shown adequately is the causal role form has in producing motion.

Let us take stock and summarize what we have found before proceeding. Aristotle's most salient observation is that different sorts of substances move in different ways. Fire rises, whereas earth falls; different plants and animals develop and mature in their own characteristic ways. The differences in these motions can only stem from internal differences in the substances that undergo them. Aristotle labels the internal character that is responsible for the motion the substance's "nature". Nature is an internal cause of motion insofar as it serves as the middle term in a syllogism whose conclusion is that a substance has a particular sort of motion. Although there are three principles of motion, Aristotle argues that matter is relative to form. Since a privation is also under-stood through the form (cf. *Metaph.* IX 2.1046b15–22), form is clearly the first principle or cause of motion. Hence, nature is form, and motion is an *attribute* of a substance, an attribute that the substance possesses through its own nature, its form. Interestingly, this form comes to be present in a matter by a process of development that is characteristic of it. The nature of something is that into which it develops, the final cause of the development. Aristotle has not yet explained how a form that is not present directs the path of develop-ment through which it comes to be present.[31] Just what sort of cause is form? And how does form cause motion?

---

31 There is a sense in which a nature is rightly called a "self-mover"; however, a nature is not an efficient cause of its *own* motion (as claimed by Irwin 1988, 94–96). The root of the latter view may be that the artisan is an efficient cause of the work of art, and Aristotle compares nature to art. However, the efficient cause of a nature is *another* nature, not itself

Once we see that the inquiry into the cause of motion has led us to nature and from there to form, we can readily understand how the rest of book II contributes to the inquiry, an issue readers rarely even try to resolve. II 3 distinguishes the four familiar causes, and it also distinguishes some twelve ways something can be any of these four causes: individual or generic, accidental or the genus of the accident, complex or simple, and any of these six potentially or actually (195b13–16). What sort of cause is the form that is something's nature? The obvious answer is the formal cause, in which case the form would be the essential nature of the substance. However, insofar as something has a form, it is not moving. So a formal cause would hardly seem able to explain why something moves when it does and the way it moves.

Although the topic of the next three chapters, II 4–6, chance and fortune,[32] seems to emerge out of the blue, these chapters contribute importantly toward explaining how nature causes motion. Some things, like the heavenly spheres, *always* move in the same way; others, such as a house, *usually* move or, rather, come to be in the same way. There is a third class that comes to be by chance or fortune. Thus, a housebuilder practicing his art on suitable material will generally produce a house, even though unusual events such as a storm, illness,

---

(II 7.198a24–27). Nature resembles art in other ways, namely, in being an end of a process of realization, as we will see. One reason that a boy's nature cannot be the efficient cause of his development into a man is that it does not exist properly until the process is complete. Likewise, when earth falls down, it is realizing its own nature or an attribute of its nature by coming to be in its proper place. (So, too, Lang 1998, 53–54, 63–64).

It follows from this reasoning that Aristotle does *not* contradict II 1's claim that nature is an internal principle of motion when, in VIII 4, he denies that elements and animals move themselves (255a15). This latter passage refers to an efficient cause. Earth is not the *efficient* cause of its own downward movement. The efficient cause here is whatever removes the obstacle that prevents earth from realizing its nature by falling. Likewise, a heavenly sphere, composed of the fifth element, has a circular motion *by nature*. Even so, it requires a distinct efficient (or final) cause, not to remove an obstacle—there is none—but to sustain the motion eternally. Unlike rectilinear motions that come to completion when a body reaches some place, a rotating sphere never comes to a new place. Always changing, it is always the same, but only in a way. The reality of the spheres' changes is evident from their effect on earth. Hence, the motion of the sphere is not a complete actuality and requires another cause. In contrast, Broadie 1988, 204–257, esp. 255–257, argues at length that Aristotle reasons circularly from the definition of motion to an eternal actuality.

32   The Greek is, respectively: τὸ αὐτόματον and ἡ τύχη. Because frequent alternative translations are, respectively, "spontaneity" and "chance", a reader who encounters the term "chance" cannot always tell which of the two Greek terms is being translated. I think that the traditional rendering I have adopted here captures contemporary usage and, thus, allows us to see that the question of whether chance is a cause in nature is a real issue.

or termite swarms could prevent him from achieving this end. But that a musician would make a house is a matter of fortune. There is nothing in the activity of a musician that would ordinarily lead to a house. In general, an event is a matter of fortune if it would ordinarily be produced through the agency of someone possessing a specific art or engaged in a specific activity, but is produced by someone with another art or engaged in another activity. The housebuilder's art ordinarily produces houses; the musician's does not. Hence, a musician who builds a house is a matter of fortune. Another of Aristotle's examples is someone collecting money for a feast who goes to the market for the sake of purchasing items, but meets there someone from whom he is able to collect money. This is fortune because an act done for one end produces an end that would typically be attained by a different act. Importantly, there would be no fortune if activities or arts did not typically attain the ends that are specific to them. Fortune is, then, a kind of privation of the regular cause (cf. *Metaph.* XII 3.1070a4–9).

Nature is like art insofar as it is a process that proceeds toward an end. Thus, a stone falls toward the ground. A boy develops into a man. If the stone hits someone when it falls, that is a matter of chance because the stone achieved a different end than the one it attains by nature. If an ox produces man-faced progeny (8.198b31–32), that too is a matter of chance because the ox generally produces offspring that resemble it, whereas man-faced progeny are naturally produced by human beings.

Just as there is fortune among rational agents, there is chance among natures. Just as fortune presupposes activity that aims at some end, chance presupposes that a nature aims at some end. To complete the analogy, chance is a kind of privation of nature; specifically, it is a privation of that nature that would produce a natural end.

Since there is chance in nature, and since chance presupposes activity for the sake of an end, there must be ends in nature. Chance is only possible insofar as a nature *has* an end. Nature, then, is a prior cause to chance (198a5–13).

What are the ends of nature? II 7 explains that nature or, rather, a form is an end because this form comes to be present in matter through the course of an individual's development. The individual comes to exist through another individual of the same form: a human being generates a human being. Thus, form is not only the end, but the efficient cause of the process of generation that realizes this end in another individual. (Were the form to come to be present in this other substance somehow without the nature that typically generates it, the generated form would be by chance.) II 7 also claims that the form is the essence and formal cause of a nature. In sum, it is in respect of his form or nature that a man generates offspring that come, in turn, through a process of development to possess the same form. In natural substances, form is the efficient, formal, and final causes. Since there are multiple ways in which the form causes motion, form can be the middle term of a syllogism in multiple ways. Importantly, the motions that form causes are generation, the course of development, and, we must add, the path of decay.

The final two chapters on *Physics* II complete the picture by explaining the motion generated by form. There is a large literature on this section, especially on II 8; but scholars do not consider these chapters in terms of Aristotle's inquiry into how nature can be form. The central question in II 8 is whether natural events are of necessity or for the sake of an end? Do the rains come of necessity? Do an animal's front teeth become sharp of necessity? Or are these events for the sake of an end? If they are of necessity, Aristotle reasons, then anything that results from the rains or the sharp teeth is not an inevitable consequence but an accident. But what happens accidentally is rare, whereas the rains usually produce the corn and an animal's front teeth are usually sharp for chewing. Hence, natural events are not of necessity. Assuming that there are only these two alternatives, Aristotle concludes that the rains and the teeth are each for the sake of an end. That end can only be the *nature*, that is, the form, which the rain or teeth serve. Moreover, Aristotle continues, where there is an end of a series, the preceding steps are all for the sake of this end (199a8–9). Since nature is like art, and art proceeds in steps toward an end, so too does nature. Thus, Aristotle, declares that if a house had been made by nature, it would have been made in the same way it is now made by art, and if something that comes by nature, say a dog, were made by art, it too would come about through the same process of development it has now (199a12–15). Each step in the series is for the sake of the next. What are these steps? The gradual production of organs that either serve the whole or are part of it. Thus, the plant grows leaves that shade the fruit and sends down roots for the sake of nourishment, and it develops other organs that serve the functioning of the mature plant (199a23–32).[33]

This is, I submit, the causal account we have been looking for. A form is an actuality. A plant that has come to possess its form is able to function as

---

33 Bolotin 1998, 47–48, denies that this sense of teleology can be identified with purposive-
    ness in nature because knowledge of organs acting to sustain a nature does not show that
    the thing was created for a purpose. He argues that *Physics* I's three-principles account
    intentionally conceals deeper questions of whether the world has come to be from noth-
    ing and, thus, the possibility of knowing nature (24). In my view, Bolotin misses the signif-
    icance of Aristotle's notion of actuality. For more on how the existence of actuality makes
    knowledge of nature possible, see Halper 1993a, 93–116.

a plant. To so function, it requires organs that contribute to its function, and those organs come to develop along with the whole organism. This process of development is governed by the end, just as the art that produces the rudder is directed by the art that uses it. Hence, the *steps* through which a matter takes on a form are determined by—or, rather, caused by—that form. The form is a cause of motion inasmuch as it determines both the path that the matter takes toward its possession and the organs that will be produced and will contribute to the overall function of the substance.

Not any matter could take on any form. To generate a plant, certain specific types of matter in certain proportions are necessary. This is the meaning of "necessity", the subject of *Physics* II 9. Properly understood, the term does not signify forces operating blindly, as Aristotle had suggested in II 8 (198b16–19). Rather, it refers to the kinds of matter that play a role in the organs whose functions either contribute to the natural substance's overall function or constitute this overall function. In order to perform this function, the nature needs organs capable of their particular functions, and they, in turn, need particular types of matter. This latter is the matter, the material cause, which is necessary for the formal cause to achieve its function. Among the material elements is the rainfall at the proper time that is necessary for the growth of the corn.

We can now see that Aristotle's initial distinction between what is necessary and what is for the sake of an end is a false dichotomy. Rain or some other source of water at the right time is necessary in respect of the development of the corn. It is an essential attribute of the corn's nature. In other words, the rains fall at the right time for the sake of an end, the growth of the crops, because the nature of the *corn* requires water to realize itself.[34] Accordingly, farmers take

---

34   Rain has its own nature, and Aristotle explains summer heat and winter rain in *Metereo-logica* I 9 without mentioning the corn, as I note in Halper 1993b, 174–175.

     Scholars have usually considered teleology apart from the development of form. For example, Broadie 1988, 79 is concerned with whether Aristotle has answered the materialist who holds that elements combine through their own natures into "a stable system" in which the elements "affect each other in such a way that they physically cohere". However, in the case she imagines, the system has its *own* form, distinct from that of its elements, a form for which the elements are necessary. If this form perpetuates itself, or even maintains itself against perturbations, as Broadie supposes, then her proposed counter-example is just Aristotle's example. For the strict materialist, every conjunction of elements is accidental and does not "form a system". Aristotle's teleology is minimal: it requires only parts that serve a larger function, which Broadie assumes. The tendency to understand teleology in terms of some good or benefit that an object receives, apart from its nature, obscures the issue.

     Sedley 1991, 179–196 argues that not only does the rain fall for corn, but the corn is for us and, indeed, the cosmos as a whole is for the sake of man. However, Aristotle is emphatic

care to plant the corn so that the rains do come at the right time. What has bothered readers about Aristotle's discussion is why what happens of necessity is accidental and how a phenomenon in the clouds could be driven by a species on earth. Following Aristotle's inquiry into the causal middle term, we can see that Aristotle's point is only that the corn's growth requires water at a particular time and that, did it not, the rainfall could only be understood through the necessity of its own nature. Aristotle is talking here about the development of a *single* nature, not some cosmic harmony.

What then is nature? It is a function, an actuality. It comes to be present in matter through a process of development that it (as present in the parent, the efficient cause) initiates in a matter. The process that that form causes is the motion of development and coming to maturity of a nature, that is, *of another like itself*. This process is as regular as the sequence of steps through which a house comes to be. Aristotle's inquiry has, at last, reached a properly causal middle term. The form *has* to cause motion because form has to be realized in matter, and like art and every other purposive activity, the realization of this end occurs in a way that is thoroughly governed by the end realized, that is by the form. From the perspective of the nature that comes to be, the *Physics* is based on the following scientific syllogism: nature is the actuality of a particular matter; the actuality of a particular matter is attained only by the developmental motion through which the particular matter comes to be actualized (that is, to have the function that is its form); hence, nature is attained only through the developmental motion through which a particular matter is actualized. As Aristotle had expressed this conclusion earlier: "nature (that is, the nature called 'generation') is the path into nature" (I 1.193b12–13; also *Metaph.* V 3.1014b16–17).

There is a question as to how the form that is not yet present can direct its own emergence in matter, but this is not an especially serious issue. The form exists before generation in another individual, the father, who sets the matter in motion in a particular way. Aristotle thinks that something can only move another thing through contact. So he has to say that the father gives the matter a motion that fertilizes it and that allows the zygote to develop on its own, provided the appropriate conditions exist (*Metaph.* IX 7.1049a13–18). Once it moves on its own, it is a nature. So the developing animal both is and is not a

---

that the end of each substance is its own nature (II 7.198b5–9) and that the cosmos has no single nature, as Judson 2005, 359–360 notes. Judson himself proposes restricting Aristotle's teleology to natural substances (348), and he ultimately rejects the idea that the rains are for the sake of the crops (p. 364). However, Judson does not discuss II 9, and he does not seem to appreciate that *every* species of plant and animal depends upon others.

nature, but in different ways. Form exists most properly at the beginning and end of the process, and only in a way in the middle. However, the form that exists in the middle is the functioning of the substance's developing organs, a functioning that transforms and matures those organs in a manner that is intelligible through the form that they come, ultimately, to realize.

With this understanding of form, we have arrived at a cause whose ascription to an individual is known immediately as a necessary truth (cf. *APo.* I 2.72a6–8, a14–16; 6.74b5–6): form causes the motion through which form comes to be realized. Obviously, such a truth cannot be deduced, but Aristotle has constructed his inquiry so as to arrive at it in a way that makes its necessity clear. Let us review the steps. We know that things are in motion, and we know that of the three principles of motion, form is primary because it accounts for the other two. But form exists together with matter in a composite. Because the composite is not eternal, the form must come to be present in the composite, and this requires that some pre-existing form act upon a matter so that the matter develops both an organ capable of performing the function that the form is and other organs capable of performing functions that sustain this primary organ. Because the material in these organs must eventually wear out, it will necessarily lose its functions, and the substantial form must cease, sooner or later, to be present in the composite. Hence, form is necessarily the cause of form's coming to be present in matter and of the course of decay through which the form ceases to be present. These processes—that is, generation, development, and decay—are the characteristic motions that the form necessarily causes. The form is, thus, the middle term of a syllogism whose conclusion is that what has the form is necessarily in motion.[35] As such the form is properly causal in so far as it accounts for the thing's necessarily

---

35   Obviously this syllogism is confined to sensible destructible substances, and these constitute a distinct genus of substance (*Metaph.* XII 1.1069a30b2). It is not a criticism of Aristotle that the heavens neither come to be nor lose their function from wear. They are a special case that he explains in *Physics* VIII. Nor is it legitimate to object that Aristotle later confines "motion" to non-substantial change (V 1.225b5–9), for this restriction represents a refinement of the inquiry, a movement that the end of I 1 alerts us to expect. Still another possible objection, equally weak, is that a substance's being in motion cannot be a premise or conclusion of a scientific syllogism because this claim is neither necessary nor always true, as premises and conclusions of scientific syllogisms must be. The ascription of motion to a substance must be atemporal, just like the ascription of two sets of teeth to human beings. In this case, we must understand a substance to be in motion if it is necessarily true that a substance must experience motion. In other words, to say that the substance is in motion is not to speak about its state at some time but to insist that at some point in its history it has come to be.

being in motion and for the characteristic motion it undergoes. The form does not, of course, account for a thing's being in motion at a particular time of day; the motion form causes stems from the thing's nature and is grasped through that nature, rather than through the motion of something else (such as the sun whose motion time measures). In general, a substance's form necessarily causes the generation and destruction of the substance's form and these latter are the essential motions of the substance. Elements like earth and fire are limiting cases. Although they can come to be from each other, their natural motion is to *maintain* their natures. When displaced, they move, "according to nature", to places proper to their natures.

If this analysis is correct, Aristotle arrives at the first principle of motion, the middle term through which there can be demonstrative knowledge, through an inquiry whose every detail furthers its end. Moreover, he does exactly what Owen and those who follow him have assumed to be impossible. He uses "common opinions" about motion in order to arrive at a necessary truth about its cause. Cognizant of contemporary discussions, we expect some formula for connecting language with the world, such as an alignment of word with object, sentence with fact, or language in general with the world. There is no such formula. Instead, we find Aristotle subjecting nature to a close examination that allows him eventually to connect a form with a thing by means of the thing's coming to possess the form, and the connection is verified by its accounting for the observed motions. We can, of course, dispute whether Aristotle is right to understand nature in terms of form and matter rather than the quantitative determinations used in contemporary science. Indeed, we might dispute Aristotle's reasoning on a number of points, but it is useless to try to do so before we have understood it. We have come to understand it by working through the details of the text with an eye toward what Aristotle himself tells us, in the *Posterior Analytics*, he is seeking, namely, the middle term.

It is important to realize that the understanding of this middle term so laboriously acquired is very general. Aristotle began by exploring the principles of any motion, and he continued to talk about the cause of substantial motion. The nature that has emerged as a cause is generic (cf. II 3.195b13–16). It will not serve for a syllogism about any particular substance. Aristotle has, though, shown how to come to understand nature, and he applies this method to his investigations of particular kinds of substance in scientific works devoted to substances such as the heavens, the elements, and the animals.

It only remains for us here to consider how this discovery of the middle term is put to work in the next stage of inquiry. This we see in the opening chapters of *Physics* III. After considering this issue very briefly, I conclude with some lessons for reading Aristotle.

IV

Whereas *Physics* I inquires into the principles of any motion, *Physics* II confines itself to substantial motion and its principle, nature. *Physics* I had given many examples of other motions. What happened to those motions that are not changes in substance?

Physics III opens with the claim that it is necessary to understand "what is motion?" (τί ἐστι κίνεσις) because one ignorant of this is also ignorant of nature (200b13–14). Evidently, Aristotle aims to use motion to test whether nature, as we now understand it, is truly a principle of motion. The rest of the *Physics* explores the character of motion, but we can confine ourselves to the first chapters of book III where Aristotle advances and explains the definition of motion. It should be noted that defining motion resembles defining the eclipse in that both are attributes rather than subjects. Moreover, just as the eclipse is defined through its cause, interposition, so too motion is defined through its cause, form. However, the eclipse is a single phenomenon; motion is many.

Aristotle's account of the definition begins by distinguishing what is only actual from what is potential and actual (200b26–27).[36] He does not illustrate the former, but he probably has in mind the unmoved movers. His examples of what is both actual and potential are the individual categories (200b27–28). That is to say, there is an actual and a potential in each category. In *Physics* I Aristotle had said that actuality and potentiality could be substituted for the three principles of motion (8.191b27–29). We have seen that each substance exists potentially and actually and that the potential substance develops into the actual substance. Apparently, Aristotle is applying this scheme to each categorial genus. In each genus, there are entities that are fully actual and entities that are potentialities for these actualities. The latter can be actualized, and the former could cease to be actualities. In the genus of substance, we saw that nature is not only the efficient cause of generation and development and their final cause, but also the path of development into a nature (e.g., II 1.193b12–13). This path is a matter of nature because it is a consequence as well as a manifestation of the nature to which it leads. Likewise, Aristotle declares here in III 1 that there is no motion apart from the things that are in motion because what changes always does so in respect of substance, quantity,

---

36   According to some manuscripts this passage makes a threefold distinction: the actual, the potential, and what is potential and actual. Although most translators follow these manuscripts, Ross follows the manuscripts that have twofold distinction in his Greek text. I think that this fits more easily into the flow of the inquiry, even though it eventually emerges that a thing can exist in three states.

quality, or place (200b32–34). He means that change always occurs *to* some *thing* and exists as a series of states of that thing, namely, as states of its substance, its quality, or one of the other categories that are present to it. There is nothing common to beings in distinct categories. Nor, consequently, can the changes in those categories—namely, qualitative change, quantitative change, and change in place—have anything in common except, perhaps, belonging as attributes to the same substance (200b34–201a1).

Having worked through the account of nature in book II, we can see that Aristotle is extending to all beings the account of substantial change he developed there by making an analogy between substance and other categorial genera. Just as each substance has a motion in accordance with its nature, namely the motion by which a matter realizes this nature, so too in the other categories there is a motion through which something in that category comes to be actualized in a matter. And just as the actual substance comes to be from a potential substance, an actual quantity comes to be from another quantity that is potentially that quantity, and analogously for changes in the other categories. In each genus, a potentiality for a form is realized when it comes to be an actuality in that genus.

Aristotle's problem is to understand how this potentiality is realized. Without explaining how he arrived at it, he introduces a definition of motion—motion is the actuality of the potential insofar as it is potential (201a10–11)—and he spends the rest of III 1–2 expounding this definition. This is not the place to explore this discussion. What matters for us is that this definition of motion combines elements of the two poles it connects. Between *inert* potential merely capable of motion and the actuality that results when motion is complete, there is a potential that is at work being potential and, thereby, in the process of becoming actual.[37] Aristotle has used the two poles, actual and potential, to find a middle between them. However we are to interpret the definition, it is an account of motion through the actuality, that is, the *form*, which is realized through the motion.

There is a difference between motion in substance and other genera. In substance, motion is the development and decay of a single individual, and what exists potentially and actually in the genus is that individual. In other genera, motion is a transition from one instance to another, for example, from a privation to a form, from black to white, both of which are instances of the genus (cf. *Metaph.* x 7). Even with this difference, the motions in other genera are analogous to those in substance in as much as there are, in each

---

37   See Kosman 1969, 40–62.

case, actuality, potentiality, and motion that is the realization of potentiality or, alternatively, form, privation, and matter (cf. *Metaph.* XII 2–3).

It is questionable whether the analogy that Aristotle uses to define motion in distinct genera can be the subject of one science because one science treats one genus and an analogy is not a genus (V 6.1016b35–1017a3). I suggest the reason all the genera of motion can be treated together in one science of physics is that they are all attributes of the categorial genus of substance (201a6–7); that is, substance either comes to be itself or serves as the matter for non-substantial motions. To this extent, even the motions in other categories are, in a way, motions of substances, and physics is concerned primarily with the motions of substances.

Nonetheless, what is really significant here is the way that in each genus a form serves analogously as the cause through which motion is understood. We have explored the way in which substantial form accounts for the characteristic processes of its own realization and its ceasing to be present. The forms in other genera also come to be present in a substance and cease to be present through paths that are characteristic of the form. These forms in non-substantial categories do not play the same causal role as substantial forms because they are not, in general, efficient causes of other things coming to acquire their forms. They are, though, formal and final causes through which the steps of their own acquisition must be understood (cf. *Metaph.* X 7). Aristotle's example of house-building helps to make this point because a change that comes through art is a motion in a non-substantial category; that is, a change in place and quality, and the steps of matter's acquiring the form of the house are dictated by the form realized. It follows, then, that all motions are analogous. Just as each species of substance has its own characteristic process of development through which its form is realized, motions in the other categorial genera are defined through a form or an actuality in that genus that dictates the process of its own realization.

V

Aristotle's works are sometimes taken to lay out a system of thought. More often, recent readers have taken them as explorations of philosophical problems that follow out clues from language and elsewhere, but often fail to reach definitive solutions. In the former case, the works are treatises that advance theses and defend them. In the latter, the *aporiai* Aristotle explores are his own, unresolved problems. We have seen that the first books of the *Physics* fall under neither of these heads. They are, rather, a carefully constructed inquiry into the cause of motion. They are guided by the method sketched in *Posterior Analytics* II, the method of using a syllogism to locate the middle term that can serve as the cause of its conclusion. Aristotle locates this cause through a dialectic that examines the common opinions of other philosophers. However, he organizes this discussion so that these opinions span the range of possibilities and can, thereby, be systematically refuted. What emerges from the dialectic is a middle term that is a necessary cause and is grasped immediately as the cause of motion.

Since the first two books of the *Physics* conduct an inquiry, the way to read them is to make the inquiry into the cause of motion along with Aristotle. We can follow his moves by thinking through what is at issue. The same method can be used to read all the works in the corpus. Often Aristotle tells us little about the steps or the progress of an inquiry. Even so, we can recognize these steps by engaging in the inquiry ourselves. To read Aristotle is to do philosophy with him. A mark of success is arriving at the problems that the text goes on to address.

This way of reading requires going beyond what is written to engage the subject written about and to reflect on it. Some scholars will insist that we have no basis for going beyond the text. They are right. However, they have not made good sense of the diverse strands of the text. In my view, Aristotle's works are not written for scholars. They are composed for philosophers and those who would become philosophers. They demand reflection on the subject matter explored, and they are, if I am right, constructed so as to guide the reader in that speculation.

CHAPTER 3

Aristotle's *Problemata*-Style and Aural Textuality

Diana Quarantotto

Abstract

According to *Posterior Analytics* II 1, scientific inquiry proceeds by grasping and resolving *problemata* of various kinds (τὸ ὅτι, τὸ διότι, εἰ ἔστι, τί ἐστι), the causal ones are its heart and focus. According to *APo.* II 14–18, part of the organization of the scientific inquiry (and hence of the construction of Aristotle's scientific treatises) consists of procedures aimed at grasping, unifying, and connecting *problemata*. The distinction between *problemata* of various kinds and the procedures aimed at grasping, unifying, and connecting them have a rhetorical, an explanatory, and a heuristic function. Arguably they lie at the root of the composition of *logoi* such as *History of Animals*, *Parts of Animals*, *Generation of Animals*, *Parva Naturalis*.

The goal of the paper is to investigate the modes of this composition (i.e., of the progressive construction of a text or inquiry) by means of an analysis of the Aristotelian notion of *problema* and an inquiry into the relations between the textuality of the *Problemata physica* (where the *problemata* occur in their "basic" form) and that of other *logoi* of the corpus. The working hypothesis is that these relations may help us to uncover (some aspects of) the process of the text construction from minimal units to extended *pragmateiai*. Moreover, since the *problema* format arises from the Socratic world of question and inquiry and, arguably, the more ancient Pythagorean *akousmata*, the paper is aimed at suggesting that the Aristotelian textuality documents a particular intermediate phase between the forms of expression characteristic of an oral culture and those proper of a world which is getting more and more alphabetized, and hence at suggesting a different image of Aristotle from the standard one: of an aural thinker, who should be read accordingly.

Introduction[1]

Posterior Analytics II opens with a list of the main questions that structure the scientific enterprise (*APo.* II 1.89b23–35), the answers to which comprise the

---

1   The translations of Aristotle's texts contained in this paper, apart from those of *PA*, are by

content of scientific knowledge. The objects of inquiry, says Aristotle, are of four different types: they correspond to questions about whether s is P, why s is P, whether s is, and what s is.

Later in the text Aristotle calls these objects of inquiry *problemata* (*APo.* II 14.98a1) and describes a series of procedures aimed at grasping, unifying, and connecting them (*APo.* II 14–18).[2] These procedures are designed to aid in the search for the causes and in the explanatory and expository unification of a subject, i.e., in the development of scientific inquiries from single questions to complex structures like those of many *logoi* of the *corpus*.

The goal of the paper is to investigate the characteristics of this construction and the presence of *problemata*, understood here as a particular kind of textual and heuristic format, within Aristotle's writings. I shall pursue this goal by means of an analysis of Aristotle's notion of *problema* and an inquiry into the relations between the textuality of the *Problemata physica* and that of other *pragmateiai* of the *corpus*.

The *problema* format arises from the Socratic world of question and inquiry, and, arguably, from even more ancient forms of expression, such as the Pythagorean *akousmata*. It could be suggested that the *problematic* aspect of the textuality of Aristotle's writings belongs to an intermediate phase between an oral culture and one where literacy is advancing more and more. Therefore the paper proposes an image of Aristotle as an aural thinker who should thus be read accordingly.[3]

This hypothesis is not new. Both the traditional image of Aristotle as a completely literate thinker who had already moved on significantly from the oral culture and the traditional contrast between a "systematic" Aristotle and a "problematic" Plato were already challenged at the beginning of the last century by Jaeger and afterward especially by Dirlmeier and Föllinger.[4] However,

---

Barnes 1991 (slightly modified). The translations of passages from *PA* are by Lennox 2001 (slightly modified).

2   Later I shall tackle the relation between the ζητούμενα of *APo.* II 1 and the προβλήματα of *APo.* II 14 and the question of whether all ζητούμενα of *APo.* II 1 are προβλήματα or not (see, below, section III).

3   The notion of "aurality" was introduced by Ong 1967. Broadly, aurality is a quality of a culture in which oral and written *media* coexist: it comprises different phases of the orality/literacy continuum between pure orality and fully achieved literacy. The notion of aurality is important and useful because it gives the dynamic compromise between orality and literacy a specific and positive status.

4   Jaeger 1912, 131–133, Dirlmeier 1962, Föllinger 1993, 263–280. Further developments of this line of inquiry can be found in: Lang 1998, 18–33, Lengen 2002, Taub 2015. Much research has also

this point of view is, apparently, still unpopular and not mainstream. This paper sets out to continue the investigation into this issue, and thereby to contribute to the research on reading strategies for Aristotle's texts.

I Aristotle's Notion of *Problema*

The Aristotelian notion of *problema* has a dialectical and interlocutory nature.[5] This is attested, first of all, by the *Topics*. The word *problema* occurs at its very beginning, where Aristotle states that the purpose of his inquiry is "to find a method by which we will be able to reason about every problem laid before us from generally accepted opinions" (*Top.* I 1.100a18–20). Further, the *Topics* provides the only definition of *problema* (there conceived of as a dialectical problem) to be found within the *corpus Aristotelicum*:

> A dialectical problem is a subject of inquiry that contributes either to choice and avoidance, or to truth and knowledge, and does that either by itself, or as a help to the solution of some other such problem. It must, moreover, be something on which either people hold no opinion either way, or most people hold a contrary opinion to the wise, or the wise to most people, or each of them among themselves.
>
> *Top.* I 11.104b1–5

Here the *problema* is defined from the point of view of its content. The main trait of a *problema* is that it is something controversial: a *problema* is a subject of inquiry for which there are convincing arguments for, against, or even no argument at all because reasons are difficult to shape. A standard example of the former is the question whether pleasure is to be chosen or not, and of the latter the question whether the universe is eternal or not (*Top.* I 11.104b8; *Cael.* I 10–12).

However, a *problema* is defined not only by the epistemic status of its content, but also by its linguistic form, by the context of its occurrence and by the role it plays in it. In the *Topics* the *problema* figures first as a question that opens the dialectical debate between a questioner and a responder. The *problema*-question concerns an alternative: it expresses two contradictory possibilities

---

been published by those scholars who have focused on the dialectical character of Aristotle's way of inquiring and writing.

5 On Aristotle's uses of the word *problema*, see Lennox 1994; Slomkowski 1997, 14–19. On the uses by his predecessors, see Flashar 1983, 297–298.

and urges a choice between them. Its general form is: "Is it the case that S is P, or is it not?" (e.g., is the universe eternal or not? Is pleasure to be chosen or not?). This is the kind of question that (like the one about whether S is), according to *APo.* II 1, represents the first phase of a *problematic* inquiry.[6] Moreover, since this question is about something controversial, the reply to it—a declarative proposition stating one of the two contradictory possibilities: "S is P" or "S is not P"—cannot help but be controversial as well. This is why it is itself a *problema*: a *problema*-answer.[7]

The task of the questioner is to refute the respondent's *problema*-answer and to prove the contradictory one, whereas that of the respondent is to withstand the refutation. The questioner poses further questions (i.e., *protaseis*-questions; *Top.* I 4.101b31–32) with the aim of substantiating the premises from which the contradictory *problema*-answer can be deduced.

The format of this reasoning can be used in many different situations, among which Aristotle includes philosophical and scientific research.[8] Indeed, according to Aristotle, "in order to discern truth and falsehood more easily on every point it is necessary to raise difficulties on both sides of a subject" (*Top.* I 2.101a34–36), i.e., to employ a refutation style of reasoning. Refutation and truth walk, Socratically, hand-in-hand:

> It is what we are all inclined to do, to direct our inquiry not to the matter itself, but to the views of our opponents; for even when inquiring on one's own one pushes the inquiry only to the point at which one can no longer offer any opposition. Hence a good inquirer will be one who is ready in bringing forward the objections proper to the genus, and that he will be when he has gained an understanding of all the differences.[9]
>
> *Cael.* II 13.294b7–13

---

6 According to Alexander, the *Topics* does not deal with the second phase of the problematic inquiry because questions about what a thing is and why it is such-and-such are not dialectical but scientific (Alexander of Aphrodisias, *On Aristotle's Topics* 62.30–63, 19; Lennox 1994, 53–77). However, a clear reference to the διὰ τί occurs in *Top.* I 11.104b16 where Aristotle describes and defines the concept of *problema*.

7 *Top.* II 2.109b24, 110a10; VII 5.155a37 ff.; VIII 3.158b16; VIII 11.161b32 ff., 162a6, 163a8 ff. See Slomkowski 1997, 16 notes 40–42.

8 *Top.* I 2.101a25–b4. Moreover, Aristotle's definition of *problema* states that a problematic dialogue may aim at truth and knowledge (*Top.* I 11.104b1–5).

9 See also *Cael.* I 10.279b7–9.

II   The *Problemata* of the *Problemata physica*

An obvious testimony of the scientific use of the *problema* format is given by those works of the *corpus Aristotelicum* that have come down to us with the title *Problemata*.[10]

The *Problemata physica*, which I shall focus on, is apparently a Peripatetic compilation. Therefore, it cannot be used as a direct document of Aristotle's inquiry. However, it can arguably be used as a testimony of it.[11] This is because we have reasons to believe that (1) Aristotle himself compiled works of this kind (indeed, on several occasions he refers to further discussion of issues in 'the problems') and that (2) the *Problemata physica*, given its Peripatetic beginnings and given Aristotle's theoretical discussions about problems in the *Topics* and the *Analytics*, stem from an original collection compiled by Aristotle himself or by his closest collaborators.[12]

The *Problemata physica* are collections of micro-inquiries into a multitude of different topics and are arranged together in a rather fragmentary way. These inquiries, like those described in the *Topics*, are a clear expression of the verbal argument between two (or more) persons.[13] They concern a debatable content and display a question-and-answer structure, which, however, is different from the one described in the *Topics*. Most inquiries in the *Problemata* are within the causal phase of scientific research[14] (i.e., the second one in the *APo*. II 1 scheme).[15] They start with questions about why X is Y, the object of inquiry

---

10   Diogenes Laertius's catalogue of Aristotle's writings lists several titles that include the word *problema* (together with thirty-eight books of *Physics* that should be our *Problemata physica*): *Problems from those of Democritus, Homeric Problems, On Problems, Reconsidered Problems.*

11   I am here employing the distinction between "document" and "testimony" traced by Rossi 1979.

12   Cf. Louis 2002, xxv–xxix; Mayhew 2011, xxi.

13   Cf. *Top.* I 2.101a27, a30. The dialogical form of the *problemata* collected in the *Problemata*, unlike the one described in the *Topics*, seems to allow for more than two interlocutors. On the group activity and interaction suggested by question-and-answer texts, doxographical texts and *hypomnema*, see Taub 2015, 430–431.

14   The exceptions are few: see Flashar 1983, 341–342.

15   In the *Problemata physica* the first phase of the research (the ὅτι question) is often omitted (whereas in the *Topics* it is the second phase that seems to be omitted; but for some evidence to the contrary, see note 6 above). The frequent omission from the *Problemata physica* of the first phase may be due to a variety of reasons. I shall come back to this point and argue that at least one of these reasons concerns the role of the *Problemata physica* in the progressive construction of a scientific inquiry.

being a phenomenon whose cause is unknown and that, as such, is something *thaumaston, atopon*, aporetic; i.e., a *problema* (*Metaphysics* I 2.982b12–20,
983a11–21).[16]

The simplest structure of a *problema* is that of a single question followed by
a single answer, which is itself sometimes expressed in interrogative form:

> Why does salt make a noise when it is thrown on fire? Is it because salt
> has a little moisture in it which is evaporated by the heat and violently
> bursting forth rends the salt? Now anything which is rent makes a noise.
>
> *Probl.* XI 26.902a1–4

More complex versions of *problemata* display an opening question followed by
a sequence of two or more answers, which are related to each other and the
initial question in one of several ways:

> Why are those who live in hot regions longer-lived? Is it because their nat-
> ural condition is drier, and that which is drier is less liable to putrefaction
> and more lasting, and death is as it were a kind of putrefaction? Or is it
> because death is due to the chilling of the interior heat, and everything
> is chilled by a surrounding medium which is colder than itself? Now in
> warm regions the surrounding air is hot, but in cold regions it is cold and
> so more quickly and effectively destroys the interior heat of the body.
>
> *Probl.* XIV 9.909b25–33

Sometimes the first answer proves unsatisfactory. Hence a second one is presented as a better hypothesis, if not a solution to the problem. Other times the
multiple answers are simply different possible solutions. In other cases, all the
answers are unsatisfactory and the problem remains unresolved. Sometimes,
finally, the answer to a question brings up a further question that in turn raises
another question, and so on: question-and-answer sequences are generated.[17]

Despite possible cases of mannerism, all these features, together with the
terminology,[18] suggest that the *Problemata* stem from the lively oral discussions
of that particular school: it gives us an insight into the group investigations

---

16   On the connections between *thauma, problema, aporia*, and contraries, see Menn 2015b.

17   On the formulaic patterns of the answers displayed in the *Problemata* and on the different
      structures of the *problemata* collected in this work, see Flashar 1983, 342–345.

18   The use of terminology characteristic of school dialectical discussions is frequent in the
      Problemata: e.g., εἰκός, μᾶλλον εἰκός, (XXI 5, 22, XXII 2), μᾶλλον εὔλογον, εὐλογώτερον (II 26,
      IX 8), πιθανόν (XXXIV 11). On this point, see Flashar 1983, 342–343.

carried out by the Peripatetics.[19] Arguably, the dialectical situation in which this form of arguing was employed was the one, or similar to the one, described by Aspasius:[20] the *problematic* investigation was carried out jointly by the teacher and the students; the students were all sitting in front of or around the teacher and tried to give answers to his questions.[21]

The development of the *problemata* by means of questions and answers—single or multiple—by objections and replies, displays that knowledge is the result of a dialectical process in an exchange between two or more persons. Although Democritus's *problematic* way of inquiring is perhaps the most direct model for the Aristotelian *Problemata*,[22] this format is also a legacy of the Socratic oral model of questioning and answering.[23] But the origin of the *problemata* (insofar as both form and setting are concerned) is, arguably, even older. Indeed, the oral teaching tradition of the Pythagorean *akousmata* seems to display a *Grundform* of the Aristotelian *problemata*: these *akousmata* had an argumentative scheme of question-and-answer and were exchanged within a circle of listeners:[24]

What are the islands of the blessed?
The Sun and the Moon.

What is the oracle of Delphi?
The Tetraktys, that is harmony, in which there are the Sirens.
(…)

---

19   On this point, see also Bodnár 2015, 3.

20   Cf. *On Aristotle's Nicomachean Ethics* 10, 30–32, Heylbut.

21   Moraux 1951, 119 argues for the trustworthiness of this report.

22   Democritus is the first to whom is traditionally attributed a writing entitled *Problemata*. In Diogenes Laertius's catalogue of Democritus's writings (DL IX 49) there is a title that includes the word *problemata* (χερνικὰ προβλήματα or χέρνιβα προβλήματα). Democritus's *Problemata*, according to Diogenes's catalogue of Aristotle's writings, had been the object of two books by Aristotle: Προβλήματα ἐκ τῶν Δημοκρίτου (On the relation between Democritus's *Problemata* and Aristotle's, see Menn 2015b).

23   See, e.g., *Theaet.* 180c–d. The Socratic legacy is clearly recognized by Aristotle himself: *Metaph.* I 2.982b12–20, 983a11–21. On the history of the *Problemata* as a literary genre, see Flashar 1983, 297–303. In Flashar's view, the problematic inquiry was already rather common since the Sophists; moreover, several Hippocratic treatises show an argumentative style that has a problematic character (e.g., *On Regimen in Acute Diseases, Epidemics*). There is also evidence that supports the hypothesis that the *problemata* originated from geometry (Slomkowski 1997).

24   Cf. von Fritz 1960, 11.

What is the right thing?

Make sacrifices.

(...)

In some *akousmata* is added the reason why one should act in a certain way. For example, you must procreate children to leave our place to another minister of the gods. In others, however, no explanation is given.

DK 58C4

III   From the *Problemata* to the Other Scientific *Logoi*: Unifying and Connecting *Problemata* (*APo.* II 1, 14–18)

All the scientific *logoi* of the *corpus Aristotelicum*, apart from the *Problemata*, display a textual structure that is not a mere collection of questions and answers. And yet, according to *APo.* II 1 and 14,[25] scientific inquiries are *problematic* in kind: they stem from and are about *problemata*. Some useful indications on how to understand this claim are given, first of all, by *APo.* II 1 itself and by *APo.* II 14–18: these chapters, I shall argue, suggest that the scientific *logoi* of the *corpus*, or at least parts of them, result from the unification of, and connection between, numerous and different basic and initial *problemata*, and hence that, within Aristotle's research plan, inquiries like those collected in the *Problemata* supply the raw material for further elaboration and organization.[26]

Before tackling these procedures of unification and connections of *problemata* and how they are used to construct progressively complex *pragmateiai*, a preliminary point must be addressed: are all the questions listed in *APo.* II 1 *problemata*?[27] Actually, the word *problema* does not occur in *APo.* II 1. The main

---

25   See note 2 above.

26   The references to the *Problemata* in Aristotle's writings seems to be compatible with this hypothesis, regardless of whether or not these are references to the *Problemata physica* that have come down to us (with one exception, they are not). On this point, see Louis 2002, xxix: "Il est vraisemblable qu'Aristote a commencé très tôt, après son entrée à l'Académie, à accumuler des notes qui' il a ensuite utilisées dans ses grands traités". On the archivial character of question-and-answer texts, see Taub 2015, 431–433. More generally, on the methods of gathering and interpreting information used at the Lyceum, see Natali 2013, 104–113. Of course, the relation between the *Problemata physica* and *APo.* II 1–18 may be investigated also from a different point of view, i.e., by inquiring into if, how, and up to what point the *Problemata physica* follow the rules about grasping, unifying, and connecting problems established in *APo.* II 1–18. I shall address this latter issue in section IV.

27   I am grateful to William Wians for pushing me on this point.

objects of scientific research are called ζητούμενα rather than προβλήματα. However, the word *problema* is clearly used in *APo.* ΙΙ 14 and thereafter to refer to two kinds of ζητούμενα, i.e., the *hoti*-questions and the *dioti*-questions. So we can conclude that at least these two questions are *problemata*. But what about the other two questions (*ei esti* and *ti esti*)? Are they *problemata* as well? Aristotle does not label them so explicitly. However, both Philoponus and Alexander think that, notwithstanding the lack of an explicit indication, all the questions listed in *APo.* ΙΙ 1 are considered by Aristotle to be *problemata*.[28] Indeed, there seem to be good reasons to believe so. After presenting in *APo.* ΙΙ 1 the four ζητούμενα as two pairs of questions and after initially describing these two pairs as related respectively to two different kinds of things (89b31–32), from chapter 2 onward Aristotle emphasizes a strong connection between them. He claims that all these questions are about the middle term (i.e., the cause): they are all searches for a middle term (90a35); they inquire either into whether there is a middle term (the *hoti* and *ei esti* questions) or into what the middle term is (the *dia ti* and *ti esti* questions) (89b36–90a7). Accordingly, Aristotle stresses that "to know what it is is the same as to know why it is" (90a31–32). This suggests that, if a *dioti*-question is a *problema*, then a *ti esti*-question is a *problema* as well, and similarly for the *ei esti*-question.

That said, there seems to remain a difference between these two pairs of questions, a difference that may be relevant to the issue about their being all *problemata* or not. According to *APr.* Ι 26–31, a *problema* is something proposed to be proved (42b27–32, 43a16–24). According to *APo.* ΙΙ 3.90b24–26, a definition (and hence the middle term, which is the definition of the first extreme: 99a21–22) cannot be proved, or at least cannot be proved in the same way and in the same sense in which other kinds of propositions can be proved. From these remarks, we may conclude that the *ti esti*-question (and the *ei esti*-question that precedes it) is a *problema* only insofar as, and in the limited sense in which, there is a proof of definitions.[29]

Let us now move to the procedures for constructing progressively complex *pragmateiai* from basic initial questions. As already emphasized, the primary instructions are given right from the start, in *APo.* ΙΙ 1: there Aristotle claims that inquiries must proceed from *hoti*-questions to *dioti*-questions or from *ei*

---

28   Philoponus, *On Aristotle's Posterior Analytics* 336.4–11; Alexander of Aphrodisias, *in Top.* 63.9–19.

29   The hypothesis that *ti esti*-questions are of a different sort from, and require a different procedure than, *hoti*- and *dioti*-questions is suggested also by *Metaph.* VII 17.

esti-questions to *ti esti*-questions, and provides an explanation of why this is so. These instructions are reaffirmed[30] and applied[31] in Aristotle's scientific research. They may be seen as basic rules for conducting a scientific inquiry. They amount to an initial, ordered, step-by-step procedure: if you want to inquire into something, first ask this and then that, but not the reverse. Moreover, after focusing—from chapter 2 onward—on the fact that all four questions are about the middle term, in chapters 14–15 Aristotle pursues and elaborates further upon the issue of the unification and connection of *problemata*, and inquires into related issues up to chapter 18.[32]

Chapter 14 opens with the issue of how to grasp problems (ἔχειν τὰ προβλή-ματα: 98a1). As we shall see shortly, "grasping problems" seems to be a preliminary step toward the solution of problems (i.e., the individuation of the cause), a step accomplished by means of dissections and divisions, and by means of generalization and comparison procedures.

Three different cases are considered. The starting point of each of them is given by the various things that are being studied (τὰ τεθεωρημένα: 98a3–4). In the first case, for instance, these various things are animals. The first step of the procedure is to posit the kind common to τὰ τεθεωρημένα: the kind "animal". The second step is to select from the dissections and the divisions the things that belong to every animal. The third is to consider the first sub-kinds of "animal" (e.g., birds, humans, horses, fish) and to select the things that belong to all the members of each of them.

The aim of this procedure is to find out *the reason why* a certain property belongs (or certain properties belong) to one or more sub-kinds of a given kind (e.g., "animal"): if every horse has the property y, and if this property belongs to the kind "animal", we can infer that horses have it *because* they are animals.

In the second case, the things that are being studied do not have a common name (98a13–15). Aristotle recommends that the inquiry tackle not only kinds that have been given a name, but also kinds that are unnamed, which he describes as "anything else [that] has been seen to belong in common". The example used here by Aristotle is that of "animals with horns". The first step of the procedure requires positing "animals with horns" as the kind that is common to the things that are being studied. Next, as in the first case, one

---

30   *PA* I 1.639b5–10, 640a10–15; II 1.646a8–12; *HA* I 6.491a7–14.

31   An example is given by the relation between *HA* (which concerns mainly *hoti*-questions) and *PA* (which concerns mainly *dioti*-questions). On this issue, see Lennox 2005, 58–70 and 2006, 294–300. On the relation between *hoti*-questions and *dioti*-questions, see also *GA* I 17.721a–721b6; *Progression of Animals* 1.704b7–10.

32   For a more recent discussion of these issues, see Lennox 2015.

should select the properties that belong to this kind, among which "having three stomachs" and "lacking upper incisors" will be found. Third, one should select what animals have horns. Having done this, one will be able to say *why* these animals (e.g., deer) have three stomachs and lack upper incisors, i.e., *because* they have horns.

The third case is barely sketched. Here the first step concerns neither a named nor an unnamed kind, but a nature (*phusis*: 98a23) that is unitary by analogy. Aristotle's example is that of pounce, fish spine, and bone, which are found respectively in different great kinds. Also in this case, one ought to select the properties that belong to each of them. Having done this, one may find a common property and hence infer that, e.g., fish have the fish spine because they have that common property.

At first sight the aim of these procedures is to find an explanation for a particular problem, i.e., a problem whose subject is a particular universal: why do deer have three stomachs? Why do horses have hearts? However, these procedures can also be seen as aimed at moving the inquiry from the level of particular problems (why do deer have three stomachs?) to the level of more general problems (why do animals with horns have three stomachs?), especially of those general problems that involve coextensive universals and are, as such, the proper objects of scientific demonstrations. For instance, moving from the fact (*hoti*) that, e.g., "deer have three stomachs" to the fact (*hoti*) that "animals with horns have three stomachs" amounts to moving from a predication whose subject is a particular universal and whose predicate extends beyond the subject to a predication in which subject and predicate are coextensive and in which the subject is the primary universal (99a34–35) to which the predicate belongs, i.e., the most general subject to which the predicate belongs as such and in itself (*APo.* I 4.73b25–74a3). On this view, grasping problems by selecting properties from dissections and divisions amounts to reformulating the initial problem in such a way that it meets the conditions for being scientifically solved.[33] The subsequent step is to look for an explanation of the new problem, which will also provide an explanation of the first one.[34]

---

33   Cf. *APo.* II 17.99a1–6, where Aristotle claims that there is not really a *problema* if something has not been demonstrated in virtue of itself.

34   In chapter 14 Aristotle does not explicitly mention the final phase of the procedure, arguably because it is not part of the "problem-grasping". The different phases of the procedure up to the final one, in which the middle term is the definition of the first extreme, are sketched in *APo.* II 17.99a16–19.

But how is the primary universal to be found? *APo.* II 14 does not answer this question. In the first case, for instance, we do not even know whether the kind "animal" is the most general kind to which the property at issue belongs, or whether there is a more general kind (i.e., we do not know whether "animal" and the property at issue are coextensive). In the second case, Aristotle seems to assume that "having horns", "having three stomachs", and "lacking upper incisors" are coextensive. What's more, he assumes that the causal relation between them is such that the first property is the cause of the others, i.e., that the first universal is the primary universal to which the other universals belong as such and in itself. In sum, there is no indication of how to discern what property follows from what and why, for instance, "having three stomachs" *follows from* "having horns" instead of being *followed by* it.

Some clues about this issue are given by the passages where Aristotle illustrates the notion of primary universal and describes the search for this primary universal as a kind of *aphairesis* (i.e., a progressive removal of properties from a subject that has the property whose cause is being searched). These passages suggest that the primary universal is searched for by means of generalization and comparison procedures. Interestingly, these procedures recall Mill's methods of induction, like the method of agreement and the method of difference:[35]

> Does it [the property 2r] belong as triangle or as isosceles? And when does it belong in virtue of this as primitive? And of what does the demonstration hold universally? Clearly whenever after removal it belongs primitively—e.g., two right angles will belong to bronze isosceles triangle, but also when being bronze and being isosceles have been removed. But not when figure or limit has been. But they are not the first. Then what is first? If triangle, it is in virtue of this that it also belongs to the others, and it is of this that the demonstration holds universally.
>
> *APo.* I 5.74a35–b4

Let us suppose that we are considering a bronze isosceles triangle that has the property 2r. In order to find the primary universal of this property, we should remove progressively the various properties of this object and see what happens, i.e., if the property 2r remains or not. By so doing we will see that "being bronze" is not the primary universal of the property 2r. Indeed, there are triangles that are not bronze and that nevertheless have the property 2r (method of difference). The same holds for "being isosceles". Moreover, since

---

35   Cf. Mill 1843, 454–455.

not all figures have the property 2r, we can exclude also "figure" from the candidates for the role of primary subject. Instead, since all and every arbitrary instance of the objects that have the property of "being triangular" have the property "having 2r" (method of agreement), we can conclude that "being triangular" is the primary universal of "having 2r".

Similarly, starting from the recognition that, e.g., deer have three stomachs (the initial *hoti*), in order to find out why they have three stomachs we must determine first of all other features that are always present in animals with three stomachs and that are instead absent from animals without three stomachs (method of agreement and method of difference, i.e., joint method of agreement and difference). By so doing, we may arrive at the preliminary conclusion that the property "having three stomachs" belongs to *all* animals that have other properties in common, i.e., "having horns" and "lacking upper incisors", and *only* to them. This would lead to the further hypothesis that these three properties are causally connected. In order to determine their causal relations (i.e., which of these properties is the cause of the others) we would have to determine which property is the one from which the others follow.[36]

Further indications about how to unify and connect problems are provided by *APo.* II 15. This chapter focuses on: (1) ways of unifying problems (i.e., ways in which problems that at first sight appear distinct turn out to be the same problem, in some sense of "same"), and (2) ways of connecting different problems. Aristotle's exposition is again very sketchy. He does not provide a complete list of these different procedures of unification and connection of problems. Insofar as the first procedure is concerned, he mentions two cases: one in which problems that are initially thought to be different turn out to have

---

36   Compare Aristotle's procedure in *PA* III 2.662b35–663a7, 663b28–664a2; III 14.674a30–
      b17. Clearly, the indications provided in *APo.* I 4–5 are not complete and exhaustive
      either. For instance, they do not help us determine the causal relation between "having
      horns", "lacking upper incisors", and "having three stomachs". They only provide a list of
      candidates for the role of cause. The same impression is given by *APo.* II 16–18, which
      focus on the relation between cause and "effect", and inquire into whether there are
      cases in which a given property belongs to more than just one primary universal (99a30–
      b7). Aristotle starts this inquiry by assuming that cause and "effect" are coextensive and
      convertible, i.e., that a given attribute belongs to *all* members of a kind and *only* to them
      (98a35–b4). This raises the question of how to determine which of two coextensive and
      convertible attributes is the cause of the other (98b4–5). The answer he gives is formal and
      does not involve a procedure we may use when searching for the cause of an attribute:
      Aristotle's only indication is that the cause has definitional priority over what is caused by
      it (98b21–24). On some central aspects of Aristotle's heuristics, see the interesting work by
      Ugaglia 2004.

the same middle term (e.g., *antiperistasis*); the other, in which a multitude of problems concerning phenomena that are specifically different and generically the same can and should make up a single problem, e.g.: Why is there echoing? Why is there mirroring? Why are there rainbows? (= Why is there reflection?).[37] The second procedure is illustrated by means of a case where several problems concerning properties that are causally subordinate to each other make up a sequence of connected problems, e.g.: Why does increased flow occur at the end of the month? Because storms occur at the end of the month. Why do storms occur at the end of the month? Because waning of the moon occurs at the end of the month.

In sum, *APo.* II 14–15—together with the preceding inquiries into the primary universal (I 4–5), into the selection of terms that are appropriate for proving particular problems (*APo.* I 27–30),[38] and the subsequent inquiries into the relation between cause and "effect" (II 16–18)—seem aimed at providing procedures to unify and connect problems, to move from particular to general and scientific problems. These procedures involve generalization and comparison, concern the scientific *hoti*, and are oriented toward the scientific *dioti*. As such, these procedures are suited to aid both in the explanatory and expository unification of a subject, and hence in the development of scientific inquiries from single questions to complex structures like those of many *logoi* of the *corpus*.

A paradigmatic example is offered by a methodological passage at the beginning of *PA* I, which concerns the standards of the inquiry into nature, the manner of its proofs (639a12–15), and the expository unification of its subjects (i.e., the desirability of avoiding needless repetition: 639a23–28). There, Aristotle raises the following question:

> ... should one take each substantial being singly and define it independently, e.g., taking up one by one the nature of human, lion, ox, and any other animal as well; or should one first establish, according to something common, the attributes common to all?[39]
>
> *PA* I 1.639a15–19

---

37   Cf. *Mete.* III 2–6. A case of this kind (i.e., in which the extremes and the middle term are in the same kind) is also mentioned in *APo.* II 17.99a6–10.

38   See Lennox 1994.

39   This question is mentioned again at 639b4–5: "the question of whether one should study things in common according to kind first, and then later their distinctive characteristics, or whether one should study them one by one straight away".

In order to answer this question, Aristotle stresses that the attributes that belong to different kinds of animals are of different types. In some cases, "the same things are present in different forms of animals, yet themselves have no difference" (639a28–29). These cases include "sleep, respiration, growth, deterioration, death, and in addition any remaining affections and dispositions such as these" (639a20–22). However, there are "other attributes which turn out to have the same predicate, but to differ by a difference in form" (639a29–b1). For instance, the locomotion of animals is not one in form: flying, swimming, walking, and crawling are different forms of locomotion (639b1–3). This means that these different types of attributes require a different treatment, i.e., a different kind of explanatory and expository unification: the first type of attribute will be explained by a cause that is the same in form for different kinds of animals, whereas the second type of attribute will be explained by several causes that are different in form for different kinds of animals, and by a common cause that is the same in kind for different kinds of animals.

This seems to be exactly what Aristotle does, for instance, in the *Parva Naturalia*, on the one hand, and in the *Progression of Animals* and in the *Movement of Animals*, on the other. The *Parva Naturalia* tackle attributes of the first type (sleep, respiration, growth, deterioration, death, etc.). The *Progression of Animals* and the *Movement of Animals* tackle an attribute of the second type (i.e., locomotion), by focusing respectively on its differences in form and its sameness in kind (704a4–9, 698a1–7). So, these treatises provide examples of how the different procedures of unification of *problemata*, outlined in *APo.*, are used in the construction of Aristotle's scientific inquiries.[40]

IV   The Problematic Inquiry in the *Problemata*: An Initial Phase of Scientific Investigation

Other data about the unification and connection of *problemata* and the construction of inquiries endowed with complex structures can be found by comparing the *Problemata* and other scientific *logoi* on the same subject. This comparison shows concretely how Aristotle's textuality changes from the *Problemata*'s basic patterns to the more complex schemes of other *logoi*. In particular, this further analysis suggests that, if considered from the point of view of

---

40   Another interesting example would be a work attributed to Aristotle, *De inundatione Nili*, which tackles a topic related to the one Aristotle uses in *APo.* II 15 to exemplify the unification of problems in the form of a sequence of distinct but causally connected problems. On the relation of this work to the *problemata* format, see Menn 2015b.

the procedures of unification and connection of problems tackled in *APo.*, and if compared with the inquiries conducted by Aristotle in other *logoi peri physeos*, the *Problemata physica* provide the testimony of an initial phase of the scientific/problematic inquiry, a phase in which basic and particular problems are mainly tackled but in which there are also signs of the applications of the procedures for grasping and unifying problems dealt with in *APo.*

In what follows I shall present five examples of thematic correspondence. Most of them show a relation of progressive development, unification, and systematization of the *problemata* being discussed: a *problema* that in the *Problemata* is dealt with as an individual case or within a rather limited context, in other *logoi* is enriched with details both from the point of view of the *hoti* and from that of the *dioti*, and is inserted into a larger integrated theoretical framework. Moreover, these changes come with a reduction in the *Problemata*'s characteristic conversational quality and also with a flatter, more didactic and linear prose. The last two cases, instead, exemplify a relation between the inquiries into the *hoti* carried out in *HA* and the causal ones of the *Problemata*.[41]

Probl. X 14[42]	*GA* IV 4.771a17–34
Q: Why is it that some animals are prolific, such as the pig, the dog, and the hare, whilst others are not so, for instance man and the lion?	In the first place it seems only reasonable to wonder why some animals produce many young, others only one. For it is *the largest animals* that produce one, e.g., the elephant, camel, horse, and the other solid-hoofed ungulates; of these some are larger than all other animals, while the others are of a remarkable size. But

41   On this whole issue, particularly interesting is *On Length and Shortness of Life*, which inquires into: why are some animals long-lived while others instead are short-lived? This treatise provides the results of an attempt at unifying many different basic problems into a single general one, i.e., at "grasping" and then at solving the problem about the length of life. Indeed, partial versions of this problem are dealt with several times in the collections of the *Problemata*: why are those who live in hot regions longer-lived? Why is it that men who have widely spaced teeth are generally short-lived? Why are men long-lived who have a line right across their palms? (*Probl.* X 48, 49; XIV 9, 10; XXXIV 1, 10). Moreover, the problem dealt with in *Long. Vit.* is the one used in *APo.* II 17.99b5–7 as a case study to inquire into whether "it is possible for there to be several causes of the same thing, but not for things of the same species".

42   *Legenda*: Q = question, A = answer, A1 = first answer, A2 = second answer, A1Q1 = first answer to the first question, A2Q1 = second answer to the first question, Ob = objection, AOb = answer to the objection.

Probl. X 14	GA IV 4.771a17–34
A: Is it because the former class has a number of wombs which they desire to fill and molds into which the semen is distributed, while with the latter the opposite is the case?	the dog, the wolf, and practically *all the fissipeds* produce many, even the small members of the class, as the mouse family. The *cloven-footed* animals again produce few, except the pig, which belongs to those that produce many. Now we should expect the large animals to be able to generate more young and to produce more semen. But precisely what we wonder at is the reason for not wondering; it is just because of their size that they do not produce many young, for the nutriment is expended in such animals upon increasing the body. But in the smaller animals nature takes away from the size and adds the excess to the seminal secretion. Moreover, more semen must be used in generation by the larger animal, and little by the smaller. Therefore many small ones may be produced together, but it is hard for many large ones to be so.

These two passages address the same *problema* (why is it that some animals are prolific while others are not so?), yet it is approached and solved differently. The *GA* passage documents a more advanced phase of the inquiry into the *hoti* and hence of the formulation and solution of the *problema*. In *Probl.* X 14 the starting question is framed quite generically with reference to just a few species of animals. Instead, in *GA* there is a longer and deeper inquiry into the kinds of animals that are prolific and those that are not: it is ascertained that large animals and cloven-footed animals produce few young, whereas small animals and all the fissipeds are prolific. After this preliminary inquiry comes the causal explanation: some animals produce few young because they are large, that is because the food is used to increase their body size rather than to produce seminal secretions; other animals instead are prolific because of their small size, i.e., because the food is employed to produce seminal secretions rather than to make their body grow.

Probl. X 53	*PA* II 14.658a15–24
Q: Why is it that in man the front of the body is more thickly covered with hair than the posterior portion, but in quadrupeds the posterior part is hairiest? A1: Is it because *all* two-footed animals have the front part of the body more thickly covered? For the birds resemble man in this respect. A2: Or is nature *always* accustomed to protect the weaker parts and is *every* creature weak in some respect? Now in *all* quadrupeds the posterior portions are weaker than the front parts owing to their position; for they are more liable to suffer from cold and heat; but in man the front portions of the body are weaker and suffer likewise under these conditions.	... in quadrupeds there is a greater abundance of hair on the back than on the under side of the body; whereas in man the contrary is the case, and the hair is more abundant on the front surface than on the back. The reason for this is that hair is intended to serve as a protection to its possessor. Now, in quadrupeds the back requires more protection, and their underside, though more noble, is smooth because of their inclined posture. But in man, owing to his upright attitude, the anterior and posterior surfaces of the body are on an equality as regards need of protection. Nature therefore has assigned the protective covering to the nobler of the two surfaces; for invariably she brings about the best arrangement of such as are possible.

The two passages address the same problem and provide essentially the same answer, at the same level of generality. They differ in the argumentative style and in the ways data are processed. The passage of the *Problemata* shows the characteristic conversational, interrogative, and aporetic qualities of the whole collection. It provides two answers, the second of which builds on the first one, and so shows the progression of the research. The *PA* passage displays an assertive, more systematic and linear style. The fact that human ventral parts, unlike those of quadrupeds, are hairier than the dorsal ones is found in both passages to result from the upright position of humans, causing greater weakness of the ventral parts, which thus need extra protection. However, in *PA* the causal explanation is enriched with additional data aimed at integrating it into the theoretical and explanatory framework of Aristotle's biology: the passage begins with a generalization about the function of hairs, refers to the greater importance of the ventral parts over dorsal ones, and mentions the theory of natural heat and that of natural teleology. In addition, the explanation is nested in a broader discussion on the function of different types of hair in different species of animals.

Probl. x 9	GA IV 10.777a31–b16
Q: Why is it that some animals bear their young quickly, but in others the period of gestation is a long one? A: Is it because the longer-lived animals come to perfection more slowly? It is the longer-lived animals that take a long time to bear their young. Ob: This is not, however, true of the longest-lived of all animals; for example, the horse is slower in bearing its young but shorter-lived than man. AOb: The reason for this is the hardness of the uterus; for the uterus of a mare may be compared to a dry soil which does not readily bring the crops to maturity.	The period of gestation is, as a matter of fact, determined generally in each animal in proportion to the length of its life. For it is reasonable that the development of the long-lived animals should take a longer time. Yet this is not the cause of it, but the correspondence holds for the most part ... The real cause of long life in *any* animal is its being tempered in a manner resembling the environing air, along with certain other circumstances of its nature, of which we will speak later; but the cause of the time of gestation is the size of the offspring. For it is not easy for large masses to arrive at their perfection in a small time, *whether they be animals or, one may say, anything else whatever.* That is why horses and animals akin to them, though living a shorter time than man, yet carry their young longer; for the time in the former is a year, but in the latter ten months at the outside. For the same reason also the time is long in elephants; they carry their young two years on account of their excessive size.

The two passages address the same problem but give different answers. GA IV 10 shows a more advanced level of investigation of, and reflection on, both the *hoti* and the *dioti*. The cause given in *Problemata* x 9 (the life span) is mentioned and rejected in GA IV 10 (which denies that life span is the cause of the times of gestation: it is a fact that happens for the most part, that is a *hoti*, and not a *dioti*). Moreover, the case of the mare—which in *Problemata* appears as a counter-example to the explanation that precedes it and for which a different and specific cause is found—is tackled in the GA passage and presented as evidence for the validity of the general explanation given there: GA IV 10 provides a general explanation that accounts also for the cases that in *Probl.* x 9 represent counter-examples to the explanation given there.

Probl. X 28	*HA* VII 4.584b36–585a3
Q: Why is it that among the other animals twins though differing in sex are just as likely to survive, but this is not so with the young of man? A1: Is it because human twins are particularly weak, for man naturally produces only one offspring at a time? A2: Now in twins it is unnatural to find a diversity of sex; and so what is most contrary to nature is also weakest.	Now among other animals, if a pair of twins happen to be male and female they have as good a chance of surviving as though both had been males or both females; but among mankind very few twins survive if one happens to be a boy and the other a girl.

The two passages concern the same facts (*hoti*), but the one from the *Problemata* provides a causal explanation whereas the one from *HA* does not. However, the *HA* passage is just a short segment of a complex inquiry aimed at collecting and organizing comparative information about the process of gestation.

Probl. X 48	*HA* II 3.501b22–24
Q: Why is it that men who have widely spaced teeth are generally short-lived? A: Is it a sign that the skull is thick? For the brain is weak if it is not well ventilated, and so, being moist, it quickly decays, just as all other things decay if they are not in motion and cannot evaporate. For this reason too man has very thick hair upon the head, and the male is longer-lived than the female because of the sutures in his skull. But we must next consider length of life in relation to other conditions.	Those [animals] that have more teeth are longer-lived as a rule; those with fewer teeth more thinly set are shorter-lived as a rule.

The two passages concern essentially the same facts. However, in *HA* the topic of widely spaced teeth is associated with the topic of their number and the argument is extended to all animals. As in the previous case, here too the *Problemata* provides the causal explanation of the fact, whereas *HA* is limited to the *hoti* phase of the research. Moreover, in *HA* the information concerning the correlation between widely spaced and scarce teeth, on the one hand, and length of life, on the other, is part of a broader and more complex investigation into the teeth and their differences in humans and other animals. However, here the *Problemata* passage likewise expresses the need for a generalization to verify the correctness of the hypothesized cause.

v   Aristotle's *Problematic* Textuality: The Presence of *Problematic* Structures in the *Corpus*

As shown in the previous section, the unification, connection, and elaboration of *problemata* into wider and more complex textual structures overshadow and reduce the conversational flow of the *problemata* and determine a flatter, more didactic and linear prose. But this transformation is not complete, nor is it pervasive. This last part of the paper concerns the role in Aristotle's philosophy of the *problemata*—understood as linguistic and cognitive structures (rather than as heuristic procedures). The aim is to corroborate the hypothesis that Aristotle's philosophy displays an aural form of thought in many significant ways, and that the *problemata* are not only a work of the *corpus*, nor are they something exceptional within Aristotle's writings, but rather they are an important and pervasive aspect of his textuality and style of reasoning. This aspect is not confined to the doxographical investigations, to *logoi* that are explicitly aporetic like *Metaph.* III, or to the lost dialogues, but characterizes large parts of the *corpus*, from *On the Soul* to *On Generation and Corruption*, from *On the Heavens* to the *Metaphysics*, from *Parts of Animals* to *Generation of Animals* and to the *Parva Naturalia*.[43] In what follows I shall present and analyze five case studies to show the widespread presence of *problematic* structures in the *corpus*.

(i) *An.* III 1.425b4–11

Q: It might be asked why we have more senses than one.

A: Is it to prevent a failure to apprehend the common sensibles, e.g., movement, magnitude, and number, which go along with the special sensibles?

---

43   Some textual evidence concerning *An.*, *GC*, *GA* is provided below. On the *Metaphysics*, see Beriger 1989, Föllinger 1993, 269–270, who also analyzes from this point of view passages from *Generation of Animals, Eudemian Ethics*, and *Nicomachean Ethics*.

Had we no sense but sight, and that sense no object but white, they would have tended to escape our notice and everything would have merged for us into an indistinguishable identity because of the concomitance of color and magnitude. As it is, the fact that the common sensibles are given in the objects of more than one sense reveals their distinction from each and all of the special sensibles.

In *An.* III 1 Aristotle carries out an inquiry into the senses and sense organs, focusing on the number of the senses. The passage quoted above appears at the end of this inquiry. It is clearly a *problema* which could well occur in the collection of the *Problemata*. Even if the questioner and the respondent are not identified, the text still has a question-and-answer structure. The question (Q) has a causal nature, and the answer (A) is a direct interrogative sentence introduced by the formula ἢ ὅπως (also used in the *Problemata*). Finally, the answer is followed by a brief counterfactual explanation. The investigation then proceeds in the following chapters on the same themes and with a similar conversational style.

(ii) *GC* I 5.321a29–b2

Q1: One might raise a further difficulty. What is that which grows? Is it that to which something is added? If, e.g., a man grows in his shin, is it the shin which is greater—but not that whereby he grows, viz. not the food?

Q2: Then why have not both grown? For when A is added to B, both A and B are greater, as when you mix wine with water; for each ingredient is alike increased in volume.

A: Perhaps the explanation is that the substance of the one remains unchanged, but the substance of the other (viz. of the food) does not. For indeed, even in the mixture of wine and water, it is the prevailing ingredient which is said to have increased in volume. We say, e.g., that the wine has increased, because the whole mixture acts as wine but not as water.

This passage is a *problema* that could easily figure in the collection of the *Problemata*. It occurs within an investigation into growth and decline, which has an aporetic style itself. The dynamics of increase and decrease is investigated using several means: direct questions and rapid shifts from direct to indirect speech; the examination of two contradictory possibilities concerning an initial hypothesis; and a demonstration of the difficulties of each (320a27–b14). Then the inquiry proceeds with a division ("it must grow by the accession either of something incorporeal or of a body": 321a5), whose parts are examined aporetically. The passage quoted above occurs when a whole series of assumptions about the nature of the subject that grows and diminishes have been examined and ruled out, leading however to some results (221a17–26). The *problema* occurs at the turning point of the argument, just before the solution of the difficulties and the definition of growth and decline. Its structure is slightly more complex than the previous *problema*. The questions are two. The first (Q1) introduces an imaginary interlocutor with the formula ἀπορήσειε δ' ἄν τις, concerns the *hoti*, and presents an alternative (πότερον ... ἤ). The second (Q2) is a why-question introduced by *diati*. Its function is to challenge the alternative posed by the first question. This challenge, however, is temporary, because the answer (A) justifies the alternative and solves the *problema*. The overall effect of the inquiry is that of the non-linear flow characteristic of oral exchange. The answer has the typical structure of the *Problemata*: it is a direct question introduced by the ἤ ὅτι formula and followed by a brief explanation.

(iii) *GC* I 3.318a13–31

Q1: Our new question too—viz. What is the cause of the unbroken continuity of coming-to-be?—is sufficiently perplexing, if in fact what passes away vanishes into what is not and what is not is nothing (since what is not is neither a thing, nor possessed of a quality or quantity, nor in any place).

Q2: If, then, some one of the things which are is constantly disappearing, why has not the universe been used up long ago and vanished away—assuming of course that the material of all the several comings-to-be was finite?

A1Q1: For, presumably, the unfailing continuity of coming-to-be cannot be attributed to the infinity of the material. That is impossible; for nothing is actually infinite, and potentially things are infinite by way of division; so that we should have to suppose there is only one kind of coming-to-be, viz. one which never fails, such that what comes-to-be is on each successive occasion smaller than before. But in fact this is not what we see occurring.

A2Q1: Why, then, is this form of change necessarily ceaseless? Is it because the passing away of this is a coming-to-be of something else, and the coming-to-be of this a passing away of something else? The cause implied in this solution must be considered adequate to account for coming-to-be and passing away in their general character as they occur in all existing things alike.

Q3: Yet, if the same process is a coming-to-be of this but a passing away of that, and a passing away of this but a coming-to-be of that, why are some things said to come-to-be and pass away without qualification, but others only with a qualification? This question must be investigated once more, for it demands some explanation.

A1Q3: (...)

This *problema* occurs in a chapter that is introduced by a *problematic hoti*-question: πότερον ... ἤ (317a32–34). The structure of the *problema* is slightly more complex than the previous ones. It consists of two questions (Q1 and Q2) and two answers (A1Q1 and A2Q1), the second of which leads to a further question (Q3). It is therefore an investigation that displays the form of a series of connected *problemata*. The two initial questions are both causal. They are not distinct questions, but different formulations of the same question. The second one seems to be aimed at clarifying the meaning of the former, as if it had not been understood completely by someone. The first answer is a confutation of a possible answer (which had already been excluded by the second question, and whose exclusion is now explained and justified). The second answer provides the solution to the *problema*. It is a direct interrogative sentence introduced by the formula ἆρ' οὖν. However, this answer raises another why-question, which in turn is followed by an answer and the *problematic* investigation continues in this way.

(iv) *GA* II 5.741a6–32

Q1: And yet the question may be raised why it is that, if indeed the female possesses the same soul and if it is the residue of the female which is the material of the embryo, she needs the male besides instead of generating entirely from herself.

A1Q1: The reason is that the animal differs from the plant by having sense-perception; if the sensitive soul is not present, either actually or potentially, and either with or without qualification, it is impossible for face, hand, flesh, or any other part to exist; it will be no better than a corpse or part of a corpse. Thus if it is the male that has the power of making the sensitive soul, then where the sexes are separated it is impossible for the female to generate an animal from itself alone, for the process in question was what being male is.

Q1bis: Certainly that there is a good deal in the difficulty stated is plain in the case of the birds that lay wind-eggs, showing that the female can generate up to a certain point unaided.

Q2: But this still involves a difficulty; in what way are we to say that their eggs live?

A1Q2: It is neither possible that they should live in the same way as fertile eggs (for then they would produce a chick actually alive),

A2Q2: nor yet can they be called eggs only in the sense in which an egg of wood or stone is so called, for the fact that these eggs go bad shows that they previously participate in some way in life.

A3Q2: It is plain, then, that they have some soul potentially.

Q3: What sort of soul will this be?

A1Q3: It must be the lowest surely, and this is the nutritive, for this exists in all animals and plants alike.

Q4: Why then does it not perfect the parts and the animal?

A1Q4: Because they must have a sensitive soul, for the parts of animals are not like those of a plant. And so the female animal needs the help of the male, for in these animals we are speaking of the male is separate. This is exactly what we find, for the wind-eggs become fertile if the male tread the female in a certain space of time. About the cause of these things, however, we shall enter into detail later.

This passage displays a particularly complex and non-linear structure, which is characteristic of the spontaneous and unrehearsed dialogue between two people. Every aspect of the issue and every point of the inquiry results from single questions and answers (rather than from a plain and monological treatment) just as it happens in a dialogue between partners tackling an issue together. The

initial question (Q1) is a causal *problema* introduced using the formula ἀπορήσειε δ' ἄν τις which brings an imaginary interlocutor into the discussion. The
question is followed by a rather long and thorough answer (A1Q1). But the question is raised again (Q1bis) with the introduction of a fact that highlights the
aporetic character of the initial question and leads to the formulation of a new
question (Q2). This new question receives three answers, two of which are in
fact refutations of possible answers (A1Q2 and A2Q2), while the third one provides the solution (A3Q2). This solution, however, is only hinted at and leads
quickly to a new question (Q3) aimed at deepening the entire research. A short
answer follows immediately (A1Q3), which gives rise to a further question (Q4)
and its answer (A1Q4).

(v) *An.* II 12.424b3–18

> Q1: The problem might be raised: Can what cannot smell be said to be
> affected by smells or what cannot see by colors, and so on?

> A1Q1: Now a smell is just what can be smelt, and if it produces any effect it
> can only be so as to make something smell it, and it might be argued that
> what cannot smell cannot be affected by smells and further that what
> can smell can be affected by it only insofar as it has in it the power to
> smell (similarly with the proper objects of all the other senses). Indeed,
> that this is so seems clear as follows. Light or darkness, sounds and smells
> leave bodies quite unaffected; what does affect bodies is not these but the
> bodies which are their vehicles, e.g., what splits the trunk of a tree is the
> air which accompanies thunder.

> ObA1Q1: But bodies are affected by what is tangible and by flavors. If not,
> by what are things that are without soul affected, i.e., altered in quality?

> Q2 (= A2Q1): Must we not, then, admit that the objects of the other senses
> also may affect them?

> Q3 (= A3Q1): Is not the true account this, that all bodies are capable of
> being affected by smells and sounds, but that some on being acted upon,
> having no boundaries of their own, disintegrate, as in the instance of air,
> which does become odorous, showing that some effect is produced on it
> by what is odorous?

> Q4: What is smelling more than such an affection by what is odorous?

Q5: Is it that air, when affected quickly, becomes perceptible, but that smelling is actually perceiving?

This passage is also characterized by the non-linear and, so to speak, immediate and random flow of spontaneous speech. It occurs at the end of *An.* II 12 where Aristotle defines "perception" as the power of taking on the forms of sensible objects without their matter. The *problema* is connected to this definition. The initial move is a *hoti*-question (Q1), which is followed by a negative answer. This answer is articulated into two parts each of which provides a distinct explanation of the proposed solution (A1Q1 and Q2Q1). At this point an objection is raised to the second part of the answer (ObA2Q1), and this objection leads to reconsidering the whole issue: it suggests the possibility that the initial question may be answered affirmatively rather than negatively. This hypothesis is in turn recast as a question (Q2) and is followed by another, which is actually a third possible answer to the initial question (Q3). The third answer raises a new issue, which is briefly examined by placing two additional questions (Q4 and Q5). The survey ends aporetically.

Conclusion: The Dialogue of (Aristotle's) Soul with Itself

All the passages analyzed in the previous section exemplify more or less complex *problemata*, which emerge from the fabric of the *logoi*.[44] Many of them are indistinguishable from those of the *Problemata* with whom they share both the structure and the formulae.[45] Sometimes they are short extracts from larger sections that have a conversational and aporetic style themselves.

The distinguishing feature of these *problemata* is that they can be read as real dialogues between interlocutors playing different roles and taking different positions: one asks questions and the other gives answers, one puts forward a hypothesis and the other raises an objection, one advances an argument and the other presents a counter-argument. The transition from one interlocutor to the other is not explicitly indicated as in texts that intentionally imitate an oral dialogue. Instead, it shows itself implicitly in the development of the discourse and in its various structures. Aristotle's interlocutor is imaginary: the discourse is, Platonically, a dialogue of the soul with itself (*Top.* VIII 14.163b9–12).

---

44   The presence of *problemata* embedded in the text is sometimes explicitly signaled by Aristotle: *Poetics* 25.1460b6 (On this passage, see Else 1967, 111–112; Janko 1987, 145).

45   On this, see Prantl 1851, 364, Flashar 1983, 345–346, Louis 2002, xxii–xxiii.

The investigation is progressive and shows the spontaneity, immediacy, and randomness of a lively discussion. Signs of this are the frequency of direct speech, the abrupt changes from direct to indirect speech, the discourse being directly addressed to an interlocutor, and especially the non-linear flow of the argument. The speech does not proceed in a flat and straight way (for example, from premises to conclusion, from data to hypothesis or from hypothesis to evidence). Instead, it advances and then goes back, it considers a hypothesis and then resumes the inquiry from the beginning because of an objection, it puts forward a thesis, develops it, and then pauses to clarify its meaning and scope, like in a real dialogue whose achievements are obtained *in itinere* and together with a particular interlocutor. The overall outcome is that every aspect of the issue dealt with and every point of the inquiry result from single questions and answers rather than from a flat, linear, and monological treatment.

These conversational structures coexist in Aristotle's textuality with aspects that are proper to a more markedly literate way of thinking. Aristotle's textuality shows the signs of a mentality that is starting to internalize the first effects of the writing technology.[46] For example, the progressive elaboration, systematization, and unification of *problemata* would probably be impossible without the aid of writing.[47] It is therefore a complex and fluid situation, which is a kind of textuality that belongs to a particular phase of Greek aurality.

The aurality of Aristotle's thought brings immediately to mind the traditional contrast between a "problematic" Plato and a "systematic" Aristotle. This opposition was already challenged at the beginning of the last century by Jaeger who described it as a false impression determined by a series of historical coincidences: the image we have of Aristotle would probably be very different if the historical accidents that led to the preservation of certain works and not of others had been different; that is, if the dialogues and the other collections of *Problemata*, listed in the ancient catalogues, had come down to us.[48] Now, the investigations into the aural and dialogical style of the so-called esoteric writings provide additional data and additional evidence against this consoli-

---

46   Of course, the dialogical one is not the only distinctive trait of an aural form of thought. On other signs of Aristotle's aural mentality, see below. On the hypothesis that Aristotle's textuality shows also other features that are characteristic of an oral/aural mentality, see Lang 1998, 18–33. On problem texts as texts that display both "openness" and "bookishness", see Taub 2015, 427–429.

47   See Koch and Oesterreicher 1985, 15–43.

48   Jaeger 1912, 131–133. See above note 10.

dated view.[49] It even seems reasonable to maintain that the presence of aural structures of thought in writings that, differently from Plato's dialogues, are not aimed at imitating real conversations is particularly significant, i.e., it is an even more indicative sign of the aural character of Aristotle's style of reasoning: indeed, these structures are not artifacts produced intentionally, but spontaneous forms of thought.

It is true that Plato's writings show a conflict between writing and speaking that does not find a close equivalent in those of Aristotle. However, it is also true that Aristotle does not neglect and underestimate orality at all. Indeed, he pays particular attention to various aspects of orality, especially to the material expression of language and its phonetic organization. For instance, the concepts of "voice" (*phone*) and "articulate voice" (*dialektos*) play a fundamental role in Aristotle's theory of language and their framing seems to be significantly influenced by the phonic and acoustic (as opposed to visual/graphic) experience of language itself.[50]

Language is described in the first place from the point of view of its production and not from that of its visual/graphic representation:[51] in Aristotle's view, language is not a combination of phonemes arranged together like beads on a string, but what results from the modification of a unitary underlying substrate (the voice) by means of *pathê* (*grammata/stoicheia*) that are thus inseparable from it.[52] Hence, in the production of language the minimal phonic units are not the *grammata/stoicheia* but the syllables (*HA* IV 9.535a27–b3, 535b33–536a4; *Probl.* X 39.895a10–11). The unity of a syllable is given by something that shows itself only in the spoken language, whereas it does not appear at all in the written one.[53] If this is true, Aristotle (just like Plato) would consider writing to be an unfaithful representation of spoken language (*Int.* 1.16a3–4), at least insofar as the material expression of language and its phonetic organization are concerned.

---

49 See above note 4.

50 E.g., every part of *logos* is defined in the first place as voice (*On Interpretation* 2.16a19–22, 4.16b26–28; *Poet.* 20) and voice is defined as the matter of *logos* (*GA* V 7.786b21–22). References to the theory of voice and articulate voice are scattered throughout the biological writings. Moreover, these theories are also dealt with in the section XI of the *Problemata* (on this section, see the recent contribution by Hagel 2015).

51 On this issue I am especially indebted to Laspia 1997.

52 Note that, thereby, Aristotle employs a model (i.e., substrate and affections) that is of fundamental importance in his whole philosophy.

53 Cf. *Categories* 6.4b32–37, where the unity of syllables is viewed as a rhythmic and prosodic feature.

Moreover, following Plato, Aristotle often employs phonetic models to illustrate his metaphysical theories.[54] The most significant and exemplary case is probably *Metaph.* VII 17.1041b11–33 where Aristotle uses the principle of unity of the syllable (i.e., an entity of the spoken and heard language rather than of the written one) as a model to explain what an *archê* and an *ousia* are.[55]

Finally, it is significant that, among sensations, Aristotle attaches particular importance not only to seeing but also, and especially, to hearing. Hearing— writes Aristotle (*Sense and Sensibilia* 1.436b3–17)—shows the differences of sound and voice, and, as such, is the more important sense for thought, and is fundamental for the processes of learning, to the point that the blind from birth are more intelligent than the congenital deaf. A similar idea is also expressed in the opening of the *Metaphysics*, which states that animals deprived of auditory faculties are incapable of learning. Also for Aristotle, then, verbal communication continues to be the main way to process and transmit knowledge.

To sum up, Aristotle's aurality is less striking than Plato's, but perhaps no less relevant.[56] It frames in the first place some aspects of Aristotle's style of reasoning and textuality, but it also determines some contents of his philosophy and, if the use of phonetic models is really significant (see note 55), it even provides important instruments and models to interpret reality.[57]

---

54   See, e.g., *Metaph.* III 3.998a20–25, 4.999b27–1000a4, 6.1002b17–22.

55   That Aristotle often employs phonetic models to illustrate his metaphysical theories is a fact. By itself this fact does not imply that the choice of this kind of model is philosophically significant. However, given the frequency of this choice, the hypothesis that it is philosophically significant seems to be worth examining. To my knowledge, few have dealt with this issue, among which an interesting contribution is offered especially by Laspia 2008.

56   On Aristotle's use, in his scientific investigations, of narrative patterns, themes, and motifs that derive from Homer, see Quarantotto 2016.

57   This paper was originally submitted to the editors of this volume in March 2012. In preparing it for publication in 2017 I felt it was necessary to preserve the original version, which of course belongs to 2012 and was written on the basis of ideas current five years ago. At the same time I must take into account important contributions that have been published during the interval. Therefore, I decided to acknowledge these more recent works in the footnotes, leaving the original text essentially unaltered. There are two works in particular that I would like to draw attention to: first, R. Mayhew's edition and translation of Aristotle's *Problems*, which was published at the end of 2011 when this paper was almost finished; secondly, the collection of essays edited by R. Mayhew that appeared in 2015 with the title 'The Aristotelian *Problemata physica*'. Some of the ideas advanced in this paper have been already published in Quarantotto 2011. I am very grateful to Emiliano Ippoliti, Monica Ugaglia and William Wians for their helpful comments and suggestions.

CHAPTER 4

Natural Things and Body: The Investigations of Physics

Helen S. Lang

Abstract

Efforts to date Aristotle's writings generally turn to their content, e.g., notions such as matter or actuality. This turn leads to the identification of this notion as early and that notion as late and so Aristotle's writings can be dated and his development identified. I suggest that there is a better way to think about this problem. Ancient Greece witnesses the development of writing and, consequently, the shift from oral culture to a "book [or scroll] culture" and I argue that considering the material conditions of writing reveals the structure of ancient texts. Against this background, I turn to Aristotle's *Physics* as a sequence of topics. Aristotle himself distinguishes "common and universal" topics, i.e., motion, the continuous, the infinite, place, void, and time, and "special attributes" that must be investigated after "common and universal" topics. The remainder of the *Physics* considers these topics. Although Aristotle never identifies an investigation of "special attributes", a case can be made that the *De Caelo* and the *De Generatione et Corruptione* provide this investigation. And so we can understand the organization of the Aristotelian corpus as reflecting the organization of physics as a science: first the investigation of common and universal topics, and then the investigation of "special attributes". But there is a problem with this view: body is common to all natural things but absent from the list of universal and common topics. In the *Physics*, Aristotle mentions but never examines body, as he investigates "things that are by nature". In the *De Caelo*, he defines physics as the science of body and investigates body. Either this construal of Aristotle's writing is wrong, or body is an anomaly within the ordering of topics, or body is a "special attribute". This paper considers this question, concluding that body is in fact a "special attribute" (a point supported by analysis of the structure of Aristotle's writing) and that it functions as a generic for physics only when abstracted from natural things.

I Introduction

Aristotle, unlike Plato, did not write "literary works" (that survive). The works that survive pose serious problems in regard to methods of composition, chronology, and how they might reveal philosophical development. Chronology has seemed the most promising starting point, especially for determining Aristotle's philosophical development. But it has proven elusive.

One method of establishing chronology identifies some concepts as "Platonic" (and so early) and others as "anti-Platonic" (and so late).[1] But "Platonic" and "anti-Platonic" are not transparent notions; even if they could be sorted out, they may not be productive. Irwin concludes: "I see no good reason to believe that he [Aristotle] spent most of his time deciding whether to agree or disagree with Plato, and hence I doubt if attention to debates with Plato or Platonism is likely to explain his philosophical development".[2] Even if Aristotle were not choosing in this sense, the assumption of a "Platonizing" Aristotle, who metamorphosed into an "anti-Platonizing" Aristotle is not supported by unambiguous evidence.[3] Even the notion of "influence" is open to interpretation. Finally, this method has failed to establish any clear "philosophical development" in Aristotle's writings.[4]

Chronology presupposes Aristotle's writings. They raise different but related questions of composition. Aristotle may have produced (a) given work(s) over

---

1 So, for example, Jaeger 1934, 297 and Solmsen 1960b, 228 both regard *Physics* VII as early (and Platonic) even though in *Physics* VII 1 Aristotle argues for a first mover that must be unmoved (rather than self-moved as Plato would have it). Solmsen 1960a, 191 argues that the arguments of *Physics* VII were replaced by the "mature" arguments of *Physics* VIII.

2 Cf. Irwin 1988, 12.

3 On how this mix occurs, and an implicit criticism of it, see Barnes 1981, 35: "That there was Platonic inspiration behind various aspects of the Apodeictic is neither disputable nor amazing. But it hardly suggests an early origin for Apodeictic: the Academy inspired Aristotle throughout his career ... and there is no reason at all to think that Academic influence betokens a pre-syllogistic stage of Aristotle's thought". Barnes may be criticizing work such as that of Solmsen 1960b, 213–235. Barnes 1994, xv continues his critique. Barnes is in turn a target (among others) of Hintikka 1996. Hintikka argues that Aristotle's earliest methodology is "called dialectical" and found in the *Topics* and *Sophistical Refutations* (87). Aristotle's early methodology leads, Hintikka continues, to "his syllogistic theory, which represents a new stage in the development of Aristotle's methodological ideas" (89). But Hintikka himself backs off the notion of two "stages" [his quotation marks] (90) and notes that the definition of a syllogism found at *APr.* I 1.24b18–20 is almost the same as that found at *Top.* I 1.100a25–27 (adding that on his view "this need not be a later change in Aristotle's original version of the *Topics*" [91–92]). Berti 1996, 130 concludes "we may say that Aristotle always professes the same conception of dialectic, in his earliest as in his latest works". For a suggested "topology" of views of Aristotle's development, cf. Witt 1996. It is hard to know what evidence would finally allow a firm conclusion to be reached.

4 Cf. Wians 1996. For an exception to this claim, cf. Chroust 1996.

an extended period of time.[5] As a result, the very notion of a "date"—and so both chronology and philosophical development—may not be altogether meaningful. These writings themselves may provide a more productive starting point.

Their survival is an astonishing fact. Were they lost to be found later or never lost at all?[6] The answer is unclear. How are we to construe their character? Did they form "an encyclopaedic series of lectures"?[7] In ancient Athens there was no notion of systematic knowledge collected into a single literary form. Even the notion of "lectures" is problematic: a lecture is spoken but we possess writings. What are they and how are they related to an oral form, such as lectures? Writing arrived in Greece well before Aristotle, but the transition from an oral culture to a culture that was in significant ways literate was slow and complex.[8] One interpretation of this transition identifies Aristotle's writings as "treatises" that served as the basis of discussion within "Aristotle's school".[9] Linking these writings to school discussion partly bypasses the problems of authorship (they may be a "communal production" within the school), dating (they were written over time), and development (within Aristotle's school, what survives is the outcome of development).

---

5   Cf. Barnes 1981, 53–54: "The *Analytics* was not composed in a year or two as a textbook: it grew organically, over a long period as a set of lectures. Thus to ask whether the *Prior* was written before or after the *Posterior Analytics* is simple-minded—it presupposes a mode of composition entirely alien to the circumstances in which Aristotle produced his philosophical *oeuvre*". We might note that some of the same issues have been raised in regard to Plato's dialogues (which sometimes serve as a model for dating Aristotle). For a review of these issues, Altman 2010, 39 provides evidence that these issues were raised in the Greek tradition, quoting Dionysius of Halicarnassus (*De compositione* 3.16): "And Plato was not through with combing and curling his dialogues, and braiding them in every which way, having reached his eightieth year" (Altman's translation).

6   Cf. Chroust 1962.

7   Cf. Graham 1987, 4.

8   See Robb 1994, 21: "Before 750 B.C., Greek society was not literate in any significant sense of the word even if, as many experts now believe, the Greek alphabet had been invented perhaps a few decades earlier than that date ... After some four centuries had passed, or by about 350 B.C., Athenian society had become fully literate, not in the statistical sense, about which we will never be adequately informed for antiquity, but in what may be termed the 'institutional' sense. Major institutions of society, especially the administration of justice and the formal education of young males in their *meirakion* years (roughly 15 to 21), had grown dependent on alphabetic literacy" (cf. also 253).

9   Cf. Owens 1978, 75–78.

Among these competing claims, the sole question for the philosopher is what difference the oral tradition and the transition to literacy make for what we call "Aristotle's writings" as philosophy and what difference it makes to the conception of philosophy that we find expressed in "the Aristotelian corpus". The problem of writing in ancient Athens, and *a fortiori* Aristotle's writings, is subject to debate, especially as it relates to an oral tradition. But recent scholarship in this area has made some progress, reaching a number of conclusions relevant to the philosophical question raised by Aristotle's writings. It is worth considering them.

The codex (what we know as a bound book) is a Roman invention of about the first century CE, although it did not become widespread until much later.[10] The earliest known desks date from about the fourth century CE and desks did not become common until about the ninth century. Prior to the codex, "convenient writing materials cannot have been as casually omnipresent as they are in our own lives".[11] Writing—and this point must apply to Aristotle's writings—was done on papyrus scrolls: it was arduous (and must have been expensive).

Many works, from Homer to Plato and Aristotle, required many scrolls. Multiple scrolls were kept together in a bucket or basket. Casson (who provides a photograph of a sculpture that depicts a bucket of scrolls) concludes that "there is no connection between the number of rolls it took to hold the text of a work and the number of books it was divided into because these vary in length, often by a great deal".[12] Sometimes scrolls are shown with tags identifying the contents; other times not. Finding the right scroll from those available in a bucket must often have been a matter of trial and error.

The production of a scroll was labor intensive. A funeral sculpture shows a man reclining, holding the scroll in both hands and reading aloud to a scribe, who is seated on a nearby stool. (Scribes also sometimes squat with a tunic pulled tight over the knees.) Aristotle's works must have been written (whoever did the actual writing) in this way.[13] A scribe, either seated on a stool or squatting, held the scroll in the left hand above the left knee, while it ran down onto the left knee, across the lap, over the right knee, and onto the floor; he wrote with his right hand on his right knee—the knee presumably defining the width of the column—and would then roll the scroll in the left hand, holding it

10   Cf. Casson 2001, 129.

11   Cf. Harris 1994, 195–196.

12   Cf. Casson 2001, 25–26.

13   Temporary slates were used by schoolboys learning to write but would hardly have been used by Aristotle's students.

up so that the newly written column, along with the one written immediately before it, could dry, as he wrote the next.

Scrolls are notoriously clumsy and hard to manipulate. Since reading and writing each require two hands to hold the scroll, they probably could not be done simultaneously.[14] Aristotle himself (*Politics* VIII 3.1337b22–27), listing the four parts of education, seems to separate them. Writing was not only arduous but also uncomfortable, and there is evidence that it was a task to be avoided.[15] Harris remarks, "One of the ironies of ancient literacy is the extent to which those at the top of the social hierarchy would often go to avoid writing".[16] Corrections, or editing, raise still further problems for scrolls. It takes two hands simultaneously to roll and unroll a scroll, and it is difficult to "find the place" within it. (The codex not only doubled the amount of space available because it was possible to write on both sides of the page but also, unlike the scroll, allowed one to "save a place" with a finger or marker, while going to another page, essentially "flipping back and forth".[17]) The assumption that Aristotle edited and rewrote his works, using the margins, making notes and corrections, is unlikely.

Reading too, while less labor intensive than writing, required considerable work, i.e., holding the scroll while simultaneously winding and unwinding it.[18] Paintings and sculpture show individuals reading. Scrolls, read across from right to left (as opposed to up and down), were written in columns and are usually shown held in both the reader's hands. Readers are almost always depicted with their mouths open, suggesting that reading was always done aloud. It resembled a recitation. Through reading, the main acquaintance with

---

14   Cribiore 1996 argues this thesis at length. She is clear about her point, which also applies to writing in ancient Athens: "Reading and writing may not have been linked in the schools or in teaching. Assumption that the two skills go together is unwarranted" (9). Even reading was difficult, given the cumbersome nature of the scroll.

15   Bagnall 1995, 25: "One might say that there was a direct correlation between social standing that guaranteed literacy and the means to avoid writing". Bagnall goes on immediately to say that "men of standing" must have done at least some, perhaps a fair amount of writing.

16   Cf. Harris 1994, 195–196.

17   Cf. Casson 2001, 129.

18   In *Theaetetus* 143a1–b2, Euclides, denying that he could remember the entire discussion, describes writing and correcting the dialogue, which he then calls a slave to read. There may be some sort of joke here about memory and reading, especially if we recall the opening of the *Parmenides*, where there is also a problem with memory, a forgotten name, and then a turn to Antiphon, who has memorized the entire dialogue and can recite it, although he currently devotes most of his time to horses (*Parmenides* 126b1–127a1). All references to Plato are to the O.C.T.

written texts remained primarily oral, e.g., a single text was read aloud to a group.[19] Indeed, even though by the time of Aristotle writing had been available for several generations, ancient culture remained oral in important ways. The shift to the written word did not simply jettison the older oral tradition; rather, the oral tradition remained a locus in which the shift to writing occurs.[20] "The invention of writing did not promote a social or intellectual revolution, and reports of the death of orality have been exaggerated".[21]

By the time of Aristotle, booksellers were thriving, suggesting that a sufficient number of texts must have been available to support the trade. Therefore, Athenian culture was seeing a new standard of literacy, whatever that may mean. Harris asks: "Who is the first truly bookish individual among the Greeks?" And he answers: "Hardly Socrates ... Some might say Euripides; but by the standards of later Greek intelligentsias, the best answer is Aristotle, for he is the first extant writer who makes it plain that he has consulted a large number of written works for himself".[22] Harris does not mention Plato, who refers to various predecessors and whose arguments may be filled with sly references that we no longer catch; but Harris is right that Aristotle is the first to record and respond to the views of his predecessors in an entirely new way and the first writer from whom we possess a significant record of writings that do not refer to or represent the oral tradition (as Plato's dialogues do).[23]

---

19   Thomas 1994, 33 remarks, "the written word in Greece was most commonly read aloud (and so accessible even to those who could not read)". She contrasts the Greek attitude to writing, i.e., suspicious, used sparingly to record laws and treatises, to that of the Romans, although in public and legal uses of writing there was some shift after the fourth century (35–37, 45–49). Cf. also Robb 1994, 233, who argues, "Plausibly some of Plato's dialogues were read aloud with success to sophisticated groups of Athenians". At *Phaedo* 97b8–c1, Socrates recounts hearing someone read Anaxagoras.

20   Robb 1994, 160 argues that "In the late fifth century, as Plato's dialogues incontestably prove, the authority of epic had not yet been displaced or even significantly diminished, a situation that the greatest of Greek prose writers and a philosopher of surpassing genius was about to challenge". Cf. also 162 ff. for the claim that in the *Ion* Plato is addressing claims that originate with Homer.

21   Cf. Bowman and Woolf 1994, 3.

22   Cf. Harris 1994, 85.

23   This view is supported by Robb 1994, 246 note 19 (whose primary interest is Plato): "In addition to the first history of philosophy and science and first accumulation of Greek constitutions, the first history of geometry and the foundation documents of botany were parts of Lyceum's ambitious endeavors. While Aristotle lived, the Lyceum even collected *didaskaliai* (the term is a reminder that dramatists were supposed to teach), records of the dramatic performances in the city and lists of victors at the Pythian games (for

Some scholars have suggested "a culture of rhetoric", i.e., a culture in which writing becomes more universal but an oral or rhetorical tradition remains central to all written expressions.[24] Literacy remained relatively rare but written texts became more widely available through recitation.[25] Written texts were memorized and recited (as we see in several of Plato's dialogues) thereby becoming available to those who cannot read or afford to own books; such recitations may have been a form of personal recollection, or entertainment, or learning, and as such would have resembled the recitation of poetry, even as it takes on new functions. "What was distinctive of classical Greek literature, which we now read in silent admiration, was that artist and audience were interacting in a dynamic and creative way through the medium of voice and ear".[26] "What was new to the Hellenistic era is, first, the multiplication of books and the mania for preservation of writing; and secondly, the establishment of primary texts from which future generations are supposed to write in their turn".[27] Aristotle's writings become central to the project of Hellenism, but they themselves originate in and so reflect the earlier oral tradition.

Within the oral tradition, recitation is a living form of memory and intellectual engagement. What is recited, while being recalled, is also being modified, expanded, improved upon, and made responsive to the audience, past and present. In short, recitation serves the function that rewriting will serve in a fully literate culture. The role of recitation, conjoined with the expense and labor of writing, suggests that what we possess as "Aristotle's writings" come at the end of the period of development, rather than exhibiting development.

What does this claim amount to philosophically for Aristotle's writings? It is widely agreed that works such as the *Physics* or *Metaphysics* are the result of editing by Aristotle's successors. Although we cannot be sure how what we

---

the last we have inscriptional evidence of the gratitude of the citizens of Delphi) ... This remarkable research activity, so manifestly based on accumulating texts—copying, studying, analyzing, and commenting on them—remained central at least through the long period Theophrastus headed the school; he died at the age of eighty-five, having guided the school almost to his final day". Cf. also Baltussen 2008, 223; Dupont 2009, 147: "During the classical era, written texts are presented often in the form of the fixation of ritualized or socially codified oral performances, that is, poems, or dialogues, or speech".

24 For a fuller (and compelling) account of what is meant by the expression "a culture of rhetoric", see Pelling 2000, 1–17.

25 For one example, Derrenbacker 2005, 27 ff. suggests a notion of a "rhetorical" culture, i.e., widespread illiteracy conjoined with an oral tradition that made literary works more widely available.

26 Cf. Robb 1994, 259.

27 Cf. Dupont 2009, 145.

possess as individual books, e.g., *Physics* II or *Metaphysics* XII, came to be collected into larger works such as the *Physics* or *Metaphysics*, the individual books probably form the basic unit of what we call "Aristotle's writing". Individual books, kept together in a bucket, may form the larger work within which editors decided on the order of the books. So for example, some works begin with a book in which Aristotle criticizes his predecessors (*Physics* I, *Metaphysics* I, *De Anima* I, just to name a few). Alternatively, one might speculate that conceptually the formation of larger works from Aristotle's individual books required the codex, i.e., the ability to move about freely in the text and, in short, the conception of a larger and more systematic work. In this case, books would have been bound into works only after the codex became widely accepted and the editor's role would be considerably larger. Not all the works need have been done in the same way. A work such as the *Physics* may have been of the first sort, the *Metaphysics* of the second. However the works came to be formed, within them the individual book is the unit of writing.

Often a book investigates a topic, defined at its beginning. Indeed, the opening lines of a book often appear as an announcement that we might think of as a mark of orality, the first line of a recitation. "There is a science of being *qua* being"; "every art and every inquiry, and likewise both action and choice, seem to be aimed at some good"; "of things that are, some are by nature and some are by other causes".[28] When related investigations are short, a single book may include more than one. Each topic is announced and the investigation presents a simple structure and clear conclusion. For example, *Physics* IV 1 opens, "Likewise, it is necessary that the physicist know place, as well as the infinite, if it is or not, and how it is and what it is" (208a26–27). *Physics* IV 6 opens saying that the same questions must be asked of void, "if it is or not, and how it is and what it is" (213a13–14). *Physics* IV 10 specifies time as coming next and this investigation is clearly complete at the end of *Physics* IV 14.

In the corpus (as we have it), just as the book is the unit of writing, the topic is the unit of investigation. Thus when the investigation is longer and more complex, the writing and the investigation coincide in a single book, e.g., *Physics* II, while shorter and less complex investigations can be combined in one book, e.g., *Physics* IV. Within a given argument, Aristotle may refer to other investigations or he may make methodological remarks that apply to more than one investigation; nonetheless, as I shall argue below, the investigations themselves, i.e., arguments that reach specific conclusions, are strictly bound by

---

28   These are the opening lines of *Metaphysics* IV 1, *Nicomachean Ethics* I 1.1094a1–2, and *Physics* II 1. All references are to the O.C.T.

the topic announced at or near the beginning. Thus, Aristotle is not systematic in the sense of reaching (a) conclusion(s) that enter different topics into
a larger construal; rather, his philosophic project is defined by an announced
topic investigated within a book, or section of a book.

In effect, the topic announced at or near the opening dominates each investigation. Here we may return to the oral character of Aristotle's writing, as
it resembles a recitation: it begins with an announcement and then lays out
the features of the investigation in an orderly forward "movement" that works
from the most important implications or features of the investigation to the
least important, often concluding with a rejection of opposing views. As a
result, subsequent arguments are defined and limited by their relation to the
announced topic. Arguments are not serial or independent of one another but
form a structure that unfolds in an orderly way from what is most important to
its immediate implications and requirements to what is less important. Recalling that one cannot conveniently move around in a scroll, we can see that this
order resembles a recitation as the scroll unrolls. This claim is crucial to the
interpretation of any particular book (its topic and investigation), any set of
books collected into a work (with the result that its topics and investigations
are also collected), and finally Aristotle's philosophical project systematically
across the works comprising the corpus as a whole.

If we take topical investigations as Aristotle's primary project, then construing relations across different investigations, or books, is solely our concern as
historians of philosophy.[29] And, if we wish to capture Aristotle's philosophical project at a fully systematic level, then however we construe these relations, the topical character of each investigation cannot be violated.[30] This
challenge is one I shall try to meet: to provide a "principle of construal" that
allows us as historians of philosophy to understand the relations across the
investigations constituting two of Aristotle's major works, the *Physics* and the
De Caelo, without violating the topical character of the individual investigations.

The *Physics* and the *De Caelo* provide a special case study for the topical
character of Aristotle's philosophy. In *Physics* II 1 Aristotle identifies "things
that are by nature" as "a substance" and "a subject" (192b33); the remainder
of this book pursues the implications of this identification. But *De Caelo* I

---

29 Again, the notion that the books form larger works, e.g., the *Physics* or *Metaphysics*, is a
     conception of philosophy that may be Hellenistic in origin. It is associated not with writing
     inquiries, but with collecting and organizing them (Pfeiffer 1968, 152).

30 For a more extended discussion of the topical character of Aristotle's works, see Lang 2009,
     3–33.

opens with the claim that the science of nature concerns body, defined as perfect magnitude.[31] "Things that are by nature", along with form and matter, disappear, apparently replaced by the examination of body and the elements. Consequently, the arguments of the *Physics* are quite different from those of the *De Caelo*; any account of them must explain both why the science of physics includes such different investigations and how they are compatible. For both works, I shall first analyze each book as topical to define its topic(s) and investigation. Proceeding in this way, as I shall argue, yields a remarkably strong sense of the coherence of Aristotle's investigations as topically defined.

In conclusion, I shall consider how the science of physics can include both the investigations of the *Physics* and those of the *De Caelo*. *Prima facie*, it is not clear how the investigations of the *Physics* insofar as they define "things that are by nature", along with their requirements, fit together with the investigations of the *De Caelo*, which identify body and all it entails as part of physics. But, as we shall see, in *Physics* III 1 Aristotle identifies the topics of the *Physics* as "common and universal", rather than "proper". But he does not define these terms or identify any "proper" investigation. He does say, though, that investigations of what is "common and universal" should be prior to investigations of what is "proper". In the final section of this paper, I shall turn to Aristotle's investigations of demonstration in the *Analytics* and *Topics*, where he does define these terms and their relations. These investigations of demonstration, I shall argue, allow us to construe the relation between the *Physics* and *De Caelo*: body is not examined in the *Physics* because it is proper rather than "common and universal". The *De Caelo* takes up what is "proper" and so follows the *Physics*. I shall also suggest that on this model we can interpret the order of Aristotle's "scientific writings" from physics to biology. I turn first to the *Physics*, then to the *De Caelo*, to consider them as ordered investigations in which the topic determines the investigation of each.

---

31   Aristotle, *Phys.* II 1.192b33–34; *Cael.* I 1.268a1–2. The "and" (καί) here may be explicative: "bodies, namely, magnitudes".

11   The Investigations of Aristotle's *Physics* I–VIII: Common and
          Universal Topics

In *Physics* I (as in the first book of several works), Aristotle opens with several
general remarks but largely reviews (and criticizes) his predecessors.[32] *Physics*
II begins his direct inquiry, opening with a clear distinction: "Of things that
are, some are by nature (τὰ φύσει) while some are by art (τὰ τέχνῃ); 'by nature'
are both animals and their parts, and plants and the simple [constituents] of
bodies, such as earth and fire and air and water; nature is a principle of motion
and rest absent from things that are 'by art', more precisely: nature is a source
and cause of being moved and being at rest in that to which it belongs in
virtue of itself and not accidentally".[33] Indeed, we have here the definition of
nature: a thing that has a nature "is a substance; for it is a subject, and nature
is always in a subject".[34] That nature is always "a substance" and "a subject"
identifies this inquiry as concerned with being in the primary sense. We may
note, anticipating *De Caelo* I 1, that body is not identified as among things that
are "by nature"; as we shall see, it is not found in the investigations of "things
that are by nature".

     Some thinkers, Aristotle continues, identify "nature and the substance of
things that are by nature" with the thing taken without arrangement, i.e., matter.[35] But whether "by nature" or "by art", matter is the thing only potentially;
we do not have a man or a bed until we have an actual man or an actual
bed; form, not matter, makes a thing actual (193a32–b6). Therefore, "the form
indeed is nature rather than the matter; for a thing is more properly said to
be what it is when it is in actuality than when it is potentially" (193a6–7).
Defining nature as form allows Aristotle to compare physics, mathematics, and
astronomy. Natural form is always found with matter and so matter too must

---

32   For two parallel cases, cf. *Metaphysics* I and *De Anima* I.

33   *Phys.* II 1.192b8–15, b21–23. Gill 1980, 147 note 18 argues that the verbal form is more
       precise than the noun form and so we may think of the second statement as replacing
       an ambiguous first account of nature. It has been claimed that the second statement is
       also ambiguous, i.e., the verb κινεῖσθαι may be either middle or passive. It has traditionally
       been taken to be passive, and I have argued elsewhere that it cannot be middle. For its
       treatment as middle, cf. Charlton 1970. For a response to Charlton and argument why this
       verb must be passive, see Lang 2009, 40–50.

34   *Phys.* II 1.192b33: καὶ ἔστιν πάντα ταῦτα οὐσία· ὑποκείμενον γάρ τι, καὶ ἐν ὑποκείμενον γάρ τι,
       καὶ ἐν ὑποκειμένῳ ἐστὶν ἡ φύσις ἀεί.

35   *Phys.* II 1.193a10–29: ἡ φύσις καὶ ἡ οὐσία τῶν φύσει ὄντων. Again nature is identified with
       substance and being in the primary sense.

be included in the study of things that are by nature.³⁶ Including matter, the physicist resembles the doctor, who includes the sinew within the study of health, and differs from the mathematician, who studies natural form apart from matter.³⁷ The inclusion of matter in the science of physics clearly implies that physics as a science deals with individuals; but the argument establishing this claim is universal—it establishes "what it is" to be a thing that is by nature—and does not consider individuals as such. "Is astronomy different from or a part of physics?" (193b25–26). The investigation of astronomy is left unclear.³⁸

Physics II proceeds with the investigation of things that are by nature, next examining the causes of things that are by nature (3.194b16: ἐπισκεπτέον περὶ τῶν αἰτιῶν). To grasp a primary cause (τὸ λαβεῖν τὴν πρώτην αἰτίαν) is to answer the question "why" (literally "on account of what"), which can be answered in four ways: (1) form, (2) matter, (3) moving cause, and (4) final cause (*Phys.* II 3.194b17–20).³⁹ The account of causes establishes the grounds for considering two proposed causes, chance and spontaneity, that analysis shows must be rejected (*Phys.* II 4–6). Summarizing ways in which the question "why" may be answered, Aristotle adds that the final cause is the form acting as a principle of motion and the moving cause, e.g., the father is the form acting from the outside to produce a new individual (*Phys.* II 7). He criticizes Empedocles, a proponent of accidental causes, and again affirms the importance of final causes (*Phys.* II 8). He concludes with an examination of hypothetical necessity, which relates to matter and its role in physics (*Phys.* II 9).

Aristotle does considerable work in *Physics* II and in this work the topical character of his investigation of things that are by nature is clear. (1) Nature

---

36   *Phys.* II 2.194a12–15; a26. The study of form as it is found apart from matter, and so apart from motion, no longer belongs to physics; *Phys.* II 7.198a27–32. Form found with matter but studied without reference to it is the subject of mathematics and form that is actually apart from matter is the subject of first philosophy or theology. Cf. also, *Metaph.* VI 1.1026a10–31; VII 11.1037a10–17; XI 3.1061a29–b1; 4.1061b18–32.

37   *Phys.* II 2.194b11–13, b32–35. For a parallel, but not identical text, cf. *Metaph.* VI 1.

38   Aristotle remarks that optics, harmonics, and astronomy are the "more natural parts of mathematics (τὰ φυσικώτερα τῶν μαθημάτων)" that contrast with geometry—"for geometry investigates natural lines but not as natural, while optics [investigates] mathematical lines, but as natural not mathematical" (*Physics* II 2.194a7–12). But the force of this comment is not clear here nor is it made clear elsewhere.

39   We generally speak of "why" in English, but the Greek reads διά τι, "on account of what", which suggests a direct, less abstract, relation than does "why". Compare this line to *Phys.* I 1.184a13, where Aristotle says we think we know a thing when we know its primary causes (τὰ αἴτια γνωρίσωμεν τὰ πρῶτα).

is defined first, an essential source of being moved and being at rest, and identified as a substance and a subject; then things that are by nature are defined primarily as form because it is actual, although matter, a thing as potential, must be included in the definition of natural things and so in the science of physics.[40] (2) Four causes answer the question "why" for natural things, conceived as a combination of form and matter, while chance and spontaneity cannot be causes (and Aristotle criticizes their leading proponent). (3) Having included matter in a secondary way within physics, its role in things that are by nature is also defined.

Aristotle announces his topic, "things that are by nature", which requires that first nature and then "things that are by nature" be defined. These definitions appear immediately; he then situates this inquiry in relation to mathematics, while raising a question about astronomy. The remainder of the investigation takes up questions that follow from the definitions of nature and natural things. This investigation "unfolds" from what is primary, the definition of nature, and the identification of natural things as primarily form, to the account of "causes" for such things, to what is less important, i.e., rejection of false claims about causes, a critique of their proponent, and the role of matter as hypothetical necessity.

Physics III 1.200b13 announces its topic straightaway: nature is a principle of motion and change, and it is the subject of our inquiry. Since nature involves motion, we must understand "motion", which appears in what is continuous as too does the infinite, which is often used to define the continuous; "in addition to these, without place and void and time, motion seems to be impossible" (200b20–21). These are clearly "common and universal" (κοινά καὶ καθόλου) to all things that are; hence, examination of them comes first, for "the examination of what is proper" (ἡ περὶ τῶν ἰδίων θεωρία) comes after that of what is common (200b21–25). The division of topics and hence investigations into "common and universal" and "proper" suggests that these kinds will not be mixed within a single investigation and that what follows here will be exclusively "common and universal". And Aristotle goes to work: he investigates motion first and then the other topics listed here as required to understand motion and ultimately nature.

Investigations of these topics, and further problems raised by them, I shall now argue, occupy *Physics* III–VIII. They follow from the definition of nature

---

40   A closer analysis of Aristotle's position lies beyond our interests in the sequence of his topics. But we may note that the combination of form and matter, which Aristotle often designates the "subject", is the weakest account of substance, although it is not thereby excluded from the rank of substance; cf. *Metaph.* VII 3.1029a30–32.

in *Physics* II 1 and placing them immediately after *Physics* II gives a clear order to the investigations—an order that reflects the definition of nature and Aristotle's list of "common and universal" topics in *Physics* III 1. Again, if we anticipate *De Caelo* I 1, we find a puzzling omission: body fails to appear as "by nature", as a cause, or as something "common and universal".[41] The topics and investigations of *Physics* III through VIII can now be considered.

Motion is the first topic; defined in terms of potency and act, its investigation is clearly universal.[42] The infinite (and by implication the continuous) is the next topic because what is moved appears to be continuous and the continuous is found with the infinite. Physics, Aristotle says, considers magnitude, motion, and time, and each must be either infinite or finite (202b30–32). Most importantly, the physicist must consider whether (or not) there is an infinite sensible magnitude, i.e., body (204a1–2).

Here "body" appears to enter *Physics* III as a topic, even though it is not included in the list of topics that must be examined, if nature is not to remain hidden. If body is a topic and so effectively added to this list, then either body would be "common and universal" after all, or a topic that is not "common and universal" is mixed in with topics that are. Either way, the investigation would be procedurally confused: the announced topic, the infinite, is set aside in the middle of an investigation to take up a different topic, body. This situation is critical for the claim that Aristotle's philosophical project must be understood as topical investigations. What is the topic of *Physics* III 4–8?

Having said that the one who examines nature must consider the infinite (202b35), Aristotle first turns to his predecessors, including not only the Pythagoreans, Plato, Anaxagoras, and Democritus, but unspecified "physicists" (οἱ δὲ περὶ φύσεως πάντες [ἀεὶ] ὑποτιθέασιν) and identifies a number of problems raised by the infinite: is it a substance or an accident, are the elements infinite, is it a principle or derived from a principle (203a1–b15)? Arguments for the infinite rest on five considerations, i.e., time, the division of magnitudes, number, coming to be and passing away, which appear to be without end, and most of all what is outside the heavens; if what is outside the heavens seems to be infinite, then body too will be infinite and there will be an infinite number of worlds; this implication raises the problems of place and void for if they are infinite, it again follows that body is infinite.[43] These implications assume that there is

---

41 Aristotle (unlike later philosophers) does not identify matter with body; matter is a thing as potential and as such is included in the definition of natural things.

42 *Phys.* III 1–3; cf. 200b25: καὶ πρῶτον, καθάπερ εἴπαμεν, περὶ κινήσεως. Cf. *Phys.* III 2.202a3: "every mover too is moved" and 3.202a14: "motion is in the movable".

43 *Phys.* III 4.203b15–30. This sentence begins τοῦ δ' εἶναί τι ἄπειρον ἡ πίστις ἐκ πέντε, which

something infinite. This assumption, as we have just seen, originates with Aristotle's predecessors. At this point in the inquiry, Aristotle has not revealed his own view; rather, he has identified a topic, the infinite, turned to his predecessors (and opponents), and now identifies the assumptions that underlie their belief in the infinite. The next words make it clear that his topic remains the infinite: the investigation concerning the infinite is problematic.[44] Impossibilities result whether we say it is or is not; if it is, then we must ask how it is, as a substance or an attribute; or if neither of these, is there something that is infinite or some plurality that is infinite (203b31–204a1).

The problem that belongs most of all to the physicist is whether there is some perceptible magnitude that is infinite.[45] Again, we must ask if the specification of the problem of the infinite to what belongs especially to physics shifts the investigation to "sensible magnitude", i.e., body? Again, the answer lies in Aristotle's very next words: "We must begin by distinguishing the many ways the term 'infinite' is used" (204a2–3). "Infinite", he continues, is applied to whatever cannot be gone through or traversed because it does not have a limit; and a thing may be infinite in respect to addition, division, or both (204a3–7). Clearly, the topic remains the infinite.

Aristotle next returns to the questions about the infinite raised by Plato and Pythagoras.[46] The infinite cannot be separate from sensible things; but if one takes it not as a magnitude or a plurality, but as a substance and not an accident, various problems follow (204a8–29). But it cannot be an accident either; the Pythagorean view involves absurdities and in any case concerns mathematical objects that do not involve magnitude (and so lie outside physics, 204a30–b1).

This inquiry is limited to sensible things and we must ask whether or not there is among them a body infinite in respect to increase (201b1–4). Belief that there is something infinite comes, as we have seen, from five considerations, most importantly that what is outside the heavens is infinite. If what is outside

---

Barnes ed. 1984 renders, "Belief in the existence of the infinite"; Hussey better captures the force of the indefinite pronoun: "The more plausible arguments for the existence of something infinite are five".

44   *Phys.* III 4.203b31. The opening words read: ἔχει δ' ἀπορίαν ἡ περὶ τοῦ ἀπείρου θεωρία (cf. *Metaph.* XII 1.1069a18). Again, Barnes ed. 1984 reads "But the problem of the infinite is difficult" while Hussey better reflects the notion of an inquiry: "Inquiry into the infinite presents difficulties".

45   *Phys.* III 4.204a1–2. The Greek here reads: μάλιστα δὲ φυσικοῦ ἐστιν σκέψασθαι εἰ ἔστι μέγεθος αἰσθητὸν ἄπειρον.

46   Pythagoras is named at *Phys.* III 5.204a33. For these arguments as also directed against Plato, cf. Ross 1950, 364.

the heavens is identified as body, then it would be a body infinite with respect to increase, i.e., going outward on and on.[47] The most likely target here is Anaxagoras. There is a general reference to "as some say" (204b23), the supposition that the infinite body is homogeneous (205a13), and Anaxagoras is named at 205a1. Aristotle begins with a point of logic: the notion of "infinite body" is contradictory because body is by definition bounded and "infinite" means unbounded (204b4–7); he concludes by unambiguously rejecting the idea of a body that is actually infinite (206a7–8). The next lines begin a new approach to the question of the infinite: it cannot be rejected altogether, and Aristotle sets out to explain how the infinite is and how it is not.

Here the argument clearly concerns the infinite, concluding: "the infinite then is in no other way but it is in this way, both something in potency and again by reduction" (206b12–13). Aristotle adds the details of his position concerning the infinite, then returns to earlier issues. The infinite turns out to be the contrary of what proponents of infinite body claim (206b33–207a7) and he compares Parmenides and Melissus (207a15); the relation of the infinite to magnitude, movement, and time is now explained and his view does not affect mathematics (207b27–34). The investigation concludes unequivocally: "but concerning the infinite, how it is and how it is not and what it is has been said" (208b22–23).

In short, Aristotle does not treat body as a topic in *Physics* III 4–8. Indeed, understanding this text as an investigation of a topic brings clarity to its logic. It begins with a clearly identified topic: the physicist must discuss the infinite (202b35–36). Aristotle takes up views that identify the infinite with body (203a36–b15), and identifies five sources of belief in the infinite (203b15–25). The fifth, what is outside the heavens is infinite body, underlies claims about infinite body and an infinite number of cosmoi (203b25–26). This problem most of all belongs to the physicist (204a1–2).

He next distinguishes how the word "infinite" is used and returns to his predecessors, sorting them out and, for the most part, rejecting their views. Arguments for infinite body have at their center a contradiction—body is by definition bounded and as infinite unbounded. The analysis of body that Aristotle now presents opposes Ionian cosmology by addresssing the fifth, most important reason for belief in the infinite. We may note that Aristotle's definition of body given in the *De Caelo*—magnitude divisible in every way— does not appear here. He is not examining body and so does not give his view or definition. A false view identifies the infinite with body. Both the claims about

---

47   Hussey 1983, xxxiii rightly takes these arguments to oppose Ionian cosmology.

the infinite and the view of body that it supports are false and must be rejected. Aristotle's own account begins at *Physics* III 6 and it unequivocally concerns the infinite.

The infinite is the topic of this investigation and Aristotle never abandons it. The arguments about body tell us nothing about Aristotle's view because they rest on his opponents' premise that identifies the infinite with body, i.e., body is infinite in regard to increase, a premise that he rejects. When he rejects infinite body (206a7–8), he has concluded his analysis of the views concerning the infinite as body, views of his predecessors, and so is ready to provide his own account of the infinite. That account, *Physics* III 6–8, concerns only the infinite. The integrity of the topical investigation is preserved.

The remaining topics listed at the opening of *Physics* III 1 are examined in order in *Physics* IV: place (1–5), void (6–9), and time (10–14). Again, while other notions, e.g., magnitude, motion, the infinite, appear within these investigations, there can be no question of the topics or the topical character of the inquiries.[48] And body again appears because of a false view.[49] But the accounts of "where" and "when", i.e., place, void, and time, examine topics that are common and universal (*Phys.* IV 1.208a29: "all suppose that things that are must be somewhere"). These topics are required by motion and motion must be understood so that what nature is will not remain hidden.[50] Hence the definitions of nature and things "by nature" provide the foundation of these investigations, starting with motion. Motion in turn raises additional topics and so is their direct, or immediate foundation, with nature as the indirect or ultimate foundation. Each investigation is clearly defined by an announced topic that defines the inquiry and the sequence of arguments that constitute it and each reaches a definition that is common and universal, bearing upon nature and things that are by nature as defined in *Physics* II 1.

But what of *Physics* V–VIII: how do these arguments relate to the topics specified at *Physics* III 1, and how can we understand the *Physics* as a whole? *Physics* V–VIII, as I shall now argue, take up further problems entailed by the definition of motion and the topics of *Physics* III. *Physics* V opens with an

---

48   *Phys.* IV 1.208a27: "Likewise the physicist must know place as well as the infinite"; 6.213a12–13: "in the same way, the investigation concerning the void must also belong to the physicist"; 10.217b29: "coming next after the things discussed is time".

49   The comparison with *Physics* III is particularly clear in the arguments concerning the void, *Phys.* IV 6–9, which Aristotle rejects in favor of place as "the where" things are.

50   Aristotle insists throughout his analysis of the void that its proponents think the void is a cause of motion (see *Phys.* IV 8.216a21–26; 9.216b24–30; 216b34–217a3; 217a5–10; cf. III 1.200b12–14).

account of the ways in which motion occurs and the claim that it requires a mover, a moved, and that in which motion occurs, i.e., place or time (224a21–23). Referring to place or time, this argument presupposes the definitions established in *Physics* IV and so "rightly" comes after them. Taking up a problem concerning requirements of motion, it presupposes its definition.[51] Insofar as it establishes a relation that always obtains, it resembles the topics of *Physics* III: it is "common and universal".

Motion always involves contraries, which raises further difficulties (225a30). Additional terms are required: "together" and "apart", "in contact", "between", "in succession", "continuous", and "contiguous" (*Phys.* V 3). Defining these terms presupposes the investigations of *Physics* III and IV, e.g., "together" requires the definition of place (226b21). Not only the terms, but also the problems of *Physics* V follow from the earlier arguments. In *Physics* III, Aristotle defines motion; in *Physics* V 4–6, he asks in what sense is motion one, or involves contrariety. These questions both presuppose the definition of motion in *Physics* III 1, which itself follows upon the definition of nature.

In *Physics* VI, Aristotle presupposes the terms, e.g., continuous and in succession, defined in *Physics* V 3 to argue that nothing continuous can be composed of indivisibles (231a23–24). Rather, "everything continuous is divisible into divisibles that are always divisible" (231b15–16). The book begins with an argument (perhaps aimed at Democritus) that a line cannot be composed of points and points cannot be in succession to one another (231a21–b10). What is continuous is not composed of parts, but is divisible into parts and likewise with magnitude, time, and motion (231b10–18). The remainder of *Physics* VI takes up further problems concerning motion arising from the fact that motion, magnitude, and time, being continuous, are also divisible. Divisibility of the continuous has been established; thus these arguments must apply to all things involving motion, magnitude, and time.[52]

Investigating the infinite in *Physics* III, Aristotle promises an account of magnitude and why every magnitude is divisible into magnitudes (207b26). In *Physics* VI 1, he keeps his promise. But for this account of magnitude, he takes up not body but points and lines. Beyond any question, the topic of this argument is magnitude not body. Indeed, body is a special case of magnitude, perfect magnitude, while this account applies to all magnitudes (*Cael.* I 1.268a6–b10; cf. *Cat.* 6.4b23–25).

---

51   At *Phys.* V 1.224b11 Aristotle refers to the definition of motion in *Physics* III.

52   This argument follows the account of the infinite at *Physics* III 4–8.

The last two investigations of the *Physics* also establish common and universal propositions. *Physics* VII, often read as a proof of a first mover, has been seen as a difficult, even inferior, book.[53] But here too Aristotle announces the topic of the inquiry in the opening line: "everything moved must be moved by something" (241b34). He first argues for this claim (242a49) and then takes up what follows from it. Using a *reductio ad absurdum* argument, he concludes that the series of moved movers cannot be infinite and so there must be a first mover and a first moved (243a30). He next argues that mover and moved must be together, citing the meaning of "together" from *Physics* V, and establishes the character of mover/moved relations for each kind of motion beginning with locomotion, the primary motion (243a39–40). That motion considered generally always requires a mover and a moved has been shown in *Physics* V, assuming the definition established in *Physics* III. Thus, *Physics* VII assumes the definitions established in the earlier books of the *Physics* to investigate the relation between mover and moved for each kind of motion. Within each kind, the conclusion obviously applies to all movers and moved things. The remainder of the book takes up the different kinds of motion and the implications of the opening proposition (e.g., *Phys.* VII 5.249b27–30). Thus the same conclusion follows as above: this investigation is topical, is clearly "common and universal", and follows from the definition of motion in *Physics* III and ultimately from the account of nature in *Physics* II.

We might pause here to note the result of understanding *Physics* VII as an investigation defined by its opening lines. It is often grouped with *Physics* VIII (and sometimes *Metaphysics* XII) as a proof of a first mover.[54] As such, it has been seen as an early Platonic effort, an "abortive attempt" to prove a first mover, replaced by the superior argument of *Physics* VIII.[55] Understanding *Physics* VII as defined by its opening line shows it to be an investigation of a specific topic, a common and universal claim stated at its opening: "everything moved must be moved by something".

---

53   Rose 1854, 199 thinks *Physics* VII is spurious, a view not widely supported. Brandis 1835–
       1866, 893 ff., Zeller 1962, 81–82 note 2, and Ross 1950, 4 see *Physics* VII as isolated or not
       really belonging in the *Physics*, although they accept it as by Aristotle. Some difficulties,
       which I shall not consider, arise from the existence of two versions of it (see Ross 1950,
       11–14).

54   Cf. Verbeke 1969, 267; Paulus 1933, 299; Owens 1966, 123; Pegis 1973, 78, 116–117.

55   For two examples, cf. Solmsen 1960b, 228; cf. also Solmsen 1960a, 191, where he says,
       "Book VII is not Aristotle's last word on these matters and … the proofs and theories
       embodied in it were later replaced by the 'maturer' insights of Book VIII" (cf. Jaeger 1934,
       297).

Like *Physics* VII, *Physics* VIII is also often read as a proof of a first mover.
But it begins with a question about motion: did motion have a beginning and
will it someday end, or is it immortal, a kind of life to all naturally constituted
things (VIII 1.250b11–15; cf. 251a5–8)? This question returns us to the account of
motion in *Physics* III and ultimately to the definition of nature as a source of
being moved and being at rest. If we keep this question in mind, both the topic
and structure of *Physics* VIII as an investigation appear clearly.

Aristotle first answers his opening question: motion and time must be eternal (*Phys.* VIII 1). He then raises three objections—perhaps he sees them as
a complete set (*Phys.* VIII 2). Two objections collapse into a single question:
why are some things in the cosmos sometimes in motion and sometimes at
rest (254b4–6). He first proves (again) that everything moved must be moved
by something (256a2)? But this argument proceeds differently from that of
Physics VII 1. Here he divides movers and moved things into kinds, arguing
that for each kind, e.g., natural self-motion or natural inanimate motion, everything moved must be moved by something. Natural inanimate motion is the
most difficult case: when heavy things go downward or light things upward,
what moves them (255a3–6)? His answer to this question has been interpreted
in different ways; however it is understood, he clearly thinks he has proven
that these things too are moved by something. Hence, he concludes that it is
universally true that everything moved must be moved by something (255b31–
256a2).

Natural inanimate motion is that of the elements, e.g., fire goes upward
and earth downward. Indeed, Aristotle uses the upward motion of fire as an
example of something that is by nature in *Physics* II 1 (192b36). He often calls
the elements "simple bodies" and so this argument, like that of *Physics* III
concerning the infinite, raises the question of whether an account of body is
introduced into the *Physics* here. The answer remains the same: "no". When
Aristotle considers "the heavy" and "the light" in the *De Caelo*, he specifically
calls them "bodies" (III 8.307b20; IV 1.307b29). The argument in *Physics* VIII 4
uses neither the word "body" nor "magnitude". This argument is intended to
prove that "everything moved must be moved by something", through an argument resting on the definition of motion established in *Physics* III. Earth,
air, fire, and water are identified as "things that are by nature" and are called
"the simple [constituents] of bodies" (τὰ ἁπλᾶ τῶν σωμάτων) at the opening of *Physics* II 1. They are treated as potency and act in the context of an
argument that reaches a universal conclusion about all things that are by
nature.

Physics VIII 5 considers the series of moved movers implied by the proposition "everything moved must be moved by something" to argue that there must

be a first mover; it must be either self-moved or unmoved and in fact it cannot be self-moved but must be unmoved (258b7). *Physics* VIII 6 answers the question with which Aristotle set out: there must be a first mover that moves its object always in the same way because it is unmoved, a first moved that is always moved in the same way and moves everything else in the cosmos; because it moves other things while being itself moved, the first moved mover produces variety in moved things, i.e., their motion starts and stops (260a12–18). Thus the initial problem is solved: an eternal unmoved mover together with an eternally and continuously moved mover explain why motion in things must be eternal, even though some things sometimes are in motion and other times are at rest. This solution both answers the question raised at the opening of *Physics* VIII 3, and explains motion in things such that "what nature is will not remain hidden".

Physics VIII 7 takes up the last objection raised in VIII 2: if motion is eternal, there must be a first motion capable of being moved eternally; what is it? Circular locomotion alone is capable of being eternal and continuous (*Physics* VIII 9). And circular locomotion can only be produced by a first mover that is indivisible, partless, and without magnitude (*Physics* VIII 10). *Physics* VIII, and so the set of investigations comprising the *Physics* as a whole, ends with a reference to magnitude as it bears on a problem raised by the claim that motion must be eternal (267b17–26).

As with *Physics* VII, the structure of *Physics* VIII becomes strikingly clear if we interpret it as an investigation defined by its opening topic: motion in things must be eternal. Its arguments presuppose definitions established in the earlier books of the *Physics*, e.g., time, magnitude, and mover/moved relations. Presupposing the investigations of these topics, it "rightly" comes after them. Without doubt, all moved things, whether moved eternally or intermittantly, are embraced by this argument.

Expressed generally, the investigations of *Physics* V–VIII follow upon the definitions of motion, the continuous, and the infinite, place, void, and time established in *Physics* III and IV. These topics are investigated so that what nature is will not remain hidden. Nature is defined in *Physics* II 1.192b21–23 as a source and cause of being moved and being at rest in that to which it belongs essentially and not accidentally. Things that are by nature are substance and a subject; therefore, these investigations reach definitions that bear on the essence of all things that are by nature. *Physics* III 1 provides a list of topics that are common and universal and these topics define the arguments that occupy *Physics* III–VIII.

Looked at in this way, the books and their investigations constituting the *Physics* seem strikingly well organized: neither a mere collection of topics nor a whole comprising a systematic exposition, the books of the *Physics* present an unfolding series of topically organized investigations that originate in the definition of nature, define the terms (or concepts) entailed by this definition and address the problems that must, given the definitions of these terms, be solved if the definitions are to stand. Aristotle announces, or specifies, a topic(s) at the outset of each investigation and it defines the inquiry that follows. Aristotle's philosophic project is not defined independently of these topics and investigations; there is no general statement concerning them or their implications taken apart from the individual investigations. The investigations themselves, each defined by its topic, each meeting the standard of "common and universal", comprise Aristotle's science of nature, as we see it in the *Physics*.

III   The Investigations of Aristotle's *De Caelo* I–IV: Body

In the corpus as we have it, the *De Caelo* immediately follows the *Physics*. But where the investigations of the *Physics* concern nature, things that are by nature (defined as form, found together with matter), motion, and a set of topics that are common and universal, *De Caelo* I 1.268a1–4 opens with its own clear and quite different claim: the science of nature for the most part concerns bodies and magnitudes, the affections and motions belonging to them and, further, their principles, as many as there are of this sort of substance (ὅσαι τῆς τοιαύτης οὐσίας εἰσίν·). Gone is nature as a principle of motion and rest, gone is form, gone is matter, and gone is the individual conceived as a combination of form and matter. The topic of the investigation appears to be body, i.e., magnitude, and what follows for this topic.

There is no explanation of how, or why, these topics work together; but the relationship between the invetigations of the *Physics* and those of the *De Caelo* is clearly complex. Aristotle continues in *De Caelo* I 1, "of things composed by nature, some are body, namely magnitude, some have body, that is magnitude, and some are principles of those having these" (268a4: τῶν γὰρ φύσει συνεστώντων τὰ μέν ἐστι σώματα). This line compares with the opening line of *Physics* II 1: "Of things that are, some are by nature (τῶν ὄντων τὰ μέν ἐστι φύσει)". While *Physics* II 1 starts from things that are, dividing them into those "by nature" and those "by art", *De Caelo* I 1 sets out from things composed by nature and proceeds to body. The topics examined in the *Physics* meet the standard of "common and universal"; but those of the *De Caelo* are things composed by nature, i.e., individuals that as such either are or have body.

As a topic, body, especially as associated with substance, presents a problem: as magnitude, body can neither be substance nor a subject; magnitude is a predicate. In Aristotle's investigation of predication, body belongs to the category of quantity, "how much" (τὸ ποσόν, *Cat.* 6). Quantity (and predicates signifying quantity) are divided into the discrete, such as grains of sand or atoms, and the continuous, such as a line, surface, or body; being continuous, body resembles not only lines and surfaces, but also time and place (4b20–25). In *De Caelo* I, body, i.e., magnitude, becomes a topic for physics and Aristotle calls bodies "this sort of substance". Body effectively moved from being a predicate signifying quantity to being a substance and a subject. Again, within the *Physics* or *De Caelo* (or *Categories*) no account is given of this shift, i.e., the shift of body from a predicate to a substance. These problems must be solved, if Aristotle's larger philosophical project is to be construed as topically defined investigations—indeed, if it is to be found coherent. After considering the investigations of body in the books of the *De Caelo*, I shall conclude by proposing a solution to this problem and suggesting that it allows us to understand the larger pattern of Aristotle's investigations in natural science, including not only physics but also psychology and biology.

The opening claim of *De Caelo* I 1, physics concerns body, is followed by its definition: a continuum is that which is divisible into parts, body is that which is divisible in every way ... therefore body alone among magnitudes can be complete [or perfect] (268a6–22). What is divisible, must also be continuous and so body must be continuous (268a28). As the Pythagoreans rightly say, body is complete, having "all directions", length, breadth, and depth (269b6–7). This investigation does not concern all magnitude, as did *Physics* VI, but only magnitude that is complete. And so, although it concerns all body, it cannot be "common and universal" in the same sense as the analysis of magnitude in *Physics* VI.

From *Physics* II–VIII to *De Caelo* I 1, the topic shifts from things that are by nature to body, but Aristotle's procedure remains the same. He announces the topic immediately, followed by a definition. *Physics* II 1 distinguishes between what is "by nature" and what is "by art" and Aristotle defines nature immediately, before proceeding to investigate whether natural things are form or matter. In *De Caelo* I 1, he specifies body as his topic and defines it immediately. He now turns to an investigation of body.

Aristotle sets aside the question of the nature of the all, i.e., the cosmos, because it concerns the infinite, a special problem in respect to its magnitude and overall bulk (μέγεθος ... τὸν σύνολον ὄγκον, I 2.268b11–13; cf. I 5–7). As the starting point of his investigation, he takes up a feature common to all bodies: in virtue of themselves, we say, all natural bodies are movable according to place.[56] This "*arche*" serves an important structural function in the *De Caelo*: it links the topic (and its investigation) of the *De Caelo* to things that are by nature (and their investigations) in the *Physics*. Indeed, motion is not defined in the *De Caelo*; rather, the definition established in *Physics* III is presupposed. Hence the definitions of both nature and motion suggest that the *De Caelo* immediately follows the *Physics* because "all natural body" may be identified with natural things, i.e., things that contain a source or cause of being moved and being at rest. Nonetheless, this identification is not made explicit—natural things are not mentioned. Furthermore, since the status of body is unclear—is it a predicate or a substance?—the justification for it is also unclear. In my conclusion, I shall suggest why body may be called a sort of substance and so replace natural things as a topic within physics. But first we must see the order of the investigations of the *De Caelo*.

Several brief arguments complete *De Caelo* I 2. All bodies are capable of locomotion, which is either straight, circular, or a mix of the two (268b17–18). Circular locomotion is around the center [of the cosmos] while straight motion can be either up, i.e., away from the center, or down, i.e., toward the center (268b20–22). Bodies are either simple (and so exhibit simple motions) or compound (and so exhibit the motion of the prevailing element). The motion of a simple body toward its proper place is natural and away from its proper place is unnatural. "Natural" and "unnatural" take Aristotle to the claim that there is an element beyond and separate from those here on earth, its nature having more honor in proportion as it is far from our world (269b13–17). Consequently, not every body is heavy or light (I 3) and while up and down are opposite, there is no opposite to circular locomotion (I 4).

Again, the structure of the argument is telling. The consideration of all natural bodies as movable takes Aristotle to the first body, i.e., the body that exhibits circular locomotion: the heaven, the eternal and most important body. Analysis of it and problems raised by it occupy the remainder of *De Caelo* I and *De Caelo* II. Again, we see the same procedure as we observed in the *Physics*. Starting from the definition of body and the starting point of movability, Aristotle arrives in short order at the first and most important of all bodies. And he considers what is most important first. Consideration of the elements, which are lower, comes later.

The first question to consider is whether there is an infinite body (I 5–6). This argument returns Aristotle to the problem set aside in *De Caelo* I 1. These

---

56   *Cael.* I 2.268b14–16: πάντα γὰρ τὰ φυσικὰ σώματα καὶ μεγέθη καθ' αὑτὰ κινητὰ λέγομεν εἶναι κατὰ τόπον· (cf. *Phys.* II 1.192b13–14).

arguments are often referred to or grouped with those of *Physics* III because in both sets of arguments, Aristotle rejects the notion of an infinite body.[57] But considering these arguments topically allows us to see them as distinct. In *Physics* III, the topic is the infinite; body comes to be included within the argument because Aristotle's opponents claim infinite body. At *De Caelo* I 5, the opposite is the case: "First, let us investigate whether there is an infinite body, as the majority of the ancient philosophers thought, or is this an impossibility" (271b2–3). The topic of body takes us to the infinite: "the infinite, then we must now discuss, opening the whole matter from the beginning" (271b16–17). The argument proper clearly concerns body: every body is necessarily simple or composite (271b18). If simple bodies are finite, the composite would also be finite; therefore, we must consider the simple bodies to see if any can be infinite, starting with the primary body and then going on to the others (271b20–25). The topic of the analysis never varies: body. Conclusions about the infinite follow from the analysis of body. (1) Body moving in a circle cannot be infinite but must have limits (273a5–6); (2) "Bodies of infinite weight or infinite lightness are equally impossible" (274a17); (3) The body of the universe is not infinite (276a16).

Aristotle's investigation of the heaven continues: why cannot there be more than one heaven (276a19). The heaven must be one and unique (I 8–9); it is ungenerated and indestructable, on Aristotle's view, and his account of this point completes *De Caelo* I (10–12). The heaven is considered as—and turns out to be—a unique individual. *De Caelo* II continues the discussion of whether the heaven comes into being or can be destroyed. As in *De Caelo* I, the treatment of the cosmos as a unique single whole and in this sense an individual is striking and, considered topically, quite different from the investigations of the *Physics*. For example, the argument of *Physics* VIII 1 establishes the eternity of motion on the basis of its definition without regard to any particular motion; only in the context of resolving an objection do we find the cosmos and the first motion. *De Caelo* I and II investigate body, specifically that of the heaven. Indeed, Aristotle now considers whether the heaven has a distinct intrinsic right and left, as the Pythagoreans claim, and concludes that it is differentiated as right and left, but differs from the Pythagoreans in defining right as where motion originates (284b7–285b27). Since circular locomotion has no contrary (and nothing non-natural can be eternal), he raises the question of why there are many circular

---

57   Cf. Hankinson 2009, 86, 99; Broadie 2009, 35–37 claims and resolves a possible contradiction between the arguments of *Physics* III and *De Caelo* I (37n19 gives a further reference on this point).

locomotions and he reaches a limited answer: they are required for generation (II 3). A fuller account, he promises, will follow later. Now a series of problems about the heavens are briefly considererd. The shape of the heavens must be spherical (II 4). There are two ways to move in a circle (clockwise or counter-clockwise); nature moves in the best way possible (II 5). The motion of the heavens is regular, not irregular (II 6). The composition, shape, and motion of the stars are considered (II 7–12). Lastly, Aristotle considers the position of the earth, whether it is in motion or at rest, and its shape (II 13–14).

The heaven, made of the fifth element aether, is the most important body. And the investigation of it comes first. In *Parts of Animals* I 5.644b23–645a7, when Aristotle compares astronomy and biology, he remarks on the superiority of the heavens as an object of study and says that he has completed this study; the evidence that would help us understand it is not as available as we would wish; now he is ready to turn to the things around us, for which there is ample evidence. The heavens are investigated first in the *De Caelo*. And within this investigation, the most important and certain points appear first, beginning with the argument that body, in this case the body of heaven, must be finite. Analysis of the stars is last not because they are unimportant but because evidence concerning them is difficult and conclusions cannot be fully supported. With these most difficult points in place, analysis of this body is complete.

De Caelo III 1 turns to "the simple bodies" (τὰ ἁπλᾶ σώματα), earth, air, fire, and water and things composed of them, i.e., the heaven as a whole, its parts, and plants and animals along with their parts (298a23–33). *Physics* II 1.192b10–11 lists things that are by nature: plants, animals, their parts, and the simple [constituents] of bodies, earth, air, fire, and water. Although *Physics* refers to the elements throughout, there is no investigation of them, except as things that are by nature or are moved.[58] The examination of elemental motion, taking the elements as the first constitutents of bodies, occupies *De Caelo* III and IV.

Again, the order of the arguments in the *De Caelo* resembles that of the *Physics*. What is most important comes first. Aristotle announces his topic, body, and defines it as perfect magnitude. The most important body, i.e., that of the all, comes first. Aristotle takes up the cosmos as a unique body alongside the problems of the heavens. Within this argument, earth is last. With earth

---

58   For a few of many examples, cf. *Phys.* II 1.192b36–193a1; IV 8.214b14–15; VIII 4.255a1–
       10, which may appear to be an exception but is not; the argument here establishes
       not elemental motion by the general proposition that "everything moved is moved by
       something".

located at the center of the cosmos, its less important bodies, including what is sublunar, is examined next (*Phys.* VIII 10.267b5–9).

If anything is generated the elements would seem to be (298b9–12). Aristotle considers his predecessors' views, which takes him from generation to the claim that the elements are composed out of mathematical planes and weightless parts; he rejects this view because natural bodies appear to have heaviness and lightness, while units can be combined neither to make a body nor to have weight (300a16–18). His own view of the elements and the necessity of considering them as body now follows.

Each simple body must have a natural motion (301a20–22). This motion entails that each must be either heavy or light (301b16–17). A comparison with the investigations of *Physics* VIII 4 is telling. In *Physics* VIII 4 Aristotle also discusses the motion of the elements, including natural and violent motion and the "fact" that each element must be heavy or light. But *Physics* VIII concerns the eternity of motion in things and the account of the elements in *Physics* VIII 4 appears within the proof of a universal claim, "everything moved is moved by something". Here in *De Caelo* III 3, he returns to the problems of knowledge and defines elements:

> Since, therefore, in every case, knowing (γνῶσις) is through first things and the elements are the first things of whatever underlies, let us investigate what sort of such bodies are elements and why (διὰ τί) and after this how many of them there are and what is their character. This will be clear when we have established what the nature of our element is. Let an element of bodies be that into which other bodies may be analyzed, present in them in potency or in actuality (which of these will yet be decided) and this [the element] is indivisible into bodies different [from it] in form.
> 302a11–18

The investigation here bears on body; the elements are examined because they are a kind of body, or a constituent of body. And on this ground, these arguments differ strikingly from those concerning motion (and the eternity of motion in things) in *Physics* VIII 4.

The elements are primary among underlying things and so the "fact" that there are indeed simple bodies, and why, is clear (III 3). Are these elements infinite in number or finite, and if finite, what is their number? The elements cannot be infinite in number (III 4). The number of elements must be limited but not reducible to one; they must be several and finite in number (III 5). The elements cannot be eternal but must be generated from one another (III 6). But when Aristotle returns to the question of the generation of the elements from one another, we find not his own view, but, again, a critique of the views of his predecessors (III 7–8). His own view is postponed.

De Caelo IV begins with its announcement: we must now consider the heavy and light (307b28–32). Body, now identified with the elements, which are movable, can be investigated as heavy and light. Yet again, Aristotle begins with the views of his predecessors (IV 2). His own account (IV 3) turns to the question why some bodies are always moved upward, some always downward, and some both up and down. *De Caelo* IV concludes with an analysis of the light and the heavy and their properties (4–6). Absolutely light is identified with always being moved upward and absolutely heavy with always being moved downward (IV 4.311b15–16). And so it presupposes the arguments of *De Caelo* I. Things exhibiting opposite motions are identified as having "opposite matter" (IV 5). And the *logos* concludes with a rejection of the view (attributed to Democritus) that the shape accounts for motion upward or downward (IV 6). The problem of the generation and destruction of the elements remains unsolved in the *De Caelo*. It is taken up, with further analysis of the elements, in the *De Generatione et Corruptione*.

In effect, the *De Caelo* investigates as body, i.e., magnitude the very things that are by nature, i.e., plants, animals, their parts, and the elements that the *Physics* studies as substance and a subject.[59] In *Physics* II, they are primarily identified as form but also include a reference to matter. The *De Caelo* studies things composed by nature, here identified as body, i.e., complete magnitude. The investigations comprising the *De Caelo* set out from the definition of body and its most important characteristic, locomotion. Aristotle then examines the most important body, the heavens, before turning to the elements and natural things as bodies composed of the elements. As such, the procedure of these books bears a striking resemblance to that of the *Physics*. Aristotle announces his topic, defines it, and sets out with what is most important in a series of arguments that unfold moving in an orderly way toward what is least imporant. These arguments are neither wholly unrelated nor part of a systematic whole. Rather, they form an ordered progression from what is most important to what is least important. And in this procedure, they resemble those of the *Physics*: they make strikingly good sense on the model of a recitation.

Aristotle tells us that what is common and universal should come first and clearly the topics of the *Physics* are these. While he says that the investigation

---

59   Aristotle calls the heavens "besouled" (*Cael.* II 2.285a29) and so it would fall under "animal" on the list of things that are by nature at the opening of *Physics* II 1.

of what is proper will come later, he never identifies such an investigation. But there is evidence that we see it here in the *De Caelo*: the investigation of body within the science of physics. I turn now to the question of how, as readers of Aristotle, we may order the topical investigations across two works, the *Physics* and *De Caelo*.

IV   Conclusion: Ordering the Investigations

As I have argued, Aristotle often opens a book with a statement of the topic that will define its investigation.[60] We have seen the internal structure of the investigations comprising the *Physics* and the *De Caelo*. These investigations are ordered, perhaps by Aristotle's editors, into works and finally these works are ordered within the corpus as we know it—the "Aristotelian corpus". I have argued above that when considered topically, the order of the books within the *Physics* and those of the *De Caelo* makes strikingly good sense. The challenge comes in ordering the works into the corpus. I shall now propose a way to understand the order of the *Physics* and *De Caelo*, i.e., why the *De Caelo* appears after the *Physics*, and why Aristotle is able to turn from things that are by nature to body. In conclusion, I shall suggest an order for the scientific writings more broadly.

In several contexts, Aristotle tells us how to order investigations: "the investigation into things that are proper" (ἡ περὶ τῶν ἰδίων θεωρία) comes after that into what is "common" (κοινά) and "universal" (καθόλου).[61] The investigations of the *Physics* are common and universal. But those of the *De Caelo* are not specified: are they common and universal, proper, or something else? Understanding different kinds of investigations will, I shall now argue, allow us to answer this question. I turn to demonstration, the topic of the *Analytics* and the *Topics*, to sort out, at least in part, the kinds and characteristics of investigations that Aristotle identifies and that we might, accordingly, expect to find in the *Physics* and *De Caelo*. To let the cat out of the bag, I shall argue that indeed the *De Caelo* is a set of investigations of what is proper to things that are by nature: body. We

---

60   Here I shall examine the *Physics* and *De Caelo*. But for another example, cf. *Metaph.* XII 1.1069a17: περὶ τῆς οὐσίας ἡ θεωρία. On this topic as determining the analysis of *Metaph.* XII, cf. Lang 1983.

61   *Phys* I 7.189b32: "for it is according to nature, he says, to investigate common things (τὰ κοινά) first and only later those things peculiar to each individual (τὰ περὶ ἕκαστον ἴδια)"; for additional examples, cf. *APo.* I 32.88b28; II 13.96b20; *Phys.* III 1.200b21–25; *PA* I 4.644a24–27.

shall now see why body can be moved from being a predicate to being a subject and as such considered as a kind of substance.

"[D]emonstration and demonstrative knowledge" form the topic of the *Analytics* and the *Topics*.[62] At the outset of the *Prior Analytics*, Aristotle defines "universal" (καθόλου): "I mean by 'universal' what belongs to all or to none [of something]".[63] In other contexts, he identifies the "universal" with knowledge and what is necessary rather than accidental.[64] After completing the inquiry into how syllogisms come to be, Aristotle takes up "the power to make [syllogisms]".[65] Here we find distinctions relevant to the *Physics* and *De Caelo*. To establish the premises for each inquiry, one must first establish the thing itself, both the definitions and "whatever is proper to it";[66] then one finds what follows the thing or again what the thing follows, and finally what cannot belong to it (43b3–5). Terms that follow a thing, e.g., "animal" follows "man" because anything that is a man is also an animal, may be divided into three kinds: (1) those predicated according to the definition, i.e., what the thing is (τί ἐστι), (2) those proper to the thing (ὅσα ἴδια), and (3) those predicated as accidents (ὅσα ὡς συμβεβηκότα κατηγορεῖται), which lie outside science and so are dismissed.[67]

---

62   Barnes 1981, 28. Cf. also Ross 1965, 287. On the relation of the *Prior* and *Posterior Analytics*, see Striker 2009, 71–72. The *Topics* too declares its relation to demonstration: "Our treatise proposes to find a line of inquiry whereby we shall be able to reason from reputable opinions about any subject presented to us, and also shall ourselves, when putting forward an argument, avoid saying anything contrary to it".

63   *APr.* I 1.24a18; cf. *Int.* 7.17a38–b16; *Metaph.* VII 13.1038b9–12. A number of issues that lie beyond the scope of this paper are raised by Striker 2009, 76.

64   *APo.* I 4.73b25–74a3; 31.87b29–39. *Phys.* I 5.189a5–6. *Metaph.* I 2.982a21–25; V 11.1018b33; XI 2.1060b20; XIII 8.1084b5. For a contrast between the universal and what is accidental, cf. *Metaph.* V 9.1017b27–1018a4. On the relation of the *Prior* and *Posterior Analytics*, cf. Striker 2009, 71–72.

65   *APr.* I 27.43a23–24: ἀλλὰ καὶ τὴν δύναμιν ἔχειν τοῦ ποιεῖν. Aristotle has clearly concluded his account of "how every syllogism comes to be and through how many terms and propositions and how each relates to another, again what sort of problem is proven in each figure and how many figures pertain to each, is clear from what has been said" (*APr.* I 26.43a16–19). Striker 2009, 189 calls *APr.* I, 27–31 "the second part of a tripartite exposition". The point of this section is how we have a "supply of deductions" (cf. 43b10–11: "the larger the supply one has of these, the more quickly one will reach a conclusion").

66   *APr.* I 27.43b1–4: ὑποθέμενον αὐτὸ πρῶτον καὶ τοὺς ὁρισμούς τε καὶ ὅσα ἴδια τοῦ πράγματός ἐστιν. I read this passage following Striker. What cannot belong to a thing can be ignored (43b5–6) and so I shall not consider it here.

67   *APr.* I 27.43b6–8. Generally speaking, what is accidental can be dismissed: it cannot be the subject of a science because it does not belong to a thing through its definition, as a property, or through a genus. Furthermore, although what is accidental may become a

In effect, to establish premises we must identify first the definition of a thing along with what it entails and then its properties.[68]

What is "common" (κοινά) is also part of demonstrative science. Like the universal, it involves the case in which everything is affirmed or denied; but, unlike the universal, what is "common" applies to all things by analogy.[69] Because both apply to every case in which a thing is affirmed or denied, "common" and "universal" sometimes appear to be identical.[70] Nonetheless, they differ because the universal expresses the essence, or kind, while what is common applies to all things in a genus.

These distinctions are explained more fully at *Topics* I 5, where Aristotle also explains what is proper. A definition signifies "a thing's essence";[71] and the essence is expressed by the universal.[72] A "property" (τὸ ἴδιον) does not signify the essence of a thing and so is distinct from the universal. But what is proper, i.e., a property, belongs to that kind of thing alone and belongs in every case.[73] Aristotle gives a clear example: it is proper to a man that he be grammatical (102a19–24); "grammatical" is never predicated of what is not a

---

proper attribute at some time or relative to something, what is accidental will never be "proper" *simpliciter*. Cf. *APo.* I 6.75a18–20; *Top.* I 5.102b4–5, b24–26; cf. *APo.* I 30.87b19–27; *Metaph.* V 9.1017b27–1018a4; *Phys.* II 4–6 rejects chance and spontaneity as causes in a closely related argument. There is some discussion in the literature as to whether "essential accidents" form an exception to this general rule. For an excellent discussion (citing *Topics* I and *Physics* II) of this tangled issue, cf. Bäck 2000, 152 ff.: "Aristotle's science consists in ways to uncover the true nature of substances, and he cashes out this project by looking for their *propria*. [*APo.* 75a18–31; 76a4–7]. But then Aristotle insists that a thing's nature, which includes its necessarily concomitant attributes, is not accidental to it [*Phys.* 192b20–23]. For him the accidental has no place in science".

68   See Striker 2009, 192–193.

69   *APo.* I 10.76a39; 32.88a37–b. The *Posterior Analytics* opens: "All teaching and all intellectual learning comes about from already existing knowledge" and takes up this claim for demonstration. Barnes 1994, xv argues that it presupposes the *Prior Analytics* and is intended to be read after it.

70   Bonitz 1955 (citing *Phys.* III, 1.200b22) suggests a number of cases in which common and universal are synonymous; cf. *An.* I 1.402b7–8; *PA* I 4.644a27; *Metaph.* VII 16.1040b23, b25, b26.

71   *Top.* I 5.101b38: τὸ τί ἦν εἶναι σημαίνων. The association of the definition and the essence is a theme across many of the investigations. For some examples, see *Top.* VII 3.153a15–22; *Phys.* II 3.194b27; *Metaph.* V 2.1013a27; 29.1024a29; VI 1.1025b29.

72   Again, this point is a theme expressed within many different investigations. For some examples, cf. *Phys.* I 5.189a7; *Metaph.* VII 10.1035b34; XI 1.1059b26–27; XII 5.1071a29.

73   *Top.* I 5.102a20. At *Top.* VI 3.140b16–26 Aristotle emphasizes that counter-predication requires that the attribute belong to everything that falls under the same species (εἶδος).

man and, although outside the definition, is predicated of every man. The relation between what is universal and what is proper is crucial to demonstrative science. Because the universal expresses the essence, it expresses the subject and the kind; what is proper is a predicate that belongs to every individual of the same kind. Because it belongs to every individual (and to no individual not of this kind), what is proper can be counter-predicated with the essence and through counter-predication can become a subject (102a18–19). As a subject what is proper can found an inquiry, a θεωρία.[74]

The universal, the common, and the proper are all first principles assumed by demonstrative science that studies what holds of them in themselves (*APo.* I 10.76b2). First principles, Aristotle argues, cannot be proven (*APo.* I 10.76a32 for a very clear example). They, and what depends on them immediately, must be assumed for scientific demonstration (*APo.* I 10.76a34; cf. *Phys.* I 2.185a12–13). But they do differ. While the universal expresses the essence, what is "proper" is predicated of every individual of a kind, i.e., the essence expressed by the universal, and what is common applies by analogy to all things in a genus (76a38–40). Starting with what is common, Aristotle gives clear examples: it is "common" that if equals are taken from equals, what remains will be equal (76a40–41). When a science considers not what is common and so across kinds, but what lies outside the definition and belongs to things in themselves, these things are "proper" (τὰ ἴδια); for example, arithmetic concerns units and geometry points and lines (76b3–5); "units", "points", and "lines" are each assumed to be and defined as a "this such" (*APo.* I 10.76b5–6: ταῦτα γὰρ λαμβάνουσι τὸ εἶναι καὶ τοδὶ εἶναι). And each has properties; arithmetic assumes the properties, or attributes, of units, e.g., odd or even, and then proves that they are through what is common and what has been demonstrated (76b6–11). "And astronomy [proceeds] in the same way" (76b11), but Aristotle leaves astronomy unexplained.

Here an important point follows concerning properties. What is proper, being an attribute, is always a predicate and so must presuppose the subject expressed by the essence; when what is proper is counter-predicated, thereby becoming a subject, the property becomes a first principle of demonstrative science. As a first principle, it founds an investigation that must also presuppose the subject expressed by the essence. The subject in effect becomes a silent partner underlying the legitimacy of the counter-predication through which the property has become a subject. "Counter-predication", particularly

---

74   *Top.* I 5.102a18–20; cf. the excellent discussion of the logic of this view in Barnes 1970, 137–140. I shall discuss counter-predication below.

what Barnes has called the "necessary tie between properties and property-owners" has been debated. But the role of counter-predication in demonstrative science cannot be in doubt: it allows proper predicates to found inquiries and thereby expands the domain of the science.[75]

But the domain of a science cannot be expanded indefinitely. If there are to be demonstrations, the number of predicates available within the demonstration must be finite (82b37–83a1). (If they were infinite, it would become impossible to achieve closure.) Here is a problem: enlarging the domain of science through counter-predication might open the door to the possibility of infinite predicates. First, Aristotle divides predicates into those that are accidental (συμβέβηκε), e.g., "the white thing is a log", and those which are *simpliciter* (ἁπλῶς), e.g., "the log is white" (83a5; a16). In the first case, we are saying something else is white and accidentally a log and in the second case the log is the underlying subject (τὸ ὑποκείμενον), which comes to be "white" (83a6–13). Again, as we just saw above, accidental predication, which clearly gives rise to an infinite number of predicates, must be set aside. Demonstrations use only the latter, *simpliciter*, form of predication (83a18–20).

Second, within demonstration a predicate either signifies what a thing is or says that it has some quality or quantity etc. (83a21–24). Predicates signifying substance are predicated of just what is that thing or just what is a particular sort of it (83a25–26). But predicates that do not signify a substance require an underlying subject; when a predicate from one of the categories is predicated of an underlying subject and belongs to every individual of this kind and to no individual not of this kind, then it is a property and can be counter-predicated (83a36–39). Indeed, Aristotle defines a property in these terms: what is predicated convertibly but does not signify the essence.[76] This definition of a property precludes accidents from ever standing as properties and Aristotle's larger point, that the number of predicates must be finite, follows. With these distinctions in hand, we may return to the *Physics* and *De Caelo*.

The accounts of the universal, the common, and the proper in the *Analytics* and *Topics* explain Aristotle's assertion in the *Physics*: the investigation of what is common and universal is prior to the investigation of what is proper. The investigation of what is common and universal must come first because it deals with substance either as essence or by analogy. In *Physics* III 1, Aristotle calls

---

75   See Barnes 1970, 137–139.

76   *Top.* I 8.103b11–12: τοῦτο γὰρ ἦν ἴδιον, τὸ ἀντικατηγορούμενον μὲν μὴ σημαῖον δὲ τὸ τί ἦν εἶναι. Cf. also 103b17–19: an accident belongs to a thing being "neither a definition nor a property nor a genus" (μήτε ὅρος μήτε ἴδιον μήτε γένος).

his arguments "common and universal". The definition of nature is "a source of being moved and being at rest". Thus motion is a universal for all things that are by nature: it is immediately entailed by the definition and so follows for all natural things. Motion in turn requires additional "terms" and they too, as required for motion, are universal for natural things: they follow the definition. Terms such as "together" may be examples of what is common. The meanings established in *Physics* VI apply to all things that are "together" and are not restsricted by definition to things that are by nature.

What is proper presupposes the subject, i.e., the substance, along with the essence and common axioms, of which it is a predicate. Because a predicate that is proper belongs to every individual, when counter-predication moves the predicate, the property, to the subject position, it presupposes an individual of this kind.[77] In effect, when a property becomes a subject, it may also become a topic; as a topic, it founds an inquiry that yields knowledge of the "underlying subject", i.e., the individual (*Topics* V 2.129b7; 130a5; 3.131a1).[78] Therefore investigations of what is proper must presuppose and follow those of what is common and universal.

The scarcity of syllogisms in Aristotle's practice of science is often remarked upon.[79] Obviously, I am not here claiming that the arguments of the *Physics* can be rendered into syllogisms. My point concerns the patterns of analysis and predication in the *Physics* and *De Caelo*. They satisfy the account of demonstration conceived as "universal", "common", and "proper" in the *Analytics* and *Topics*. At *Prior Analytics* I 27, Aristotle notes that in order to establish the premises for each inquiry, one must first establish the thing itself, both its definitions and whatever is proper to it. Striker comments (in agreement with Ross[80]) that the plural "definitions" may refer to "two terms for each proposition, or by reference to dialectical debates".[81] But in the actual practice of the *Physics* we see a different meaning: the several definitions reached in the investigations of the *Physics* bear on the common and universal terms entailed by the definition of nature so that "what nature is will not remain hidden".

The investigation of what is proper remains. Unlike the common and universal, the proper is predicated of individuals and defined *via* its relation to every individual of a kind and to no individual of any other kind. This rela-

---

77   For problems that go beyond the bounds of this paper with the notion of "counter-predication", cf. Barnes 1994, 177–179.

78   See Barnes 1970, 136.

79   See Barnes 1981, 19–20.

80   See Ross 1965, 384.

81   See Striker 2009, 192.

tion, as Sorabji argues, implies that a property belongs to a species necessarily.[82] When this relation obtains, a property can be counter-predicated, i.e., moved to the subject position. Consequently, the examination of a property must be an examination of individuals. Aristotle's assertion that of natural things, some are body, some have body, and some are principles of those having body effectively identifies body as a property of things that are by nature.

"Counter-predication" suggests an order between the investigations of the *Physics* and those of the *De Caelo*.[83] Those of the *Physics* are common and universal: nature, things that are by nature, and what is required so that these do not remain hidden. Body is absent from them. In the *Categories* and again in the *De Caelo*, body is defined as quantity, i.e., perfect continuous magnitude. It is absent from the *Physics* because by definition it is not a substance and a subject and so lies outside the essence of natural things. Body, however, must belong to each and every thing that is by nature and to no other things, e.g., god or soul. (Things that are "by art" also have body and are movable insofar as they are made out of natural things and in this respect [*Phys.* II 1.192b19–20].) Therefore, body meets the criteria of what is proper and so can become a topic through counter-predication with things that are by nature. Hence the claim of *De Caelo* I 1, i.e., physics concerns body, witnesses that counter-predication has occurred: an investigation of body is included within the science of physics, as we see in the *De Caelo*.

In short, we can understand the inquiries of the *Physics* as examining what is "common and universal" to things that are by nature while the *De Caelo* investigates what is "proper" to such things, i.e., body and its elements, thereby expanding the domain of physics from what we see in the examination of topics that are common and universal. The investigations of the *Physics* come first, followed by those of the *De Caelo*. Understanding the *Physics* and the *De Caelo* as well as the relation between them in these terms both respects the

---

82 Sorabji 1981, 211: "an *idion*, i.e., a predicate which belongs to all and only the members of a species, but which does not enter into the species' definition, belongs to that species necessarily".

83 Barnes 1981, 19–20 notes the problematic relation between the logic and Aristotle's scientific work: "On the one hand, the theory of demonstration was designed primarily as a method for the presentation and transmission of scientific truths ... and many of Aristotle's treatises attempt to systematize and transmit the truths of science ... on the other hand, those [scientific] treatises notoriously contain few syllogisms ... But by and large, the logic of the *Analytics* has had little discernible effect on the structure of Aristotle's scientific reasoning". But there are many ways beyond the syllogistic form in which the logic may be reflected in the substantive treatises.

topical character of Aristotle's investigations and identifies the presupposed principle that underlies the pattern of their organization.

Here we can understand both the order of topics within the *Physics* and the organization of the corpus. The rules of demonstration precede the actual practice of science; so the logic opens the corpus. In *Metaphysics* VI, Aristotle, seeks the principles and causes of the things that are *qua* being. He concludes that if there were no separate substance, physics would be the first science (1.1025b2–3; cf. also IV 3.1005a21–b1). And physics is first after the logic. Among the sciences, physics is the most universal because it considers all things that are by nature, including plants, animals, their parts and the elements earth, air, fire, and water. Defining physics as an inquiry into nature that primarily bears on form but also includes matter, Aristotle defines common and universal topics that determine the topics and investigations of the *Physics*.

The *Physics* is followed by the *De Caelo*. It too, as its first line declares, is the science of nature. It extends our knowledge of "things composed by nature" by taking up body, a predicate in the category of quantity, that must belong to every thing that is by nature and to no thing that is not by nature. The *De Caelo* takes what is proper to things that are by nature as "body", and makes it the topic of investigation. The announcement that opens *De Caelo* I 1, is a case of counter-predication. The investigation of body leads to a consideration of the elements, the underlying constitutents of all body, and so ultimately of all things that are by nature (and nothing that is not by nature).

In the *De Caelo*, Aristotle promises an account of generation, specifically the generation of the elements from one another. He keeps his promise in the *De Generatione et Corruptione*, which follows the *De Caelo*. In the corpus as we have it, the *De Generatione* is followed by the the *Meteorologica*. Its opening lines list what has been accomplished thus far and define the topics to be examined here. Topics on this list are easy to recognize: the first causes of nature, all natural motion, the stars, the bodily elements, how they change into one another and generation and corruption generally (338a20–23). Meteorology remains. "It is concerned with events that are natural, though their order is less perfect than that of the first of the elements of bodies" (338b20). These remaining problems, including the Milky Way, comets, meteors, winds and earthquakes, thunderbolts, whirlwinds, and fire-winds, come last because their order is less perfect than that of the first of the elements of bodies. When these topics have been examined, Aristotle will turn to plants and animals to complete the examination that had been set out at the beginning (339a7–10). The beginning here is presumably things that are by nature in *Physics* II 1. The topics that comprise physics taken at its broadest within the corpus begin with what is "common and universal" proceed to what is "proper" and conclude with what is less perfectly ordered than the elements. This sequence of topics reflects the procedure identified in *Physics* III 1 and can be understood in terms of demonstrative science and counter-predication defined in the *Analytics* and *Topics*.

In the corpus as we have it, the *De Anima* follows the *Meteorologica* (I omit spurious works). *De Anima* I 1 begins with an explicit reference to nature: the knowledge of the soul admittedly contributes greatly to the advance of truth in general, and, above all, to our understanding of nature, for the soul is in some sense the principle of animal life (402a5–7). This introduction resembles that of the *Physics* and *De Caelo*: nature is first, then properties and consequences of soul for animals. Having studied nature as common and universal and proper, Aristotle now takes up a part of nature. "For we seek to investigate and to know its [soul's] nature, i.e., its substance, then as many things that follow concerning it; of these, some properties seem to be affections of the soul and some belong to animals through this [soul]".[84] *De Anima* I concerns his predecessors while in *De Anima* II Aristotle makes a fresh start to distinguish "what soul is and what would be the most common account of it" (412a5–6: τί ἐστι ψυχὴ καὶ τίς ἂν εἴη κοινότατος λόγος αὐτῆς). The three books of the *De Anima* define soul, define the senses and their object, and, raise, and for Aristotle answer, a series of questions about sensation and thinking.

Taking soul's nature and substance first and searching for the most common definition of it suggests that we are starting a new science. But this science examines one kind of those things that are by nature and so presupposes physics. In effect, an inquiry into plants and animals "cuts off" a part of things that are by nature (cf. *Metaph.* IV 1.1003a21–26). This part, things having soul and so life, is now a science comprised of topics to be investigated in the same order as physics. Soul, like form, comes first and its "most common" or general account comes first.

The *De Anima* is followed by the *Parva Naturalia*, opening with *De Sensu*, which in its turn refers back to the *De Anima* (436a1)—saying that what has been established may now be assumed—and takes up activities that are common to all or proper (ἴδιαι) to some (463a4). Ross 1973, 1 remarks that "practically the whole of the topics to be discussed are there [*De Sensu* 1] set forth". As he makes the point clearly: "the special senses are discussed not merely as relative to sense but in their own proper nature as modifications of external reality ... In fact, in the whole of this treatise we seem to be immersed in details, and

---

84   *An.* I 1.402a7–10: ἐπιζητοῦμεν δὲ θεωρῆσαι καὶ γνῶναι τήν τε φύσιν αὐτῆς καὶ τὴν οὐσίαν, εἶθ' ὅσα συμβέβηκε περὶ αὐτήν· ὧν τὰ μὲν ἴδια πάθη τῆς ψυχῆς εἶναι δοκεῖ, τὰ δὲ δι' ἐκείνην καὶ τοῖς ζῴοις ὑπάρχειν.

there is less of the wide generalisation and speculative insight which charac-terise Aristotle's chief psychological work" (2). The exact organization of the problems in the *De Sensu* may be open to debate; but it is surely striking that Aristotle explicitly sets out from the most common account of soul and then turns to what is more proper and presupposes this common account.

The *Parva Naturalia* ends with the short treatise *On Youth, Old Age, Life and Death, and Respiration*. This work opens with a reference to the *De Anima* (467b14) and concludes with a reference to physics: in regard to health and disease, not only the physician but also the physicist, up to a certain point, must give an account of the causes and to this extent the inquiries are co-terminous (480b22–26). In effect, the topics of the *Parva Naturalia* may be seen as a subset of "things that are by nature".

Following the *Parva Naturalia*, we find the biological works. The first, *Historia Animalium* begins not with a topic but with a distinction: of the parts of animals, some are simple ... others are complex (486a5–6). And the discussion of parts begins immediately. In effect, what we know generally as "Aristotle's biology" constitutes an extended examination of the parts, i.e., bodies, of animals, first generally, and then the parts used in movement, and finally genera-tion. The order of these works parallels that of the science of physics. What is common and universal, soul as form and first entelechy of the body, is exam-ined first; activities involving both soul and body, e.g., memory and recollection, come next; an examination of body, both common and proper, completes the biology.

This order returns us to the point raised at the beginning of this paper: what can be said of the chronology of Aristotle's writings? "Very little". But the purpose of chronology lies in the evidence it might provide concerning the order of Aristotle's works. Considering Aristotle's "writings" as they reflect an oral tradition and the material conditions of writing in ancient Athens during the turn from orality to literacy is an approach that yields quite positive conclusions.

The remainder of Aristotle's corpus clearly presents challenges. But the scientific treatises seem strikingly well organized. The key to their organization lies in taking them as defined by topics that are then investigated. The topical character of the investigations may well have its origins in the ancient oral tradition. But if Aristotle is not "the first truly bookish individual", he is certainly among the first. His demonstrations may be evaluated by the standards he himself defines in his investigation of demonstration, the *Analytics* and *Topics*, as "common" and "universal" and "proper".

CHAPTER 5

Surrogate Principles and the Natural Order of Exposition in Aristotle's *De Caelo* II

Mariska Leunissen

Abstract

In his account for why stars and planets move in different directions, Aristotle reasons that if the universe is to move eternally in a circle, it must have a center that remains at rest, and that if there is to be such a center, "it is necessary that earth exists: for this rests at the center" (*De Caelo* II 3.286a20–21). Interestingly, this proposition about the position and the immobility of earth is not a pre-established fact: instead, "we must assume it for now, and later there will be a demonstration about it" (286a21–22: νῦν μὲν οὖν ὑποκείσθω τοῦτο, ὕστερον δὲ δειχθήσεται περὶ αὐτοῦ). Aristotle relies on the same assumption later on (*Cael.* II 8.289b5–6: "let it be assumed—ὑποκείσθω—that the earth is at rest"), but does not demonstrate it until at the very end of book II (*Cael.* II 13.293b15–17: "it remains—λοιπόν—to speak about earth ..."). I argue for a dual role of the use of ὑποκείσθω—of which there exists currently no paper-length discussion in the scholarly literature—as both an explanatory and an expository principle by elucidating its use in this particular example from the *De Caelo*.

Aristotle's treatises are full of propositions that need to be assumed for now—and that thereby perform an immediate explanatory role in the arguments in which they are used—but that are ultimately, unlike the true first principles of a science, demonstrable. It is my contention that the reason why Aristotle posits these propositions as "surrogate principles" instead of demonstrating them immediately has nothing to do with their epistemic status (they *can* be known through a demonstration). Rather, it has to do with his wish to preserve what he thinks is the proper order of exposition that is to be followed both within and among treatises. The example from the *De Caelo* mentioned above provides an especially interesting case, because here Aristotle connects the order of exposition to the hierarchical order of nature itself. Aristotle thus postpones his demonstration concerning earth because his writing needs to reflect the *scala naturae* that exists among the heavenly bodies, and this requires him to discuss the attributes of the universe as a whole before those of its parts, to discuss stars before planets, and to discuss earth last, because it is the least honorable heavenly body in existence.

© KONINKLIJKE BRILL NV, LEIDEN, 2017 | DOI: 10.1163/9789004340084_007

My paper consists of three sections. In section one, I discuss in more detail the use of ὑποκείσθω in the *De Caelo* passage and next, in section two, provide some context for it by comparing it to other uses in Aristotle's natural treatises that connect it to his concern for preserving the proper order of exposition (in *Physica* VIII 7.260b15–29 and *De Partibus Animalium* IV 10.689a5–14). Finally, in section three, I show that Aristotle's concern with the proper order of exposition in the *De Caelo* is in fact a concern for tracking a *natural* order in this treatise (and not merely a didactical or conceptual one, as discussed by, e.g., Burnyeat 2001 and 2004, and Lennox 2010). This involves drawing an analogy between this case and (1) Aristotle's use of the human body as a road map for his discussion of the parts of animals in *De Partibus Animalium*, according to which parts that are ranked "first" on the human body have to be discussed first and parts that are "last" have to be discussed last; and (2) his use of the hierarchical scale of different levels of 'perfection' among animal kinds as a guide for the order in which to discuss the different modes of reproduction in *De Generatione Animalium*. I also draw brief attention to Aristotle's own account of the lowly status of Earth and the center it occupies in *De Caelo* II 13.293b6–15, and thereby round off my argument that this is why he discusses earth last.

I   **Surrogate Principles in Aristotle's Sciences**

In the *Posterior Analytics*, Aristotle explains that every science makes use of two kinds of first principles (*archai*).[1] These are axioms (*axiômata*), which are common to all sciences and need to be grasped by anyone who wants to learn something, and theses (*theseis*), which are proper to each science and therefore need to be grasped by the students of that science. This latter category divides into definitions (*horismoi*), which identify and demarcate the subjects of that science, and into hypotheses (*hypotheseis*), which are propositional assertions about those subjects, stating that they exist or that something is the case about them. Importantly, none of these first principles are themselves demonstrable (otherwise, demonstrative knowledge would face an infinite regress).[2] Instead, humans come to know first principles in some other, non-demonstrable way that presupposes the possession of experience and involves the operation of our intellect.[3] In his scientific treatises, Aristotle frequently appeals to these

---

1   See especially *APo.* I 2.72a14–24 and I 10.76a31–b11.

2   See, e.g., *APo.* I 2.72a15; I 3.72b18–22; I 9.76a17–25; and I 10.76a31–32.

3   See *APo.* II 19; cf. *APr.* I 30.46a17–27, *Cael.* III 7.306a5–17, and *GC* I 2.316a5–10. Aristotle's account of how humans come to know the first principles is tantalizingly obscure; for a recent discussion, see Ferejohn 2009.

first principles as part of his strategy to generate knowledge of a particular domain,[4] but he also makes use of another (third?) kind of "principle" that he claims "we must assume for now" at this stage of the argument, but that "will be demonstrated later". The propositions Aristotle introduces in this way thus resemble in some ways the indemonstrable hypotheses from the *Posterior Analytics*, but are in fact demonstrable.

Let me offer two examples of cases where Aristotle appeals to these "surrogate principles" in the natural treatises. First, in arguing for the primacy of locomotion among the different kinds of motion that exist in *Physics* VIII 7 (260b15–29), Aristotle uses as one of the premises the claim that "it is possible for [motion] to be continuous" (260b23–24: δυνατὸν δὲ συνεχῆ εἶναι). However, unlike the other premises Aristotle uses in this argument, the claim about the possibility of continuous motion is not a pre-established fact, but something that "will be demonstrated later"; "for now", Aristotle says "let it be assumed" (260b24: δειχθήσεται δ᾽ ὕστερον· νῦν δὲ τοῦτο ὑποκείσθω). This demonstration, then, is offered in the latter half of the same chapter (see especially 261a28–31) and in the next (see *Phys.* VIII 8.261b27–262a12; esp. 261b27–28: ὅτι δ᾽ ἐνδέχεται εἶναί ... λέγωμεν νῦν). Second, in the *Parts of Animals*, Aristotle similarly postpones the demonstration of the proposition that the male semen and the female menses are residues, while assuming its truth for the present purpose of showing that the organs for the excretion of residues are the same as those for sexual reproduction:

> Nature uses the same part for the excretion of the moist part of the residue and in connection with reproduction ... The cause is that the seed is something moist and a residue: let this be assumed for now, and later there will be a demonstration about it (τοῦτο δὲ νῦν μὲν ὑποκείσθω, ὕστερον δὲ δειχθήσεται περὶ αὐτοῦ). And in the same manner are also the menses in females and that by which seed is discharged: there will be a definition concerning these things later as well, for now let it just be assumed that also the menses in the female are a residue (διορισθήσεται δὲ καὶ περὶ τούτων ὕστερον, νῦν δὲ ὑποκείσθω ...).
>
> *PA* IV 10.689a5–14

Since the seed and the menses are both moist, Aristotle argues, it is "in accordance with the account" (*PA* IV 10.689a17: κατὰ λόγον) that nature uses the same

---

4   On the use of first principles in Aristotle's (natural) science, see especially Bolton 1987, 120–166; Gotthelf 1987, 167–198; Lennox 2001a, *passim*; Leunissen 2010a, 119–135.

parts for their secretion. The surrogate principle is again explicitly used as an explanatory premise in the argument (cf. the use of αἴτιον in 689a8), while its demonstration is provided not in a later chapter but in another treatise, i.e., in *Generation of Animals* I 17–20.

As it turns out, Aristotle's treatises are full of propositions that need to be assumed for now[5]—and that thereby perform an immediate explanatory role in the arguments in which they are used[6]—but that are ultimately, unlike the true first principles of a science, demonstrable. The reason, then, why Aristotle postpones these demonstrations and relies on "surrogate principles" instead cannot have anything to do with them being non-demonstrable, since the propositions in question *can* be scientifically known through demonstrations (even though providing those demonstrations might be a lot of work or difficult to do).[7] I shall argue that Aristotle postpones a proper demonstration of the knowledge expressed by these surrogate principles in those cases where providing this demonstration now would—in one way or another—disrupt what he considers to be *the proper order of exposition* that is to be followed both within and among treatises. For instance, in the examples discussed above, the primacy of locomotion needs to be established before the possibility of continuous motion, because a demonstration of the latter entails a discussion of the nature of locomotion itself: the "if it is"-question and the "what it is"-question (cf. *APo.* II 1.89b23–25) cannot be separated in this instance. And demonstrations concerning reproductive parts belong properly to a *methodologically later* treatise that deals specifically with animal generation; their demonstration

---

5 Aristotle typically introduces these "principles" through the present imperative ὑποκείσθω, but does not have a technical name for them. (The substantivated participle, τὰ ὑποκείμενα, refers to the subjects of predications or to underlying realities of things, and there is no noun form of the verb that parallels, for instance, the derivation of ὑπόθεσις from ὑποτίθημι.) For ὑποκείσθω as introducing "surrogate principles," see *APo.* II 13.96b8–13; *Cael.* I 7.275a28–b1; *EE* II 1.1219b28–32 and 1220a22–24; *EN* II 2.1103b31–33, V 1.1129a11, and VI 1.1139a6; *GA* V 3.782a28–29; *GC* II 10.336a24–25; *Insom.* 1.459a11–12 and 2.460a32–b2; *Mete.* II 6.363a30–31; *Phys.* IV 11.219a29–30; *Rhet.* I 11.1369b33–1370a1; and *Sens.* 7.447a17–18. Cf. also *Cael.* I 3.269b18–19 and II 4.287a11–12.

6 Cf. *EE* II 11.1227b23–25: "we posit that … but we must assume it just as a principle (ὥσπερ ἀρχὴ τοῦτο ὑποκείσθω)".

7 Most demonstrations are offered later, either in a later chapter or in a methodologically later treatise. For cases where what needs to be assumed has already been demonstrated in a methodologically *earlier* treatise: see *Sens.* 1.436a1–6 (referring back to *On the Soul*) and *Pol.* VII 1.1323b40–1324a4 (referring to the *Ethics*). Sometimes Aristotle suggests that the truth of what is assumed can be made clear through *induction* rather than demonstration: see *EE* II 1.1218b37–1219a2 and *Phys.* I 2.185a12–14.

now would violate the order of exposition and the division of explanatory tasks among the various biological treatises (as outlined in, for instance, PA IV 14.697b26–30 and GA I 1.715a1–18; I return to this issue below).[8] In other words, it is my contention that the role of these surrogate principles in Aristotle's scientific treatises is *as much explanatory as expository*: they allow Aristotle to generate the required piece of knowledge at the appropriate stage of an argument or explanation, but without disturbing the proper order of exposition.

In the remainder of this paper, I will discuss in detail one more example of Aristotle's use of such "surrogate principles" in the natural treatises, namely his use of the assumption that the Earth rests at the center of the universe in *Cael.* II 3.286a21–31, which is demonstrated a few chapters later, in *Cael.* II 13–14. This example from *On the Heavens* provides an especially interesting case, because here Aristotle connects the order of exposition to the hierarchical order of nature itself, such that what is more important by nature ought to be discussed first and what is least important by nature ought to be discussed last. Aristotle thus postpones his demonstration concerning Earth because his writing in this particular case needs to reflect the *scala naturae* that exists among the sublunary and heavenly bodies, and this requires him to discuss the attributes of the universe as a whole before those of its parts, to discuss stars before planets, and to discuss Earth last, because—within this class at least—it is the least honorable body in existence. I believe that in this case, then, the use of surrogate principles allows Aristotle to preserve first and foremost the *natural* order of exposition—with the didactic or conceptual one following suit—that guides the second book of *On the Heavens*.

II   Surrogate principles in *On the Heavens* II

Aristotle's use of "surrogate principles" in the second book of *On the Heavens* occurs in the middle of an argument that tries to establish that the reason why the heavenly bodies move in different directions is that these different motions each serve their own, specific purpose (Aristotle introduces this question, and the teleological strategy for answering it in *Cael.* II 3.286a3–8).[9] The argument

---

8   On didactic and conceptual concerns driving the order of exposition, see Burnyeat 2001, 111–120 and 2004, 13, 19–23; on the distribution of explanatory tasks among the natural treatises and how this influences the order of exposition, see Lennox 2001b, 323 and 2010, 4–5.

9   On this argument and its reliance on teleological principles (in this case, the principle that "each thing that has a function is for the sake of that function"), see Leunissen 2010a, 160–165.

starts out by identifying the function of the first motion, i.e., that of the outer sphere carrying the stars:

> The activity of god is immortality, and that is everlasting life. In consequence it is necessary that an eternal motion belongs to the divine (ὥστ' ἀνάγκη τῷ θείῳ[10] κίνησιν ἀΐδιον ὑπάρχειν). Since the universe is such (for its body is a divine thing), for that reason it has a circular body, with which it naturally moves in a circle for eternity.
>
> *Cael.* II 3.286a8–11

Aristotle reasons that, if the function of the divine is immortality, and if the universe is divine, then the function of the universe is immortality. Furthermore, if being immortal is the defining function of the universe, then it is a necessary prerequisite for it that it possesses an eternal motion. That is, for the universe as a whole to be able to perform its defining function or its activity of being immortal, it has to perform at least one kind of eternal motion, and the only kind of motion capable of uniform eternal continuity is motion in a circle.

However, this only explains why *part* of the universe—namely the outer, celestial sphere—moves with one motion, not why there are several other motions performed by its other parts, and so Aristotle continues by laying out another complicated chain of arguments that progresses in six steps, two of which involve the use of a surrogate principle. Starting with the conclusion taken from the first part of the explanation, which is the necessity of there being an eternal motion of the outer sphere in order for the universe to be immortal, Aristotle "deduces" the following claims (*Cael.* II 3.286a13–b2):

(a)   If there is to be a body that moves in a circle eternally, it must have a center that remains at rest.

(b)   For there to be a fixed center, the existence of earth is a necessary condition.

(c)   If there is to be earth, then it is a necessary consequence that there is also fire (for earth and fire are contraries, and if the one exists, so does the other).

(d)   If there is to be fire and earth, then it is a necessary consequence that the two other elements exist (for water and air are in a relation of contrariety to each of the other two elements).

---

10   I follow Leggatt 1995, 227 in reading θείῳ instead of θεῷ with most manuscripts.

(e)   From the existence of the four elements it necessarily follows that there must be generation (for none of the four sublunary elements can be everlasting).

(f)   If there must be generation, then it is necessary that there exists some other motion.

According to this account (which Aristotle sums up in *Cael.* II 3.286b6–9), generation is a necessary consequence of the existence of sublunary elements, and their existence is a necessary condition for there to be an eternal, cyclical motion of the outermost sphere of the universe. However, having established that it is necessary for there to be generation, Aristotle turns the argument around, and reasons that if there is to be generation, then it is conditionally necessary for there to be other motions, because the motions of the outermost sphere alone cannot cause generation. Accordingly, generation must be what is produced by all the other motions (namely, the motions of the planets). Thus, the universe must possess one eternal motion in a circle—performed by the outer sphere carrying the fixed stars—for the sake of realizing its immortality; but it must also possess other motions—performed by the inner spheres carrying the planets—if there is to be generation.

The surrogate principles come in at step (b) and at steps (c–d) of the argument as reconstructed above. First, at step (b), Aristotle argues that, since whatever is made out of aether itself cannot remain at rest, there has to exist a *second* element besides aether, the natural motion of which is to move toward the center and then to remain at rest at that center. Aristotle concludes that this second element has to be earth, "for this is at rest at the center" (*Cael.* II 3.286a20–21: ἀνάγκη τοίνυν γῆν εἶναι· τοῦτο γὰρ ἠρεμεῖ ἐπὶ τοῦ μέσου). However, that it is in fact earth that remains at rest at the center is not something Aristotle has already established: instead, "we must assume it for now, later there will be a demonstration about it" (*Cael.* II 3.286a21–22: νῦν μὲν οὖν ὑποκείσθω τοῦτο, ὕστερον δὲ δειχθήσεται περὶ αὐτοῦ). Next, at step (c–d), Aristotle infers from the existence of earth the existence of the other three elements, while building upon the assumption that "each of the elements has a contrariety in relation to each" (*Cael.* II 3.286a29–30), which is again something "we must assume for now", whereas the attempt to demonstrate it is announced to follow "later" (*Cael.* II 3.286a30–31: ὑποκείσθω δὲ καὶ τοῦτο νῦν, ὕστερον δὲ πειρατέον δεῖξαι). Clearly, *without* the assumption of these propositions, Aristotle would not have been able to explain why the motions of the lower spheres exist (the argument does not quite amount to a demonstration, as Aristotle is well aware of, but it is intended to provide an explanation of some sort: *Cael.* II 3.286a7: ἡ δ' αἰτία; 286b6: διὰ τίνα αἰτίαν). On the other hand, any kind of truth or plausi-

bility of the explanation Aristotle does provide is itself conditional on the truth
of the surrogate principles, which has not been established yet. So why, then,
does Aristotle postpone their demonstrations, if these surrogate principles are
in fact demonstrable?

For the present purposes, I will focus on the first of these two surrogate
principles, which is also the most central to the second book of *De Caelo*: not
only does the truth of the argument in *Cael.* II 3 depend on it, it also makes
another appearance in a later chapter where it is used to reject the possibility
that both the stars and the universe as a whole are at rest (see *Cael.* II 8.289b5–
6: "let it be assumed that the Earth is at rest"; τὴν δὲ γῆν ὑποκείσθω ἠρεμεῖν), but
again without its demonstration being immediately forthcoming. In fact, the
proposition is not demonstrated until in the last two chapters of the second
book:[11] Aristotle announces the project at the beginning of *Cael.* II 13 (293a15–
17: "it remains to speak about Earth, of its position, and whether it is among
the things that are at rest or among those that move, and about its shape"),
lists the different opinions that exist on the issue of the Earth's rest or mobility
in the middle of that chapter (see especially *Cael.* II 13.293b15–32 and 294a10–
21), and finally settles the issue in *Cael.* II 14 (296a24–297a7: "Let us first say
whether it has motion or rests"). This final argument is again complex and takes
up the first half of the chapter: Aristotle first argues for the impossibility of
Earth moving (for instance, if the Earth moved, it would have to be by a motion
that is enforced on it, but enforced motions do not last forever, whereas the
universe is everlasting; and, if the Earth moved, it would have to undergo at
least two motions, but this does not fit with the phenomena) and then appeals
to empirical evidence supplied by the mathematical astronomers to claim that
Earth in fact rests at the center.

Obviously, Aristotle's "demonstration"—if it even amounts to that—of the
proposition that the Earth rests at the center of the universe is long, and
providing it earlier—in the midst of the explanation of why there are several
motions of the universe in chapter 3—would certainly have disrupted the
flow and the *clarity* of the argument there; postponing this demonstration is
certainly a pragmatic thing to do. However, there are reasons to believe that this
is not the full story. After all, Aristotle *could* have decided to start the second
book with a discussion of the attributes of Earth, then move on to the other
heavenly bodies, and conclude with a discussion of the universe as a whole.
Instead, Aristotle first discusses the attributes of the universe as a whole (*Cael.*

---

11   The second surrogate principle concerning the contrary relation between the elements is
      (presumably) demonstrated in GC II 3–4.

II 1–6: the universe is eternal; possesses the dimensions left and right, above and below; moves forward in circular, regular motions; and is spherical in shape); then discusses the attributes of the heavenly bodies (*Cael.* II 7–12: the heavenly bodies are made of aether; are spherical in shape; move in virtue of the spheres in which they are fixed; differ in relative speeds by which they move and in complexity of motions); and concludes with an exposition of the attributes of Earth (*Cael.* II 13–14: the Earth rests at the center of the universe, is motionless, and spherical in shape). As I will suggest in the sections below, this particular order of exposition is *deliberate* and is supposed to reflect a certain *natural order* among the heavenly bodies themselves; using a surrogate principle thus allows Aristotle to observe this proper, natural order of exposition.

III   Natural Order in Aristotle's Biology

The claim that Aristotle's natural treatises follow some deliberate plan of exposition is not controversial: the first chapter of the *Meteorology* (*Mete.* I 1.338a20–339a10) famously lays out a "map" of what topics ought to be pursued in what order within Aristotle's natural science as a whole,[12] and most individual treatises contain cross-references forward or backward to the topics discussed in other treatises. Presumably, the "macro-level" order presented in these passages reflects Aristotle's views about how these individual treatises are related to each other conceptually or didactically, that is, about which treatise the student of nature should read first, and which next, if he is to be able to follow and gain understanding from the explanations provided in them. Aristotle's *On the Heavens* is no exception: the *Meteorology*-passage mentioned above places the study of "the ordered motions of the stars up above" provided in the first two books *in between* the study of the *Physics*, which deals with "the first causes of nature and with all natural motion", and the study of "the bodily elements, their numbers and kinds, and their change into each other" and of "becoming and perishing in general", which are provided in the last two books of *On the Heavens* and in *On Generation and Corruption*. However, at the "micro-level", that is, at the level of the organization of materials *within* the individual chapters and sections of the natural treatises—and especially when those materials involve large amounts of natural entities and their attributes (say, all attributes of the heavenly bodies, all parts of animals, or all modes of reproduction)—

---

12   For discussions of this passage and its significance for the order of exposition among Aristotle's natural treatises, see the references in note 8 above.

such didactic concerns may not yield specific enough norms for determining the order of exposition (for instance, it is not clear whether there is any didactic advantage in learning the function of eyes before that of feet). This means that Aristotle has to get his—additional—norms for determining the order of exposition from elsewhere, such as, for instance, from the hierarchical order of nature itself.[13] This relation between the order of exposition and the order of nature is clearest in Aristotle's biological works; let me discuss two prominent cases before returning to the issue of order in *On the Heavens* II in section 4.

First, when Aristotle discusses the *parts* of animals—both when presenting the facts about them in the *History of Animals* and when explaining why they belong to the animals they do in the *Parts of Animals*—he uses the *human body* and the natural, hierarchical order of its parts as a guideline for the organization of his exposition.[14] The justification for doing so, as Aristotle explains in both treatises, is not just that the human body is better known to us, but also that the human body is the only sublunary body that has its parts organized in accordance with nature: taking the human body as a guideline for determining the order of exposition thus does not only make didactic sense, it is also the most natural way to proceed.

For instance, in his introduction to the discussion of the parts of animals in the *History of Animals* (I 6.491a14–26), Aristotle explains that we should start by enumerating the parts on the *human* body, as they are epistemologically speaking "closer to us" and visible to everyone, but also because proceeding in this way will somehow preserve "the proper order" (491a24–25: ὅμως δ' ἕνεκεν τοῦ μὴ παραλιπεῖν τε τὸ ἐφεξῆς ... λεκτέον τὰ μέρη ...). The next couple of chapters proceed to discuss the facts about the non-uniform parts that are visible on the human body and that are common to both male and female (HA I 7–16; see especially I 15.494a19 and I 16.494b18–21), while moving from the parts on the head to the bottom. Nearing the end of this enumeration, Aristotle states that the position of these parts on the human body are again clear enough for perception to see, but that he nevertheless must specify them, for the same reason he had given earlier, which is to make sure that "the proper order is accomplished" (HA I 15.494a20–24; a24: ἵνα περαίνηται τὸ ἐφεξῆς). Aristotle

---

13   My claim is *not* that following the natural order of things is completely independent of any didactic or conceptual concerns (what is more clear to us may well coincide with what is more honorable by nature, in which case natural order and didactic order run together), or that there are no other guiding principles for the order of exposition; rather it is that one *important* principle in determining the order of exposition when dealing with natural entities and their attributes is the hierarchical order given by nature itself.

14   On this point, see Lennox 1999, 8–10.

never explains what exactly he means by this "proper order", but he clearly takes
it to be normative for determining in what order the various parts need to be
discussed *and* ties this order of exposition to their actual, natural order and
position on the human body (cf. *HA* I 16.494b19–20: τὰ μὲν οὖν μόρια ... τοῦτον
τέτακται τὸν τρόπον). Aristotle does, however, explain that this ordering of parts
on the human body is the order that is most in accordance with the natural
dimensions of the cosmos, such that the upper parts in humans correspond
with the natural up of the universe, etc.:

> Humankind has more than other animals the upper and the lower [parts]
> distinguished with a view to the natural locations (πρὸς τοὺς κατὰ φύσιν
> τόπους): for what is up and below [in humans] has been ordered (τέτακται)
> with a view to what is the up and the below of the universe. And in the
> same way [humankind] also has the front and back [parts] and the right
> and left [parts] in accordance to nature (κατὰ φύσιν).
>
> *HA* I 15.494a26–b1; a26–31

This, then, provides a natural ordering of the visible (external)[15] human body
parts (*HA* I 15.494b1–4): "After the head there is the neck, next the chest and
the back, the one in the front and the other in the back. And next to those are
the belly and the loins and the sexual parts and the haunches, next the thigh
and the shin, and last, the feet". Interestingly, Aristotle's *Parts of Animals* follows *more or less* same order of exposition in providing explanations for the
presence and differentiations of the external, non-uniform parts of animals,
and provides a very similar set of justifications for following this order. Aristotle's treatment of the external, non-uniform parts starts in *PA* II 10, where he
states that "we must now speak as if we are again at a beginning, starting first
from the primary things" (*PA* II 10.655b28–29: νῦν δὲ λέγωμεν ... ἀρξάμενοι πρῶτον ἀπὸ τῶν πρώτων). As it turns out, "first among firsts" are again the parts of
humankind:

> So both because of this [i.e., the fact that humankind has one of the most
> polymorphic appearances and partakes most in the divine] and because
> the shape of the external parts of humankind is most familiar, one must
> speak about him first. For it is directly the case also that in this kind alone
> the natural parts are in accordance with nature (τὰ φύσει μόρια κατὰ φύσιν

---

15   For the internal parts, Aristotle relies on analogies with animals close to human beings:
      see *HA* I 16.494b19–24.

ἔχει), and that what is above for him is with a view to what is above for
the universe; for humankind alone among animals is upright.

PA II 10.656a9–13

After this, Aristotle starts his discussion of the external, non-uniform parts and
loosely follows the natural order of the parts as introduced in the *History of
Animals*, moving from the parts on the head down to the neck (in *PA* II 10–III 2),
then discussing both external and internal parts on the trunk or thorax—first
those in between the chest and the back (in *PA* III 3–13) and next those around
the belly (*PA* III 14–IV 4; the discussion of the sexual organs is postponed)—and
concludes with the remaining appendages, the arms and legs (*PA* IV 9–10).[16] In
this way, Aristotle again uses the parts on the human body and their natural
ordering on the body as his way to organize his explanations.

Second, when Aristotle discusses the different *modes of reproduction* of animals (i.e., live-bearing, egg-laying, and grub-producing) in *Generation of Animals* II–III, he uses the hierarchical scale pertaining to their levels of "perfection" as a guideline for determining which mode to discuss after which.
Roughly speaking, the exposition of *Generation of Animals* as a whole follows
the chronological, causal order of the coming to be of animals: Aristotle starts
with a discussion of the first principles of sexual reproduction, continues by
explaining the various modes of reproduction and embryogenesis, and concludes by explaining the mechanisms of sexual differentiation and heredity,
the phenomena surrounding birth, and, finally, the occurrence of affections of
the more and the less after the animal is born.[17] However, when discussing the
different modes of reproduction that exist concurrently among different animal species Aristotle has to turn to a different principle of exposition; as he
points out at the beginning of this discussion (*GA* II 4.737b25–27): "Now we
must start first from the first [animals]: and *first are the perfect animals* (ἔστι
δὲ τὰ τέλεια ζῷα πρῶτα), and such are the live-bearing animals and first among
them humankind".

Apparently, live-bearing animals and, in particular, *human* live-bearers need
to be discussed first, because they rank first in terms of perfection, and the

---

16   The *precise* order of exposition in the *PA* is actually more complex than that of the *HA*,
       in part because Aristotle interrupts his discussion of the external, non-uniform parts in
       blooded animals frequently to discuss those parts in non-blooded animals or to diverge to
       internal parts (see Lennox 1999, 8–9 and 16 note 10); but roughly speaking, the exposition
       moves from head to toe, taking the human body as a paradigm.

17   On Aristotle's concern for tracking the chronological order of causation in the *GA*, see
       Leunissen 2010b, 52–57.

order of exposition follows the most perfect kind of reproducers to the less perfect kinds. By "perfection" Aristotle has in mind the level of completeness of the offspring by the time it is cast out of the mother (i.e., whether it has all its necessary parts and is already sexually differentiated or not), which is itself determined by the level of perfection of the material nature (including its level of internal heat) that animal has. Earlier, Aristotle had differentiated between three different types of material nature found among animals and claimed that each of them gives rise to a particular mode of reproduction (*GA* II 1.732a25–733a32): moist and pure blooded animals become live-bearers, dry and earthy blooded animals become egg-layers, and dry bloodless animals become grub-producers. Within these three groups, the possession of more or less internal heat further differentiates the levels of perfection, thus giving rise to a *scala naturae*. As Aristotle puts it (*GA* II 1.733a32–33): "it is necessary to understand how *well and orderly* (εὖ καὶ ἐφεξῆς) nature has rendered generation". According to this natural hierarchy, the animals that are hottest, moistest, and purest are *the most perfect*[18] and possess the most perfect mode of reproduction, whereas the ones that are colder and dryer are least perfect and reproduce less perfectly. And, from II 4 onward, Aristotle uses this natural hierarchy to organize his discussion of the various modes of reproduction: he starts with the live-bearing animals, using embryogenesis in humankind as his paradigm (in the remainder of book II), then turns to egg-layers—first birds (in *GA* III 1–2; cf. *GA* III 1.749a10–15 and *GA* III 2.754a15–20), then fish, since the latter are even less perfect than birds (in *GA* III 3–8; cf. *GA* III 3.754a20–26); and concludes with the grub-producing insects (*GA* III 9–10; see esp. *GA* III 9.758a26–29), and the spontaneously reproducing testacea (*GA* III 11; cf. *GA* III 11.761a12–13).[19]

In short, nature provides all kinds of hierarchies in its organization from which Aristotle can draw so as to find normative principles for the organization of his own writings in those cases where didactic or conceptual concerns yield no particular preference for discussing one natural entity or its attribute before another. I think that something similar is the case in the second book of *On the Heavens*, so let me return to that text.

---

18   Cf. *GA* II 1.732a16–23 and *Resp.* 13.477a15–25, where Aristotle calls animals with more heat "more honorable" (τιμιώτερα), and ascribes to them a "more honorable" soul and [material] nature, while singling out humans as being the hottest and purest.

19   Interestingly, Aristotle introduces his discussion of the different modes of reproduction in the *History of Animals* (*HA* V 1.539a4–15) as needing to follow the *exact opposite order* (moving from testacea to insects, then to fish, birds, and live-bearing animals, and lastly to humankind; cf. the use of ἐφεξῆς in 539a10), for the apparently pragmatic reason that humankind involves the longest discussion.

IV   Natural Order in Aristotle's Cosmology: Why Earth Should be
        Discussed Last

That Aristotle is following a specific, deliberate order of exposition in *On the Heavens* II can be gleaned from the clear section-breaks he provides between chapters 6 and 7, where he moves from a discussion of the attributes and motions of the universe as a whole to the *following* discussion of the nature, shapes, and motion of the stars (see *Cael.* 289a8–13: ὅτι μὲν οὖν ... ὁ οὐρανός ... ἐπὶ τοσοῦτον ἡμῖν εἰρήσθω. περὶ δὲ τῶν καλουμένων ἄστρων ἑπόμενον ἂν εἴη λέγειν ...), and between chapters 12 and 13, where he turns to the discussion of the *remaining* topic, the attributes and motions of Earth (see 293a11–17: ἀλλὰ περὶ μὲν τῶν ... ἄστρων εἴρηται ... λοιπὸν δὲ περὶ τῆς γῆς εἰπεῖν ...).[20] And, on one occasion, Aristotle uses the term ἐφεξῆς to indicate that his exposition follows a certain preferred sequence (*Cael.* II 6.288a14: ἐφεξῆς ἂν εἴη τῶν εἰρημένων διελθεῖν; cf. *Cael.* I 12.281a28). However, more is needed to show that this order of exposition traces a natural hierarchy among heavenly bodies, analogous to that among sublunary living beings, according to which demonstrations concerning the "lowest" body, Earth, ought to be postponed until the very end of the book.

Unfortunately, Aristotle never specifies what exactly his preferred order of exposition is, or why prefers it. However, there are indications that Aristotle believes that the heavenly bodies are hierarchically ordered *and* that Earth is the lowest among them. For instance, Aristotle tries to provide an explanation for why the heavenly bodies move with different complexities (some bodies have many motions, some few, and one performs no motion) by *likening* the various heavenly bodies to different kinds of sublunary beings which require various complexities of motions to achieve the good, if they can achieve it at all (see *Cael.* II 12.292b1–25; b1–2: "This is why it is necessary that we consider also the action of the heavenly bodies as being of the exact same sort as that of animals and plants"). The analogy is complex, and does not quite do the work Aristotle wants it to do,[21] but the hierarchical picture implied by analogy is clear enough: in the sublunary realm, humans who are in the best state form the top of the hierarchy, next come the other humans, then all other animals, and plants are at the bottom. Analogously, the outer sphere carrying the fixed stars forms the top of the hierarchy in the heavenly realm,[22] next come five planets (i.e., Saturn, Jupiter, Mars, Venus, and Mercury), then the Sun and the Moon,

---

20   Book I similarly provides frequent "signposts": see, e.g., *Cael.* I 2.268b11–14; I 5.271b1;
      I 8.276a18–19; and I 9.272b27–29.

21   On this analogy and its problems, see Leunissen 2010a, 165–168.

22   Aristotle had already explained earlier that the further away something is from "the things

and, at the bottom, comes Earth. According to this account, Earth holds the same lowly natural status as plants, because it is furthest removed from the good and is not even able to get close it, which explains why it does not move at all—any motion would be in vain (*Cael.* II 12.292b15–20).[23]

The lowly status of Earth comes up also in the next chapter, where Aristotle reviews the common opinions about its position (*Cael.* II 13.293a17–b15; cf. *Mete.* II 1.353a34–b6). Aristotle states that there are many people who in principle agree with the Pythagoreans, who deny that the Earth is positioned at the center of the universe, because these people think that "it is befitting that the most honorable region belongs to the most honorable thing" (293a30–32: τῷ γὰρ τιμιωτάτῳ οἴονται προσήκειν τὴν τιμιωτάτην ὑπάρχειν χώραν), and that fire is more honorable than earth. Interestingly, Aristotle shows the wrongness of this line of thinking, not by denying that fire is more honorable than earth, but by denying that the *spatial* center of the universe is the most important location. Instead, Aristotle appeals to the way "center" is used with regard to animals, where the most important location is the *natural* center, which does not necessarily coincide with the spatial center (293b6–8): "And yet we better assume that—just as in living beings the center of the living being and that of its body are not the same—so too are things with regard to the whole universe". In his biology, Aristotle employs as one of his teleological principles the proposition that "nature always places the more honorable things in the more honorable locations, where nothing greater prevents it" (see, e.g., *PA* III 4.665b20–21), and uses it, for instance, to explain the location of the heart at the center of the *necessary*[24] body (665b23)—at a place that is "originative" (665b18: ἡ θέσις αὐτῆς ἀρχικὴν χώραν). In the universe, then, the corresponding natural center—which is something "primary and honorable" (293b11: ἀρχὴ ... καὶ τίμιον)—is to be found *on the outside*, in that which limits everything and which is furthest away from the spatial center, which holds the lowest or last position (293b12: τόπου μέσον ἔοικε τελευτῇ). There is thus no contradiction between Aristotle's view and between those who hold that the most honorable position should be occupied by the most honorable body: the spatial center of the universe is the

---

here," the more honorable its nature is (*Cael.* I 2.269b13–17) and that the upper region is "more divine" than that which is below (*Cael.* II 5.288a4–5).

23   Cf. perhaps Aristotle's use of ἐφεξῆς in *GC* II 4.331b2–4, referring to the natural order of the elements, working downward from Fire, to Air, to Water, and finally to Earth.

24   The "necessary body" includes the head and thorax, which enable the performance of the vital functions of nutrition and perception, and excludes the limbs: the natural center thus does not coincide with the spatial center of the animal if one takes its *entire* body into account.

least honorable position and is therefore a fitting location for the Earth, the least honorable among the bodies under discussion.

In conclusion, by using a surrogate principle about the position of Earth in *Cael.* II 3, Aristotle is able to negotiate his concerns for following the appropriate order in his expositions—which in this particular case tracks the *natural order* among heavenly bodies themselves—and the demands created by his overall aim of providing scientific explanations. The proposition that the Earth rests at the center of the universe is needed for the explanation of why the heavenly bodies move with different motions, but its demonstration needs to wait until its appropriate place at the very end of the book: a fitting location for such a lowly body.

CHAPTER 6

Arrangement and Exploratory Discourse in the *Parva Naturalia**

Philip van der Eijk

Abstract

Aristotle's works on sleep and dreams provide striking examples of what Charles Kahn has called, in relation to the *De anima*, the *Parva Naturalia* and the zoological works as a whole, "the progressive character of the exposition" in Aristotle. Both on a macro-level and, as will be shown in this paper, within the confines of a more restricted investigation, Aristotle's works on the soul and on living beings often display a careful structure, possibly motivated by didactic and/or rhetorical considerations, in which arguments and ideas gradually unfold in the course of a thought process that the reader is meant to go through. This thought process is informed by explanatory principles familiar from Aristotle's psychology but also guided by expository techniques such as the dialectical reviewing of current opinions, the aporetic raising of puzzles, the gradual refinement of descriptions and definitions, and the use of repetition and cross-referencing. This paper aims to show that close analysis of the role of these expository principles in Aristotle's discussion of sleep and dreams is illuminating not only for our appreciation of Aristotle as a writer, but also of crucial importance for the interpretation of specific passages that on the face of it seem to be in conflict with other passages or problematic in other respects. In particular, it will study the importance of the rhetorical principle of arrangement (*taxis*) in the exposition of Aristotle's ideas as a means to enhance the persuasiveness of the views he wishes to put forward.

* I am grateful for comments and suggestions on earlier versions of this paper from audiences in Berlin, Rome, and Göteborg, and for exchanges with Markus Asper (who kindly sent me an unpublished chapter from his Habilitationsarbeit on Peripatetic prose writing), David Bloch, Wei Cheng, Sabine Föllinger, and Thorsten Fögen. The research project from which this paper has arisen was supported by the Alexander von Humboldt Foundation.

I   Reading Aristotle and Hermeneutic Scenarios

Reading Aristotle is a fascinating but also, at times, frustrating and infuriating experience. This is not just because of the complexity of the philosophical issues he addresses. One often feels that Aristotle could have made the lives of his readers (ancient as well as modern) a bit easier. Indeed, as a writer, Aristotle does not have a very good reputation. He has often been accused, in antiquity as well as in modern times, of carelessness and sloppiness, of repetitiveness or brevity to the point of obscurity.[1] What is particularly irritating is that Aristotle could have done a much better job, for, as is well known, he is reported by Cicero to have been a skilful writer of elegant, fluent prose.[2] But Cicero's judgment applies, in all likelihood, to the works that were meant for a larger audience and that were in the form of dialogues, perhaps similar in elegance to Cicero's own philosophical dialogues. Unfortunately, these works survive only in fragments, and it is difficult to appreciate their style based on such meagre evidence.[3] What does survive are Aristotle's so-called esoteric works, usually referred to as *pragmateiai*,[4] the writings that were presumably not meant for circulation beyond his own circle of fellow philosophers and students. It is widely believed that this latter point accounts for their unpolished style and poor state of organization. And it has often been suggested that the texts as we have them represent Aristotle's own notes, which he used as the basis for his lectures and seminars and that were supplemented by oral elucidations that have not found their way into the texts as we have them (or, alternatively, the notes taken by a student or scribe during the lecture or seminar and revised afterward).[5]

---

1   Föllinger 2012, 237–238 offers an overview of some assessments of Aristotle's prose; see also Asper 2003; Rapp 2013, 297–299. On ancient judgments about Aristotle's obscurity, especially among the Neoplatonist commentators, see Kanthak 2013, 179–183.
2   *On the Nature of the Gods* II 37.95, which compares Aristotle's writing to a "stream of gold" (*flumen orationis aureum*).
3   For an attempt, see Schickert 1977.
4   Although conventional, the term *pragmateia* is not very helpful as a genre category, as it does not do justice to the great variety of textual forms in the Aristotelian corpus, as Lengen 2002 convincingly shows; see also van der Eijk 2013. Asper 2003 suggests "Schulskript", a text that is the collective intellectual property of a school and that remains subject to usage and revision within this environment.
5   The latter possibility is considered by Asper 2003: the Peripatetic writings are "Niederschrif-ten ... die der schulöffentlichen Kommunikation eher nachfolgten als vorausgingen" and that served the purpose of "Konsenssicherung".

Yet this explanation is not completely satisfactory, nor is it entirely fair. For it does not explain why some allegedly esoteric Aristotelian texts (or parts of them) do display abundant evidence of careful design and literary crafting. There are sections in Aristotle's *Metaphysics*, in the *Nicomachean Ethics*, in the *Parts of Animals*, and in the *Generation of Animals* (to mention just some examples) that display undeniable care and craft in style, arrangement and overall architectonic structure, which makes them suitable and even potentially attractive to wider audiences.[6] They testify to Aristotle's ability to engage his readers in long, sustained reasoning, to present ideas and arguments in ways that attract and keep their attention and that are conducive to the text being more easily engaged with, understood, and accepted; and they demonstrate that Aristotle, at least on a number of occasions, put that ability into practice also in his *pragmateiai*.

What is particularly striking is Aristotle's use of arrangement, one of the cardinal principles recognized by ancient rhetorical theory (*taxis, dispositio*).[7] The order in which Aristotle presents his arguments, the way in which he revisits and refines them, and even the order of these refinements themselves, is by no means arbitrary but displays a keen sense of didactic and rhetorical skill. This vital role of arrangement in enhancing the clarity, interest, and persuasiveness of the argument is what I should like to explore further.

In doing so, I should like to make a connection with what Charles Kahn has called "the progressive character of the exposition" in Aristotle.[8] The idea underlying this formulation is as follows. Both on a macro-level and within the confines of a more restricted investigation, Aristotle's works often display a careful structure, possibly motivated by pedagogic and/or rhetorical considerations, in which arguments and ideas gradually unfold in the course of a thought process that the audience is meant to go through. This thought process

---

6   See the studies by Lengen 2002; Schütrumpf 1991; Föllinger 1993, 2005, 2012; van der Eijk 1997; Verdenius 1985; Dirlmeier 1962; Bodéüs 1993, chapters 4 and 5. While in some of these cases, one may suspect that Aristotle's own personal involvement plays a special role, this explanation does not work for all passages of this kind.

7   On Aristotle's discussion of *taxis* in oratory (in *Rhet.* III 13–19), and on its potential relevance to the arrangement of his own philosophical writings, see Rapp 2013, 297–301. Of course, a speech for a lawcourt, in a political assembly, or at a funeral, is different from a philosophical or scientific *pragmateia*; nevertheless, some general principles such as clarity, comprehensibility, and a certain degree of interest and attractiveness to captivate the audience's attention apply also to technical writing, especially if there is a didactic component involved. Arrangement plays a vital role here.

8   See Kahn 1966, 51.

is informed by explanatory principles that are familiar from Aristotle's philosophy (and that the audience is sometimes explicitly reminded of, but which are often implicitly presupposed) but also guided by expository techniques such as the dialectical reviewing of current opinions, the aporetic raising of puzzles, the use of tentative answers and suggestions, arguments and counterarguments, the gradual refinement of descriptions and definitions, and the use of repetition and cross-referencing.

This more positive evaluation of Aristotle's writing style, in particular the dynamic, progressive structure of his argument, has an important methodological advantage, for it makes it easier and more natural to apply to our reading of Aristotle one of the key principles of textual interpretation. This is the assumption—which can be seen as a variant of the well-known principle of charity—that the author is in control of his or her material, both intellectually and in terms of its formal and literary organization and presentation, and that any difficulties in the explanation of the text are, at least in the first instance, the interpreter's problem, not the author's.[9] On this assumption, until the contrary is proven, everything in a text is intentional, or at least meaningful and functional,[10] and there is no point in speculating as to whether certain elements or features of the text are meant to be there or whether their presence is, as it were, by accident, or the result of later editorial intervention. Thus the assumption is that the text as we have it is the product of careful design and crafting by a writer who possesses the necessary linguistic and literary competence and who knows what he is talking about. And we make this assumption not so much because we believe that all texts are perfect, but for methodological reasons. In order to abide by the rules of rigorous scholarly interpretation,

---

9   For a classic statement of the principle of charity, see Davidson 1984, chapter 13. I am aware that this assumption is controversial and that it is rejected in several streams in literary studies that question the whole concept of authorial intentionality ("the intentional fallacy"). Without going into this debate here, I would say that, even if it is questionable whether an author's intention can be recovered in the process of interpretation, there can be no doubt that authorial agency is a major explanatory factor in the production of a text that has to be taken into account. Furthermore, the principle of charity is a valuable starting point in that it encourages attempts at maximizing or optimizing the text as it stands, and seeing how far one gets before giving in to alternative hermeneutic scenarios such as the assumption of later interpolations, plural traditions, etc. The analysis that follows below is an attempt to do just that.

10   I use "functional" here to take account of the objection that it may not be possible to determine whether specific elements or features of a text (e.g., the ambiguity of a particular passage) were put in by the author on purpose.

and in order to arrive in a transparent manner at a plausible, defensible, and justifiable hypothesis as to what the text is meant to say or how it is meant to work, we have to start from the assumption that the text is in good shape. This is simply a code of interpretive practice. If we did not make this assumption, we would get onto a slippery slope and interpretation would be in danger of becoming an arbitrary process in which, at any time, a reader may decide to read a passage in a different way by taking it as a later interpolation or by assuming that, at a particular place, the author has not applied the finishing touches to his work.

There are, of course, cases where this assumption needs to be qualified or even suspended. There can be good evidence, both internal and external, that the text as we have it is not a finished product, or that it is a combination of material from different sources put together without much care and organization. In such cases, the application of the hermeneutic principle mentioned above might be felt to be problematic and artificial. But unless there is such evidence, we should start from the assumption that everything in the text is functional, for the methodological reason mentioned: if we do not make this assumption, there is no common basis for debate and argument in case of disagreement about the reading of specific passages.

These considerations are relevant to reading Aristotle, for as I already indicated, it has often been argued that Aristotle's works present exactly such a case in which there are good reasons to question the assumption that the texts as we have them represent a unified, accomplished product. Some of Aristotle's texts read like rough drafts; some arguments give the impression of not being fully elaborated; and there is also, at times, a fair bit of repetition and duplication. Even when it comes to the subject matter, one sometimes feels that Aristotle's handling of the material, at least as far as it shows from the text, is not entirely satisfactory. There are cases where one wonders whether a particular problem, or aspect of a problem, has escaped his attention, and where one feels that if he was aware of this problem, he should have mentioned it and brought it to bear on his discussion or, alternatively, where one wonders whether he deliberately does not discuss the problem for reasons to do with the argumentative strategy. This, of course, is a more general hermeneutic problem that also arises with other ancient philosophers and scientific writers. The question in such cases is whether the author's failure to do what we expect him to do is the result of lack of control of the subject matter, or carelessness of presentation, or the result of a deliberate strategy of refraining from a discussion of issues that might complicate the argument or jeopardize the conclusions reached. The significance of that latter possibility becomes greater when other passages elsewhere in Aristotle's works demonstrate his awareness of problems that seem absent from the passage under investigation. To say that this is just *our* problem, as modern readers of Aristotle, and that what is unclear, ambiguous, or problematic for us may not have been so for Aristotle's intended audience, who were native speakers who lived and worked in Aristotle's close vicinity, does not help very much, as the examples that follow below show, quite apart from the fact that we have very little evidence as to what such ancient readers of Aristotle were expected to be able to take on board.[11]

In the past, one way of dealing with such cases was to assume that Aristotle had changed his mind and that his views had developed. This "genetic" approach to Aristotle has had its champions in twentieth-century scholarship, but it has gone out of fashion. I mention it here because it is, essentially, an extension, on a macro-level, of the view that the author's work as we have it is not an entirely finished product: it presupposes that the corpus or œuvre of an author as a whole does not, in the form in which we have it, represent a coherent unity of doctrine and style but shows evidence of the author's intellectual development, in which some tensions and inconsistencies have remained unresolved. Similarly, on the micro-level of an individual treatise or text, one may sometimes wonder whether the text represents a coherent unity or whether it shows evidence of the author, as it were, thinking aloud and developing his or her thoughts while writing, with the result that certain tensions or problems in the argument are not completely smoothed out.[12]

II   Rhetorical and Didactic Motivations for Aristotle's Ways of Writing

Today, however, different interpretive paradigms reign, and the prevailing way to account for apparent omissions or tensions that is more popular with current

---

11   Most of the evidence for the actual reception of Aristotle's works in antiquity is of a later date (see Kanthak 2013), and whether Aristotle's students and readers in the Lyceum in the fourth century BCE had less difficulty coping with the problems and obscurities that later commentators were struggling with is hard to say. To answer this question properly would require a comprehensive investigation into the presuppositions that Aristotle appears to make in the various stages of the argument in a large number of his writings; this might make it possible to reconstruct the background knowledge that Aristotle presupposed his audience to possess and their "horizon of expectations". In the absence of such an investigation, much of what we assume about the capacities and limitations of Aristotle's intended audience is little more than speculation.

12   On this latter point, in relation to Aristotle, see Föllinger 2012, drawing on recent developments in "Schreibforschung", e.g., Eigler et al. eds. 1990.

readers of Aristotle, and of most ancient authors, is to assume that the author has left things out, or unresolved, or unspecified, on purpose. This may be for didactic reasons: when an author is addressing an audience of students, for example, or non-experts, he or she may feel that for pedagogic reasons it is advisable not to make the argument too complicated. Alternatively, there may be rhetorical reasons: the author may have been manipulative and, like a cunning orator, have omitted evidence or arguments that could weaken the views he or she wishes to put across. Whatever one may think about the implications of this latter view for our assessment of an author's integrity or honesty, there certainly is a rhetorical dimension to Aristotle's works, too: there are many cases where it is undeniable that he wants to persuade, to score points, especially in polemical contexts where he is criticizing and discrediting rival views.

My feeling is that in the study of Aristotle as a writer, these different scenarios should be carefully distinguished from one another. It makes quite a difference whether we attribute textual features to the text being meant as a teaching tool for a group of students (and, within that category, for beginners or for more advanced students), or to the text being the product of a rhetorical speech act intended to persuade an audience of certain views and to discredit certain rival views. Furthermore, it makes quite a difference whether we attribute textual features to the text being orally presented to a group of students, or meant to be studied in written form, either privately in a library or in a class or small group.

When considering these scenarios, we need to bear in mind that we are not that well informed about teaching practices in the fourth century BCE in general, and in the Lyceum in particular, or about the exact ways in which texts were believed to suit these practices.[13] Indeed, in many cases we do not even know for sure whether a text was actually meant for teaching purposes; it often remains a hypothesis based on our evaluation of certain textual features that, we believe, make best sense on that assumption. In framing such a hypothesis, we should be careful not to retroject our own preconceptions and preferences for specific styles of teaching onto the ancient material. For example, we may think today that teaching is more effective when it is interactive and when the discourse is, at least superficially, of an exploratory nature, open-minded

---

13   For a classic survey of the evidence see Lynch 1972; for a more recent account of intellectual life in the Lyceum see Natali 2014; for the philosophical schools more generally see Dorandi 1999. On Aristotle's own occasional remarks on philosophical teaching, e.g., in the *Nicomachean Ethics* and the *Parts of Animals*, see Kullmann 1974, 107–122 and Bodéüs 1993, 83–122.

and open-ended. In this way, we may feel, students are more likely to be engaged and encouraged to make an active contribution to what is seen as a collective intellectual enterprise, in which the students and the teacher stand in a relationship of *Augenhöhe*, and in which, when the process is completed, the audience will share in a communal sense of achievement and satisfaction. But of course this is just one specific view on teaching, whose popularity is only a recent phenomenon; teaching practices and fashions were very different not that long ago and they have varied, and will continue to vary, greatly from one timeframe and one culture to another.

Yet I would argue that it is not anachronistic to apply the term "exploratory" to Aristotle's method of instruction, and that there are good reasons to believe that he used this method in order for his audience to go through a learning process. It has often been observed that many of Aristotle's writings, or at least certain sections of them (especially the opening chapters), are characterized by such a tentative, cautiously seeking, open-ended and non-dogmatic attitude, and he has even been commended for this.[14] I would suggest that this is very similar to what in discourse analysis is referred to as "exploratory discourse",[15] and that it is illuminating to look at Aristotle's writings from this point of view,

---

14   E.g., by Ackrill 1981, 1–2: "It is true that Aristotle often adopts a headmaster's style, and speaks with assurance as if on the matter in hand final truth has been achieved ... Nevertheless, through most of his works there also rings, more or less loudly, the note of caution and of questioning: much remains obscure or uncertain, the answers to one set of problems throw up new ones, on important issues arguments seem evenly balanced". On the alternation between dogmatism and uncertainty in ancient philosophical and scientific texts in general, see Lloyd 1987.

15   See van der Eijk 1997, 81–82, drawing on Kinneavy 1971, who coined the term, though without endorsing in all detail Kinneavy's schematic distinctions between exploratory discourse, informative, and scientific discourse as species of "referential discourse", which in turn is distinguished by Kinneavy from "persuasive (rhetorical)", "expressive", and "literary" discourse. In my view, the very use of exploratory discourse can be part of a rhetorical strategy aimed at persuading the audience of certain views by involving them in a collective, open-minded investigation, or of a didactic strategy aimed at making students acquire certain insights and arrive at certain conclusions. By exploratory discourse I mean a text (or a section of a text) that approaches a topic in an essayistic, tentative, non-dogmatic, and non-definitive manner. This does not mean that everything remains provisional or that no presuppositions are made: it means that in a particular stage of the investigation, questions are touched on rather than answered, and approaches are attempted rather than pursued to the very end. As such, exploratory discourse shows affinities with the well-known "raising of puzzles" (διαπορεῖν) characteristic of many Aristotelian investigations.

not only for reasons of pragmatic linguistics but also because it may shed light on difficulties in the philosophical interpretation. For it means that individual passages need to be seen within the context in which they stand, e.g., in a particular stage of an argument, and within the rhetorical or didactic strategy they are meant to serve, but also in relation to other stages of that argument in other parts of the text. It further means that a text as we have it may not give Aristotle's fully comprehensive views on the matter in question, and that there is a certain occasional, *ad hoc* character to the way in which a particular subject is dealt with.

III   Orality, Thinking Aloud, Dialogue, Exploratory Discourse

Before looking at examples, we need to consider some further methodological points related to formal approaches to Aristotle's writings, and some alternative explanations for some of their features. First of all, the scenarios mentioned above—intended for oral or written presentation, intended for teaching purposes, intended to persuade an audience of certain views, and to discredit certain rival views—are, of course, not incompatible. For one thing, there is a rhetorical dimension to teaching as well.[16] When producing a text on a particular subject matter that is meant to provide instruction to an audience, the author acts and participates in a discursive, i.e., literary, cultural, and intellectual context and setting. In order for the text to work in such a setting, to attract and keep the audience's attention, to facilitate a hearing or reading that is interesting, agreeable, and persuasive, or deliberately provocative, or instrumental in making the audience react and behave in a particular way (e.g., signing up for a course, abandoning a particular lifestyle, and choosing a new way of life), the author of such a text needs to persuade the audience of his or her competence (both technical and literary), his or her moral integrity, and the plausibility of his or her theses and arguments. In this sense, didactic texts have a rhetorical dimension as well, not only in their more polemical sections, where the author attempts to persuade the audience of certain views or to discredit certain rivals (e.g., in the preface), but also in their overall linguistic, stylistic, and structural organization.

To return to the example of the open-ended, exploratory style of teaching, the use of such discourse in a teaching setting may itself be regarded as a rhetorical feature, and its appreciation may vary: one may applaud a teacher

---

16   For further elaboration of this point for Roman technical writing, see Fögen 2009.

for engaging his or her students by means of an open-minded and interactive mode of teaching rather than through a dogmatic, schoolmasterly, *ex cathedra* style; but a more cynical view one could take is that such open-mindedness is only apparent and in reality just constitutes a clever trick. Such somewhat cynical assessments have sometimes been made, for example, of the early Platonic dialogues: although the dialectical discussion is explicitly justified as a means of ensuring that the interlocutors have the opportunity to express disagreement at any time, one sometimes cannot but feel that the actual course of the Socratic discussion is manipulated by leading questions and other deceptive strategies. It would merit further investigation to what extent similar strategies may be detected in the more exploratory, "dialogic" parts of Aristotelian works.

In this connection, it is worth observing that the tentative nature of Aristotle's investigation has sometimes also been taken as evidence of an oral setting, although I agree with the editors of this volume that the density of most of his works makes it difficult to believe that they were meant for oral presentation—at least not in the form in which we have them. They may, however, be meant to reflect or imitate such an oral setting, just as we may think of a Platonic dialogue as being meant to imitate (and perhaps slightly idealize) the oral conversation in which people engage in a philosophical investigation.[17]

The tentative nature of some of Aristotle's writings raises the related question of to what extent the texts, in the form in which we have them, reflect the process of their composition. The alternative is to view them as essays imitating such a thought process, just as, again, a Platonic dialogue may be seen as an attempt to imitate the step-by-step reasoning process that someone goes through during the examination of a philosophical question or issue. Aristotle's works do indeed convey an impression of spontaneity and improvisation, which has been well described by Sabine Föllinger:

> The treatment of a question is sometimes not subject to strict planning, even if its introduction, for example in the form of a prepared list of questions, suggests this. Rather, a new approach is suddenly undertaken from a different perspective, a question connected with the topic is opened or,

---

17   See, however, the important qualifications by Föllinger 2012, 238: "Dirlmeier already spoke of the 'oral style' which the *pragmateiai* display ... The manner of representation produces the impression of being present in a dialogue. But no imitation of a dialogue takes place, as in Plato's works or in Aristotle's dialogues ... Rather, the to-and-fro of the argumentation conveys the impression to the reader that an exchange is taking place with an imaginary interlocutor". Later on (240), she describes this as "imaginierte Mündlichkeit".

after a question seems to have been dealt with, further confirmation or justification is added.

FÖLLINGER 2012, 240

Unannounced changes of plan, *ad hoc* explanations and afterthoughts are what Aristotle's style is notorious for. The traditional explanation for these features is that they simply reflect the genesis of the writings as we have them and that Aristotle did not carry out a final revision in which everything would smoothly fall into place. Yet, again, rather than attributing this to Aristotle's hasty, improvising, or even careless way of writing, we may consider as an alternative explanation that these features are stylized and functional and serve a didactic aim.[18]

Exploratory discourse, like the *essai* or the "essay" as literary genres that were developed and used (alongside the dialogue) in the early modern period, cultivates the unpredictability and open-endedness of the investigation, which allows for changes of plan, the abandoning of attempts that do not lead anywhere. As such, it can be very effective and illuminating. But exploratory discourse is a tricky business. The author has to be careful not to pitch the level too low for the audience he or she is addressing, as it may easily give a patronizing impression. Moreover, in using exploratory discourse, the author needs to be careful not to be open to the criticism that the discourse invites the audience to think about a problem that at the end turns out not to have been a genuine problem at all. For readers or hearers of such a text may feel that they have been misguided and have wasted their time.

Thus an attempt to make sense of the formal features of Aristotle's writings by reference to a didactic or rhetorical strategy they may have been meant to serve also has to assess the likelihood that such a strategy may actually be successful. What I mean by "successful" is best shown by a comparison with the practice most of us are familiar with from our daily lives as members of an academic community. Imagine someone presenting his or her work informally to an audience of colleagues as a "dry run" for a more formal presentation at a conference. At such a rehearsal, we give our colleague the feedback that is needed in order to improve the paper before the final presentation. We consider the paper's clarity and persuasiveness, its suitability for the audience

---

18 Cf. Föllinger 2012, 240: "The heterogeneity in the implementation shows how writing as a medium of discursive thinking leads to a further development of oral and dialectical approaches, for instance in the form of a hierarchic list of questions put forward at the beginning of the investigation, and how at the same time a certain spontaneity and immediacy of the thinking process is maintained".

it is addressing; we look at the structure and style and make suggestions for clarification of the wording and for simplification (especially if the paper is meant for oral presentation). We look at the order and the arrangement, and wonder whether certain points are better placed earlier or later in the paper, again bearing in mind that at an oral presentation, the audience will not be in a position to remember exactly the sequence in which certain points are made. If there is a handout or a PowerPoint presentation, or illustrations, diagrams, or statistics, we look at the appropriateness of this material to the presentation of the paper itself and make suggestions as to where and when they are best inserted. We judge such a paper not only on its intellectual merit but also on its effectiveness. Will it work? Will it be effective in getting the points across? Will it achieve its goals?

My suggestion is that we look at Aristotle's texts in this way. What are the aims that Aristotle seems to have set himself in a particular treatise? How successful is the text in achieving these aims? Could it have been improved?

In this way, we may get around the methodological problem I mentioned at the beginning, i.e., that the hermeneutic principle that authors are in full control of their material often seems in such blatant contradiction with our experience of reading Aristotle, or in other words, the problem of being unduly charitable to Aristotle's literary achievement. We still start on the assumption that the text is the product of careful design and crafting; what we do in analyzing the text is to try to bring to light just this careful design and crafting. In doing so, we will be patient and suspend judgment, allowing Aristotle to finish his argument before we start criticizing. We then judge the text on its merits in achieving the aims we believe the author had set himself.

In the end, such a judgment of Aristotle's achievement as a writer of philo-sophical prose is likely to be nuanced. On the one hand, there may be cases where we run out of patience and cannot but conclude that he *is* sloppy and careless, and that his prose is obscure or even positively confusing.[19] On the other hand, there may also be cases where patience pays off and where, ulti-mately, we can credit Aristotle with successful philosophical writing and/or teaching. As the papers in this volume demonstrate, the evidence of such suc-cessful philosophical writing may be greater than has been assumed in the past.

---

19   His use of examples or analogies is a case in point. As every reader of Aristotle knows, the examples he gives are sometimes even more obscure than the points they are meant to elucidate; or, while illuminating in some respects, they are complicating or even mis-leading in other respects. If one of the defining features of a good teacher is the ability to illustrate abstract problems by means of examples, this casts serious doubts on Aristotle's didactic skills.

In an earlier study, I tried to show how Aristotle's works on sleep and dreams illustrate aspects of Aristotle's methodology and approach.[20] In particular, I argued that there is a progressive unfolding of the question of the relationship between sleep and sensation (αἴσθησις). Aristotle's initial claim that there is no sensation in sleep is qualified in a number of ways as the investigation proceeds, and when we get to the end of the treatment, it turns out that there are various modes in which the sensitive part of the soul can, after all, be affected during sleep. In the end, my assessment of Aristotle's way of handling the topics was positive, though not 100 percent favorable: some tensions remained unresolved and could have done with more explicit clarification, e.g., the question of whether the term ἐνύπνιον is used, in *On Divination in Sleep*, in a narrower or more general sense than in *On Dreams*; and it was not quite clear why Aristotle left these questions unresolved. I ended up giving Aristotle the benefit of the doubt by suggesting various solutions to the problem that he might have mentioned if he had been asked for clarification; and I suggested that, on balance, our appreciation for Aristotle's open-mindedness with regard to empirical evidence, the ἔνδοξα of other respectable thinkers, and his enthusiasm to provide *ad hoc* explanations, should outweigh our insistence on clarification of some of the remaining issues.[21]

Building on these ideas and methodological considerations, but also slightly qualifying them, I will now in the rest of this paper look at two further examples of Aristotle's expository techniques, with particular attention to his use of arrangement (*taxis*) and exploratory discourse. In doing so, I will try to spell out the various hermeneutic options and moves that present themselves as we

---

20   See van der Eijk 2005a.

21   Van der Eijk 2005a, 202–203: "In the course of his argument, Aristotle sometimes arrives at explanations or conclusions which implicitly modify or qualify things he said earlier on without recognising this explicitly or revising his earlier formulations. Instead, he simply goes on, eager to explain as much as he can and carried away by the subtlety and explanatory power of his theories, but without bothering to tell us how these explanations fit in with what he said earlier on. This may be an argumentative, 'dialectic' or perhaps even didactic strategy (we should not forget that Aristotle's extant works derive from the teaching practice, and that they are very likely to have been supplemented by additional oral elucidation). Alternatively, it may be a matter of intellectual temperament or style. However this may be, it is undeniable that Aristotle in his works on sleep and dreams, as in his biological works at large, sometimes shows himself an improviser of *ad hoc* explanations, constantly prepared to adapt his theories to what the phenomena suggest. This inevitably means a lower degree of systematicity than we would perhaps regard as desirable; on the other hand, the elasticity of his explanations, and his readiness to accommodate new empirical observations, are things for which he is to be commended".

read the text and the questions it raises. The examples are taken from Aristotle's works *On Dreams* and *On Divination in Sleep*. The practical reason for this is that I have worked on these texts before and therefore feel in a better position to consider them from the point of view of formal and literary analysis than with a text with which I am less familiar: for such analysis can only be undertaken in conjunction with a thorough investigation of the philosophical and scientific contents. Yet I would argue that the examples have a wider significance and can be paralleled by many similar cases in other Aristotelian writings.[22]

IV   Repetition and Refinement of One and the Same Argument in *On Divination in Sleep*

My first example is taken from *On Divination in Sleep*, a short but fascinating and challenging text in which Aristotle discusses the phenomenon of prophecy in sleep. The text lends itself well to an analysis along the lines set out above, for it shows evidence of careful design, while at the same time leaving a number of questions unresolved. As will become clear shortly, the text appears to be meant for an audience that is familiar with a number of Aristotelian tenets and presuppositions that are not spelled out but that must be accepted in order for the argument to work. Yet at the same time, the audience is also clearly meant to learn a number of things it did not know yet, and hence it is interesting to study the methods by which Aristotle leads his audience to specific insights and conclusions.

A remarkable ingredient of this text is Aristotle's emphatic, repeated criticism of the idea that prophetic dreams are sent by the gods (θεόπεμπτα). This idea was widespread in the Graeco-Roman world, even among intellectuals, and Aristotle's insistent criticism is therefore significant. For the purposes of this paper, it is important to look at the precise form in which Aristotle's criticism is presented and at the different contexts in which it occurs. In his rejection of the idea that prophetic dreams are sent by a god, Aristotle repeatedly uses what appears to be the same argument. This argument is

---

22   As David Bloch suggests to me, a close parallel to my first example can be found in *On Memory and Recollection*, where Aristotle points out on three occasions that the difference between memory and recollection is shown by (what he presents as) the fact that people who are good at remembering are usually different from people who are good at recollecting (449b6–8; 450b1–11; 453a4–14). My second example, about the long and aporetic method of trying to determine which part of the soul is affected in *On Dreams*, can be paralleled by *Mem.* 449b30–450a25 and *An.* III 3.

concerned with the *distribution* of the phenomenon, and it goes as follows: if prophetic dreams were sent by the gods, one would find them not among ordinary, simple-minded people but among the most superior and intelligent of people. However, prophetic dreams are found among ordinary, simple-minded people; therefore, dreams are not sent by the gods.

Elsewhere, I have discussed the philosophical and theological presuppositions of this distribution argument (which is found elsewhere in Aristotle as well), its logical structure (in the form of a *modus tollens* argument: if A, then B; not B; therefore not A), and its usage, in a very similar context, by the author(s?) of the medical texts *On the Sacred Disease* and *Airs, Waters, Places* in his (or their?) criticism of the attribution of phenomena such as epilepsy and impotence to divine agency.[23] What interests us in the present paper is the question of how the distribution argument actually works in *On Divination in Sleep* and how it is used, for there are slight variations in the way in which it is phrased; the question is whether these variations serve a purpose in their different contexts and in the overall strategy of the argument.

Let us look at the first occurrence, right at the beginning of the text (462b12–26):[24]

Περὶ δὲ τῆς μαντικῆς τῆς ἐν τοῖς ὕπνοις γινομένης καὶ λεγομένης συμβαίνειν ἀπὸ τῶν ἐνυπνίων, οὔτε καταφρονῆσαι ῥᾴδιον οὔτε πεισθῆναι. τὸ μὲν γὰρ πάντας ἢ πολλοὺς ὑπολαμβάνειν ἔχειν τι σημειῶδες τὰ ἐνύπνια παρέχεται πίστιν ὡς ἐξ ἐμπειρίας λεγόμενον, καὶ τὸ περὶ ἐνίων εἶναι τὴν μαντικὴν ἐν τοῖς ἐνυπνίοις οὐκ ἄπιστον· ἔχει γάρ τινα λόγον· διὸ καὶ περὶ τῶν ἄλλων ἐνυπνίων ὁμοίως ἄν τις οἰηθείη. τὸ δὲ μηδεμίαν αἰτίαν εὔλογον ὁρᾶν καθ᾽ ἣν ἂν γίνοιτο, τοῦτο δὴ ἀπιστεῖν ποιεῖ· τό τε γὰρ θεὸν εἶναι τὸν πέμποντα, πρὸς τῇ ἄλλῃ ἀλογίᾳ, καὶ τὸ μὴ τοῖς βελτίστοις καὶ φρονιμωτάτοις ἀλλὰ τοῖς τυχοῦσι πέμπειν ἄτοπον. ἀφαιρεθείσης δὲ τῆς ἀπὸ τοῦ θεοῦ αἰτίας οὐδεμία τῶν ἄλλων εὔλογος εἶναι φαίνεται αἰτία· τοῦ γὰρ περὶ τῶν ἐφ᾽ Ἡρακλείαις στήλαις ἢ τῶν ἐν Βορυσθένει προορᾶν τινας ὑπὲρ τὴν ἡμετέραν εἶναι δόξειεν ἂν σύνεσιν εὑρεῖν τούτων τὴν ἀρχήν.

Concerning the divination that takes place in sleep and which is said to occur on the basis of dreams, it is not easy to frown upon it nor to believe in it. For on the one hand, (the fact) that all, or many, people suppose that dreams have something significant about them lends (the matter)

---

23   See van der Eijk 1994, 256–261 and 294–295; van der Eijk 2005b, 239–244.

24   All quotations from *On Divination in Sleep* and *On Dreams* follow Siwek's edition (1963), with occasional departures (listed in van der Eijk 1994, 100).

credibility, as something that is claimed to be the case on the basis of experience. Moreover, that concerning some things divination in dreams exists is not unreasonable, and hence one might have the same opinion about other dreams. Yet on the other hand, (the fact that) we do not see any reasonable cause by which it could occur, this is what makes us doubt. *For that it is a god who sends (these dreams), apart from being unreasonable in other respects, and that he sends (these dreams) not to the best and most intelligent but to ordinary people is absurd. However, if one eliminates the cause that comes from the god, none of the other causes appears to be reasonable; indeed, as for some people foreseeing things happening at the Pillars of Heracles or at the Borysthenes, it seems to be beyond our comprehension to find the origin of these [cases].*

This section is introductory and aporetic, and is clearly meant to make the reader think about a difficult problem. The problem is presented in the form of a dilemma. On the one hand, there are good reasons (empirical as well as theoretical) to believe that there is such a thing as divination in sleep; on the other hand, the (apparent) absence of a plausible explanation for the phenomenon makes one doubt. Whether this absence is genuine or only apparent is left open in the text by the expression "the fact that we do not see" (τὸ δὲ μηδεμίαν ... ὁρᾶν), and the implication may well be that the text is going to provide such a plausible explanation, or at least make a contribution toward it. Aristotle then explicates his claim about this (apparent) absence of a plausible explanation, again weighing two considerations against each other: on the one hand, the explanation that attributes these phenomena to gods sending such dreams is unacceptable on rational grounds; on the other hand, if one dismisses the explanation that attributes the phenomenon to a god, no other explanation can be found that accounts for the (alleged) fact that some people have prophetic dreams about events happening at the other end of the world. Stylistically, we may note the "integrative" use of the first person plural in "our comprehension" (τὴν ἡμετέραν ... σύνεσιν) in 462b25, and of a topic and comment structure (which may, but need not, be regarded as evidence of oral presentation) in the repetition of τοῦτο ("this is what makes us doubt") in 462b19 and of τούτων ("these cases") in 462b26.

In this context of raising doubts and puzzles, the "aporetizing" stage familiar from many Aristotelian investigations, the argument about the distribution of prophetic dreams is striking both for the presuppositions it makes and for the vagueness with which it is phrased. Indeed, when reading this argument, our first reaction may well be resistance. Why, we may ask, would we have to suppose that if gods sent dreams to people, they would target intelligent and morally eminent people rather than ordinary people? After all, we can think of various reasons why the gods might deliberately wish to reveal the future to ordinary and simple-minded people rather than to people who are very clever. In Plato's *Ion*, for example, we find the idea that the gods use incompetent poets as channels for their revelations so that the audience will understand that it is not the poet's own skilful imagination but a message of a higher order (534c7 ff.); and a variation of this idea occurs in the *Timaeus*, where divination is said to be given to the irrational, desiderative part of the soul (71a4). Christian readers may be reminded of Matthew 11:25, where Jesus says that God has deliberately revealed his message of salvation to simple people and concealed it from the wise, or of St. Paul's insistence on God's purposive use of human folly as a channel of his revelation (1 Corinthians 1:19–29). So, as modern readers of Aristotle, we may raise our eyebrows when reading the presupposition underlying this argument. Our sympathy to Aristotle's argument may not become greater when we read the phrase "apart from being unreasonable in other respects" (πρὸς τῇ ἄλλῃ ἀλογίᾳ), which comes across as a rather lazy, arrogant remark, casting doubt on a claim without substantiation and only acceptable to those who relate the idea criticized here to theological insights expressed elsewhere in the Aristotelian corpus.[25]

While this interpretive puzzle may just be *our* problem as modern readers of Aristotle but not problematic for those who share certain Aristotelian theological assumptions, Aristotle's claim about the alleged distribution of prophetic dreams among certain kinds of people seems even more dubious. How can this claim be justified, we might ask? Has he done empirical fieldwork? Has he interviewed a certain number of people by means of a questionnaire? Or is he just arguing on the basis of a prejudice? Surely every person has a prophetic dream every once in a while? And it would require some research to come to firm conclusions about the distribution of the phenomenon, about the relevant criteria to distinguish certain groups from others and about the possible causes to account for the phenomena. None of these points are raised in the text.

Yet on closer inspection—and here the vagueness comes in—it is not so clear what the text actually says. First, there is a question about the meaning of οἱ τυχόντες, which can either mean "random" people (thus potentially including intelligent people as well) or "ordinary", "simple-minded people" (thus excluding intelligent people). Semantically, both interpretations are possible, as are

---

25   It is very doubtful that the "theology" of the Unmoved Mover is of any relevance to the interpretation of this passage here; Aristotle seems to be arguing on a more "popular" level of religious beliefs, similar to *Nicomachean Ethics* x 9.1179a21 ff.; see van der Eijk 2005b, 243–244.

the possibilities to take μὴ ... ἀλλά as "not to these but to those" or as "not only to these but also to those".[26] One is tempted to wonder whether this ambiguity is intentional or whether it is due to our lack of ability to determine the exact semantic meaning of the Greek phrasing here. Likewise ambiguous is the status of the two parts of the sentence: is Aristotle confronting the *idea* that gods send dreams to people with the (alleged) *fact* that such dreams are found (also, or even exclusively) among ordinary people, or is he confronting the *idea* that gods send dreams to people with the *idea* that such dreams are found (also, or even exclusively) among ordinary people?[27] On the first interpretation, he is confronting an idea with (alleged) empirical counter-evidence; but then, as critical readers of Aristotle, we may immediately raise questions about the factual basis for this argument. If τυχόντες is interpreted as "random" people, we may be inclined to give Aristotle the benefit of the doubt, for we might say that the onus of proof is on those who wish to argue that prophetic dreams occur with a particular kind of people. But if τυχόντες is understood in the narrower sense of commonplace, simple-minded people, and if μὴ τοῖς φρονιμωτάτοις is understood not as "not only" but as "not", the onus of proof seems to lie with Aristotle. Aristotle does not satisfy our desire for clarification or justification here. Is this our problem? Or would the text have been equally ambiguous to Aristotle's original audience? And is the ambiguity intentional? Is Aristotle being provocative?

Possibly. But we also need to consider the second interpretation, according to which he is pointing to the absurd combination of two ideas within one and the same theory. Again, the text is not clear on these two options. As we have just seen, there was the Platonic theory according to which the gods deliberately send divination to people who do not have the rational capacities to think of these themselves and are just a medium through which the divine message comes. Aristotle may well be criticizing implicitly a Platonic idea, and his then audience may well have been expected to be able to pick this up and cast a knowing glance at each other. If this is how the text is to be understood, there is no ambiguity, though we may feel that this is a bit of an over-interpretation. If we decide that the text *is* ambiguous, we are again tempted to wonder whether this is intentional on Aristotle's part, meant to challenge his audience. The alternative would be to regard it as one of his "slips", little hints that betray, so to speak, Aristotle's not entirely satisfactory treatment

---

26   For detailed discussion of these questions, see van der Eijk 1994, 256–261.

27   Cf. J.I. Beare's translation in the Oxford Translation: "it is absurd to combine the idea that the sender of such dreams should be God with the fact that those to whom he sends them are not the best and the wisest, but merely commonplace persons".

of the subject. Yet deliberate ambiguity may well be part of Aristotle's rhetorical purpose in the opening section of the text, and the preliminary stage of the discussion makes it less urgent to make a decision as to which of the various interpretive options is to be preferred.

After this introductory section, in which a number of things are left hanging in the air, Aristotle sets out his positive views on the subject. He begins by considering the different possible ways in which dreams about future events and the actual future events they (appear to) predict may be related to each other. First, he lists the theoretical possibilities: dreams may be causes of events; dreams may be signs of events; and dreams and events may coincide without being related as causes or signs (462b26–463a3). He then examines the possibility that dreams may be signs of events, and he considers examples in which this may be the case; likewise, he does the same for the possibility that dreams may be causes of events (463a3–30). He is positive about these possibilities, and he not only provides empirical evidence but also logical explanations, using terms such as "reasonable" (εὔλογον, 463a6, οὐκ ἄλογον, 463a23), "clear" (φανερόν, 463a20), and even "necessary" (ἀνάγκη, ἀναγκαῖον, 463a20, a27). His first explicit conclusion is drawn in 463a30: "In this way, then, it is possible for some dreams to be signs as well as causes" (οὕτω μὲν οὖν ἐνδέχεται τῶν ἐνυπνίων ἔνια καὶ σημεῖα καὶ αἴτια εἶναι).

This sentence, however, is introduced by the particles μὲν οὖν, and it is followed by a sentence introduced by the particle δέ: "but the majority (of cases) appear to be matters of coincidence" (τὰ δὲ πολλὰ συμπτώμασιν ἔοικε); and the contrast is marked further by the opposition between "some" (ἔνια) and "many" (πολλά). Again, the impression is conveyed of balancing the positive and the negative, the affirmative and the sceptical elements in the investigation. And it is clear that, at least here, the sceptical part of the argument carries greater weight, as the use of "many" (πολλά, 463a31, 463b6, 463b9) and "all" (πάντα, 463b1) indicates. Aristotle goes on to point out that most cases of prophetic dreams seem to be matters of coincidence; and he gives as examples of dreams that are "extraordinary" and that are concerned with events such as a sea battle or events taking place at great distance. He says very clearly that the events apparently predicted by these dreams (contrary to those discussed in 463a3–20) do not have their origin within the dreamer; the audience is reminded of the remark in 462b24 about the dreams foreseeing events taking place at the Pillars of Heracles, the implication being that there is, indeed, no "origin" (ἀρχή) to be found of these co-occurrences: they are just a matter of coincidence.

This section (463a31–b11) breathes a different tenor from the previous sections: Aristotle expresses himself in terms of likelihood (ἔοικε, 463b1; εἰκός, 463b4; μᾶλλον δ᾽ εἰκός, 463b5–6); he also uses the phrase τί κωλύει, "what prevents?" (463b5), which may just be a rhetorical way of putting things but may also be a deliberately cautious expression.[28] The only more affirmative statement comes in 463b9–11, where he says that his account also explains why many dreams are not fulfilled, since coincidences occur neither always nor for the most part, a point that had already been anticipated in 463a2–3 by the statement that coincidences (i.e., the particular coincidence of two specific items) occur neither always nor the most part.

The conclusion that most cases of (apparently) prophetic dreams are cases of coincidence and that, for this reason, most dreams do not come true, provides the basis for Aristotle's second encounter with the idea of god-sent dreams in 463b12–18:

Ὅλως δὲ ἐπεὶ καὶ τῶν ἄλλων ζῴων ὀνειρώττει τινά, θεόπεμπτα μὲν οὐκ ἂν εἴη τὰ ἐνύπνια, οὐδὲ γέγονε τούτου χάριν, δαιμόνια μέντοι· ἡ γὰρ φύσις δαιμονία, ἀλλ' οὐ θεία. σημεῖον δέ· πάνυ γὰρ εὐτελεῖς ἄνθρωποι προορατικοί εἰσι καὶ εὐθυόνειροι, ὡς οὐ θεοῦ πέμποντος, ἀλλ' ὅσων ὥσπερ ἂν εἰ λάλος ἡ φύσις ἐστὶ καὶ μελαγχολική, παντοδαπὰς ὄψεις ὁρῶσιν· διὰ γὰρ τὸ πολλὰ καὶ παντοδαπὰ κινεῖσθαι ἐπιτυγχάνουσιν ὁμοίοις θεωρήμασιν, ἐπιτυχεῖς ὄντες ἐν τούτοις ὥσπερ ἔνιοι ἁρπάζουσιν ἐρίζοντες· ὥσπερ γὰρ καὶ λέγεται "ἂν πολλὰ βάλλῃς, ἄλλοτ' ἀλλοῖον βαλεῖς", καὶ ἐπὶ τούτων τοῦτο συμβαίνει.

In general, *since some other animals have dreams too, dreams cannot be sent by a god*, nor do they exist for this purpose; they are, however, beyond human control, for the nature (of the dreamer) is beyond human control, though not divine. A sign of this is that *quite simple-minded people are capable of having foresight and of having clear dreams, which suggests that it is not a god who sends them, but rather that all people who have, so to speak, a garrulous and melancholic nature, see all kinds of visions (in their sleep).* For on account of their being subjected to many movements of various kinds, they hit upon images that resemble (future events), their success in dealing with these being similar to the way in which some people snatch away the prize in a competition: for as the saying goes, "if you throw the dice many times, you will throw a different result every time".

---

28   463b5–6: τί γὰρ κωλύει καὶ ἐν τοῖς ὕπνοις οὕτως; μᾶλλον δ' εἰκὸς πολλὰ τοιαῦτα συμβαίνειν. See
      also 464a9–10, where the tone is more affirmative: "nothing prevents" (οὕτως οὐδὲν κωλύει
      κίνησίν τινα καὶ αἴσθησιν ἀφικνεῖσθαι).

At the beginning of the passage quoted, Aristotle marks a transition in the argument by means of ὅλως δέ, "Generally speaking ...". This transition is first of all meant to meet a possible reaction to the conclusion just reached, namely that for the "extraordinary" cases such as those just mentioned, one might be tempted to attribute them to a god; thus the argument mirrors that in 462a24–26, where Aristotle argued that, if one eliminates the explanation that attributes dreams such as those predicting events happening at the Pillars of Heracles to a god sending them, no other explanation seems available. At the same time, the words "in general" also give the argument a wider scope, not just restricted to the exceptional cases referred to in the previous section.[29] Aristotle's point here seems to be that invoking divine agency only in exceptional cases is a flawed argumentative strategy: if the gods were involved in sending dreams, they would not do so only in special cases, nor would the distribution of dreams among certain kinds of people be the way it is.[30]

The distribution argument is here used in two ways. First, Aristotle argues that since some animals also dream, dreams are not sent by the gods. Again, this argument is based on some presuppositions that remain unarticulated in *Divination in Sleep*, namely that dreams in animals are not sent by the gods and that, if some dreams can be shown not to be of divine origin, this will apply to all dreams in general (ὅλως). And again, readers of Aristotle (both ancient and modern) may feel some resistance against this argument. Why would it be obvious that the gods do not send dreams to animals? This view was not unheard of in the ancient world and can be found among Pythagoreans. And why would it be obvious that, if some dreams were not sent by the gods, this applied to all dreams in general? After all, one might think that it is not necessary that *all* dreams are god-sent, or that it is not necessary that *all* dreams are prophetic. Classification of dreams into various types was popular in the ancient world. It is already found in Homer, in the well-known metaphor of the gates of horn and ivory in the *Odyssey* (xix 560 ff.), which distinguishes between true and false dreams (and one may think of Zeus's deceptive dream sent to Agamemnon), and in the fourth book of the medical work (attributed to Hippocrates) *On Regimen*, which differentiates between dreams of a divine origin and dreams that have a physical origin (chapter 89). Later Greek thought on dreams made even more elaborate distinctions between various kinds of dreams. Aristotle does not address these counter-arguments, and background

---

29   The traditional chapter division in most modern editions is somewhat unsatisfactory here as it disrupts what is, in reality, a continuous argument.

30   For a detailed interpretation of the argument here and its underlying presuppositions, see van der Eijk 1994, 289–297.

information is needed in order to see why they would not impress him: the idea seems to be that it is unacceptable, within Aristotle's ideas about gods and about nature, that a god incidentally and *ad hoc* uses a natural phenomenon to serve a purpose that is different from its normal, natural goal. It is possible that Aristotle took it for granted that his audience would be familiar with these presuppositions. But as a modern reader of the text one may find that it is somewhat unsatisfactory that we do not get this background information presented here.

Yet there is also a second, more positive point to be made concerning the argument about the distribution of dreams among humans: for some of the ambiguities that characterized the first presentation (462b20–25) have here disappeared. Aristotle clearly presents as a fact, not just as an idea held by others, that quite simple-minded people have prophetic dreams; and he clearly refers to people who are positively simple-minded (εὐτελεῖς), not to random people, which may include intelligent as well as simple-minded people. And the reason for this also becomes clear now, for he explains foresight in sleep by reference to the specific nature (φύσις) of certain kinds of people. For while, perhaps, an intelligent person may sometimes have a prophetic dream (which may be a matter of coincidence), in the case of the simple-minded people there is a clear tendency or capacity, as marked by the ending *-ikoi* in the adjective προορατικοί. And his reference, in the next sentence, to "people with a garrulous and melancholic nature" underscores this, again, with the reference to their nature (φύσις) showing that in their case there is a natural, constitutional explanation for the phenomenon. The conclusion is that in these cases, foresight is just a matter of what we would call statistical probability and thus, in Aristotle's terms, still a matter of coincidence (σύμπτωμα): the more images one sees, the greater the likelihood that one may encounter an image that happens to correspond with an actual event in the future. And since some people, by nature, have more associative minds, they see more images and have therefore a greater chance to see the future. The implication—which is, however, not spelled out in the text—is that such cases of foresight belong to the category of coincidences, i.e., dreams stand to the events they resemble as συμπτώματα.

Aristotle goes on (in 463b22) to say that the fact that many dreams are not fulfilled is in no way surprising.[31] This point had already been made in 463b9–11;

---

[31]   ὅτι δ᾿ οὐκ ἀποβαίνει πολλὰ τῶν ἐνυπνίων, οὐδὲν ἄτοπον· Again, contrary to editorial practice, it is better not to introduce a new paragraph here but to print the texts as one continuous argument. On paragraph marking in Aristotle, see Netz 2001.

but it becomes more understandable in connection with the other point just made: that many dreams do not come true is *therefore* in no way surprising. And the implication is that, on the assumption that prophetic dreams are sent by the gods, the undeniable fact that most of them remain unfulfilled does actually pose a problem, at least to those who share some fundamental beliefs about what sort of things may or may not be attributed to gods. There is an enlightened tenor noticeable here, in expressions such as "in no way surprising" (οὐδὲν ἄτοπον, 463b23), whereas the occurrence of prophetic dreams among simple-minded people was labeled ἄτοπον ("out of place", "surprising", "contrary to expectation", "absurd") in the context of the theory that attributed prophetic dreams to the gods (462b22).[32] This enlightening tenor continues in the following lines, where Aristotle goes on to point out that this—the non-occurrence of the predicted event not being at all surprising or problematic, 463b22–23—even applies to the hypothetical scenario in which the fulfilment of the dream would have presented a case in which the dream is related to the actual event as its cause or its sign; for even in such scenarios, Aristotle argues, there is a possibility that the event signified by the sign does not happen as a result of interference by other, more powerful movements. Likewise, the process of a cause leading to an effect may be overruled by other, more powerful causes. Aristotle then makes another generalization (ὅλως), saying that, "In general, that which was about to happen (τὸ μελλῆσαν) is not the same as that which will actually take place in the future (τὸ ἐσόμενον)" and thus sounding a more general note of caution about the uncertainty of prediction in the light of the contingency of some future events. At the same time, he insists (ὅμως) that this does not mean that in such cases the use of the terms ἀρχή and σημεῖον is inappropriate, for they apply to genuine situations that are different from situations in which the resemblance of a dream with an actual future event would have been a matter of coincidence. The point of this insistence is probably to enhance the rhetorical plausibility of Aristotle's own theory by showing that his account of divination in terms of cause and sign still stands. But the reference to causes and signs also leads on to the next section (463b31 ff.), in which Aristotle returns to the kinds of cases he had already been dealing with in 463a31 ff., and which he had explained there as a matter of coincidence:

---

32   462b20–22: τό τε γὰρ θεὸν εἶναι τὸν πέμποντα, πρὸς τῇ ἄλλῃ ἀλογίᾳ, καὶ τὸ μὴ τοῖς βελτίστοις καὶ φρονιμωτάτοις ἀλλὰ τοῖς τυχοῦσι πέμπειν ἄτοπον.

περὶ δὲ τῶν μὴ τοιαύτας ἐχόντων ἀρχὰς ἐνυπνίων οἵας εἴπομεν, ἀλλ' ὑπερορίας ἢ τοῖς χρόνοις ἢ τοῖς τόποις ἢ τοῖς μεγέθεσιν, ἢ τούτων μὲν μηδέν, μὴ μέντοι γε ἐν αὑτοῖς ἐχόντων τὰς ἀρχὰς τῶν ἰδόντων τὸ ἐνύπνιον, εἰ μὴ γίνεται τὸ προορᾶν ἀπὸ συμπτώματος, τοιόνδ' ἂν εἴη μᾶλλον ἢ ὥσπερ λέγει Δημόκριτος εἴδωλα καὶ ἀπορροίας αἰτιώμενος.

As for dreams that do not have such origins as we described,[33] but origins that are extravagant in time, place, or size, or in none of these respects but without those who see the dream having the origin in themselves: if foresight of the future (in these cases) does not occur as a result of coincidence, it is more likely to be as follows than as Democritus says, who adduces idols and emanations as causes.

The terms in which Aristotle defines the field of investigation here are virtually identical to those (stated in 463b1–2) in which he had introduced the category of cases in which dreams and the events they appear to predict are related to each other as συμπτώματα (τά τε ὑπερβατὰ πάντα καὶ ὧν μὴ ἐν αὑτοῖς ἡ ἀρχή, ἀλλὰ περὶ ναυμαχίας καὶ τῶν πόρρω συμβαινόντων ἐστίν). There is, however, one slight but potentially significant difference: whereas in 463b1–2, the dreams themselves are called "extraordinary" (ὑπερβατά), in 464a1–4 it is their ἀρχαί, their origins or starting points, that are said to be extraordinary (ὑπερόριαι).[34] Here, he seems to be envisaging the same kinds of dreams but under the presupposition that prophecy is not due to coincidence. Note, again, the topic-comment style of composition: the topic is announced by περί, "as for", the comment is expressed by a conditional clause followed by a main clause in which the subject is vaguely to be understood from the preceding cluster, referred to as τὸ προορᾶν, "foresight". Note also the cautious—but perhaps ironical, or quasi-modest—phrase "it is more likely to be as follows (τοιόν δ' ἂν εἴη μᾶλλον) than as Democritus says".

Then the explanation itself follows (464a4–24):

ὥσπερ γὰρ ὅταν κινήσῃ τι τὸ ὕδωρ ἢ τὸν ἀέρα, τοῦθ' ἕτερον ἐκίνησε, καὶ παυσαμένου ἐκείνου συμβαίνει τὴν τοιαύτην κίνησιν προϊέναι μέχρι τινός, τοῦ κινήσαντος οὐ παρόντος, οὕτως οὐδὲν κωλύει κίνησίν τινα καὶ αἴσθησιν ἀφικνεῖσθαι πρὸς τὰς ψυχὰς τὰς ἐνυπνιαζούσας (ἀφ' ὧν ἐκεῖνος τὰ εἴδωλα ποιεῖ καὶ τὰς

33   There is a difficulty as to what τοιαύτας ... ἀρχάς ... οἵας εἴπομεν refers to; for discussion, see van der Eijk 1994, 306–307.

34   On the significance of this difference, see van der Eijk 1994, 307.

ἀπορροίας), καὶ ὅπῃ δὴ ἔτυχεν ἀφικνουμένας μᾶλλον αἰσθητὰς εἶναι νύκτωρ διὰ τὸ μεθ' ἡμέραν φερομένας διαλύεσθαι μᾶλλον (ἀταραχωδέστερος γὰρ ὁ ἀὴρ τῆς νυκτὸς διὰ τὸ νηνεμωτέρας εἶναι τὰς νύκτας), καὶ ἐν τῷ σώματι ποιεῖν αἴσθησιν διὰ τὸν ὕπνον, διὰ τὸ καὶ τῶν μικρῶν κινήσεων τῶν ἐντὸς αἰσθάνεσθαι καθεύ-δοντας μᾶλλον ἢ ἐγρηγορότας. αὗται δ'αἱ κινήσεις φαντάσματα ποιοῦσιν, ἐξ ὧν προορῶσι τὰ μέλλοντα καὶ περὶ τῶν τοιούτων, καὶ διὰ ταῦτα συμβαίνει τὸ πάθος τοῦτο τοῖς τυχοῦσι καὶ οὐ τοῖς φρονιμωτάτοις. μεθ' ἡμέραν τε γὰρ ἐγίνετ' ἂν καὶ τοῖς σοφοῖς, εἰ θεὸς ἦν ὁ πέμπων· οὕτω δ' εἰκὸς τοὺς τυχόντας προορᾶν· ἡ γὰρ διάνοια τῶν τοιούτων οὐ φροντιστική, ἀλλ' ὥσπερ ἔρημος καὶ κενὴ πάντων, καὶ κινηθεῖσα κατὰ τὸ κινοῦν ἄγεται.

Just as when something sets water in motion or air, and this moves some-thing else, and when the one has stopped exercising motion such a move-ment continues until it reaches a certain point, where the original moving agent is not present, likewise *nothing prevents* a certain movement and sense-perception from arriving at the dreaming souls, proceeding from the objects from which he (Democritus) says the idols and the emana-tions proceed, and in whatever way they arrive, (nothing prevents them from being) more clearly perceptible at night, because during the day they are scattered more easily—for at night the air is less turbulent because there is less wind at night—and from bringing about sense-perception in the body because of sleep, for the same reason we also perceive small movements inside us better when we are asleep than when we are awake. These movements cause appearances, on the basis of which people fore-see the future even about these things. This is also why this experience occurs with simple-minded people and not with the most intelligent. For it would present itself both during the day and to intelligent people, if it were a god who sent (these dreams). But *in the way in which we have explained it, it is quite plausible* that it is simple-minded people who fore-see the future; for the mind of such people is as it were empty and devoid of everything, and once set in motion, it is carried away by whatever it is that sets it in motion.

Everything seems to fall into place now: the (alleged) fact that it is simple-minded people rather than intelligent people who have such prophetic dreams, can now be accounted for by reference to the psychological mechanism described. The (alleged) distribution of the phenomenon would be problem-atic if we were to assume that gods sent dreams; but in the way Aristotle explains it, it is entirely plausible (οὕτω δ' εἰκός, 464a22). Readers of Aristotle may still feel inclined to raise the counter-objection that surely, occasionally,

an intelligent person may have a prophetic dream every once in a while. But
by now, they can be satisfied that this counter-argument can be addressed in
two ways: (i) we are here in the restricted context of dreams about "extraordinary" cases, not the cases of dreaming about bodily states and dreaming
about actions that the dreamer himself is going to perform in the future; (ii)
we are here concerned with dreams in which there are, after all, some causal
connections between dream and event, and foresight is not just a matter of
coincidence.

It is not that Aristotle takes the trouble to spell this all out, and again the
text is highly challenging in terms of what it demands from its readers for a
full comprehension of the points made. But it may help to remind ourselves,
again, of what Aristotle said in the beginning (462b24–26) about the puzzling phenomenon of people dreaming about future events occurring at the
Pillars of Heracles (clearly an example of an extreme, ὑπερόριος case), "finding the origin of which" was said "to *appear* (italics mine) to be beyond our
understanding" (ὑπὲρ τὴν ἡμετέραν εἶναι δόξειεν ἂν σύνεσιν εὑρεῖν τούτων τὴν
ἀρχήν). This perplexity now turns out to be only apparent: for while, half-way
through the argument, Aristotle seemed to dismiss these cases as matters of
coincidence, he now offers an alternative explanation where the result is not
a matter of coincidence (μὴ ἀπὸ συμπτώματος, 464a4–5) and where the ἀρχή of
the phenomenon *can* be found. Hence the variation in formulation between
463b1, where dreams were said to be ὑπερβατά, and 464a1, where the ἀρχαί
of dreams were said to be ὑπερόριαι, a subtle syntactical difference that now
turns out to be functional. It also turns out that this explanation only works
for people with low intellectual capacities, for their specific state of mind—
their διάνοια, as 464a22 puts it, or their φύσις, as 463a17 called it—is needed
to explain their receptivity to the small movements arriving over great distance.

We see here a further reason why the distribution argument is employed
three times: it is not just used for polemical purposes (against the idea that
dreams are sent by the gods) but it also plays a constructive role in Aristotle's
positive explanation of foresight under certain circumstances. For whereas
the case of an intelligent person having a prophetic dream about something
actually happening the next day at the Pillars of Heracles can only be regarded
as a matter of coincidence, the case of a simple-minded person having a
prophetic dream about something actually happening the next day at the
Pillars of Heracles may *also*, alternatively, be the result of the mechanism of
transmission of movement described in 464a4–19.

Aristotle then proceeds to provide an additional argument by referring to
the contrast between day and night: if the gods were the senders of messages

about the future, they would provide them during the waking state rather than during sleep (464a19–20); and this reduces the likelihood that the gods are in any way behind the phenomenon of prophetic dreams, whereas Aristotle's own explanation of the phenomenon in terms of the transmission of movements due to atmospheric circumstances gives their nightly appearance a greater likelihood. Again, the presupposition that gods, if they revealed the future to people at all, would prefer to do so by day rather than by night is taken for granted in this context, but it can be connected with Aristotle's ideas about gods elsewhere in his works.[35]

Aristotle's argument thus has a strong "enlightening" tenor: after initial difficulties, all puzzles are resolved and phenomena that are difficult to account for in other theories are shown to make perfect sense within the account Aristotle has given. Thus the initial rhetoric of uncertainty, openness, and exploration gives way to a rhetoric of confidence and achievement, clearly marked by the final words of the treatise: "We have now discussed divination on the basis of dreams in its entirety (περὶ πάσης)" (464b18).

v   Explanatory Principles and Expository Techniques in *On Dreams*

My second example is taken from *On Dreams*, the treatise that precedes *On Divination in Sleep* in the *Parva Naturalia*. I can be briefer here, since I have already covered some of this material in earlier work, where I also discussed the apparent doctrinal tensions between the two treatises.[36] I will leave those issues aside and focus here on what in our editions is presented as the first chapter of *On Dreams*, which provides a further example of exploratory discourse in Aristotle (458a33–459a22). Yet this time, alongside expository techniques such as those we have already seen above, we also encounter a stronger, more explicit use of explanatory principles. In this opening part of the text, Aristotle addresses the question of which part of the soul dreaming is an "affection" (πάθος):

> Μετὰ δὲ ταῦτα περὶ ἐνυπνίου ἐπιζητητέον, καὶ πρῶτον τίνι τῶν τῆς ψυχῆς φαίνεται, καὶ πότερον τοῦ νοητικοῦ τὸ πάθος ἐστὶ τοῦτο ἢ τοῦ αἰσθητικοῦ.

---

35   See van der Eijk 1994, 319.
36   See van der Eijk 1994, 36–38 and 62–67.

> After this, we must investigate the dream, and first of all to which (part) of
> the soul it appears, and whether this affection belongs to the intellectual
> or to the sensitive (part).

This very question, and the conceptual background it presupposes (parts of the
soul, affection), is familiar from other Aristotelian psychological writings; and
indeed the whole chapter contains a number of such explanatory principles
well known from other parts of Aristotelian philosophy, such as the concept of
phantasia, or the idea of something being the same in extension but different
in essence or definition (459a15–17). Indeed, Aristotle explicitly marks the close
connection with other works by means of a cross-reference to his discussion
of *phantasia* in *On the Soul* (459a15). Clearly, he is not addressing an audience
of beginners here, and the integrative use of the first person plural "we" is
clearly meant not so much in the sense of "we human beings" but rather "we
researchers".

 Yet it is once again striking how undogmatic and open-minded Aristotle's
approach to the object of investigation is. The chapter provides a good illustra-
tion of Aristotle's "problematizing" approach. He considers two possibilities,
i.e., that dreams belong either to the sensitive or to the rational part of the
soul, and he takes it for granted that these are the only options. Yet after less
than one page, both these possibilities have been rejected: in 458b9, we read
that "It is clear that we do not perceive anything in our sleep; therefore, it
is not by means of sensation that we perceive the dream". And immediately
following on from this, he says "nor is it by means of opinion" (δῆλον ὅτι οὐκ
αἰσθανόμεθα οὐδὲν ἐν τοῖς ὕπνοις· οὐκ ἄρα γε τῇ αἰσθήσει τὸ ἐνύπνιον αἰσθανόμεθα.
ἀλλὰ μὴν οὐδὲ τῇ δόξῃ). There is a kind of chiastic structure here: first we get
considerations (458b3–9) on account of which we conclude that it is not by
sensation that we dream (458b9–10); then we first get the conclusion, "Nor it is
it by means of opinion", which is followed by a number of arguments (458b10–
25). The arguments themselves are not in all cases easy to understand,[37] but
the conclusions are clear enough, and they are marked by the use of δῆλον: "it
is clear (δῆλον) that we do not perceive anything in sleep, and therefore it is not
by sensation that we perceive dreams" (458b9). And in 458b24–25: "It is therefore clear (ὥστε δῆλον) that not every image that appears in sleep is a dream
and that what we think (in sleep) we think by opinion" (ὥστε δῆλον ὅτι οὐκ ἐνύπνιον πᾶν τὸ ἐν ὕπνῳ φάντασμα, καὶ ὅτι ὃ ἐννοοῦμεν τῇ δόξῃ δοξάζομεν). In other
words, dreaming does not come about through *doxa*, for the working of *doxa*

---

37   For a detailed discussion, see van der Eijk 1994, 139–147.

in sleep is manifest in the thoughts that may accompany dream images. At 458b25, then, we are back to square one.

Aristotle then makes a fresh start, again using δῆλον right at the beginning of the sentence, and suggesting that an inspection of the phenomenon of error (ἀπάτη) may shed light on the problem: "At least so much is clear on all these things that the same [part, faculty] by which we are deceived even in the waking state, when we are in a state of illness, that this very same [part, faculty] causes this affection (i.e., error) also in sleep" (δῆλον δὲ περὶ τούτων ἁπάντων τό γε τοσοῦτον, ὅτι τῷ αὐτῷ ᾧ καὶ ἐγρηγορότες ἐν ταῖς νόσοις ἀπατώμεθα, ὅτι τοῦτ' αὐτὸ καὶ ἐν τῷ ὕπνῳ ποιεῖ τὸ πάθος). But then immediately an objection is raised against this suggestion, as indicated by ἀλλά (458b29–459a1):

> ἀλλ' εἴτε δὴ ταὐτὸν εἴθ' ἕτερον τὸ φανταστικὸν τῆς ψυχῆς καὶ τὸ αἰσθητικόν, οὐδὲν ἧττον οὐ γίνεται ἄνευ τοῦ ὁρᾶν καὶ αἰσθάνεσθαί τι· τὸ γὰρ παρορᾶν καὶ παρακούειν ὁρῶντος ἀληθές τι καὶ ἀκούοντος, οὐ μέντοι τοῦτο ὃ οἴεται. ἐν δὲ τῷ ὕπνῳ ὑπόκειται μηδὲν ὁρᾶν μηδ' ἀκούειν μηδ' ὅλως αἰσθάνεσθαι.

> Yet regardless of whether the imaginative [part] of the soul and the sensitive [part] are different or identical, it is no less the case that [this affection, i.e., error] does not take place without seeing and perceiving something, for erroneous seeing and hearing take place when someone sees and hears something that is really there, except that it is not what one thinks it is. Yet the assumption is that in sleep there is no seeing nor hearing nor indeed perceiving at all.

The question of whether the *phantastikon* and the *aisthêtikon* are identical or different arises because the faculty or part that is responsible for error that was left unnamed in the previous sentence (τῷ αὐτῷ ᾧ ... ἀπατώμεθα, ... τοῦτ' αὐτό ...) is, in fact, *to phantastikon*. This is left implicit here, but readers familiar with Aristotle's psychology will probably be expected to work this out for themselves. The question is suspended here, probably because whatever the answer to it may be, it does not address the problem posed by the following objection, i.e., that perceptual error requires the presence of perception. The answer to the question is given only later, at the end of the chapter in 459a16–17, when the objection raised in the present passage (458b29–459a1) has been dealt with. In that final section of the chapter (459a15–22), we will also hear that it is, after all, the imaginative part of the soul (*to phantastikon*) that is affected in the case of dreaming, and thus represents a crucial factor to the solution to the puzzle. Yet in the present stage of the argument (458b29–459a1), Aristotle immediately raises an objection to the suggestion that dreaming may be a matter of *phantasia*. We may suspect that the reason for this arrangement is that the suggestion that dreaming may be a matter of *phantasia* has to be subjected to refinement before being capable of acceptance, i.e., it needs to be demonstrated how it stands up to the scrutiny expressed in the objection raised against it at the earlier stage of the investigation.

The interceding discussion is meant to achieve just that: for Aristotle postpones the solution to the puzzle and makes a few more points that are necessary (459a1–8):

ἆρ' οὖν τὸ μὲν μὴ ὁρᾶν μηδὲν ἀληθές, τὸ δὲ μηδὲν πάσχειν τὴν αἴσθησιν οὐκ ἀληθές, ἀλλ' ἐνδέχεται καὶ τὴν ὄψιν πάσχειν τι καὶ τὰς ἄλλας αἰσθήσεις, ἕκαστον δὲ τούτων ὥσπερ ἐγρηγορότος προσβάλλει μέν πως τῇ αἰσθήσει, οὐχ οὕτω δὲ ὥσπερ ἐγρηγορότος· καὶ ὁτὲ μὲν ἡ δόξα λέγει ὅτι ψεῦδος, ὥσπερ ἐγρηγορόσιν, ὁτὲ δὲ κατέχεται καὶ ἀκολουθεῖ τῷ φαντάσματι;

Could it be, then, that it is true that there is no seeing [in sleep], but that it is not true that sensation is not affected [in sleep], and is it possible both for vision and for the other senses to be affected [in sleep], and that each of these [affections] somehow impinges on the sense faculty, as it does to someone in the waking state, yet not in the same way as to someone in the waking state? And [could it be that] on some occasions opinion says [in sleep] that [what appears in sleep] is false, as it does in people who are awake, while on other occasions it is withheld from doing so and follows the appearance?

Aristotle here tentatively suggests a solution that meets the various objections raised. He raises it in the form of a question (ἆρ' οὖν), and he uses cautious expressions such as "in a certain way" (πως) and "is it possible" (ἐνδέχεται). He suggests ways in which sensation, without being *active* in sleep (which was the point of the first section: 458b3, χρῆσις), may nevertheless be capable of being affected (πάσχειν) in sleep, and he suggests ways in which opinion (*doxa*) may be operational in sleep after all. At the same time, he is careful to point out that the ways in which sensation and opinion may be involved are different in sleep from how they are in the waking state, and he goes on to say that it is this difference whose understanding is crucial to the solution to the problem (459a8–11):

ὅτι μὲν οὖν οὐκ ἔστι τοῦ δοξάζοντος οὐδὲ τοῦ διανοουμένου τὸ πάθος τοῦτο ὃ καλοῦμεν ἐνυπνιάζειν, φανερόν. ἀλλ' οὐδὲ τοῦ αἰσθανομένου ἁπλῶς· ὁρᾶν γὰρ ἂν ἦν καὶ ἀκούειν ἁπλῶς. ἀλλὰ πῶς δὴ καὶ τίνα τρόπον, ἐπισκεπτέον.

That the affection we call dreaming is not (an affection) of the judging nor of the thinking (part? person?) is evident (φανερόν), then. Yet neither can it be an affection of the perceiving (part? person?) in an unqualified sense, for then it would be seeing and hearing in an unqualified sense. Rather, we must investigate in what sense and in what way [it is an affection of the perceiving part/person].

This reads as if the suggestion just made in the preceding lines (459a1–8) is temporarily left hanging in the air and as if Aristotle recapitulates points he has already made before (as the particle combination μὲν οὖν indicates). The mention of *doxa* is probably prompted by the fact that *doxa* has just been mentioned in the previous sentence. Clearly, then, dreaming is not a matter of opinion or judgment. This leaves sensation as the remaining possibility; but the crucial point—and this is the insight gained from the tentative section 459a1–8—is how and in what manner dreaming can be said to be an affection of the sensitive part of the soul. This is an understandable line of thought. But then, somewhat surprisingly, a new thought is being introduced:

ὑποκείσθω μὲν οὖν, ὅπερ ἐστὶ καὶ φανερόν, ὅτι τοῦ αἰσθητικοῦ τὸ πάθος, εἴπερ καὶ ὁ ὕπνος· οὐ γὰρ ἄλλῳ μέν τινι τῶν ζῴων ὑπάρχει ὁ ὕπνος, ἄλλῳ δὲ τὸ ἐνυπνιάζειν, ἀλλὰ τῷ αὐτῷ.

It must be assumed, which is evident anyway, that if sleep is an affection of the sensitive part of the soul, [dreaming] must be an affection of the sensitive part of the soul as well. For it is not that sleep occurs with one living being and dreaming with another, but they occur with the same living being.[38]

One might react by saying that this is fair enough; but one may feel that it is somewhat late for Aristotle to introduce this point at this stage, especially when it is so "evident" (φανερόν). That sleeping is an affection of the sensitive part of the soul had, indeed, been pointed out in *On Sleep and Waking*, a treatise that precedes *On Dreams* and with which, we may assume, Aristotle took his audience to be familiar. So why has it not been introduced earlier if it is so important and relevant? Has Aristotle exaggerated his use of exploratory discourse and have we been wasting our time?

---

38   On the various interpretive problems in this sentence, see van der Eijk 1994, 153–154.

Perhaps the answer is that Aristotle regards the relevance of this consideration, i.e., that sleeping is an affection of the sensitive part of the soul, for the investigation about dreams not as something immediately obvious, but as something that needs to be spelled out. This is indicated also by 459a20: "for we call dream the image that appears in sleep" (τὸ γὰρ ἐν ὕπνῳ φάντασμα ἐνύπνιον λέγομεν). Aristotle is cautious here, and does not take things for granted. We can easily imagine this remark being made in the form of a question in a Platonic dialogue. It is part of his step-by-step method of reasoning. And the reasons for this caution will become clear enough later on in chapter 3 of *On Dreams*, when he discusses borderline experiences between sleeping and waking and wonders to what extent such experiences can be regarded as dreams (462a8–31). Yet there is also a more pedagogical reason, again to do with *taxis*, the order of the exposition, why Aristotle did not introduce this "argument from sleep" at an earlier stage; for if he had stated right at the beginning that, since sleep is an affection of the sensitive part of the soul, dreaming must be so too, this would have sounded very dogmatic, and it would have made the whole discussion of the role of *phantasia* and *doxa* in sleep completely superfluous. Moreover, it is much more satisfactory and rhetorically persuasive to arrive at the conclusion that dreaming is an affection of the sensitive part of the soul after the most important alternative—that it might be an affection of the rational part of the soul—has been eliminated. Having shown that dreaming cannot be an affection of the rational part of the soul, it *must be considered as established* (ὑποκείσθω) that it belongs to the sensitive part of the soul. This establishment is strengthened by the consideration—which had already been established in the previous treatise—that sleep, too, is an affection of the sensitive part of the soul.

Aristotle then draws the conclusion that dreaming is an affection of the sensitive part of the soul in its capacity as the imaginative part of the soul:

> ἐπεὶ δὲ περὶ φαντασίας ἐν τοῖς Περὶ ψυχῆς εἴρηται, καὶ ἔστι μὲν τὸ αὐτὸ τῷ αἰσθητικῷ τὸ φανταστικόν, τὸ δ᾽ εἶναι φανταστικῷ καὶ αἰσθητικῷ ἕτερον, ἔστι δ᾽ ἡ φαντασία ἡ ὑπὸ τῆς κατ᾽ ἐνέργειαν αἰσθήσεως γινομένη κίνησις, τὸ δ᾽ ἐνύπνιον φάντασμά τι φαίνεται εἶναι (τὸ γὰρ ἐν ὕπνῳ φάντασμα ἐνύπνιον λέγομεν, εἴθ᾽ ἁπλῶς εἴτε τρόπον τινὰ γινόμενον), φανερὸν ὅτι τοῦ αἰσθητικοῦ μέν ἐστι τὸ ἐνυπνιάζειν, τούτου δ᾽ ἡ φανταστικόν.
>
> 459b13–22

Since we have talked about imagination in *On the Soul*, and since the imaginative [part] is identical to the sensitive, yet being is different for the imaginative and the sensitive [part], and since imagination is the movement that takes place on account of sensation in actuality, and since the dream appears to be an image (for we say that a dream is the image that appears in sleep, either in an unqualified sense or occurring in a particular way), it is evident that dreaming is an affection of the sensitive [part], yet this in its capacity of the imaginative [part].

Thus Aristotle's argument is once again carefully structured, and all the cautions, qualifications, and also counter-arguments from the preceding sections are being addressed; moreover, it turns out why they have been raised, and why it is important to have considered them at the appropriate place and stage of the argument. He clarifies the relationship between sensation and imagination by reminding his audience of what was said in *On the Soul*; he also resolves the difficulty about there no being sensation in actuality in sleep by showing that there does not have to be such actuality (ἐνέργεια) of sensation for *phantasia* nevertheless to take place (γίνεσθαι); he establishes a connection between dreaming and *phantasia* on the basis of ordinary language; and he picks up the point about the special way in which such dream images may come about, thereby anticipating (but the audience does not know this yet) clarifications and definitions that will become relevant later on in the argument.

Conclusion

I hope to have shown that analyzing Aristotle's methods as a writer in this way is not a matter of being unduly charitable to his practice as a pedagogic teacher of philosophy. His use of exploratory discourse, characterized by caution and a searching attitude in the manner in which ideas and arguments are presented, and his use of arrangement, repetition, and refinement are recurrent and effective features in the Aristotelian *pragmateiai* we have studied. I am confident that this kind of research can be extended to other Aristotelian writings and, indeed, to other authors of scientific treatises, for example Galen.[39] And my

---

39   See van der Eijk 2013, 169 in relation to Galen: "Depending on the circumstances, subject matter and rhetorical strategy, an author can choose to create an impression of openness and unpredictability of the outcome of the investigation; he may even emphasize the difficulty or complexity of what he is examining, e.g., by raising questions or stating that things are difficult or by otherwise sounding caution. In Aristotle, for example, this 'raising of problems' (διαπορεῖν) is part of the dialectical stage of the discussion and has an important epistemic, heuristic purpose. Alternatively, it can be motivated by pedagogic considerations, trying to involve an audience of students into a collective intellectual

sense is that further analysis of Aristotle's methods of exposition will reveal more aspects of his repertoire of techniques as a persuasive instructor and will contribute to a better appreciation of the communicative and pragmatic aspects of Aristotelian philosophizing.

---

challenge or to instil a sense of seriousness and devotion. Yet it can also arise from a desire, on the author's part, to create a sense of suspense: as the investigation proceeds, the difficulties and complexities become bigger and bigger and the reader is made curious and led to wonder where it will all end—and then suddenly there is a breakthrough in the argument, everything falls into place and the solution to all the difficulties has been found. Such a technique of creating suspense followed by resolution can, of course, enhance the audience's admiration for the masterly and seemingly magical skills of the lead-investigator; and if the investigation has been presented as a collective enterprise, the audience will share in the success and there will be a communal sense of achievement and satisfaction".

CHAPTER 7

The Place of the *De Motu Animalium* in Aristotle's Natural Philosophy

Andrea Falcon

Abstract

The opening lines of the *Meteorology* suggest that Aristotle was centrally concerned with the integration of a range of different natural investigations into a single program of study. This essay will attempt to illustrate how this integration is achieved by looking at the place of the *De Motu Animalium* (hereafter *De Motu*) in Aristotle's natural philosophy. At least at first sight, this short but difficult treatise does not seem to be a very promising case. It has been argued that the *De Motu* does not belong to natural philosophy (or to any other Aristotelian science for that matter). On this interpretation, the *De Motu* would be an "interdisciplinary work" or even "a [deliberate and fruitful] departure from the *Organon* model" (Martha Nussbaum, Aristotle's *De Motu Animalium*. Princeton 1978: 113). Hopefully, a fresh look at the opening lines of the *De Motu* will help, not only to establish *that* it pertains to natural philosophy, but also to show *how* it contributes to the explanatory project pursued by Aristotle.

Introduction

We have already discussed the first causes of nature and all natural motion, also the stars ordered in the motion of the heavens, and the bodily elements, [establishing] their number, nature, and mutual transformation, and generation and perishing in general. There remains for consideration a part of this investigation that all earlier thinkers called meteorology. It is concerned with events that are natural, though their order is less perfect than that of the first element of bodies. They take place in the region nearest to the motion of the stars, such as the Milky Way, the comets, and the inflamed and moving portents. It studies also all the affections we may posit common to air and water, and the kind and parts of the earth and the affections of its parts. These shed light on the causes of winds and earthquakes and all the consequences the motions of these kinds and parts involve. Some of these things puzzle us while others

admit of explanation in some degree. Furthermore, it is concerned with
the falling of thunderbolts, whirlwinds, fire-winds, and the other recurrent affections produced in these same bodies by concretion. Once we will
have gone through these things, we will consider whether we are somehow able to give, in accordance with the method indicated, an account of
animals and plants, both in general and separately. Once this is discussed,
perhaps the whole of what we established at the outset will be completed.

> *Meteorology* I 1.338a20–339a10

By definition a sketch does not contain all the information one might want,
or even all the information one might need. The sketch offered in the opening
lines of the *Meteorology* is no exception to the rule. These lines are not meant to
give us a complete list of investigations, let alone a complete list of writings that
correspond to those investigations. I illustrate this point with two examples.
First, we are told that the study of nature is not complete without a study
of "animals and plants, both in general and separately". Yet we are not told
what it takes to study animals and plants, and study them both in general
and separately.[1] Second, there is no reference to the study of the soul in the
opening lines of the *Meteorology*. In fact, it is far from obvious that this study
is conceived by Aristotle as an integral part of the explanatory project outlined
by the philosopher. Some scholars have maintained that the *De Anima* can be
fully integrated within the study of animals. On their view, the role of the *De
Anima* is equivalent to a philosophical introduction to the study of life. Others
do not deny that the study of the soul is relevant to the study of life but contend
that the significance of the *De Anima* goes beyond the boundaries of the study
of nature. This dispute cannot be settled on the basis of what is said in the
opening lines of the *Meteorology*. The absence of an explicit reference to the
De Anima could be a deliberate choice on the part of Aristotle. But it could also
be a consequence of the fact that Aristotle is content to give us a sketch of his
larger research project with an emphasis on how the investigation he is about
to launch (what he calls meteorology) fits within it.

    Although it lacks in detail, the sketch offered in the opening lines of the
Meteorology is very important. In particular, it is clear evidence that Aristotle
was centrally concerned with the integration of a range of different investigations into a single explanatory project. In this essay, I will attempt to illustrate
how he envisioned this integration in the case of the *De Motu*. I will try to show

---

1   For a full discussion of the explanatory project conveyed by the words "animals and plants,
both in general and separately", I refer the reader to Falcon 2015a, 75–91.

that the interplay of general and particular investigations is a key structural principle in the organization of the science that Aristotle has outlined at the outset of the *Meteorology*.

I   The *De Motu* from Valentin Rose to Martha Nussbaum

At least at first sight, the *De Motu* does not seem to be a very promising case for the sort of project I have just described. In the nineteenth century, its authenticity was often disputed. Among other things, it was not clear how this work contributed (if at all) to Aristotle's natural philosophy. To my knowledge, Valentin Rose was the first to deny that the *De Motu* was a work by Aristotle in his monograph on the order and authorship of Aristotle's writings.[2]

For Rose, the *De Motu* is a truly anomalous work—a work that belongs neither to physics narrowly understood (*Physics, On the Heavens, On Generation and Corruption*, and *Meteorology*) nor to biology (*History of Animals, Parts of Animals, Generation of Animals*, and *Progression of Animals*). Rose emphasized what he called the "metaphysical" dimension of this treatise. By "metaphysical", he meant the general nature of the investigation conducted in the *De Motu*, which is a study of animal locomotion at the most general level, including a comparison with celestial motion (chapters 3–4). In addition, Rose noted that the *De Motu* had an ethical dimension as well. By his lights, the discussion of the so-called practical syllogism (chapter 7) as well as the treatment of voluntary, involuntary, and non-voluntary motion (chapter 11), had ethical relevance. In sum, the *De Motu* was an "eclectic" work. By this Rose meant that the *De Motu* was not an original work by Aristotle but rather a Peripatetic reworking of Aristotle's physics with an infusion of metaphysics and ethics.[3]

Edward Zeller was generally critical of how Rose achieved his results. In the second edition of *Die Philosophie bei den Griechen*, Zeller introduced Rose's book with the following words: "a learned and ingenious work, which, even apart from the opaque presentation, would have a far greater value had its

2 Rose 1854, 163 ff. In the years immediately before the publication of Rose's book, the order of Aristotle's writings on natural philosophy was discussed in Prantl 1843 and Spengel 1848, 143–167. Neither one considered the possibility that the *De Motu* might be a spurious work.

3 Rose went on to argue that the doctrine of the connate πνεῦμα is a post-Aristotelian innovation. In the end, his overall argument against the authenticity of the *De Motu* was twofold. The *De Motu* is (1) a reworking of Aristotle's natural philosophy, with an infusion of metaphysics and ethics, and (2) an attempt to update this natural philosophy in the light of the medical discoveries of the Hellenistic time (most notably, the doctrine of connate πνεῦμα).

author proceeded with greater circumspection and less self-confidence".[4] Despite this cautionary remark, Zeller endorsed Rose's conclusion that the *De Motu* was a spurious work. Interestingly enough, Zeller did not use the perceived heterogeneity of the contents of the *De Motu* as an argument against its authenticity. Instead, his case was entirely based on the reference in the *De Motu* to a work on the preservation of connate πνεῦμα (*De Motu* 10.703a16–18). Zeller took this to be a reference to the opening lines of the *De Spiritu*, which he regarded as a spurious work.[5]

In the first of the five essays attached to her edition of the *De Motu*, Martha Nussbaum recalls the interpretation offered by Rose, as follows: "the *De Motu* is a strange, interdisciplinary work and accords so poorly with what we know Aristotle believed that it cannot be genuine".[6] Unlike Rose, Nussbaum has no doubt that the *De Motu* is an original and important work by Aristotle. At the same time, she agrees that "the [*De Motu*] does indeed represent a departure from the *Organon*'s system but a deliberate and fruitful one".[7] Rose was right after all, and the *De Motu* is a strange, if not even aberrant, work. According to Nussbaum, "it will not do simply to conclude that Aristotle added to his works on natural science an appendix that he had not, at some earlier point, envisaged".[8]

The interesting twist suggested by Nussbaum is that the *De Motu* entails a significant revision of Aristotle's philosophy of science. By her lights, the *De Motu* is "a blend of cosmological and biological speculation".[9] Her choice of words is quite interesting. It is meant to capture the unique nature of the investigation conducted in the *De Motu*. This work begins by recalling the cosmological truths established in *Physics* VIII. Those truths are treated as axiomatic starting points in the *De Motu*. The latter is primarily (but not exclusively) concerned with biology. Nussbaum does not simply argue that the theorems proved in the *De Motu* pertain to biology. It is very important to her argument that those biological theorems entail a refinement of the cosmological truths established in the *Physics* VIII. In other words, the truths established in the *Physics* and recalled at the beginning of the *De Motu* are

---

4   Zeller 1862, II, 42 note 1 [my translation].
5   But the putative reference to the *De Spiritu* is far from being compelling evidence against the authenticity of the *De Motu*. It is possible to regard the *De Spiritu* as a later attempt to fill a lacuna in the biological corpus prompted by the reference in the *De Motu*.
6   Nussbaum 1978, 113.
7   Nussbaum 1978, 114.
8   Nussbaum 1978, 109.
9   Nussbaum 1978, 108.

not just reiterated in the study of animals, and the detailed knowledge about the movement of animals achieved in the *De Motu* does not simply confirm the doctrine of self-motion advanced in *Physics* VIII. Speaking of *Physics* VIII, Nussbaum says that "its arguments have gaps that can be filled only by an adequate account of animal motion and its relationship to external goals and eternal necessities. The [*De Motu*] undertakes to provide such an account, grounded on the specific data of the preceding biological works".[10]

It is clear that Nussbaum has an answer not only to the question of whether the *De Motu* is to be integrated within Aristotle's natural philosophy but also to the question of how the interplay of general and particular investigations Aristotle's philosophy is to be understood. By her lights, general accounts of the sort given in *Physics* VIII are at most "vague sketches" or "incomplete accounts". They are preliminary accounts that ought to be followed by a study of the relevant particulars. The study of these particulars does not simply complete these general accounts; it may also entail a revision of these accounts.

Nussbaum defends the following claims: (1) the *De Motu* is an authentic work by Aristotle; and (2) it entails (a) a revision of Aristotle's philosophy of science, as well as (b) a restriction of the general account of self-motion offered in *Physics* VIII. In the pages to follow, I will challenge both (2a) and (2b). I will argue that the *De Motu* fits well within Aristotle's explanatory project. In a nutshell, my view is that the *De Motu* exemplifies the distinctively Aristotelian idea that explanations ought to be given at the proper level of generality.

II   Werner Jaeger and the Traditional Reading of the *De Motu*

I will return to the interpretation advanced by Nussbaum shortly. First, however, I would like to recall the traditional reading of the *De Motu*. By "traditional reading" I mean the reading that was prevalent before the authenticity of the *De Motu* was disputed by Rose.

Before Rose, the *De Motu* was often assimilated to the short essays that are collectively known as *Parva Naturalia*.[11] This reading was restated by Werner

---

10   Nussbaum 1978, 120.

11   Rose offered three objections to the assimilation of the *De Motu* to the *Parva Naturalia*. (1) The plan of the *Parva Naturalia*, as can be reconstructed from cross-references at the beginning of *On Sense-perception* and the *On the Length and Shortness of Life*, is a complete and relatively self-sufficient whole and the *De Motu* is not part of this plan. (2) The reference to a work on the movement of animals, transmitted by the manuscript tradition at the end of the *On Divination in Sleep* and often taken as evidence that the

Jaeger. In 1913, Jaeger edited the *De Motu* (along with the *Progression of Animals*, and the *De Spiritu*) for the Bibliotheca Teubneriana. The very same year, he published an extraordinarily rich and ambitious article entitled "Das Pneuma im Lykeion". In this article, Jaeger defended the authenticity of the *De Motu*.[12] A full discussion of the results reached in this article goes beyond the scope of this paper. Here suffice it to concentrate on its first part.[13] By looking at the cross-references at the end of the *De Motu*, *Progression of Animals*, and *Parts of Animals*, Jaeger found traces of two Aristotelian courses in biology. The first would comprise the following works: *History of Animals*, *Parts of Animals*, and *Generation of Animals*. The closing words of the *Parts of Animals* would be evidence of this course, in which a close link between the *Parts of Animals* and the *Generation of Animals* was envisioned:

> Regarding the parts, then, on account of what cause each of them is present in the animals has been stated with respect to all animals considered by kind. Having established these things, the next step is to go through the things that concern their generation.
>
> *PA* IV 14.697b27–30

Traces of a second course would be preserved at the end of the *De Motu* and the *Progression of Animals*:

> We have given the causes of the parts of each of the animals, of the soul, and also of sense-perception, sleep, memory, and movement in general; it remains to speak about generation.
>
> *MA* 11.704a3–b3

> The things that concern the parts of the animals, both the others and those involved in the progression of animals and all change in place, are in this way. Having established these things, the next step is to study the soul.
>
> *IA* 19.714b20–23

De Motu can be assimilated to the *Parva Naturalia*, is a later editorial addition. (3) The "metaphysical nature" of the *De Motu* does not fit well with the contents of the *Parva Naturalia*.

12   Jaeger 1913b, 30–73.

13   In the second part, Jaeger argued that Aristotle had a theory of πνεῦμα, and that this theory was borrowed from the medical tradition. In the third part, he contended that this theory was modified in the Hellenistic Peripatos on the basis of subsequent medical discoveries.

This second biology course would include the following writings: *History of Animals, Parts of Animals, Progression of Animals, De Anima, PN1*,[14] *De Motu, On Generation of Animals*, and *PN2*.[15] The reader should note that this second course would have not only expanded on the first but also recommended a different sequence of topics. In particular, the close link between the *Parts of Animals* and the *Generation of Animals* envisioned in the first course would be, if not broken, at least significantly loosened.

Jaeger was not the first interpreter to point to the discrepancy between the last sentence of *Parts of Animals* and what we read at the end of the *De Motu* and the *Progression of Animals*.[16] What is new in his approach is the attempt to reconcile this tension by employing the hypothesis that the extant biological works may belong to different chronological layers. An evaluation of his hypothesis does not concern us here. What is immediately relevant to our discussion is how the *De Motu* contributes to the explanatory project pursued by Aristotle in the second, expanded biology course. According to Jaeger, in the second course the *De Anima* would look forward to the *De Motu*. Jaeger found evidence for this reading in a passage toward the end of the *De Anima*. There, in dealing with animal locomotion, and in connection with desire,

---

14 *PN1* is an abbreviation for the following short studies: *On Sense-perception, On Memory, On Sleep, On Dreams, On Divination in Sleep*. For this abbreviation, see Rashed 2004, 185–202.

15 *PN2* stands for *On Length and Brevity of Life, On Youth and Old Age and Respiration*. Cf. Rashed 2004, 185–202.

16 For instance, Francesco Cavalli dealt with this discrepancy in his book on the order and number of the parts of Aristotle's physical theory (*De ordine et numero partium ac librorum physicae doctrine Aristotelis*, published in Venice between 1490 and 1495 [GW 5832]). Cavalli condemned the passage at the very end of the *Parts of Animals* (IV 14.697b29–30: "having established these things, the next step is to go through the things that concern their generation"). Although not universally accepted, this order was adopted in a number of important Renaissance editions of Aristotle, including the Juntine edition of Aristotle and Averroes. This is not a place for a full discussion of the scholarly debate on the closing words of the *Parts of Animals*. Here I am content to say that the relationship of the *Parts of Animals* and the *Generation of Animals* is not an illusion created by an editorial artifice. On the contrary, the systematic cross-references between these two works strongly suggest that Aristotle envisioned a division of labor between the *Parts of Animals* and the *Generation of Animals*. But this does not mean that these two works exhaust the *dioti*-stage of the investigation of animals. Tellingly, when the *Progression of Animals* and the *De Motu* were translated for the first time by William of Moerbeke (ca. 1260), his translations initiated an intense debate on how these two new texts (they were unknown at the time) contribute to Aristotle's explanatory project. For an introduction to this instructive debate, I refer the reader to Falcon 2012, 521–539, which contains a discussion of the new data presented in De Leemans 2011.

Aristotle refers to another work. He envisions a division of labor between the
De Anima and this other work:

> as for the tool by which desire moves [the animal], this is already [some-
> thing] bodily, which is why one has to inquire about this [tool] in the
> [study of the] functions common to the body and the soul.
>
> *An.* III 10.433b19–21

Before Rose, it was not uncommon to read this passage as containing a reference to the *De Motu*.[17] As a matter of fact, this reading was already known to
Averroes. In his long commentary on the *De Anima*, Averroes writes: "Aristotle
spoke about this in the *De Motu*, but this treatise did not come to us, apart from
a little part of Nicolaus's summary".[18] Jaeger revived this reading. *Contra* Rose
and Zeller, he re-established the broken link between the *De Anima* and the *De
Motu*.

The traditional reading defended by Jaeger invites an integrated study of
the *De Motu* and the *De Anima*. Unfortunately, Jaeger did not elaborate on
how he understood such an integrated study. We have to look somewhere
else for guidance on how such a study should be pursued. Klaus Corcilius
has recently offered an integrated study of *De Anima* III 9–11 and the *De
Motu*.[19] He has argued that the *De Motu* and the *De Anima* are two parts of
the same explanatory project. While the latter is concerned with the soul as
form of the body, the former deals with what is common to the body and
the soul. In his own words, the *De Anima* consists in a search for principles
("Prinzipienfindung"), whereas the *De Motu*, along with the *Parva Naturalia*, is
concerned with the application ("Anwendung") of those principles to the study

---

17   Of course, Rose was aware of the tradition that connects the *De Motu* to the end of the
      De Anima. He did not dispute the authenticity of the passage in the latter work. Instead,
      he argued that when Aristotle is looking forward to a study of "the functions common to
      the body and the soul", he is not referring to the *De Motu* but to the *Parva Naturalia* as a
      whole. In other words, the *De Motu* would be a later attempt to fulfill a promise made by
      Aristotle in his *De Anima* (and fill a lacuna left in his explanatory project). This reading is
      endorsed by H. Bonitz: "quae omisit Aristoteles, ea autem autor libri de *Motu Animalium*
      videtur voluisse explere" [*Index Aristotelicus* 99.19–20].
18   Cranford 524.54–62. The reader should keep in mind that the *De Motu* and the *Progression
      of Animals* were not known in the Arabic world. How did Averroes know of the existence
      and contents of the *De Motu*? In all probability, he gathered this information from the
      epitome of Aristotle's philosophy written by Nicolaus of Damascus (first century BCE).
      This epitome was quite popular in the Syriac and Arabic traditions.
19   Corcilius 2008.

of what is common to the soul and the body. By his lights, the *De Anima* and the *De Motu* are not just different investigations; rather, they are different *kinds* of investigations.[20]

The idea of an integrated study of the *De Anima* and the *De Motu* on the basis of the model offered in the *Parva Naturalia* is encouraged by the reference in the third book of the *De Anima* to a study of the functions common to the body and the soul. The expression "common to the body and the soul" is used at the beginning of the treatise *On the Senses* to refer to the contents of the *Parva Naturalia* (*Sens.* 1.436a7–8). In order to understand how the *De Motu* and the *De Anima* may be integrated into a single explanatory project, we need to recall the opening lines of the short essay *On Sense-perception*:

> [s]ince it was determined earlier about the soul considered in itself and about each of the powers of the soul considered with respect to the soul, it is next to be investigated about animals and everything that has life, as to what are their specific and what are their common activities.
>
> *Sens.* 1.436a1–5

This passage suggests that Aristotle has already moved away from a study of the soul, and that he is about to engage in a different kind of investigation. While in the *De Anima* Aristotle was concerned with *the soul*, he is about to engage in a study of *ensouled beings*. Note, however, that Aristotle is still working within the theoretical framework established in the *De Anima*. For one thing, Aristotle is not only invoking, explicitly and unequivocally, the *De Anima*; he is also building, here (as well as in the rest of the *Parva Naturalia*), on the results established in his investigation of the soul:

> So let's assume what has been said about the soul, and let's speak about the rest, and first about what is first.[21]
>
> *Sens.* 1.436a5–6

---

20 Corcilius 2008, 36. Jaeger makes a similar distinction, when he speaks of the *De Anima* as being concerned with "reine Psychologie", and of the *Parva Naturalia* and the *De Motu* as dealing with "Psychophysiologie". See Jaeger 1913, 36.

21 In this passage, Aristotle is crystal clear that not just this work but all the essays that are collectively referred to as *Parva Naturalia* depend for their theoretical framework on the results achieved in the investigation of the soul. A quick study of the references to the *De Anima* in the *Parva Naturalia* confirms this impression. The results achieved in the former work are explicitly recalled, and assumed as explanatory starting points in the latter.

A full discussion of how the project of an integrated study of the *De Anima* and the *De Motu* is carried out by Corcilius goes emphatically beyond the scope of this paper. It is telling, however, that this project is pursued by concentrating on the second part of the *De Motu* (chapters 6–11), to the exclusion of the first part (chapters 1–5).[22] The justification given for not taking into account the first part of the *De Motu* is that these five chapters do not specifically treat animal locomotion. Rather, they are concerned with Aristotle's general theory of motion, and more specifically with his theory of self-motion.[23] This interpretative approach comes dangerously close to denying the integrity of the *De Motu*. Instead, we need to approach the *De Motu* in a way that helps us see how this work is one, continuous argument. I would like to suggest that progress toward this interpretative goal is possible if we remain open to what Aristotle tells us in the opening lines of the *De Motu*.[24]

III   *Physics* VIII and the *De Motu*

The picture of integration offered in the opening lines of the *De Motu* is quite different from the one outlined at the beginning of the work *On Sense-perception*. While conceptual proximity to the treatise *De Anima* is stressed at the outset of *On Sense-perception*, the opening lines of the *De Motu* make contact with *Physics* VIII:

> Now, it was determined earlier that the source of all other motions is
> that which moves itself, and of this that which is not subject to motion,
> and that the first mover must be unmoved, when it was determined

---

22   This part begins with a reference to the *De Anima*, which is invoked for the thesis that the soul is not subject to motion, except by accident (700b4–6). I will return to this reference in due course.

23   Corcilius 2008, 243 and 288.

24   Here I am content to sketch out what I perceive as problematic in the attempt to offer an integrated study of the *De Anima* and *De Motu* on the basis of the model of the *Parva Naturalia*. A great deal more could be said on the attempt to assimilate the *De Motu* to the *Parva Naturalia*. Since I will not pursue this issue further, a few words of clarification are in order. I do not deny that in the course of his investigation of the soul Aristotle looks forward to the *De Motu*, and looks forward to it as a study of what is common to the body and the soul. In other words, it is not my intention to block the route that takes us from the *De Anima* to the *De Motu*. Rather, my first and foremost concern is to alert the reader to the existence of another route to the *De Motu*. A main goal of this essay is to see what we can learn about Aristotle's explanatory project as a whole by taking this route.

concerning eternal motion, whether or not there is such a thing, and if
there is, what it is. But this has to be grasped not only with a general
account but also with respect to the particular and perceptible things, on
account of which we also seek the general accounts and which we believe
they have to fit.

MA 1.698a8–14

Nussbaum is right in insisting on the importance of this passage for an overall interpretation of the *De Motu*. However, her reading of this passage as an
attempt to apply cosmology to the study of animals misses the point. For one
thing, Aristotle never speaks of biology and cosmology as two separate, or even
separable, sciences.[25] In fact, Aristotle actively discourages the thought that
biology and cosmology are distinct Aristotelian sciences. His language is carefully crafted to avoid giving the impression that the study of animals is an
autonomous science. There is no doubt that Aristotle could have chosen to refer
to the study of animals as a science. For one thing, he does refer to the study of
animals as a μέθοδος.[26] But it is significant that Aristotle does not call it a science (ἐπιστήμη). Instead, he insists, quite pointedly, on presenting the study of
animals as contributing directly to the science that he calls ἐπιστήμη φυσική.[27]

The strong integration of biology within Aristotle's physics finds confirmation in the opening lines of the *De Motu*. In approaching this work, one should
begin by stating the obvious, namely that Aristotle is concerned with animal
motion as a certain kind of motion (κίνησις). While obvious, this assumption is
often overlooked. And yet, it is this assumption that enables Aristotle to invoke
the general account of motion developed in *Physics* VIII. At least in the *De
Motu*, Aristotle is simply blind to the distinction between cosmology and biology, and using this distinction does not help us to make progress toward understanding the place of the *De Motu* in Aristotle's explanatory project. Instead, I
suggest adopting the distinction between general and special physics. I believe

---

25 For a still helpful reaction to this aspect of Nussbaum's interpretation of the *De Motu*,
     I refer the reader to Kung 1982, 65–76. The reader will find a recent reflection on the
     exchange between Joan Kung and Martha Nussbaum in Lennox 2010, 1–23.
26 The passage is found at the end of the *On Length and Shortness of Life*: "It remains to
     investigate youth and old age, life and death. Once this is done, the investigation (μέθοδος)
     of animals will be concluded" (*Long. Vit.* 6.467b5–9).
27 Aristotle is fully aware of being innovative and of going beyond anything done before him.
     At the same time, he is careful to remind his reader of the unity of his explanatory project.
     For a discussion of this double aspect of his engagement with what *we* call Aristotle's
     biology, I refer the reader to Lennox 2005, 55–71 and Lennox 2010, 1–23.

that this second distinction is more helpful in discussing a key structural principle in the science that Aristotle calls ἐπιστήμη φυσική.

Physics VIII is general physics.[28] The opening lines of the *De Motu* apply to *Physics* VIII the two-stage investigation sketched out at the outset of *Posterior Analytics* II.[29] The two stages of the investigation are the εἴ ἐστι (whether it is) and the τί ἐστι (what it is). *Physics* VIII 1 is an attempt to answer the εἴ ἐστι question with respect to eternal motion.[30] By the end of the chapter, Aristotle is confident that this question is to be answered in the affirmative. More directly, Aristotle is confident that he has achieved the result that there was not a time when there was no motion and there will not be a time when there will be no motion (VIII 1.252b5–6). By establishing that there is eternal motion Aristotle has also established that there is a fact that calls for an explanation.[31] His work toward answering this question begins in *Physics* VIII 3. This chapter marks also the beginning of his attempt to answer the τί ἐστι question.[32] In his attempt to answer that question, Aristotle offers a general treatment of motion. Among other things, he establishes that self-motion is the origin of all other motion, and that self-motion displays some internal structure, namely the structure of a mover and a moved thing (*Physics* VIII 5). Aristotle treats this general truth about motion as an axiom in the opening lines of the *De Motu*. In addition, he also takes as axiomatic that there must be a mover that is unmoved at the beginning of the chain of motion. Aristotle establishes this truth in *Physics* VIII 6.

---

28   That the *Physics* deals *in general* with nature and motion is suggested by Aristotle himself. In recalling the general truth that motion is divisible in ever-divisible parts, Aristotle refers his reader to what is said in general (καθόλου) about nature (*Phys.* VIII 5.257a34). In all probability, this is a reference to *Physics* VI.

29   For a full defense of this reading of *Physics* VIII, I refer the reader to Falcon 2015b.

30   The opening words of *Physics* VIII introduce the εἴ ἐστι question as follows:
     Did motion ever come into being without having existed before, and does it perish again in such a way that nothing is in motion? Or is it that motion neither comes into being nor perishes but instead has always been and always will be (being present in things as something immortal and unceasing, like a kind of life of all things that are constituted by nature)? (*Phys.* VIII 1.250b11–15)

31   Note, however, that in answering the τί ἐστι question Aristotle is doing more than just setting up an explicable fact—that there is eternal motion. He is also doing some preliminary work toward explaining that fact. I take this to be the main (but emphatically not the only) aim of the dialectical discussion of the views of his predecessors (Anaxagoras, Empedocles, and Democritus).

32   It is telling that the starting point of the second stage of Aristotle's investigation is why (διά τι) some things are sometimes in motion and sometimes at rest. For the equivalence between τί ἐστι questions and διά τι questions, see *Posterior Analytics* II 2.90a14–23.

That Aristotle considers *Physics* VIII general physics finds a strong confirmation in the opening lines of the *De Motu*. There, Aristotle promises to show how the account of motion given in general fits (ἐφαρμόττειν) the relevant particular cases. This promise is fulfilled in the rest of the *De Motu*, which is regarded as a special study resulting in detailed knowledge about animal motion. Following a suggestion made by Nussbaum, one might take these lines as a promise to test the general truths of motion in the rest of the *De Motu*. I resist this suggestion. I do not think that Aristotle makes this promise because he believes that the general truths offered in *Physics* VIII need to be confirmed, let alone tested, in the study of animals. Nor do I think that the general account offered in *Physics* VIII is incomplete in any other way. On the contrary, I think that this account is informative and is lacking nothing—except, of course, the sort of detailed knowledge that only a careful study of the particular cases can supply.[33]

By now, it should be clear that the opening chapter of the *De Motu* is an important methodological passage. In this chapter, Aristotle is recommending the integration of the general account of motion offered in *Physics* VIII with the body of detailed knowledge that is achieved in the study of animal motion. At least two points can be made on the basis of what Aristotle says in the opening lines of the *De Motu*. The first point is this: Aristotle is asking for more than just harmony, or absence of conflict, between *Physics* VIII and the *De Motu*. He is setting himself the task of showing that the account offered in the *De Motu* is an articulation of the general truths established in *Physics* VIII. Moreover, precisely because the *De Motu* is an articulation of a more general account, the account of animal motion is expected to flesh out the general account offered in *Physics* VIII. The second point has to do with the translation of the Greek δι' ἅπερ in line 698a14. Nussbaum does not do justice to the Greek in her translation. Aristotle is not saying that it is through the particular cases and perceptible objects that we go on to look for the general

---

33   Consider the case of the *De Anima*, where Aristotle makes it clear that a general account by itself is not sufficient to provide knowledge. With reference to the common account of the soul given at the beginning of the second book of the *De Anima*, Aristotle emphatically says that "it would be ridiculous" to stop at such a general level of analysis (II 3.414b25–28). He adds that "the account of each type of the soul is the most appropriate account of the soul" (II 3.415a12–13). The second claim taken in isolation may suggest that the general account of the soul is superseded, once a specific account for each type of soul becomes available. The context, however, makes it clear that Aristotle is not rejecting the most common account. He is only rejecting an account of this type that is not followed by an account that is specifically tailored to each type of soul. For more on this topic, see Falcon 2010, 167–181.

account.[34] Rather, he is saying that it is on account of the particular cases and perceptible objects that we go on to look for general accounts of the sort that Aristotle gives in *Physics* VIII. Nussbaum places an emphasis on the fact that the particular cases provide evidence for the general account he offered in *Physics* VIII. The alternative translation does not exclude that the general investigation offered in *Physics* VIII is based on a careful observation of the particular cases, but it suggests, in addition, that an interest in the particulars provides the motivation for the general investigation offered in *Physics* VIII. This investigation is offered because we are interested in the particular cases. In other words, the particular cases remain the ultimate explanatory goal of the project pursued by Aristotle in his physics. It is because we want to explain the particular cases that we have to develop accounts of the sort offered in *Physics* VIII.

IV   *De Motu* and *Progression of Animals*

Aristotle's natural philosophy begins to look like a complex business crucially involving the interplay of general and particular investigations.[35] Note, however, that the picture of integration presented so far does not do full justice to the opening lines of the *De Motu*. In particular, I have not discussed the crucial stretch of text that comes immediately before the passage in which Aristotle makes contact with *Physics* VIII:

> As to the motion of animals, what belongs to each kind [of animal], what their differentiating features are, and what the causes of the attributes that belong to each [kind] of animals are—all of this was investigated elsewhere. Now it is to be investigated in general the common cause (τῆς κοινῆς αἰτίας) of moving with any motion whatsoever (κίνησιν ὁποιανοῦν), since among animals, some move by flying, some by swimming, some by walking, and some in other ways.
>
> MA 1.698a1–7

---

34   Nussbaum 1978: "it is through these [*sc.* the particular cases] that we go on to look as well for general explanations, which we believe must be in harmony with them". This translation would be acceptable if the transmitted text had the genitive δι' ὧπερ. Cf. Barnes 1982, 223.

35   In light of what I have said above, it should be clear that Aristotle is committed to the unity of general and particular physics; he is also recommending the following, double movement: (1) from the particular to the universal, and (2) from the universal to the particular.

In this passage, Aristotle promises an account that will explain animal motion by pointing to a *common* cause (*MA* 1.698a4). This account will explain the movement of animals *in general* by giving the common cause of their moving with *any movement whatsoever* (*MA* 1.698a4–5). On the one hand, it is fairly obvious that the account Aristotle is about to give is a special account in the sense that it is concerned with a special type of motion, namely animal motion. On the other hand, it is clear that this account is still general in the sense that it is expected to map on all types of animal motion.

What Aristotle says in the opening lines of the *De Motu* may help to address a frequent dissatisfaction with the text. This dissatisfaction is expressed by Martha Nussbaum when she complains that "the physiological side of the *De Motu* is oddly vague and abstract".[36] While I have no objections to the claim that the account offered in the *De Motu* is abstract, I contend that this account is not vague, sketchy, or even incomplete. On the contrary, it is precisely what one should expect given what Aristotle is trying to explain. The sort of physiological details Nussbaum would like to find in the *De Motu* would be out of place there. Consider, for example, how the concept of joint is introduced in the *De Motu* (chapter 1): Aristotle has invoked the *Physics* VIII for the view that a self-mover is the origin of motion, and the origin of motion in a self-mover is something that is unmoved. The joint is introduced as an origin of motion. *Qua* origin of motion, the joint is a point of rest. It is by using the joint as a point of rest that not just the relevant bodily part but also the animal as a whole can move. In commenting on this passage, Nussbaum complains that more details would be needed to make the concept of joint really informative. She is quite specific about what she would like to find in the *De Motu*. She would like to find details about how tendons and muscles are attached to bones, and how the joints are realized in this kind of bodily support. But these are exactly the sorts of concrete physiological details that would be out of place in the *De Motu*. Aristotle's goal is to provide an account mapping on all animal movement. Hence, this account has to be reached without exploiting anything specific to any type of animal motion.

What Aristotle says in the opening lines of the *De Motu* indicates, clearly and unequivocally, that this work does not exhaust, and is not intended to exhaust, the topic of animal locomotion. On the contrary, it is natural to read the opening lines of the *De Motu* as implying that a detailed causal investigation of animal motion has to be part of a fully developed theory of animal locomotion. Moreover, it is natural to read these lines as conveying the expectation that the

---

reader of the *De Motu* is already familiar with this detailed causal account. But where does Aristotle supply it? A possible answer is that this account is offered in *Progression of Animals*.

We often take this treatise as an appendix to *Parts of Animals*. This reading is certainly encouraged by the fact that *Progression of Animals* is introduced as a causal study of the *parts* involved in animal locomotion:

> One should investigate *the parts* useful to animals for their motion from place to place.
>
> *IA* 1.704a4–6

Furthermore, there is no doubt that the very end of the treatise reinforces the idea that *Parts of Animals* and *Progression of Animals* work as a team in the explanation of the parts of animals:

> The things that concern the *parts* of the animals, both the others and those involved in the progression of animals and all change in place, are in this way.
>
> *IA* 19.714b20–22

Yet we should not be blind to the fact that *Progression of Animals* is kept separate from *Parts of Animals*. This fact cannot be explained away as a mere accident of the manuscript transmission or as the result of a later editorial decision. There are at least two good reasons why we should refrain from thinking of *Progression of Animals* as a mere appendix to *Parts of Animals*. The first is that the opening lines of *Progression of Animals* announce an independent and self-contained investigation of animal locomotion. No attempt is made there to establish contact with *Parts of Animals*. On the contrary, the treatise begins with a clear set of questions to be answered in the course of the investigation on the basis of a theoretical framework explicitly introduced for this purpose in *Progression of Animals*.[37] The second reason for loosening the tight

---

37   This theoretical framework consists of the following three starting points:

(1) Nature does nothing in vain but always the best from what is possible with respect to the οὐσία of each kind of animal;

(2) There are six dimensions (διαστάσεις) grouped into three pairs: up/down, front/back, and left/right;

(3) The origins (ἀρχαί) of motion are pulling and pushing.

Given my emphasis on the integration of general and special investigations of motion,

relationship that is often assumed to exist between *Progression of Animals* and *Parts of Animals* emerges from a close study of cross-references. There are four explicit references to *Progression of Animals* in the extant corpus of Aristotelian writings. Three of these references are in *Parts of Animals*. Tellingly, they are references to *another* causal investigation.[38] Moreover, they describe *Progression of Animals* as a study of πορεῖα or even κίνησις.[39] Either way, the reference is to a work on locomotion rather than to a work on the bodily parts involved in locomotion. However, the attempt to cast the content of *Progression of Animals* as an investigation of animal locomotion is not unique to *Parts of Animals*. The fourth reference is found in the treatise *On the Heavens*. There, Aristotle refers to the *Progression of Animals* as a study of the different *modes* of animal locomotion.[40]

While no one has ever disputed that *Progression of Animals* contributes to the study of animals, there has been some concern about the exact place of this work in Aristotle's explanatory project. We do not really know why *Progression of Animals* is kept separate from *Parts of Animals*. However, progress toward answering this question can be made if we keep in mind that *Progression of Animals* contributes to an integrated study of motion.

v   **Natural Philosophy as a Multi-layered Explanatory Project**

In the first book of the *Parts of Animals*, Aristotle is quite emphatic on the need to provide explanations of certain features of animal life ranging across different species of animals. According to Aristotle, such common explanations are necessary not only to avoid tedious repetitions but also to shed light on salient explanatory features that might be otherwise missed. His examples are sleep, respiration, growth, decline, and death (I 1.639a19–20). Interestingly enough, Aristotle adds the following crucial remark: in studying what is common, we should not overlook the fact that there are important articulations that also have to be taken into account. In this context, Aristotle introduces

---

the third starting point is the most interesting one. This principle is established in the context of a general physics (*Physics* VII) and is applied to the study of a special type of motion: animal motion (*Progression of Animals*).

38   *PA* IV 11.690b15 and IV 11.692a17: πορεῖα; *PA* IV 13.696a10–13: πορεῖα and κίνησις.

39   The reference to a study of πορεῖα and κίνησις in *PA* IV 13.696a10–13 looks like a conscious attempt to present the content of *Progression of Animals* as a study of a special type of motion, namely animal locomotion.

40   *Cael.* II 2.284b13: κινήσεις.

animal locomotion (πορεῖα) as a correction against the danger of oversimplification. A study of animal locomotion has to be a study of the different ways in which animals move around (11.639b1–3).

This methodological remark is often read as a theoretical motivation for the investigation conducted in the *Progression of Animals*. I have no objections to this reading. I hasten to add, however, that the opening lines of the *De Motu* suggest that it is not sufficient to explain swimming, flying, walking, and the like. In addition, the student of nature should look for a common causal account of animal motion. This is the task that Aristotle sets for himself in the *De Motu*.

Aristotle's natural philosophy begins to look like a multi-layered explanatory project crucially involving the integration of general and particular investigations. I have highlighted three causal accounts of motion (κίνησις): (1) the general account of motion offered in *Physics* VIII; (2) the special account that gives the common cause of animal motion (*De Motu*); and (3) the special account that deals with the causes of the different forms of bodily displacement, namely swimming, flying, walking (*Progression of Animals*). These accounts are causal in the sense that their aim is to explain the φαινόμενα by grasping the relevant cause(s).

Now that we have established that Aristotle's natural philosophy has both a general and a special component, it is time to return to the interpretation defended by Martha Nussbaum. We have seen that, in addition to defending the authenticity of the *De Motu*, she has put forward a certain view of the interplay between general and special investigations. By her lights, the general account offered in *Physics* VIII is a preliminary account, which is to be followed by a study of the particular cases. Moreover, the latter does not simply complete the general account offered in *Physics* VIII; it also entails its revision. But we have seen that there is no reason to think that, when Aristotle is asking us to integrate his causal accounts into a single explanatory project, he is asking us to revisit the results reached in *Physics* VIII. In particular, the general account developed in *Physics* VIII does not depend for its confirmation on the results achieved by the special accounts. To clarify this last point, it may be helpful to introduce a model for how to think about general physics. The model is given in the *Posterior Analytics*.

In *Posterior Analytics* I 4–5, Aristotle tells us that we have proper knowledge of the fact that triangles have the sum of their internal angles equal to two right angles only if we know that this property belongs to every triangle *qua* triangle. Since this geometrical property belongs to all triangles, it belongs to equilateral, isosceles, and scalene triangles. But it does not belong to these triangles in virtue of the fact that they are equilateral, isosceles, or scalene. It belongs to them because they are triangles. Aristotle employs this example to show that there is a common explanatory level beyond that of equilateral, isosceles, and scalene triangles, and that we reach this common explanatory level by ignoring those facts that are specific to equilateral, isosceles, and scalene triangles. More precisely, we ignore those facts that make these triangles equilateral, isosceles, or scalene by treating them *as* triangles. We can use this geometrical example to shed light on the nature of what we have called general physics. What is important, and must not be overlooked, about this example is that the study of triangles is not about triangles other than equilateral, isosceles, and scalene. On the contrary, those triangles *are* the object of this study, except that they are considered *in abstraction* from those properties that make them equilateral, isosceles, and scalene triangles. In a similar way, when we engage in the sort of study that I have called general physics, we are concerned with concrete physical objects, except for the fact that we study these objects in abstraction from their specific properties. The geometrical example employed by Aristotle helps us see that the results achieved in the context of general physics do not depend for their confirmation on anything that may be achieved at the level of special physics. More directly, the explanation of the property of having the internal angles equal to two right angles is secured by Aristotle without exploiting anything specific or peculiar to either equilateral, isosceles, or scalene triangles. To put it differently, their being equilateral, isosceles, or scalene does not contribute to our understanding of why they have the property in question. Hence, we can speak of a scientific autonomy of general physics.[41]

With this point in place, we can return to the general account of motion offered in *Physics* VIII. This account commits Aristotle to the following three theses:

1.   An animal moves itself in the sense that one part of the animal moves another (259b1–3);
2.   There is a first unmoved mover and cause of self-motion in the animal (259b15–17);
3.   Although unmoved, this mover is moved in an accidental way; more directly, by being in a body moved from place to place it too happens to be in successive places (259b18–20).

---

41   Helpful remarks on how this geometrical example may help us understand how the study of animal motion is conceived by Aristotle can be found in Wilson 2000, 14–52.

There is no doubt that the first unmoved mover in the animal is a soul. Aristotle stops short of making this identification in the *Physics* VIII. This important feature of the soul is fully discussed only in the *De Anima*. In light of this fact, it is not surprising to find out that the *De Motu* refers to the *De Anima* for a discussion of whether the soul is moved (*MA* 6.700b4–6). I will not elaborate on how important this thesis is for Aristotle's theory of the soul.[42] What is relevant to the present discussion is that the *De Motu* builds on the doctrine that the soul moves as an unmoved mover—a doctrine about the soul that is defended in the *De Anima* by appealing to a general truth about motion presented in *Physics* VIII.[43] The *De Motu* expands on this doctrine by showing how the soul moves the body. But I cannot find anything in the *De Motu* that restricts, modifies, or implies in any other way a rethinking of either the general truth of the *Physics* or the doctrine of the soul defended in the *De Anima*.[44] On the contrary, the insight that the soul imparts motion as an unmoved mover is restated in a memorable way toward the end of the *De Motu*. In particular, the animal is likened to a well-governed city:

> One should consider that the animal is organized as a well-governed city. For once order is established in the city, there is no need of a separate monarch who has to watch over each of the happenings; rather, each [citizen] does his own [task] as ordered, and one thing happens after another thing because of established practices. The very same thing happens in animals because of nature and in virtue of the fact that each of the parts, since they are so organized, naturally does its own task. So there is no need of a soul in each of them, but, since the soul is in some bodily origin, the other [parts] live in virtue of being naturally attached to it while they perform their own task because of nature.[45]
>
> *MA* 10.703a30–b2

---

42   For a full discussion of the implication of this thesis for Aristotle's theory of the soul, I refer the reader to Menn 2001, 83–139.

43   It is very telling that Aristotle opens his discussion of the *De Anima* by recalling the claim that the mover need not be moved (I 2.406a3–4). Although Aristotle is content to say that this result was established earlier, there is no doubt that this is a reference to *Physics* VIII.

44   The same conclusion is reached in Morison 2004, 67–80.

45   Failure fully to appreciate how the idea of the soul conveyed by this image is to be integrated with the theory of the soul defended in the *De Anima* has played a role in the debate on the authenticity of the *De Motu*. For more on this debate, I refer the reader to Nussbaum 1978, 7–8.

VI   Conclusion

I have argued that the *De Motu* is far from being a "strange" or "eclectic" work as suggested by Valentin Rose and Martha Nussbaum. On the contrary, this work is a vivid example of the distinctively Aristotelian idea that explanations ought to be given at different levels of generality. This idea is a key explanatory principle in Aristotle's natural philosophy.[46]

I do not want to downplay how difficult the *De Motu* is. However, it seems to me that the difficulties we experience depend, at least in part, on approaching the text with a ready-made distinction between physics and biology. We often think that Aristotle has left four great works on physics (*Physics, On the Heavens, On Generation and Corruption*, and *Meteorology*), a biological corpus that includes the three great works on animals (*History of Animals, Parts of Animals, Generation of Animals*), and a few other minor treatises, including the *De Motu, Progression of Animals*, and the so-called *Parva Naturalia*.[47] I have suggested that not only the *De Motu* but also the explanatory project that Aristotle calls ἐπιστήμη (or φιλοσοφία) φυσική is impervious to the distinction between physics and biology. Instead, I have argued that this project is best understood as having a general as well as a special component. General physics is a study of nature and motion at the most general levels. Such a study is offered in the eight essays that are collected in Aristotle's *Physics*. The other physical writings can be usefully regarded as contributing to special physics as they deal with a special aspect of the physical world. The *De Motu* is no exception to the rule. This work deals with animal motion on the crucial assumption that animal motion is a special type of motion.

---

46   It can be found outside the study of nature as well. In the *Nicomachean Ethics*, the general account of virtue is illuminated and flashed out with the help of the relevant particular cases. For helpful comments on this often overlooked aspect of Aristotle's account of ethical virtues, see Gotthelf 2008.

47   I refrain from listing the *De Anima* because this work enjoys a unique status in Aristotle's thought. Here suffice it to say the opening lines of the *De Anima* introduce the study of the soul as contributing *to all truth*, but most especially to truth about nature, as the soul is a principle of animals (I 1.402a4–7). In other words, the *De Anima* contributes most obviously to the explanatory project that Aristotle calls ἐπιστήμη (or φιλοσοφία) φυσική because in order to study life optimally one must engage in the study of the principle of life, the soul. At the same time, however, the *De Anima* contributes to theoretical knowledge emphatically beyond this ἐπιστήμη.

CHAPTER 8

Is Aristotle's Account of Sexual Differentiation Inconsistent?*

William Wians

Abstract

Many scholars have found Aristotle's explanation of parental resemblance in *De Gener-atione Animalium* to be inconsistent with the hylomorphic theory of sexual differentia-tion developed in GA I. The later passage claims that the female imparts motions of her own through the material she contributes, while the earlier account seems to assign all form-imparting motions to the father, limiting the female's contribution to passive, inert matter. I shall argue that the alleged inconsistency should instead be understood as reflecting the GA's overall plan of exposition, which makes IV 3 the final refinement of definitions of male and female advanced provisionally in Book I. I propose to locate GA IV 3 within two larger contexts of a carefully constructed exposition. Most immedi-ately, IV 3 belongs to the sequence of argument beginning at the start of book IV dealing with sexual differentiation. But the issues in IV reach back to the very beginning of the GA and the definition of male and female as stated there (which raises but post-pones the question of parental resemblance). Scholars who regard Aristotle's account as inconsistent—and even many who don't—have failed to appreciate the progressive unfolding of an Aristotelian exposition.

Aristotle's explanation of parental resemblance in *De Generatione Animalium* IV 3 (*GA*) appears on its surface to conflict with the hylomorphic differentiation of male and female with which he operates in the treatise up to that point. In his general account of reproduction in *GA* I–II 3, Aristotle seems to limit the female's contribution to passive, inert matter, assigning all form-imparting motions to the father. Even as late as the first two chapters of Book IV, a sharp separation of male and female along the lines of active and formal vs. passive

---

* I would like to thank Jim Lennox and Devin Henry for comments on a much earlier confer-ence version of this paper, Alan Bowen for helpful suggestions on an earlier written draft, Brill's anonymous referee for incisive comments, and my co-editor Ron Polansky for a very careful reading of the penultimate draft.

and material seems to be maintained. But then in a controverted passage in GA IV 3, Aristotle unexpectedly attributes to the female motions of her own through the material she contributes. The apparent inconsistency and the passages giving rise to it have become a crux in understanding both Aristotle's embryology and his hylomorphic theory.

The most forceful case charging Aristotle with inconsistency was made by Furth, who, after an extended analysis of the relevant passages, attributes the inconsistency to Aristotle's "male-chauvinism".[1] Other commentators have sought to defend Aristotle against inconsistency or at least diminish its effects. Cooper, approaching the issue from the metaphysical question of substantial form, denies there is any inconsistency, arguing that despite the evident language of IV 3 the mother contributes no actual motions of her own, even when the offspring is female.[2] Similarly, Reeve defends the "canonical doctrine" that the female contributes no form by arguing that Aristotle attributes "complex tendencies" to the potential movements in the female menses but no actual movements to the embryo.[3] Arguing against an inconsistency, Morsink claims that the introduction of maternally imparted movements in GA IV 3 is an intentional qualification meant to account for real world deviations from the hylomorphic theory's ideal case of a male offspring resembling the male parent.[4] Gelber argues that the female contributes motions inherent in the menstrual blood, but does not contribute form at either the species or subspecies level.[5] Others suggest, not always on clear grounds, that not all aspects of the offspring's observable form come from the father's contribution. Thus, Mayhew uses Aristotle's observations of wind-eggs in certain fowl along with brief but suggestive remarks on GA IV 3 to argue for the "rich contributions"

---

1   Furth 1988, 127–141. Prior to Furth, Lesky 1950, 152–154, charged Aristotle with inconsistency (though not with sexism); see Furth 132 note 22 for further citations. Against the charge of sexism frequently leveled against Aristotle by feminist critics, see Tress 1996, Cook 1996, Mayhew 2004 (reviewed in Wians 2005), and Henry 2007, with a critical rebuttal in Nielsen 2008. I give only passing attention in this paper to the question of Aristotle's sexism.

2   Cooper 1988. See also Matthews 1986 and Witt 1985. Powerful rebuttals to Cooper in favor of an active female contribution can be found in Coles 1995, 71 note 73 and especially 81–88; and Gelber 2010, 203–209.

3   See Reeve 1992, 198–207.

4   See Morsink 1982, 127–143.

5   Gelber 2010. My solution is in one respect closest to Gelber's, in that I also emphasize the inherent motions of the female menses. But while our readings of IV 3 are similar, Gelber does not appreciate the implications of Aristotle's exposition in the GA, especially with regard to statements of male and female as principles prior to IV 3. Doing so would, I believe, support her case against the need to posit sub-specific forms in Aristotle.

made by the female, though he admits that he leaves the question of how best to read IV 3 unsettled.[6] Balme speaks vaguely of the female contribution as "primarily material plus a secondary formal influence",[7] with IV 3 making explicit what had earlier only been implied.[8] Yet despite their many insights into the female's contribution, none of the defenders can fully explain how the earlier and later passages are related and why the two portions of the GA seem so at odds. At best, they give an incomplete defense of Aristotle's position.[9]

I shall argue that the alleged inconsistency in fact reflects the nature of GA's overall expository structure, a structure in which Aristotle's full theoretical position is revealed only through a progressive unfolding that extends over the entire treatise. In speaking of an expository structure and an unfolding position, I am making a distinction between what I shall call explanatory and expository principles.[10] Explanatory principles include the four causes, the operations of heat and cold, the priority of the actual over the potential, the primacy of male over female, and the principle that nature is everywhere a cause of order. Equally pervasive are expository principles. These are derived from Aristotle's convictions about proper sequence and pedagogical method, principles formulated to move from initially plausible assumptions and opinions so as to make what is more knowable by nature more knowable to us. Expository principles shape both the overall order of the treatises and the structure of individual treatises and so carry direct consequences for how the arguments in a treatise should be read. A treatment of issues raised earlier in a treatise may be preliminary and left intentionally incomplete, in need of later supplementation. Conversely, the argument of a later section may be derived from explanatory principles guiding the exposition as a whole, but at the same time develop and articulate those principles beyond what had been stated at ear-

---

6   See Mayhew 2004, 45–49.

7   See Balme 1987, 292.

8   A more fully worked out statement of this position can be found in Henry 2006. For a critical response to Balme's position, see Lloyd 1990, 17–24.

9   Interestingly, the basis of my approach is expressed in the last paragraph of Henry's article. There he states that "However neat and tidy the traditional interpretation may be, *when we trace Aristotle's reproductive hylomorphism through the GA* we find that it clearly does not divide the contributions of the mother and father exhaustively into matter and form" (Henry 2006, 286; my italics). Tracing Aristotle's hylomorphism through the stages of its expository unfolding is precisely what I propose to do, in a way that will go beyond the few suggestive steps Henry takes in that direction.

10   Key ideas in this paragraph are borrowed by the introduction to this collection.

lier stages of the inquiry. This implies that Aristotle's full position cannot be plucked out of a single passage, early or later, but must be found in a progressive unfolding of an argument the stages of which may extend over many chapters.[11]

The key to my resolution of the alleged inconsistency in the GA is based on the claim that the biology in general and the GA specifically operate according to both explanatory and expository principles. I propose to locate Aristotle's explanation of parental resemblance within two larger expository contexts in the GA, one nearer the problematic passage, the other more remote but also more comprehensive. Most obviously, the account in IV 3 belongs to an argument sequence beginning at the start of Book IV that poses as its central problem the differentiation of male and female in the more perfect animals. But Aristotle's overall exposition does not start there. The issue of parental resemblance addressed in IV 3 is already raised but postponed in the course of setting out the preliminary, endoxic definition of male and female introduced in GA I 2. My analysis will show that, rather than creating an inconsistency, IV 3 marks the completion of a comprehensive exposition designed to work out implications of explanatory principles left intentionally incomplete until that point. Consequently, no one part of the argument can be adequately assessed apart from the full exposition. Scholars who regard Aristotle's account as inconsistent—and even those who don't—fail to appreciate the progressive unfolding of Aristotle's exposition.

I

Before turning to the two contexts within the GA, I would like to situate the *Generation of Animals* within the larger sequence of treatises to which it belongs. It is widely recognized that the GA is part of a carefully organized series of investigations into living things, what Düring called "Aristotle's great course in biology".[12] Various passages in the biology point to an overarching plan according

---

11   My approach to the GA is indebted to Lang's close reading of the *Physics* and *De Caelo* (Lang 1998). Describing what she calls a method of subordination (11–27), Lang argues that Aristotle's basic unit of argument is the extended *pragmateia* or *logos*, which announces a set of issues and topics in a programmatic introduction, which are then investigated in a continuous development from that point, with specific arguments subordinated to the particular problem or topic they address.

12   Düring 1943, 34–35. The relation between the sequence formed by the biological treatises and Aristotle's pedagogical principles is noted by Tress 1996, 34.

to which the biological works have been arranged (e.g., *De Partibus Animalium* (*PA*) II 1.646a8–12 (cf. I 1.640a33–b4); *De Incessu Animalium* 1.704b7–10; *GA* I 1.715a1–16—a passage we shall examine in detail).[13] Extensive as the biological sequence is, it is part of a still more comprehensive plan encompassing all the works on nature. The fullest description of the plan comes at the beginning of the *Meteorology* (*Mete.* I 1.338a20–339a10).[14] There Aristotle describes a sequence that begins with the first causes of nature and natural motion, and proceeds through the orderly motions of the heavens, to the four elements, growth and decay, shooting stars, and winds and earthquakes. It finishes with plants and animals "both generally and separately" (*katholou te kai chôris*; 339a7–8; see also *Mete.* IV 12.390b15–23; *PA* I 5.645a4–7). It is not hard to map this plan onto parts of the surviving corpus. It begins with the *Physics*, leads to the *De Caelo*, proceeds to *De Generatione et Corruptione* and *Meteorology*, and concludes with the works on biology.[15] As its own programmatic opening makes clear, the *GA* stands as the final treatise in the sequence.[16] Having dealt with the other parts of animals "both those in common (*koinê*) and separately (*chôris*) about the parts as peculiar to each kind",[17] three of the four causes of

---

13   In an excess of caution perhaps reflecting a time when programmatic passages and cross-references were often held in suspicion, Balme 1992, 127 brackets the *GA*'s entire opening passage, saying it "may be post-Aristotelian". Fortunately, he has not been followed in this attitude.

14   Johnson 2005, 8 calls this passage Aristotle's syllabus for the study of nature. He notes that the progression of treatises proceeds along a scale of increasing complexity. For an extended discussion of the passage and the sequence it envisions, see Falcon 2005, 1–7. Aristotle's emphasis that one must follow the appropriate sequence both in investigating and in teaching is underlined by Burnyeat 2004.

15   Whether the *HA* belongs in the sequence has been controversial, given its appearance as an open notebook for observations prior to theorizing. But some version of this work is invoked as a preceding part of a larger sequence by *PA* II 1.646a8–12; see also *De Incessu Animalium* 1.704b7–10, previously cited. The *De Anima*, which one might say is positioned at the threshold of second and first philosophy but at the same time would precede the biology in the great sequence, is a problematic member for quite different reasons. See Polansky 2008, 7, 9–11, 36–37; also *De Sensu* 1.436a1–22.

16   Nothing in my argument hinges on the *GA*'s date of composition relative to the other biological works.

17   My translations of *GA* I–II 3 follow Balme; those for later parts of the *GA* follow Platt's translation in Barnes ed. 1984, both with important modifications noted. In the case of this line from the beginning of the *GA*, I translate *koinê* as "in common" instead of Balme's "generally". We shall return to distinctions between *koinê* (vs. *katholou* or *holôs*) and *chôris*, the idea behind which will play an important part in my resolution of the problem addressed in this paper.

their parts have been examined. There remains only the cause of motion in the sense of reproduction, which according to Aristotle's plan (*logos*) has been left until last (*GA* I 1.715a1–16).

Beyond its place in the overall sequence, the *GA* posesses it own internal structure and organization.[18] While this is generally recognized, the depth of its structure and the subtlety of its organization have not been sufficiently appreciated. Working out the details of its organization will, of course, be a major concern. For now it is sufficient to mark out four stages at which the *GA* can be divided at the broadest level.

From the beginning of the *GA* to the end of II 3, Aristotle focuses on the characteristics common (*koinêi*) to animal reproduction, particularly the role of male and female as principles, the differences in their sexual parts, and the nature of the seed each contributes to the embryo. The second major stage runs from II 4 to the end of book III. In it, Aristotle explores how these and related topics manifest themselves in the main groups into which animals are separated—first in internally viviparous animals (II 4–8), then oviparous birds and fish (III 1–8), and finally (III 9–11), he says, "it remains to speak of insects and testacea according to the plan laid down" (*kata tên huphêgê- menên methodon*, III 9.758a27–28).[19] A third stage, which is contained in the fourth book, considers questions of sexual differentiation, parental resem- blance, monstrosities, and matters related to gestation. The fourth and final stage occupies book V and, despite what commentators have often seen as a random tying up of loose ends, exhibits a reasonably well worked out inves- tigation of variations not directed toward a final cause but produced by the interactions of the many causal factors, particularly the material and the mov- ing causes (V 8.789b15–20), involved in reproduction.[20] It is within this overall structure that I shall locate the account of parental resemblance.

---

18   Thus I disagree with Balme 1992, 127, who claims that "the thread [of I–II 3] has been obscured by some ancient editor who believed it to be a descriptive anatomy".

19   The plan was laid down over the first twenty lines of II 4, with Aristotle setting out on the second stage of the investigation at 737b24.

20   On the purpose and structure of book V, see Gotthelf and Leunissen 2010, including remarks for the overall unity of the *GA*.

II

Aristotle's account of parental resemblance cannot be understood apart from the two larger contexts of which it is a part. The opening lines of IV 3 make clear that the account is a continuation of what has preceded it in book IV:

> The same causes (*hai autai aitiai*) must be held responsible for the facts that some children resemble their parents, while others do not (some being like the father and others like the mother, both in the body as a whole and in each part) ...
>
>   IV 3.767a36–37

The "same causes" referred to are not just the differences between male and female, but the causes of those differences. These were advanced over the course of IV 1–2, and constitute the immediate context of Aristotle's account. We shall examine them in detail in due course. But before doing so, it is necessary to note that the fourth book as a whole opens by placing itself within a much larger plan, its first line echoing the very first line of the entire treatise:

> We have thus spoken of the generation of animals both in terms of what is common (*koinêi*) and separately (*chôris*) in all the different classes. But since male and female are separated in the most perfect of them, and since we say that these powers (*dunameis*) are principles (*archai*) of all living things, both animals and plants, but some have them unseparated and others separated, we must speak first of the origin (*tês geneseôs*) of the sexes in the latter. For while the animal is still imperfect in its kind, the distinction is already made between male and female.[21]
>
>   IV 1.763b20–26

The passage accomplishes two things. First, Aristotle signals the completion of one phase of the exposition and the shift to a new phase. He has dealt with animal generation on the basis of both what is *koinêi* and *chôris*.[22] This

---

21   Platt does not translate *dunameis* at b23 (proleptically substituting "the sexes"), while Peck 1942 translates it as "characteristics". But Platt over-translates the accusative *archas* in the same line as "*first* principles" rather than simply as "principles". It is important not to do this so as to be able to render the contrast between principles and first principles at 766a30–b3 (where Aristotle explicitly contrasts the sexes as [non-first] principles with the heart as first principle).

22   Platt translates *koinêi* as "generally". But what Aristotle refers to are parts or features of

corresponds to the two major stages into which the GA can be divided up to this point, with the parts common to reproduction in animals occupying GA I–II 3 and specific variations in parts dealt with from II 4 to the end of III.

Second, the opening lines of IV 1 identify the problem that will now be the subject of investigation.[23] The problem arises from the fact that male and female are distinct in the most perfect animals. This is not, of course, the first time Aristotle has drawn attention to the distinction. From the beginning of the GA, male and female were said jointly to be the principles of reproduction in all living things, including both animals and plants, with the fact of their differentiation central to the arguments in both I 17–21 and II 1–3. Now at the start of book IV, and with a *scala naturae* of degrees of perfection in the background, Aristotle states that an explanation of the origin of sexual differentiation is necessary. Because male and female are principles of all living things, the explanation will apply to all animals and plants. Though the distinction can be hard to observe in lower species, it is plainly evident in the highest animals—so much so that the passage concludes with a further *phainomenon* observable by any careful investigator regardless of theoretical commitments: male and female are distinguished already in the developing embryo of these highest kinds.[24]

Aristotle proceeds to supply an extensive critical survey of expert opinion on the question of the origin of the sexes (763b27–765b6). Each predecessor, though ultimately mistaken, is said to have captured some portion of the truth. Anaxagoras held that the difference between male and female existed already in the seed, but said the seed comes only from the male; Empedocles claimed that heat gave rise to males and coldness to females, but made the uterus the source of the heat due to menstrual fluid being greater in quantity than

---

reproduction that are common or shared across the different kinds of animals. I will reserve "generally" as a translation for *holôs* and *katholou*, which refer in effect to what is true in most cases or for the most part. See also Aristotle's use of *koinêi* to refer to those parts, attributes, and conditions common to different species (often in contrast to parts treated *chôris* is each kind of animal). *Mete.* I 1.339a7–8; *PA* I 1.639a16–b6; *GA* I 1.715a1–3; IV 10.778a10–12.

23   Recall here Lang's "method of subordination". Such subordination will be evident in much that follows.

24   Clearly, if the phenomenon of sexual differentiation were apparent mainly in the lower animals and plants, a different sort of explanation would be forthcoming. In that case, sexual difference would represent a deviation or falling away from the ideal nature always strives for. As we shall see, the purpose served by differentiation is to allow the higher animals to imitate more fully the motions of the eternal heavens.

semen; Democritus saw differentiation arising from whichever seed "prevailed" (*kratêsê*) over the other, but made the seed a single, uniform thing.

Aristotle concludes his survey with a qualfied endorsement of the general idea that heat and cold are in some way causes of the differences between male and female (765b2). But this, he says, is not an adequate way of putting it:

> Yet to put it this way is to lay hold of the cause from too far away (*porôthen*); we must draw as near to the primary causes (*tôn prôtôn aitiôn*) from those things that have been admitted (*ek tôn endechomenôn*) as possible.[25]
>
> IV 1.765b4–6

Aristotle does not deny that hot and cold are causes; indeed, these are fundamental factors in his natural philosophy generally and in his own solution to the problem. But stated baldly as "hot and cold" they are not sufficiently informative as an explanation of sexual differentiation. Rather, he will draw on the positive results of the dialectical survey to find principles closer to the specific problem at hand, something that will presumably involve heat and cold.

This leads to a short but key transition marking the beginning of Aristotle's own position. The transition is just two sentences:

> We have, then, spoken in a different work (*proteron en heterois*) of both the body as a whole and its parts, both what each part is and for what reason it exists (*ti te hekaston esti kai dia tin' aitian*). But male and female are distinguished by a certain capacity (*dunamis*) and incapacity (*adunamia*).[26]
>
> IV 1.765b7–9

In the first sentence, Aristotle places his own account of sexual differentiation within a larger context. Indeed, it is a much larger context, for it carries us back momentarily to the beginning of the entire sequence of the biological works and signals the precise way in which what he is about to say departs from what he has said up to this point. In saying that he has treated the body as a whole

---

25   Both Platt and Peck render the phrase *ek tôn endechomenôn* as "as much as is possible". But coming at the end of a dialectical survey that has arrived at a degree of consensus between Aristotle and his predecessors, I think a more literal translation is appropriate. I thank Alan Bowen for this suggestion.

26   Aristotle's language here echoes that of *Posterior Analytics* II 1–2. For a similar parallel with the *APo.* and the earlier discussion of *sperma*, see Bolton 1987, especially 151–164.

and its parts elsewhere, Aristotle is pointing back not just to the beginning of the *GA*, but to the plan announced as far back as the *PA*.[27] From *PA* II onward, each animal part was indeed explained in terms of the positive function it was able to perform (*PA* II 1.646a10–12; 647a1–3). As we shall see shortly, the same approach has been followed in the *GA* up to this point specifically with regard to male and female as principles. Through the first three books of the *GA*, Aristotle has explained these parts in terms of their positive powers and functions, of the *dunamis* each part possesses and the *ergon* it serves.

The second sentence signals that this positive approach is not adequate to explain sexual differentiation and the phenomena surrounding parental resemblance in the higher animals. In place of identifying the positive capacities of different parts, Aristotle will now employ a distinction between having a power or capacity and not possessing that specific capacity. The concept of the female's *adunamia* had in fact been introduced at I 20.728b16–21, where the female is said to be incapable of concocting the nutriment into semen. But the idea entered the discussion as an aside and is not used subsequently in the first two stages of the *GA*. Returning to the distinction here marks a crucial departure (I do not say an inconsistency) from what had been Aristotle's standard mode of explanation. With it commences the final portion of the explication of male and female as principles of animal reproduction. To see that this is so, and by it to see why Aristotle's overall position is not inconsistent, we must follow the steps of the exposition of male and female from its beginning.

III

The first stage of the progressive exposition begins immediately after the *GA*'s opening programmatic remarks. It is worth noting that the first chapter of the *GA* does not explicitly identify male and female as *archai*. Rather, *GA* I 1 is confined to a survey of the *phainomena* of animal generation, carefully dividing animals into those that are formed by the union of male and female and those that are not, with some generalizations and brief details regarding the main groups making up each division. Only in the opening lines of I 2 does Aristotle posit male and female as the *archai* of generation, explicitly identifying them as the initial starting points for an extended and staged investigation:

---

27   Peck 1942 also sees these lines as pointing back to the first book of the *GA* and to the *PA* as a whole.

Of the generation of animals we must speak as various questions arise in order in the case of each, and we must connect our account with what has been said. Based on what was said above, we may at a minimum set down (*ouk hêkista theiê*) as the starting points (*archai*) of generation the female and the male, the former as having the efficient cause of generation, the latter the material of it.[28]

> I 2.716a3–7

Aristotle here sets down the thesis that will become the subject of a structured sequence. Based on their prominence (but not ubiquity) in animal reproduction, male and female may be set down as the starting points of generation. As such, they become at the same time the starting points for an extended investigation. He immediately offers as evidence calculated to be "most persuasive" (716a8) the apparent fact that both male and female produce and emit "seed" (*sperma*).[29] This leads to a first preliminary definition of the two terms, "by a male animal we mean that which generates in another, and by female that which generates in itself" (716a14–15), which is made plausible (though hardly proved) by appealing to a mythological *endoxon* that identifies the Earth as female and mother, and the sky and Sun as male and father (716a15–17).

Aristotle then offers a fuller description of male and female in I 2, distinguishing between them in no fewer than four ways—by their respective definitions, *dunameis*, functions, and physical parts:

> Male and female differ in their definition (*logos*) by each having a separate faculty (*tôi dunasthai heteron hekateron*), and to perception by their particular parts. By definition the male is the one able (*to dunamenon*) to generate in another, as said above; whereas the female is the one able to generate into itself and out of which comes into being the offspring previously existing in the generator. And since they are differentiated by a faculty and by their function (*dunamei kai ergôi*), and since instruments are needed for all functioning, and since the bodily parts are the instru-

---

28   Here I translate *archai* as starting points rather than principles to suggest a parallel between the starting points of generation and the starting points of Aristotle's inquiry. Male and female are not at this point fully articulated *principles* of a demonstrative science but endoxic starting points of the investigation.

29   More will be said about the ambiguity of *sperma* shortly. At this point I would simply say the ambiguity is not inappropriate for the preliminary stages of the inquiry, and that the concept receives clarification and refinement at later stages.

ments to serve the faculties, it follows that certain parts must exist for union and production of offspring. And these must differ from each other, so that consequently the male will differ from the female.

I 2.716a16–26

I have quoted this passage at length because it is key to recognizing the nature of Aristotle's exposition. The distinction between male and female in terms of their *dunameis* and *erga* is obviously preliminary. It is an *endoxon*, a distinction more familiar or better known to us initially in virtue of its being perceptible (716a20; also 716a32). As an *endoxon*, it is a presumed fact for which an explanation must now be sought—the *hoti* in need of the *dioti*, as the *Posterior Analytics* would put it. Positing male and female as starting points raises questions rather than solving them, and so sets the program for the subsequent investigation.

Unpacking and refining this phenomenologically and endoxically inspired definition becomes the task of the first major stage of the *GA* in books I and II. Everything from the beginning of I 3 to the end of II 3 forms a sequence of puzzles arising from the differences between male and female and their parts, with each puzzle leading to the next. The investigation begins in I 3–11, where Aristotle considers why sexual parts display such great variety in their visible structure, i.e., in terms of what is familiar to us in virtue of their being perceptible. I 3 summarizes the variety of sexual parts, with 4–7 surveying differences in testes, and 8–11 those of the uterus. Only in I 12 does Aristotle turn from external structures to the internal, asking why the uterus is always internal while testes are sometimes internal and sometimes not. I 13 considers why the passage for excretion of waste sometimes coincides with the sexual part; the short chapters 14–16 extend the discussion to bloodless animals.

From I 17 to I 20 Aristotle investigates a network of questions pertaining to the issue of "what is the nature of the seed generally (*holôs*)" (I 17.721b4).[30] These chapters provide striking anticipations of problems addressed in IV 1–3, particularly in their consideration of the fundamental difference between male and female contributions to generation as well the issue of parental likeness.[31]

---

30   Here Aristotle speaks generally (*holôs* or *katholou*, though the latter term is not used here) about what most but not all animals exhibit rather than of what they have in common (*koinê*). Mayhew 2004, 31–37 surveys Aristotle's use of key "spermatic" terms, taking his cue from Balme 1992, 131.

31   Morsink 1982, 127 perceptively calls chapters I 17–19 Aristotle's "unfinished argument", which concentrates only on the absurd consequences of pangenesis. For an extended analysis of the argument of this section, see Bolton 1987.

It is notable, however, that while the general investigation rejects rival theories and argues for important claims such as that the seed is a residual form of blood (not a waste product), Aristotle does not offer anything like a full explanation for parental resemblance or for the difference between the sexes. The closest he comes to explaining parental likeness is half a sentence that claims that it is "natural" for the offspring to resemble the parents given that the seed, as highly concocted blood, is capable of nourishing all the parts (I 19.726b13–14). In fact, several times Aristotle directs the reader to a later portion of the GA for a fuller account of these matters (I 17.723b25; 724a6–7; 19.726b18–21).[32]

In I 21–23, which conclude book I, Aristotle asks how male and female contribute to generation. This would seem to be another plausible place in which to address the question of parental resemblance. Indeed, this is a key passage for those who find earlier and later parts of Aristotle's account inconsistent. But the terminology should give us pause. I 21 says that on general grounds (holôs), the female is passive and moved, while the male is active and moving. Aristotle is quite clear that he is offering a generalization "so that the extremes (ta akra) of each of the two is grasped" (I 21.729b14).[33] In other words, he is highlighting the conceptual difference between male and female as sharply as possible, ignoring other differences or similarities at this point in the investigation. Surely by this remark Aristotle leaves room for—if not actually promises—further specification and refinement.

The unpacking continues in book II, which turns in its opening lines to the problem of sexual differentiation. But, as before, male and female are distinguished on the basis of their different positive capacities:

> That the male and female are the principles of generation has been previously stated, as well as what is their power and their definition (dunamis kai ho logos tês ouias). But why is it that one thing becomes and is male, another female?[34]
>
> II 1.731b19–21

---

32   These passages should be compared to II 1.731b23, where Aristotle provides an explanation of sexual differentiation in terms of the final cause but postpones an explanation in terms of necessity and the efficient cause due to the material constitution of male and female. I shall return to this passage shortly.

33   Ta akra are literally the highpoints or summits. The phrase can refer to the extreme terms in a proportion and to the limiting cases in a range of possibilities. In the Prior Analytics, ta akra are the extreme terms of a syllogism bound together by means of the middle term. We shall see that the meson between these extremes is provided later in GA IV 3.

34   See also II 4.738b18–23, where the distinction in terms of positive powers is again repeated.

Before answering this question, he distinguishes between two sorts of explanation. One is in terms of the necessities arising from the efficient and material causes, the other explains in terms of the that-for-the-sake-of-which, the final cause. Famously, Aristotle proceeds (731b24–732a25) by pointing to a principle "from above" (*anôthen*) to explain the final cause behind the distinction between male and female: that perishable things take part in reproduction so that the species may enjoy a kind of immortality, and that among higher animals it is better that the male, as conveyer of form, be separated from the inferior female, which provides the matter. But he is absolutely clear that this is not the whole story, explicitly postponing until later an explanation of differentiation in terms of the moving and material causes (731b22). There can be no doubt that the explication of the difference between male and female is incomplete and that a full accounting in terms of the four causes must wait until a later stage of the exposition.

At this point, however, the exposition moves in a different direction. In II 2, Aristotle says one may puzzle over the nature of semen. One might be surprised by this claim, in that semen had been discussed extensively in I 17–23. But again the method of subordination is at work. In the earlier section, the question was whether or not the seed came from every part of the body. Now the question pertains to semen's material constituents: though in one sense, the material of semen is blood, more fundamentally it is a combination water and *pneuma*, air or breath warmed by the natural heat of the body. The investigation into semen continues in II 3, where Aristotle turns to the question of how *nous* is transmitted from parent to offspring. Only at the end of II 3 does Aristotle complete his general explication of the *dunameis* of male and female, explaining them in terms of *pneuma*, the three faculties of soul, and the distinction between potential and actual. In short, at no earlier point can the explication of the distinction between male and female be considered final or complete. The first major stage of the *GA* amounts to a progressive elaboration and refinement of a preliminary definition first introduced in *GA* I 2.[35]

With this pattern of explanation in terms of positive powers in mind, we can now understand how IV 1's distinction between a *dunamis* and an *adunamia* functions in the overall exposition. The distinction between a capacity and an incapacity with respect to concocting blood is central to the argument of the rest of the chapter and thus to the resolution of the *aporia* posed but left unresolved by his predecessors surveyed at the beginning of this stage of the exposi-

---

35   I will pass over the second major stage of the *GA*, which begins at II 4 and treats male and female in the different kinds according to their (positive) powers and functions.

tion in IV 1. But there is no inconsistency between the new distinction and the previous definition highlighting the female's positive capacity (of which the brief transition had served as a reminder). The female does not suffer an absolute incapacity, an inability to effect any change at all. After all, the female's blood is itself a concocted product, with its own *dunameis*, representing the stage at which food taken into the digestive system has been turned into utilizable nourishment. Rather, the *adunamia* represents the upper limit to an inherent positive power. Indeed, he says a few lines later, "able" and "unable" are spoken of in many senses, so that a given faculty is able to produce its effect to a lower or higher degree (766a2–3). The female's *adunamia* is a carefully qualified incapacity, namely, an inability to work blood up to its final, purest stage (*katharon*, 765b36), which on his view is what semen is. In other words, the female is not a purely passive material receptor.

Because the *adunamia* is qualified and not absolute, it does not imply that the female is totally incapable of imparting movements. Indeed, Aristotle said as much in II 5, in explaining the phenomenon of so-called wind-eggs in some species of birds. According to Aristotle, the male and not the female imparts the sensitive soul, the possession of which is the necessary condition for animal life (see also *An* II 2.413b1–4). But in some birds, the motions belonging to the nutritive soul are sufficient on their own to begin (though not to complete) the development of the embryo even without the male, so that "the female can generate up to a certain point unaided" (II 5.741a18).[36] He even entertains the possibility, based on reports from fishermen, that in some species of fish the female might be fully capable of reproducing without the male, though he says no reliable evidence has yet been found.[37]

The female, in other words, is a cause and a principle, as Aristotle has maintained from the beginning; only with respect to the highest degree of concoction is she found lacking. She is a mover imparting motions of her own, an *arche*, simply not a *first* mover with regard to generation—the female's contribution must (first) be moved by the contribution of the male.[38] But once

---

36   Even earlier, he had remarked without further explanation that the females of some birds "can generate to a certain extent, for they do form something" (I 21.730a30–31). On wind-eggs and the female contribution to generation with regard to the nutritive vs. the sensate soul, see further Mayhew 2004, 45–47. Gelber 2010, 198–202 points out why it is doubtful that the female contributes the nutritive soul in an unqualified way, as the nutritive soul in actuality.

37   The fact that Aristotle does not reject out of hand female parthenogenesis as an impossibility mitigates to some extent the *a priori* sexism with which other aspects of his account are charged.

38   I therefore disagree with Cooper's argument that movements are in every case due to the

the vital motions of the fully concocted semen are introduced and make the material supplied by the female into a living embryo, the female's own positive capacity, i.e., the nutritive motions present in her material, is sufficient in the ordinary course of development to maintain the fetus. This is just what the endoxically inspired preliminary definition of the female in I 2 had implied, though without adequate explanation.

This suggests that the exposition of Aristotle's biological *pragmateia* has been worked out at a level of detail that determines what is said and left unsaid over a very large expanse of writing. Defining the female in terms of a positive capacity was part of an extended investigation into the *dunameis* of each sex. But the capacities of male and female cannot explain sexual differentiation. They are instead a result of it.

IV

We may now return to IV 3. As we saw, the chapter opens with a contextualizing transition. The full passage lists the range of phenomena to be accounted for using the causes previously identified:

> The same causes (*hai autai aitiai*) must be held responsible for the facts that some children resemble their parents, while others do not (some being like the father and others like the mother, both in the body as a whole and in each part); and that they resemble these [the parents] more than remoter ancestors, and resemble those more than any chance individual; and that males more resemble their fathers, females their mothers; that some, though resembling none of their relations, yet do at any rate resemble a human being, but others have not even the look (*tên idean*) of a human being but already a monstrosity. For even he who does not resemble his parents is already in a certain sense a monstrosity; for in these cases nature has in a way departed from type (*parekbêbeke ek toû genous tropan tina*).[39]
>
> IV 3.767a36–b8

---

semen. In this I am influenced by the analysis of Aristotle's position in Coles 1995, 71–74. See also the criticism of Cooper in Gelber 2010, 203–209. Morsink 1982, 132–135, argues that in book IV Aristotle extends the meaning *dunamis* far beyond its ordinary usage employed previously.

39   The contrast between humans and monstrosities in b4–6 shows that Aristotle has parental resemblance in humans mainly in mind.

The long list of phenomena provides a nice example of how explanatory factors not identified at one stage of an exposition can influence the exposition at a later stage. Working backward through the list, one can see that it amounts to a series of dichotomous divisions reflecting a deviation from the norm or ideal at each level of the division. The offspring is either monstrous or human; if human, it resembles either remote ancestors or the parents; if it resembles the parents, it is more like either the mother or the father; if the offspring is male, it is either more like the mother or like the father. In effect, the problem of parental resemblance briefly noted previously but left unexplained will now be addressed in its full complexity.[40]

It should be clear now that the causes alluded to include motions residing in the female's contribution and that (whatever its other obscurities and shortcomings!) Aristotle's account of parental resemblance is not *ad hoc* or inconsistent in any obvious way. But IV 3 also relies on a crucial idea from IV 2. It seems that not just any male and female in a species can reproduce successfully. Although male and female are to be distinguished as a whole (*holôs*), yet there must be a certain correspondence (*summetria*) or ratio (*logos*) between male and female if they are to produce offspring (GA IV 2.767a13–17).[41] If heat predominates too much (*lian kratoûn*) it dries up the liquid; if it is very deficient (*polu elleîpon*) the combination fails to set. In a biological version of the doctrine of the mean adapted to the question of fertile and infertile couples, Aristotle says that there must be a due mean between these extremes (*ton toû mesou logon*). As long as the extremes of too much heat and too much cold are avoided, an offspring can be produced.

This allows us to return to IV 3 and refine the question being asked there. What happens when a mix within the acceptable middle range is achieved, when one or the other contribution predominates, but not so much as to render the fetus unviable? Given IV 2, we know there is a due proportion. But given the nature of the mean as a range between extremes, there is no exactly specifiable midpoint. Of course one or the other contribution must predomi-

---

40 Morsink 1982, 132 notices that the list of phenomena to be explained corresponds to the objections Aristotle had raised against pangenesis theory in I 18. This is a further sign of the level of detail at which the exposition has been worked out.

41 The notion that a due proportion is needed between the contributions of male and female was mentioned in passing as early as I 18.723a26–31 and I 19.727b11–12. Indeed, the first of these passages looks like a pointer to the present chapter. The need for a proper proportion between male and female contributions is noted by Reeve 1992, 202. Cooper 1988, 67–68, on the other hand, argues that the notion of *summetria*, while assigning an important role to the female, comes well before any mention of motions in the menses.

nate: the offspring must be either male or female. Aristotle's theory of parental resemblance—or we may say more precisely, familial resemblance—is the answer. In a long and intricate argument,[42] Aristotle combines the principle of proportionality with the female's qualified incapacity fully to concoct blood to explain the differentiation into male or female, and the resemblance to father or mother, or to more distant ancestors. At the same time, the argument also saves the appearances captured correctly though partially in earlier accounts—the Anaxagorean idea of male and female capacities inherent in the parental seeds, and the Democritean principle of predominance.

As for what constitutes a due proportion, Aristotle is not explicit,[43] though Furth came close to seeing the explantion without recognizing it—in fact, criticizing it as part of the alleged overall inconsistency. All material things are composites of form and matter. But the concepts of form and matter are always relative to a given level of analysis, as is the resulting composite of the two. That is to say, when one considers a uniform part of the body, say for example blood, the form is the essence of blood, while the matter is water and earth. The blood itself as a uniform part is a composite. When one considers a non-uniform part such as a hand, the form is (say) the function of the hand, while the matter is (a composite of) blood and flesh. Blood is matter from the latter perspective, and formed composite from the former. Now both the male's semen and female's menses are forms of blood, differing (as we saw) in that the former is more highly "concocted" than the latter. But as forms of blood, both are also composites of form and matter (this is the point that Furth saw without grasping its significance). Thus, while it is correct to say that the female's contribution serves as the matter in generation, it would certainly not be correct to say that the *katamenia* is unformed matter.[44] Rather, as IV 1 said, it is not *fully* formed in this one respect: it is blood less purified than the male's

---

42   Some of which, as Lloyd 1990, 18 says, is "desperately indeterminate". Here our understanding may be limited by the loss of Aristotle's treatise *On Growth and Nutrition* (see GA V 2.781b2–3). But neither Lloyd nor Furth sees how closely the account of IV 3 follows from principles in IV 1 and IV 2, much less from the earliest stages of the investigation. Furth in fact calls the account in IV 3 a "surprise".

43   It should be noted that a *summetria* of hot and cold functions as a major causal explanatory principle in his overall natural science; see for instance *Phys.* IV 3.246b4–6. In GA IV 10, Aristotle suggests that the varying effects of hot and cold in the sublunary sphere are the attenuated influence of heat in the outer cosmos (IV 10.777b26–778a2).

44   A point expressed nicely by Gelber 2010, 201: "That which plays the role of the matter for a change will itself be something *of some sort*, a hylomorphic composite of form and matter" (emphasis in the original).

semen. Though in the general terms of a hylomorphic dichotomy the menses is to be identified with the concept of matter, it has its own form and powers, making it the kind of part it is.[45]

It is important to say "in general terms" for another reason. For not just any chance combination of sperm and menses will produce a viable offspring. As Aristotle had said in an earlier passage, the specific combination of active agent and materials must naturally (*pephuke*) be suited to one another if generation is to take place (*GA* II 6.743a21–25). This clearly implies that semen and the menses encounter each other as more and less dynamic composite substances, not as pure activity on the one hand and pure passivity on the other. A viable *summetria* or *logos* must be achieved within a range of consonant pre-existing motions derived from each contribution.

The inherent dynamism of both male and female contributions is probably why, regardless of which set of motions predominates, certain motions continue in what geneticists would call a masked fashion. Judging from the phenomenon of grandparental likeness, these motions persist beneath the surface, ready to assert themselves in future generations. Aristotle's account is admittedly sketchy here, one point on which pretty much all commentators agree. But it would seem that the motions of the grandparents' seed (both male and female) are not fully effaced by the formal properties of the parental seed. Their potential to impart enforming motion persists, just as one might say the vibrating strings of a piano, struck with the sustaining pedal being held, color and materially affect the sound of strings that are subsequently struck.[46]

Is there anything predictable in these interactions? Aristotle strongly implies that there is not, at least at the level of a particular pair of parents. Though their interactions would be mechanically determined, I am inclined to say he would regard them as wholly unpredictable, particularly with regard to non-

---

45   Thus, when at the conclusion of a long passage at I 20.729a21–33 Aristotle calls the female menses *protê hulê*, he is picking out its role at the broadest conceptual level (cf. *kata ton logon*, a23–24) as proximate rather than formless matter; see Peck 1942, 111 note "e", Balme 1992, 152, and Mayhew 2004, 42. Relevant too is *Metaph.* VII 16.1040b5–9: The parts of animals are not *ousiai*, but rather *dunameis*, for they exist "all of them" (*panta*) as matter, implying that from the standpoint of the living composite being, both menses and semen are matter.

46   The continuation of soul-motions across generations raises the interesting possibility of a kind of immortality for the individual soul, or at least for potentialities residing in a particular soul. Whether these motions attenuate over time and even cease (rather like Cebes' weaver who outlives many cloaks but eventually dies) is not a question that Aristotle raises.

essential characteristics. After introducing the idea of the reproductive mean in IV 2, Aristotle enumerates a series of phenomena that strongly suggest there would be little predictability. An individual's constitution is crucial, but so is the person's age and health. Even the waters one drinks and the direction of the wind at the time of conception can influence the outcome. These are no doubt the sorts of instances that prompt Aristotle to say, at IV 10.778a5–10, that nature's intention to achieve a *summetria* of hot and cold in living things can be frustrated by both the indeterminacy of matter (*aoristos tês hulês*) and the mutual interference of a multiplicity of causal factors. Though this passage refers specifically to the female's contribution and so may be used as further evidence of Aristotle's sexism, it shows as well that the material contribution should be understood as not merely passive. It is a particular kind of enformed matter, with capacities and motions inherent to its own nature.[47]

When Aristotle sums up this stage of the argument in IV 3, he commends certain predecessors who expressed imprecisely the reason for cross-generational resemblance for at least recognizing a multiplicity of potential causal factors (IV 3.769a25–769b1).[48] In a passage recalling the earlier criticism of positing hot and cold as causes of male and female, he continues:

> But if we assign only one manner of causation, it is not easy to give the causes of everything—of the origin of male and female, why the female is often like the father and the male like the mother, and again the resemblance to remote ancestors, and further the reason why the offspring is sometimes unlike any of these but still a human being, but sometimes, proceeding further on these lines, appears finally to be not even a human being but only some kind of animal, what is called a monstrosity.[49]
>
> IV 3.769b3–b9

---

47 Despite what I take to be the inherent unpredictability of mixing of motions, Aristotle in book V does offer a general account of differences such as hair color and voice pitch that arise at the individual level due to the interactions. See further Gotthelf and Leunissen 2010.

48 Compare Aristotle's endorsement of this idea with the position in certain Hippocratic treatises that the constituents of the human body, though blended, retain their specific natures. See further Lloyd 1983, 89–94. Coles 1995 develops numerous parallels between the GA and Hippocratic embryological treatises.

49 The chapter concludes by applying the theory to the case of monsters—offspring who appear not even to be human but only some kind of animal.

Unless this passage is seen as the conclusion of a long-unfolding exposition, the account in IV 3 could easily seem *ad hoc* and inconsistent with earlier stages. Aristotle in book I *had* identified one causal role for each parent, defining the male's contribution as active, formal, and moving, the female's as passive and material. But that was a preliminary endoxic definition, treated as such from the moment it was put forward. It was refined and developed over the course of *GA* I 3–II 3. But even then its treatment was not complete, for Aristotle had not accounted for it in terms of all four causes, nor fully explained the distinction between male and female in the highest animals. Not until book IV does Aristotle do that. The argument there finally completes the preliminary working definition by suggesting that each parent contributes motions to the conception, though in varying degrees, and that these motions somehow preserve motions from the non-dominant parent's seed, and even from the grandparents and more distant ancestors. Only when we reach the end of a sequence begun at the start of the *GA* do we fully understand the role of male and female as principles of generation announced at the beginning.

CHAPTER 9

The Concept of *Ousia* in *Metaphysics* Alpha, Beta, and Gamma*

Vasilis Politis and Jun Su

Abstract

The aim of this article is to examine Aristotle's use of the term *ousia* in books Alpha, Beta, and Gamma, and, by doing so, to establish what is Aristotle's basic concept of *ousia* in the *Metaphysics*. We shall argue for the following claims. First, contrary to a long and dominant critical tradition, which principally relies on the first two chapters of Gamma and largely ignores the use of the term *ousia* in books Alpha and Beta, Aristotle's basic concept of *ousia* in the *Metaphysics* is not the concept of *that which being is* or *that which determines that which being is*. Secondly, book Beta, the book of *aporiai*, serves both to develop the project of Alpha and to prepare for the first two chapters of Gamma, and it does so also in regard to the concept (or concepts) of *ousia* in Alpha and in Gamma. Thirdly, the question "What is being?" and the concepts *that which being is* and *that which determines that which being is*, so familiar from Gamma, are introduced in Beta as a result of and in order to address and engage with a particular *aporia*. Finally, Aristotle's concept of *ousia* in the *Metaphysics*, including the concepts *that which being is* and *that which determines that which being is*, are, in a strong sense, *aporia*-based; that is, they can be understood *only* by understanding and engaging with certain *aporiai*.

1   Introduction

How are we to understand the term *ousia*, as it is introduced in the *Metaphysics*? How are we to do this, if we do not want to appeal, straight away, to Aristotle's account of *ousia* from later on in the work, in particular by appealing to Gamma 1–2, and without looking further ahead? What, in any case, is wrong with appealing to Gamma 1–2 and answering that, as we know from these two chapters, Aristotle's concept of *ousia* in the *Metaphysics* is, if not

---

*   For instructive and helpful critical comments, we are grateful to David Meissner, Ronald Polansky, and Pantazis Tselemanis; also, and especially, to the anonymous referee.

identical with, then closely related to the question "What is being?" and the concept *that which being is*? For, as Aristotle argues in Gamma 2, the concept of *ousia* is the concept of that special kind of being (or those special kinds of being) that determines *that which being is*. Is there, especially if we look to Aristotle's use of the term *ousia* in books Alpha and Beta, reason to question the answer based on Gamma? If we should find that there is reason to question this answer, then this would be a significant finding, if only because this is an answer that critics commonly give, and give so readily as to betray that they consider it beyond question. In recent times, critics have been beholden to this answer (we may call it the Gamma-based reading of Aristotle's concept of *ousia* in the *Metaphysics*) especially since Owen's 1960 paper.[1]

It is remarkable that as early as the end of chapter 2 of book Alpha (see 983a21–23) Aristotle says that he has now stated what is his overall project and task, the task of searching for *sophia*, and whereas he has countless times used the terms *aitia* and *archē* to characterize and articulate this task, he has not once used the term *ousia* up to this point in the *Metaphysics*. When, in the remainder of book Alpha, he uses the term *ousia*, which he does quite a number of times, he does so always with reference to other thinkers, especially Plato. In book Alpha Aristotle appears to be using the term *ousia*, in the main at any rate, to refer to the essence of a thing, and he goes out of his way to point out that this is how he is mostly using it. He is not using it here to refer to the essence of being, but to essence in general and of any thing.

This should, at least, make us wonder how, as if all of a sudden, book Gamma introduces the question "What is being?" and the concept *that which being is* and, as a consequence, the concept of *ousia* to mean *that which determines that which being is*. Or are we simply to suppose that there is no relation and no link

---

1   Owen 1960; Kirwan 1971, 75: "Book A, which they [*sc.* the editors of the *Metaphysics*] set at the beginning, describes the aim of the philosophy as the removal of surprise and perplexity by supplying 'knowledge of original causes', and assesses the work of Aristotle's predecessors in that field. After the short book designated α, B outlines a set of 'perplexities', most of which get examined, more or less directly, in the rest of the treatise. Γ thus stands, by the traditional ordering, at the start of Aristotle's main discussion of metaphysics; it announces its subject matter in the first chapter; and its argument is hardly more dependent on what has preceded than on other parts of Aristotle's work". Likewise Barnes 1995, and many others. Cf. also Brentano 1975 originally 1862, 1: "For first philosophy must begin with a determination of the sense of the name 'being', if indeed its object is being *qua* being, as Aristotle claims repeatedly and with great definiteness ... Thus, as he himself says (*Metaph.* VII 1.1028b2), Aristotle researches and investigates in the books of the *Metaphysics* always only one question, namely, what is being?" On the other hand, compare and contrast Ross 1923, 154–155, and Ross 1924, lxxvi–vii. We do not wish to include Ross in the Gamma-based reading.

between the concept of *ousia* in book Alpha and the concept of *ousia* in book Gamma? Before we are drawn to any such conclusion, or to the closely associated conclusion that there is no apparent relation or link between Aristotle's project as characterized in Alpha and the project as characterized in the opening chapters of Gamma, we should, at least, wonder whether such a relation and link is perhaps provided in book Beta, the book of problems and *aporiai*.

11   Problems with the Gamma-Based Reading of the Concept of *Ousia*

There are, we think, serious problems with the Gamma-based reading of Aristotle's concept of *ousia* in the *Metaphysics*. We shall articulate them summarily in this section, before attending to them properly and fully later.

But first let us remind ourselves of what one shall find that Aristotle's concept of *ousia* is, if one relies on book Gamma and its opening two chapters. Aristotle begins book Gamma with the assertion that there is a science of being *qua* being; that is, of what it is for something—anything—to be, and to be a being. In the second chapter he raises, and begins to respond to, some problems about the very idea that being—all beings and all of being—can be the subject of a single enquiry, investigation and science; problems that are due in part to his own views from the *Categories* and in part due to views that he shares with other thinkers.[2] What is distinctive of Aristotle's way of resolving these problems is his proposal that being has a *pros hen* structure. This is the proposal that all beings divide into beings that depend (cf. ἤρτηται, 1003b17), for their being beings, on other beings, and beings that do not depend, for their being beings, on other beings. These latter are, in this sense, *primary beings*, or what Aristotle calls *ousiai* (1003b18), in that they are that which determines what it is for something to be or, simply, what being is (where "x determines Y" is equivalent to "Y depends on x"). If, therefore, one relies, for establishing Aristotle's basic concept of *ousia* in the *Metaphysics*, on the Gamma-based account of *ousia*, then one shall find that Aristotle's basic concept of *ousia* in the *Metaphysics* is the concept of *that which determines that which being is* and is closely related to the concept *that which being is*.

We think there are serious problems with relying on the Gamma-based account of Aristotle's concept of *ousia* for establishing Aristotle's basic concept of *ousia* in the *Metaphysics*.

---

2   For a recent account of these problems, which argues that they are due not only to Aristotle's views but also to views he takes himself to share with others, see Politis and Steinkrueger 2017.

The First Problem. If we suppose that we can, straight away, use the opening chapters of Gamma to establish Aristotle's basic concept of *ousia* in the *Metaphysics*, then *either* we will suppose that Aristotle's task in the *Metaphysics* as characterized in book Alpha involves the question "What is being?" and the task of enquiring into that which being is, and this supposition is questionable; *or* we will suppose there is no apparent relation or link between Aristotle's project as characterized in Alpha and the project as characterized in the opening chapters of Gamma, and this is not an attractive view.

This problem relies on the supposition that, based on the way in which Aristotle characterizes his project, the search for *sophia*, in book Alpha, this project does not involve and is not associated with the question "What is being?" or with an enquiry into *that which being is* or into *that which determines that which being is*. We think that a careful reading of book Alpha will readily confirm this supposition (as we shall argue in the next section).

On its own, this problem may not seem especially serious. Even setting to one side the difficult question of whether the division of the *Metaphysics* into these books goes back to Aristotle, or indeed whether these three books (Alpha, Beta, and Gamma) belong together originally, one may respond to the apparent problem by arguing that in book Alpha Aristotle does not want to do more than give an introductory and partial account of *sophia*, and that he intends to complete and drive home the account of *sophia* in the opening chapters of Gamma. One may even, in a positive spirit of pluralism, urge that there is no reason to suppose that there is a single basic concept of *ousia* in books Alpha, Beta, and Gamma of the *Metaphysics*, rather there are at least two basic concepts of *ousia* in these books, *one* being the concept of *the primary cause of a thing's being the way it is*, from book Alpha, *another* being the concept of *that which determines that which being is*, from book Gamma, and urge that both concepts are basic in the sense that neither is derivable from the other and, indeed, each can be understood perfectly well without reference to the other. That is, one need not be particularly troubled by the idea that there is no apparent relation or link between Aristotle's project as characterized in Alpha and the project as characterized in the opening chapters of Gamma.[3]

---

3   See Owen 1960, 179–180 and 192 and Kirwan 1971, 75. Contrast this with Ross 1923, 155 and Madigan 1999, xxii–xxxviii.

This may be an adequate response to the first problem, were it not for the extended part of the *Metaphysics*, which we refer to as book Beta, the book of problems or *aporiai*, situated between Alpha and Gamma.[4] Book Beta is not a cut-and-paste list of problems, and problems that may be more or less relevant to Aristotle's project; on the contrary, it is a series of problems that serve to articulate the project. There is good reason for thinking that book Beta serves both to develop the project of book Alpha and to prepare for the first two chapters of book Gamma, and that it does so also in regard to the concept (or concepts) of *ousia* in Alpha and in Gamma.

This takes us to:

> **The Second Problem.** It is wrong to suppose that we can, straight away, use the opening chapters of Gamma to establish Aristotle's basic concept (or concepts) of *ousia* in the *Metaphysics*. This is because: (1), Aristotle's basic concept (or concepts) of *ousia* in the *Metaphysics* can be properly understood only by establishing how it is (or they are) related to Aristotle's basic project in the *Metaphysics*, the project of searching for wisdom, *sophia*; (2), the series of problems in book Beta serves to articulate this project; and (3) book Beta serves both to develop the project of book Alpha and to prepare for the first two chapters of book Gamma, and it does so also in regard to the concept (or concepts) of *ousia* in Alpha and in Gamma.

It should be noted that point (1) under this problem is common ground between us and the Gamma-based reading; indeed, this point will be accepted by most critics. It is, therefore, the addition, to (1), of points (2) and (3) that creates a problem for the Gamma-based reading.

III   The Concept of *Ousia* in Book Alpha

(i) Let us begin by considering how Aristotle characterizes his project in book Alpha and what is the place of the concept of *ousia* in this characterization and this book.

At the end of Alpha 2 Aristotle says:

---

4   Book Beta is so situated even if one supposes that the insertion of Alpha-elatton goes back to Aristotle.

It has been stated (εἴρηται), then, what is the nature of the science we are searching for, and what is the mark (ὁ σκοπός) that our search and our whole investigation (μέθοδον) must reach.

983a21–23

Aristotle, therefore, takes himself to have provided, by the end of Alpha 2, a characterization of the basic project and task of the *Metaphysics*; this being the task that he has, from the beginning of Alpha, referred to as *sophia* and the search for *sophia*. He has identified the search for wisdom, *sophia*, with the search for first causes (*aitiai*) and principles (*archai*), and has identified a variety of marks of causes and principles and of the search for causes and principles. It is remarkable that the term *ousia* is not used in the first two chapters of Alpha; and that, no less clearly, the concepts *that which being is* and *that which determines that which being is* are absent from the opening of the *Metaphysics*. This has to be important, especially in view of Aristotle's statement at the end of chapter 2. It is undeniable that the term *ousia* is not used in the first two chapters of Alpha, and that by the end of the second chapter Aristotle takes himself to have introduced his project and task of the *Metaphysics* and at least some of its basic concepts. Indeed, if we put together these two facts, we might go as far as inferring that the concept of *ousia* does not belong to the basic concepts of the *Metaphysics*. But let us set to one side this remarkable consequence.

Let us consider what happens in the remainder of book Alpha, with regard to Aristotle's further articulation of the project and his use of the term *ousia* in this articulation. Having, in chapters 1 and 2, characterized the project of searching for wisdom as being the search for first causes and principles, and having identified a variety of marks of causes and principles and of the search for them, Aristotle now, in the remainder of the book, examines what his predecessors have thought on the matter of causes and principles. It is a good question why Aristotle thinks that this examination is called for at this juncture, that is, immediately following his characterization of his project. There are a number of indications, in the remainder of book Alpha and also at the opening of book Beta, that Aristotle's examination of the views of his predecessors on the topic of causes and principles is not simply critical and preparatory but is part of what he considers the positive and constructive character of his own project and enquiry.

Let us briefly remind ourselves of the structure of the remainder of book Alpha. Aristotle opens chapter 3 by referring to the *Physics* and by remarking that that work contains an "adequate" (cf. ἱκανῶς, 983a33) account of causes and principles. It does so especially because of its commitment to the four basic causes, or causal elements, that he distinguished there (see 983a33–b1; see also 985a10–13 for a similar reference to the *Physics*). He then turns, for the remainder of the book, to the question of what his predecessors have thought on the matter of causes and principles, and in particular whether, to what extent, and how clearly and distinctly they have distinguished these four causes or causal elements. The remainder of the book is divided into a primarily expository account of the views of his predecessors on this issue, culminating in his account of Plato's views (chapters 3–7), followed by a critical appraisal of their views—first the views of the thinkers before Plato (chapter 8), then Plato's views (chapter 9). The book ends with a brief conclusion (chapter 10), in which Aristotle again refers to the *Physics* (993a11). He concludes book Alpha with the notable observation that he will need to consider how one may be properly puzzled on the matter of causes and principles, and remarks that he will need to consider this with a view to making progress with his own puzzles (*aporiai*). This is clearly a forward-looking reference to book Beta and especially the general methodological reflections, at the opening of Beta 1, on the role of *aporia* in the search for wisdom.[5]

All this is quite familiar to the student of the *Metaphysics*. Nevertheless, we already have arrived at something important, especially if we consider (as we shall, presently) that whereas in book Alpha following chapter 2 Aristotle uses the term *ousia* a number of times, he does so always with reference to other thinkers, and especially Plato, and uses it, in the main, to refer to the essence of a thing. Clearly, the *Physics*, to which he refers at the beginning, in the middle, and at the end of Alpha following chapter 2, occupies a major place in this book. No less conspicuously, the *Categories* is absent, or practically so; there is only one reference to the *Categories* in book Alpha, which is at 992b18–22. This, if anything, ought to give us pause before we appeal to the account in book Gamma to establish Aristotle's basic concept of *ousia* in the *Metaphysics*. For it is familiar that the account of *ousia* in book Gamma depends on the *Categories*; it does so because at least one problem to which this account of *ousia* is intended to provide an answer is a problem that is due to views that Aristotle has defended in the *Categories*.

---

5 It may be said that the forward reference at the end of book Alpha (993a25–27) may be to Alpha-elatton rather than to Beta; if, that is, we may suppose that Alpha-elatton may have been inserted by Aristotle. We do not find this plausible. The wording in 993a25–27, surely, anticipates the wording at the opening of book Beta, as Ross points out both in his classic translation (1928) and in his commentary (1924, 213 and 222). See Laks 2009, 28–30 and Cooper 2012, 351–354.

(ii) We now turn to Aristotle's use of the term *ousia* in book Alpha. The aim is not to examine, in detail and for their individual sake, each of the relatively numerous occurrences of this term, but to consider them sufficiently to be able to do two things. First, to be able to assert with confidence that there is not anything in Aristotle's use of the term *ousia* in book Alpha that indicates that this term denotes, or may denote, the concept of *that which being is* or the concept of *that which determines that which being is*. And, secondly, to be able to give a general account of what Aristotle means by *ousia* in book Alpha of the *Metaphysics*.

To begin with, it is worth repeating that there is not an occurrence of the term *ousia* in book Alpha, before chapter 3; and this means that Aristotle introduces the term entirely in the context of his examination of the views of his predecessors on the matter of causes and principles, and that he does not use it in his basic account of his project, an account that he takes himself to have presented already by the end of chapter 2.

Of the thirty plus occurrences of the term *ousia* in book Alpha, four, including the first and the last occurrences, stand out by the fact that Aristotle indicates, clearly and explicitly, that he is using the term to refer to the essence of a thing; which he refers to here both under the label τὸ τί ἦν εἶναι[6] and the label τὸ τί ἐστι.[7] How significant are these occurrences? They are, we think, very significant; and much more so than the rate of four over thirty plus might suggest.

First, it is clear that when Aristotle uses *ousia* here to mean essence, he does so because he is associating the term *ousia* with one of the four causes, or causal elements, that he has distinguished in the *Physics*; namely, the formal cause. Why does he not use his own preferred terms for "form", that is, *eidos* or *morphē*? Apparently, for two reasons. First, in his own favored way of speaking from the *Physics*, these terms, *eidos* and *morphē*, are used in opposition to the term *hulē*, or "matter"; and he does not want to presuppose this contrastive use of the term *ousia* when discussing the views of his predecessors. Secondly, even according to his own use, the terms *eidos* and *morphē* are not synonymous with, or interchangeable with, the terms τὸ τί ἦν εἶναι and τὸ τί ἐστι. Rather, Aristotle will, later in the *Metaphysics*, raise the question of whether the essence of a thing is its form, or whether it is, instead, its matter; and he will argue, as opposed to assuming, either that the essence of a thing is its form as opposed to its matter or, at any rate, that the essence of a thing is primarily its form and only secondarily its matter.

---

6 I 3.983a27–28; I 7.988a34–35; I 10.993a18.

7 I 8.988b28–29.

Secondly, a large number of additional occurrences of the term *ousia* in book Alpha (in addition, that is, to the four mentioned) are situated in the context of either expounding or criticizing the views of Plato and Platonists, and in particular their commitment to Forms and their view that a cause is a Form.[8] It should be clear, both from book Alpha and from elsewhere in the *Metaphysics*, that Aristotle considers Platonic Forms to be, precisely, essences. Platonic Forms are, he thinks, essences, on a characteristically Platonic account of essence; an account that Aristotle considers, at least in part, mistaken. This is clear especially from the opening of chapter 6 of book Alpha (987a29–b10), when he considers how and on what reasoning Plato arrived at the theory of Forms. He argues that Plato arrived at the theory of Forms on the basis of two distinct and independent premises: first, the commitment to definitions and essences, a commitment the original stimulus for which, he thinks, was Socrates; and, secondly, the view that physical things are subject to such extreme instability as not to be capable of having an essence, a view the original stimulus for which, he thinks, was Cratylus. There is no doubt both that Aristotle shares in Plato's first commitment, the commitment to essences, and that what he rejects is the second view that he ascribes to Plato, namely the "flux view".[9] This, rather than any misgivings about Plato's commitment to essences, is why Aristotle rejects Plato's theory of Forms. We may, therefore, suppose that in these occurrences too, that is, the numerous occurrences of the term *ousia* when he expounds and criticizes a Platonist account of essence, Aristotle is using the term to refer to the essence of a thing.

Thirdly, a number of additional occurrences of the term *ousia* in book Alpha, in addition, that is, to the original four and to the Platonist-specific ones, are situated in the context of either expounding or criticizing the views of the Pythagoreans.[10] And it is evident that Aristotle treats the Pythagoreans as being, basically, proto-Platonists.

However, it would be wrong to conclude that the concept of *ousia*, in book Alpha of the *Metaphysics*, is the concept of essence. This would be wrong even if in all the occurrences of the term *ousia* in Alpha Aristotle had used this term to mean the essence of a thing. The reason is that when, in book Alpha, Aristotle uses the term *ousia* to mean the essence of a thing, he does so not because he

---

8   E.g., I 6.987b18–19; 988a10–11; I 7.988b1–2; I 9.991b3–4.

9   Let it be noted that we mean to leave it an open question, first, whether Plato is really committed to a flux thesis, and, secondly, if he is, whether this commitment can, as Aristotle apparently thinks it can, serve to contribute to the justification of the theory of Forms.

10   E.g., I 5.987a18–19.

immediately identifies the two concepts, but rather because he considers that, first, it is the form of a thing that has the best claim to being the cause of the thing's being the way it is, and, secondly, it is the form of a thing, as opposed to its matter, or at any rate primarily the form of a thing, that determines what the thing is and its essence.

It is, therefore, important that there are, in fact, some occurrences in book Alpha, even if not numerous, in which the term *ousia* is not used to mean the essence of a thing.[11] Some of these are as we would expect them to be, given that Aristotle has associated *ousia* with what is regarded by this or that thinker as the primary cause of a thing's being the way it is. Here he is thinking, especially if not exclusively, of the so-called natural philosophers (οἱ φυσιολόγοι), and consequently he is using *ousia* to mean the underlying matter of a thing. There is also the odd passage in which *ousia* is used to mean the moving cause and the final cause.

Finally, there are a number of remaining occurrences of the term *ousia* in book Alpha in which it cannot, at least not so readily, be identified with any one of the four Aristotelian causes or causal elements. These include some of the uses of the term *ousia* in the context of the Pythagoreans and some of the uses of this term in the context of the Platonists. Without going into the matter in any substance or detail, we can readily recognize that here Aristotle is using the term *ousia* to refer either to *number*, or to *the one*, or to *being*.

(iii) We may conclude that, first, Aristotle introduces the term *ousia* in the *Metaphysics* with reference to and as part of addressing the question "What is the primary cause of a thing's being the way it is?" And, secondly, nowhere in book Alpha does Aristotle use the term *ousia* in association with the question "What is being?", or with an enquiry into *that which being is*, or to denote *that which determines that which being is*. Indeed, this question and these concepts are absent from book Alpha.

It would, however, be wrong simply to assume that in book Alpha Aristotle identifies the concept of *ousia* with the concept of *the primary cause of a thing's being the way it is*; or, in general, simply to assume that he provides, or intends to provide, a single well-defined concept of *ousia*. We are left, rather, with an important question, namely, whether these occurrences of the term *ousia* in book Alpha can be brought under a single well-defined concept, and whether Aristotle intends them to be brought under a single well-defined concept. If it were not for the presence of book Beta, which follows immediately upon

---

11   E.g., I 3.983b10; I 4.985b10; I 8.988b28–29.

Alpha and is referred to at the end of Alpha, one would, no doubt, be invited to respond to this problem by looking further and deeper into the use of the term *ousia* in Alpha. We shall not, however, proceed in this manner. Rather, we want to turn to book Beta. For we shall argue that when, in book Beta, Aristotle articulates *aporiai* that crucially involve the term *ousia*, he does so in such a way as to show that he does not suppose that a single well-defined concept of *ousia* can be established prior to and independently of recognizing and engaging with such *aporiai*. This is reason to doubt that Aristotle intends to provide a single well-defined concept of *ousia* in book Alpha of the *Metaphysics*.

IV   The Concept of *Ousia* in Book Beta, and Its Relation to Alpha and Gamma

(i) *Ousia* in Beta. We want to argue that book Beta serves both to develop the project of book Alpha and to prepare for the first two chapters of book Gamma, and that it does so also in regard to the concept (or concepts) of *ousia* in Alpha and in Gamma.[12]

While the term *ousia* is not used in all the *aporiai* of book Beta, it is used in some; and used in such a way that, clearly, the articulation of the *aporia* depends on it. The *aporiai* in which the term *ousia* is used include some of the very major *aporiai* in Beta, such as the fifth and the twelfth. Our aim is not to consider all the *aporiai* in Beta in which the term *ousia* is used. Rather, we want to identify some *aporiai* in Beta in which the term *ousia* is used and which, as we shall argue, serve either to develop the project of book Alpha (this, we shall argue, is the case with regard to the fifth *aporia*) or to prepare for the first two chapters of book Gamma (this, we shall argue, is the case with regard to the twelfth *aporia*).

What must a reader know, with regard to the meaning of the term *ousia*, to understand an *aporia* in Beta in which this term occurs? This seems to be a relevant question to ask, if we want to consider Aristotle's concept of *ousia* here. One thing that is meant, in general, by a concept, C, associated with a term, T, is just this: a concept, C, associated with a term, T, is that which a person must know in order to understand sentences in which term T is used in a particular context. And this is very much the concept of a concept that we need here.

---

12   For a detailed and thoughtfully structured review of the main literature on this issue, see Madigan 1999, xxxiii–viii.

It may be said that all that the reader must know, with reference to the term *ousia* as it functions in the *aporiai* in Beta in which it occurs, is the everyday meaning of the term *ousia* and its cognates, or, at any rate, the everyday meaning of the terms *on, to on, onta, ta onta*, etc. However, this view is questionable when one is dealing with questions, and questions that involve the term in question (in this case, *ousia*), and questions that serve to articulate *aporiai*, and *aporiai* that their author considers fundamental to his or her enquiry, and *aporiai* that very much depend, for their being *aporiai*, on the use of the term in question—these being characteristics of book Beta of Aristotle's *Metaphysics*. We have gone some way toward showing how questionable this is, inasmuch as we have seen that it is hard, not to say impossible, to have even a minimal understanding of the use of the term *ousia* in book Alpha of the *Metaphysics*, unless one engages in Aristotle's project of searching for wisdom and considering what this search is and involves; and unless one follows Aristotle in associating wisdom (*sophia*) with *aitia*-involving knowledge; and unless one follows Aristotle in asking: *What is it that we need to know, in regard of a thing, O, to be able to explain (= give the aitia) why the thing is as it is? Is it the matter of the thing? Its form or essence? The origin of the process of motion that led to it? Its final end? Or something else altogether (such as* number, unity *and the like)?*— and last but not least, unless one recognizes that the series of problems in book Beta serve to articulate further the project set out in book Alpha.

(ii) The Relation to Alpha. We want to argue that book Beta serves to develop the project of book Alpha, and that it does so also in regard to the concept of *ousia* in Alpha. We shall concentrate on the fifth *aporia*,[13] in its own right and in relation to two or three passages from toward the end of book Alpha: 8.988b22–26 (together with 989b21–29), and 9.992b18–22.

Consider the following lines from chapter 8 of book Alpha:

> Those, then, who posit that the all is one and one sort of nature (μίαν τινὰ φύσιν), which they suppose to be matter (ὡς ὕλην) and bodily (σωματικήν) and in possession of magnitude (μέγεθος ἔχουσαν), clearly go astray in many ways. For they posit only the elements (στοιχεῖα) of bodies and fail to posit elements for non-bodily things—since indeed there are non-bodily things too.[14]
>
> 988b22–26

---

13   997a34–998a19; in the summary at III 1.995b18–27 it is listed as the fourth *aporia*.

14   ὄντων καὶ ἀσωμάτων is bracketed by Jaeger, who considered it as a *varia lectio* of τῶν δ'

Aristotle repeats what is basically the same point in a somewhat longer passage a little later in Alpha, 989b21–29, but in which he replaces the opposition between *sōmata* ("bodies") and *asōmata* ("non-bodily things") with the opposition, which he clearly considers equivalent, between *aisthēta* ("sense-perceptible things") and *ouk aisthēta* ("non-sense-perceptible things").

What is the relevance of these lines, for considering the relation between book Alpha and book Beta? The lines from Alpha 8 suppose that there are also non-bodily things, in addition to bodily things (cf. "since indeed there are non-bodily things too", ὄντων καὶ ἀσωμάτων, 988b25–26). But this supposition is turned into a problem in the fifth *aporia* of book Beta; it takes the place of the one side of a dilemma with apparently good, and equally good, reasons on both sides.

Let us turn to the fifth *aporia* of book Beta. Aristotle casts the principal question that states this *aporia* as follows (*the Principal Dilemma*):

> whether one ought to maintain that *only* sense-perceptible *ousiai* exist OR that there are other ⟨*ousiai*⟩ in addition to these.
>
> 997a34–35

We should note that the question in the Principal Dilemma is *not* whether *ousiai* are sense-perceptible or non-sense-perceptible; it is the question whether or not, in addition to sense-perceptible *ousiai*, there are also non-sense-perceptible *ousiai*. The significance of this will become apparent. Aristotle goes on to argue that this question is not merely a grammatical dilemma but that there are substantial and serious reasons on both sides. Without going into the very considerable detail of his argument, we may note a number of important points.

First, he immediately associates it with another dilemma, and one that makes particular reference to Platonist views (*the Subordinate Dilemma*):

> And whether *ousia* is to be taken in one way only (μοναχῶς) OR there are several types of *ousiai*, such as in the case of, for example, those who maintain both Forms and Intermediates, the latter being said to be the subject matter of the mathematical sciences.
>
> 997a35–b3

ἀσωμάτων οὔ. We regard it as important to keep the traditional text (which was read by Alexander 1989, 98).

Secondly, he comes down equally hard against both sides of both dilemmas. Thirdly, the Principal Dilemma appears to presuppose that there are sense-perceptible *ousiai*. For it is remarkable that Aristotle does not make logical room for what, on the face of it, appears to be a third option, namely, that there are only non-sense-perceptible *ousiai*. We ought to wonder how Aristotle can allow himself to disregard this option, if, as in general he recognizes, it cannot be ruled out that *ousia* is something that is not sense-perceptible. This cannot be ruled out, especially if, as Aristotle does here, one is considering also the Platonist position, which, on Aristotle's account of it elsewhere, says that there are only non-sense-perceptible *ousiai*, in a relevant sense of *ousia*. Our response to this remarkable fact—that Aristotle presupposes that there are sense-perceptible *ousiai* and disregards the possibility that there are only non-sense-perceptible *ousiai*—is this: We need to understand the way in which Aristotle uses the term *ousia* here, in this *aporia*, in such a way that it is indeed obvious—even to the Platonist—that there are, also if not only, sense-perceptible *ousia*. This, we may note, implies that we cannot understand the term *ousia* in its present use to mean *that which determines that which being is*, or in some such sense. For, if we so understand it, then it is not obvious that there are sense-perceptible *ousiai*. This is not obvious, as Aristotle recognizes, especially if one is engaging with Platonists, who deny that there are sense-perceptible *ousiai* in some such sense of *ousia*. One might suggest that the term *ousia* here is not meant in a particularly heavy or committal sense, a suggestion that finds some support in the fact that in book Alpha (8.988b25–26) the supposition was formulated simply in terms of *onta*.

Fourthly, the Principal Dilemma appears to presuppose that there are *ousiai*. For it is remarkable that Aristotle does not make logical room for what, on the face of it, appears to be a fourth option, namely, that there are not any *ousiai* at all. Perhaps the claim that there are not any *onta*, that is, that there is nothing at all, is not worth taking seriously. For it is surely obvious that something exists. But while it may be obvious that there are *onta*, it is not so obvious that there are *ousiai*. That depends on what is meant by the term *ousia* in this *aporia* and how heavy and committal this term is supposed to be as used here.

Does Aristotle simply assume that there are *ousiai* or is this, on the contrary, something that he argues for? That Aristotle argues for the claim that there are *ousiai* is apparent if we go back to book Alpha and to the following passage from Alpha 9:

> In general, if we search for the elements of the-things-that-are without distinguishing the many ways in which things are said to be, it will be

impossible to find them, especially if the search is conducted on the basis of the question of *what* elements the-things-that-are are derived from. For it is surely impossible to apprehend from out of what ⟨elements⟩ "acting" or "being acted on", or "the straight", are derived, *rather, if elements can be discovered at all, it will be only the elements of ousiai.*

992b18–22; our emphasis

It is apparent that this passage provides an argument for the claim that there are *ousiai*; and an argument that, apparently, prepares for the fifth *aporia*, since that *aporia* assumes that there are *ousiai*.

Aristotle's argument for the claim that there are *ousiai* (992b18–22) relies on the idea of searching for the elements, and therefore for the causes, of things. For we may take Aristotle to suppose that all elements (*stoicheia*) are causes (*aitiai*), even without taking him to suppose that all causes are elements. This shows that Aristotle's argument for the claim that there are *ousiai* relies on his project as he has been characterizing it from the beginning of book Alpha, that is, as the project of searching for the primary causes of things. And since this argument from book Alpha apparently prepares for the fifth *aporia* in book Beta, we may suppose that this *aporia* in Beta likewise relies on the project of searching for the primary causes of things, and does so also in its use of the term *ousia*. We may suppose, therefore, that in the fifth *aporia* of book Beta Aristotle is using the term *aporia* in a way that is continuous, if not identical, with the way in which he has been using it in book Alpha.

Aristotle's argument in this passage (9.992b18–22) for the claim that there are *ousiai* relies on the claim that, if the-things-that-are (taken either individually, or in their totality, or both) have elements, then this will be because *ousia* has elements. We may suppose that the term *ousia* here means *the primary cause of a thing's being the way it is.* But is causal primacy the only primacy that is meant? This is not so clear. The reference to the claim that the things-that-are (*ta onta*) are said in many ways, and so to the *Categories*, suggests that it is not the case that only causal primacy is meant, since this claim from the *Categories* introduces a sense of primacy but not causal primacy.

We cannot suppose, however, that Aristotle's argument in this passage (A 9.992b18–22) for the claim that there are *ousiai* relies on the Gamma account of *ousia*, which associates *ousia* with *that which being is* and which says that *ousia* is *that which determines that which being is.* We cannot suppose that the *Categories* claim, which says that the things-that-are (*ta onta*) are said in many ways, implies the account of *ousia* in *Metaphysics* Gamma 1–2. We cannot suppose this, even if we suppose (as we may on one reading of the *Categories*) that in the *Categories* Aristotle distinguishes not simply several categories, but *ousia* on the one hand, and several other categories on the other; and that he claims that there is a dependence of the items in the other categories on *ousia*. As is familiar, it is difficult to understand the dependence in question in the *Categories*. On one understanding, it is dependence with regard to existence; on another understanding, it is dependence with regard to essence; on yet another understanding, it is dependence with regard to both essence and existence. But on no understanding is it dependence with regard to what it is for something to be and so involving the concepts of *that which being is* and *that which determines that which being is*.

We may also recall that when we considered the fifth *aporia* we found positive reason to deny that, in that *aporia*, Aristotle can mean by *ousia*, *that which determines that which being is*. The reason was that in that *aporia* Aristotle presupposes that there are sense-perceptible *ousiai* and disregards the possibility that there are only non-sense-perceptible *ousiai*, and he could not presuppose this and disregard that possibility, if he meant by *ousia*, *that which determines that which being is*.

(iii) Let us sum up so far. We have found that book Beta, and the fifth *aporia* in particular, serves to develop the project of book Alpha, and that it does so also in regard to the concept of *ousia* in Alpha. Book Beta serves to develop the project of book Alpha in at least two recognizable and significant ways. First, certain suppositions in book Alpha, which may look like simple assertions when made in that book—such as the supposition that there are also non-bodily and non-sense-perceptible things, in addition to bodily and sense-perceptible things—are turned into elements of problems, and argued to be questionable, in book Beta. These are problems in which the term *ousia* is used and used for the very articulation of the problems. Secondly, certain apparent presuppositions of certain *aporiai* in book Beta—such as the presupposition that there are *ousiai*—have already been argued for in book Alpha, even if we need not suppose that the argument is intended as conclusive.

> **Weak Conclusion:** This shows that book Beta serves to develop the project of book Alpha, and that it does so also in regard to the concept of *ousia* in Alpha.

Perhaps we go can further, and suppose that:

> **Strong Conclusion:** understanding and engaging with certain *aporiai* in Beta *is necessary* for understanding the concept of *ousia* in Alpha.

That depends. It depends on how different, and how significantly different, we consider the concept of *ousia* in Alpha to be, depending on whether or not we take account of how it is taken up and developed in Beta. If the answer is "Not so different", then we shall be happy to concede that we have failed to defend also the Strong Conclusion and be content to have defended the Weak Conclusion. If, on the contrary, the answer is "Very significantly different", then we shall have defended the Strong Conclusion. We shall leave this choice to the reader, while noting that, in our view, the difference between supposing that a proposition (and one that depends for its meaning on the use in it of a term, T, here the term *ousia*) has the force of a simple assertion and, on the other hand, supposing that it is the one side of a two-sided, whether-or-not question with apparently good, and equally good, reasons on both sides—an *aporia* in this sense—is a major and very significant difference.

(iv) The Relation to Gamma. We want to argue, finally, that the question "What is being?" and the concepts *that which being is* and *that which determines that which being is*, so familiar from Gamma, are introduced in Beta and introduced as a result of and in order to address and engage with a particular *aporia*, the twelfth *aporia*.

Remarkably, the term τί τὸ ὄν (used to mean either the question "What is being?" or the nominalization based on this question, that is, to mean *that which being is*) occurs prior to book Gamma. It does not occur in book Alpha, but it occurs twice in book Beta. It occurs twice in the twelfth *aporia* (which is found in III 5.1001b26–1002b11) and in this *aporia* only: first in 1001b28; and again in 1002a27–28. In both occurrences the term τί τὸ ὄν is adjacent to the term *ousia*. The two terms—τί τὸ ὄν and *ousia*—are part of a single conjunction whose two conjuncts are closely related and, apparently, intended to be equivalent (assuming, of course, that the *kai* is to be read epexegetically). In the first occurrence,

τί τὸ ὄν καὶ τίνες αἱ οὐσίαι τῶν ὄντων (5.1001b28–29);

and in the second occurrence,

τί τὸ ὄν καὶ τίς ἡ οὐσία τῶν ὄντων (5.1002a27–28).

It is plausible, therefore, to suppose that here the term *ousia* is used to mean: *that which being is* or even *that which determines that which being is*.

Remarkable as this is, it does not immediately imply that the question "What is being?" and the concepts *that which being is* and *that which determines that which being is*, so familiar from Gamma, are introduced in this *aporia* of Beta and introduced as a result of and in order to address and engage with this *aporia*. All we have shown, by appeal to the use of the terms τί τὸ ὄν and *ousia* in this *aporia* in book Beta, is that in a particular *aporia* in book Beta Aristotle begins to speak of *ousia* in the sense in which he speaks of *ousia* in book Gamma. But this, one might object, is not to show that he does so as a result of and in order to address and engage with that *aporia*.

We want to address this objection by looking closer at the twelfth *aporia*. The short, succinct and dilemmatic formulation of the question that states this *aporia* (as opposed, that is, to the dilemmatic argument that follows the question and whose purpose it is to show that the question articulates an *aporia*) is as follows:

> An *aporia* that follows upon these [i.e. the previous *aporiai*] is this: whether numbers and bodies and planes and points are some sort of *ousiai* (οὐσίαι τινές), or not.
>
> 1001b26–28

There is no reason to suppose that the term *ousia*, in the question that states this *aporia*, is used to mean *that which being is* (τί τὸ ὄν), much less *that which determines that which being is*. All we may immediately suppose is that it means *that which is, in one way or another, primary*. The concept *that which being is* has not been introduced so far in the *Metaphysics*, or associated with the term *ousia* and the concept of *ousia*; and, going by the question alone that states this *aporia* (i.e. the lines quoted above), we have no reason to think that it is introduced at this precise point in book Beta, that is, in the question that states the twelfth *aporia* (as opposed, that is, to what follows this question and argues that the question articulates an *aporia*).

This obviates the following objection: the association of *ousia* with *that which being is* and *that which determines that which being is* occurs already in the question that states the *aporia*; it is, therefore, a presupposition of the *aporia* and not something the *aporia* prepares for. We are happy to concede that, *if* (i) the association of *ousia* with *that which being is* and *that which determines that which being is* occurs already in the question that states the *aporia* and is a presupposition of the *aporia* and not something that the *aporia* prepares for, *then* (ii) this association is compatible with thinking that, whereas it is true that in a particular *aporia* in book Beta Aristotle makes this association, we cannot suppose that he does so as a result of and in order to address and engage with the *aporia*. But the antecedent, (i), is false; it is not the case that: the association of *ousia* with *that which being is* and *that which determines that which being is*

occurs already in the question that states the *aporia*. On the contrary. The association of *ousia* with this concept, τί τὸ ὄν, is made *after* the question that states
the *aporia*, and made for the purpose of exhibiting apparently strong reasons
for answering the question in the affirmative. Here is what Aristotle says:

> If these [i.e., numbers, bodies, planes, or points] were not *ousiai*, then it
> would escape us *what being is* (τί τὸ ὄν) and of what sort the *ousiai are*
> (τίνες αἱ οὐσίαι).
>
> 1001b28–29

Aristotle's point here is this, and it is thoroughly striking: if we do not suppose
that *ousiai* (in the sense of that which is, in one way or another, primary) are
such things as numbers, or bodies, or planes, or points, then it entirely escapes
us even *what being is*, that is, what we mean by "to be" and what we take
ourselves to be asking when we are asking "What is there?" (*not*: when we are
asking "What is being?").

  This, we submit, shows that the association of the term *ousia* with the
concept *that which being is* is not presupposed in this *aporia*; on the contrary,
the association is made as a result of and in order to address and engage
with the *aporia*. We may conclude that the question "What is being?" and the
concepts *that which being is* and *that which determines that which being is*, so
familiar from Gamma, are introduced in Beta and introduced as a result of and
in order to address and engage with a particular *aporia*.

(v) We have argued that the question "What is being?" and the concepts *that
which being is* and *that which determines that which being is*, so familiar from
Gamma, are, as a matter of fact, introduced in Beta and introduced as a result
of and in order to address and engage with a particular *aporia*. This implies that
(the Weak Conclusion) *one way* of understanding this question and these concepts is by understanding and engaging with certain *aporiai*. May we go further,
and suppose that (the Strong Conclusion) *the only way* of understanding this
question and these concepts is by understanding and engaging with certain
aporiai?

  It may be said that, had the opening, that is, the Gamma-preceding books of
the *Metaphysics* been lost, we would get along perfectly well starting with book
Gamma and understanding Aristotle's basic concept of *ousia*, in this possible-
world *Metaphysics*, on that basis. We have no wish to deny this. The question,
therefore, is this: How different is the basic concept of *ousia* in this possible-
world *Metaphysics* from the basic concept of *ousia* in the actual *Metaphysics* as
we know it? If the answer to this question is "Not so very different", then we shall

be happy to concede that we have failed to defend also the Strong Conclusion and be content to have defended the Weak Conclusion. If, on the contrary, the answer is "Very significantly different", then we shall have defended the Strong Conclusion. We shall leave this choice to the reader, while adding one final question and a suggestion for an answer.

The critical question at this point, we would like to suggest, is this: Whence the impression—which one may well have and which is common to a long tradition of critics—that the concept of *ousia* in book Gamma, as *that which determines that which being is*, which is introduced in Gamma by reference to the question "What is being?" and the concept *that which being is*, can be understood perfectly well without reference to any *aporia*, such as those in book Beta? The source of this impression, we would like to suggest, is the supposition—apparently common to the same tradition—that all we need to understand in order to understand the question "What is being?" and to understand the concept *that which being is* are the everyday concepts of *to on*, *on*, *onta*, *ta onta*, etc. But this supposition is eminently questionable, at any rate if what we are considering is the actual *Metaphysics* as we know it. For it begs a notable question: whether, in asking the question "What is being?" at the opening of book Gamma of the *Metaphysics*, Aristotle is engaged in something like an analysis of an everyday concept.

CHAPTER 10

Aristotle's *Nicomachean Ethics* is a Work of Practical Science*

Ron Polansky

Abstract

From beginning to end, the *Nicomachean Ethics* is a work of practical science. While few deny this, its implications remain unclear. I argue that practical science should not rely on any theoretical principles. This position has been insufficiently appreciated and defended. I acknowledge that the practical treatises are largely consistent with the theoretical books, and even that they might not have been written had Aristotle not worked out his theoretical positions. Nonetheless, they do not depend upon them or ever appeal to them explicitly for any sorts of principles. This does not preclude his using points from the logical works within practical science, as in any of the theoretical sciences, but theoretical conclusions and premises are out of bounds. This is important for understanding the argumentation of this treatise itself, for appreciating Aristotle's commitment to practical science as science, and for defending the ethical writings from claims that they are outmoded based on superseded theoretical positions. After elucidating the first book of the *Nicomachean Ethics*, I turn to later sections that might be supposed dependent upon theoretical conceptions.

> ... it is a lack of training to be unable to distinguish, in regard to each subject, between those arguments which are appropriate to it and those which are foreign.
>
> *Eudemian Ethics* 1217a8–10

> Ethics, however, is not the only branch of philosophy which the Aristotelian scheme of things kept apart from physics. Another is theology or first philosophy.
>
> BURNYEAT 2008, 274

* Friendly discussions with David Reeve, Devin Henry, Greg Salmieri, and Jon Buttaci, along with suggestions by an anonymous reviewer, have been very helpful in the development of this contribution.

From beginning to end, the *Nicomachean Ethics*, along with the *Eudemian Ethics*, the *Magna Moralia*, and the *Politics*, are works of practical science. Though few if any interpreters simply deny this, its implications are not so well appreciated. Commentators often suggest that practical science crucially depends upon premises borrowed from the theoretical works. For instance, Alasdair MacIntyre claims that the *Nicomachean Ethics* relies on Aristotle's "metaphysical biology",[1] and Bernard Williams takes it to rest on no-longer-viable theoretical positions.[2] It therefore becomes relatively easy to dismiss many of Aristotle's practical writings, if they in fact require antiquated theoretical principles. Or commentators hasten to look to theoretical works for illumination when they contend with difficult passages in the practical writings. But should genuine practical science as science not have its own principles, and hence stand on its own, thereby avoiding the suggested vulnerability or requiring clarification from outside its own field? Did Aristotle really suppose that he needed to rely upon theoretical principles and notions in developing practical science, or would he carefully refrain from using foreign principles and concepts in practical science?[3]

---

1   See MacIntyre 2007, 58, 148, 162, 196–197.

2   Williams 1993, 161: "For Aristotle, ethics is based on psychology, even biology" and Williams 1985, 52: "Aristotle saw a certain kind of ethical, cultural, and indeed political life as a harmonious culmination of human potentialities, recoverable from an absolute understanding of nature. We have no reason to believe in that. Once we lose the belief, however, a potential gap opens between the agent's perspective and the outside view". Irwin 1988, 23–25 holds that Aristotle's ethics can only go beyond "pure dialectic" and have "objective principles" if it uses the results of first philosophy and even that "the correct use of his method, and the correct interpretation of his metaphysical principles, do not justify the implausible conclusions that he claims to derive from them" (and see 351–352 and 358–365; cf. Henry and Nielsen eds. 2015, esp. 22–23 and Scott 2015, 153 note 21 referring to Irwin 1980, Whiting 1988, Shields 2007, Bostock 2000). Lawrence 2006, 58 states more cautiously, "the criticism of Aristotle's account as 'super-objective,' as dependent on metaphysics for its alleged objectivity, has some grounding. *Yet* there is nothing essentially metaphysical about Aristotle's *project* ... That Aristotle's own best thoughts on these topics should strike us as in part 'metaphysical' does nothing to unseat the project and stop us using it to deliver a quite ordinarily objective answer about how best to live, neither too indeterminate nor too specific".

3   *Posterior Analytics* I 7 makes clear that each science should have its own sorts of principles, unless there is definite subordination, as optics to geometry. Kraut 2014, 3.2 says pertinently that Aristotle "never proposes that students of ethics need to engage in a specialized study of the natural world, or mathematics, or eternal and changing objects. His project is to make ethics an autonomous field, and to show why a full understanding of what is good does not require expertise in any other field".

To my knowledge it has not received much attention, in the way I shall be considering it; that is, considering what it means that practical sciences are based on their own sorts of principles without dependence on theoretical notions.[4] Consequently, many readings of the ethical and political writings misconstrue important arguments through assuming that they presuppose theoretical principles and ideas for their justification and elucidation. I look at what appear to be potentially problematic sections of the *Nicomachean Ethics* to support my way of reading this work as practical science. I hope to show that none of this practical science hangs on antiquated and superseded natural science or metaphysics. This is important for understanding the argumentation of the *Nicomachean Ethics* itself and for appreciating Aristotle's commitment to practical science as science. I concentrate initially upon the first book of the *Nicomachean Ethics* and then turn to some other sections that might seem reliant upon theoretical concepts. If I succeed as intended, we should no longer see incautious references to theoretical positions in commentary on the practical writings or hear loose talk of ethical "theory".[5]

My contention requires some initial clarification. I readily admit that the practical treatises are generally consistent with Aristotle's theoretical positions, and even that they might not have been written had he not worked out his theoretical sciences, for he has hardly forgotten the rest of his thought when he comes to the practical books. I even accept that key positions in the practical treatises are unannounced applications of some of his theoretical views.[6] And,

---

4   In contrast with my approach, Shields 2015, 236–237 (cf. Leunissen 2015, 216–217) says, "Aristotle expects the politician, whose primary goal as politician is purely practical, to be a theoretician as well. In some respects, at least, this study seems to require intimate familiarity with the soul's essence and inner structure, the sort of knowledge, then, that we would rightly expect only of the accomplished soul-scientist ... Aristotle is not committed to the view that a science's practical orientation precludes its practitioners from engaging in theoretical study. Rather, precisely because correct action requires a correct understanding of the ends of action, practical science will sooner *presuppose* theoretical understanding and so demand rather than preclude it". I instead contend that Aristotle only requires for practical science, besides good rearing and habituation of his audience, what he presents in his ethical treatise. A related project to mine, only limitedly undertaken here, challenges the frequent comments by interpreters that Aristotle's remarks display prejudices and assumptions of his own age and culture. A successful practical science should also escape such objections.

5   Even in the marvelous attack on modern ethics in Anscombe 1958 she holds that ethical thought awaits progress in moral psychology.

6   Below I consider that Aristotle might not have written the *Ethics* without already having worked out his theoretical positions. That some key views in the *Ethics* are unannounced applications of theoretical principles, consider the way the four causes are clearly in play,

of course, the *Nicomachean Ethics* concludes that the theoretical is the best life, yet, as we shall see, not by relying on theoretical principles. Hence, the practical works do not and need not ever explicitly appeal to the theoretical works for any sorts of principles. In fact, Aristotle is scrupulously methodologically attentive to the distinctions of the sciences and deliberately avoids references to theoretical positions in the practical context. He may freely use points from the logical works as fair game for practical science, as for any of the sciences, but theoretical conclusions and premises are out of bounds.[7]

That Aristotle keeps theoretical assumptions out of practical science goes along with his novelty in writing a treatise on ethics. His predecessors, with the possible exception of Socrates and Plato, were not generally careful to keep theoretical views out of their practical thought. The Pre-Socratics routinely link their cosmic reflections with comments about how humans should live (see, e.g., Heraclitus B2, B114, Empedocles B115, Philolaus B11, Diogenes of Apollonia B5). Plato may seem to align with Aristotle since the Forms can be causes

---

though Aristotle does not appeal to his presentation of the four causes in the *Physics* or his defense in the *Metaphysics* that there are but these four sorts of causes. I contend that further theoretical clarity about such notions makes no contribution to practical science and is not anticipated in its students.

7   Henry and Nielsen eds. 2015, 12 say, "The focus of the present volume is on the extent to which Aristotle's ethical treatises make use of the concepts, methods, and practices developed in the *Analytics* and the other scientific works" (cf. 2). I agree that practical science accords with the approaches suggested in the logical works, and so can be science, since science depends on demonstration through causes, even if the demonstration may pertain to what holds only for the most part (about demonstration in physics or ethics concerning what holds for the most part, see Henry 2015, esp. 185–188). Yet I deny their further claim that Aristotle appeals in practical science to theoretical principles from other sciences. They suggest that whenever in the practical sciences Aristotle deals with topics universally and seeks definitions that this amounts to a theoretical component of practical science: "Knowledge of ethical universals— what happiness is, what virtue of character and thought require, and the sphere and function of the individual virtues—helps us become better people. Therefore, seeking definitions is time well spent from a practical perspective. It is not an idle theoretical exercise" (10). They assert: "It is certainly true that ethics is not a theoretical science in the sense that it does not aim at knowledge for its own sake ... But it doesn't follow from this that practical disciplines lack a theoretical component" (3; cf. Henry 2015, 169 note 1 and 170 note 5), and they state, "the fact that we come to *love* final ends by pursuing them over the course of our lives does not mean that these ends cannot be examined from a theoretical point of view, that is, from the point of view of first principles of action" (10). This very questionably assumes that for Aristotle all science as science, since science involves first principles that hold universally, i.e., necessarily or for the most part, is theoretical. On such a dubious view even the productive sciences, such as carpentry, must have a "theoretical component".

of changeable things and standards for human emulation, yet it is debatable whether Plato really rests his ethical thinking, which derives from the eudaemonist approach initiated by Socrates,[8] on metaphysical positions. Socrates perhaps differs from his predecessors by turning from the cosmic to focus more exclusively on human affairs, as Aristotle indicates in *Metaphysics* 987b1–2 and 1078b17–19. But Socrates would not be completely exemplary for Aristotle, if Socrates did not have any theoretical science, which could mean his practical science is confused about its own domain.[9]

The arguments that Aristotle's *Ethics* is somehow theoretically based take several forms: (1) Aristotle depends upon and utilizes his theoretical positions in his arguments in the ethics, for only thus can he go beyond a "dialectical" treatment and attain objectivity. Practical science needs grounding in theoretical principles; (2) Since in writing the ethics Aristotle deals with universals rather than getting to particulars, the work must be theoretical. Practical wisdom, if narrowly defined in *NE* VI as the capacity to deliberate means to ends, would not enable Aristotle to work out his ethical positions, so development of the ethics is a project of theory; (3) Even if Aristotle's practical science need not rely on theoretical principles, he could offer a more fully developed and precise science were he to take the "longer route" and employ worked out theoretical positions in his ethics. Scott says, "Aristotle's ethics *could* be further grounded in his metaphysics and psychology";[10] (4) Since the highest happiness is the theoretical or contemplative life, in defending it and advocating it Aristotle must be engaged in theorizing. I shall be attacking each of these arguments.

I   *NE* I is Free from Theoretical Assumptions

The opening book of the *Nicomachean Ethics* seeks to establish the first principle of practical science, that is, to show *that there is* a human end or goal, the highest human happiness (*eudaimonia*), and also to give some preliminary account of *what it is*. The project begins with the treatise's very first sentence:

---

8   See Vlastos 1991, chapter 8.

9   Tessitore 1996, 128 note 28 says, "Strauss maintains that Aristotle, unlike Plato, succeeded in founding political science as a practical discipline in a way that does not make it dependent upon theoretical science". I do not believe, however, that Plato in fact made practical thought depend upon theoretical positions since these are largely absent from the so-called "Socratic dialogues".

10   See Scott 2015, 214.

Every art and every inquiry, and similarly every action and choice, is
thought to aim at some good; and for this reason the good has rightly
been declared to be that at which all things aim.[11] πᾶσα τέχνη καὶ πᾶσα
μέθοδος, ὁμοίως δὲ πρᾶξίς τε καὶ προαίρεσις, ἀγαθοῦ τινὸς ἐφίεσθαι δοκεῖ· διὸ
καλῶς ἀπεφήναντο τἀγαθόν, οὗ πάντ' ἐφίεται.

1094a1–3

By speaking of art and inquiry, and then action and choice, Aristotle deals with
characteristically *human* efforts. Only metaphorically do the beasts or gods
engage in these. What is emphasized is that each of these is directed toward
some end or objective relevant to the sort of enterprise that it is. Human doing
always has a goal in view. Aristotle hardly denies that beasts seek ends through
perception and desire, yet he starts to suggest how human doings differ from
those of the beasts. Art, inquiry, action, and choice, as engaged in by humans,
involve thought or reasoning.[12] Humans distinctively have an end in view for
which they could give some account. Perhaps because every human project
aims at some good, it has plausibly been declared that *all things* aim at the
good (cf. x 2.1172b9–15). In a theoretical context for Aristotle this means that
every being seeks to be as much like divine being as it can be at its level of
being, and for Plato it might mean that the Idea of the Good is the principle
of all else. Yet Aristotle will soon reject the Idea of the Good, while allowing
that human projects utilize both non-living and living things as means to their
ends. So, from the *practical* perspective, humans use all things for their good.[13]
He here takes advantage of the possibility of all things having ends, in addition
to humans engaging in projects with ends, to emphasize ends.

    Among human ends some are *activities* that are ends in themselves, but oth-
ers are products or works (*erga*) that result from human efforts to produce them

---

11   All translations of Aristotle are from Barnes ed. 1984.

12   In the biological works Aristotle may speak of action (*praxis*) in regard to the beasts, but
      the ethical writings distinguish human action from anything the beasts or even human
      children are involved in since human action requires deliberation and choice (see *NE*
      III 2.1111b6–10; cf. Leunissen 2015, 215n4).

13   In theoretical contexts Aristotle indicates that each natural being aims to be as like the
      divine being as is possible for it (see, e.g., *An.* II 4), and in *Metaph.* XII 10 he suggests that
      the entire cosmos is ordered. But only in a practical context will he say that everything
      is here for humans (see *Politics* 1256b15–32). In *Physics* 194a33–36 he merely says that
      humans use everything as if for their purposes. Hence Sedley 1991 mistakenly supposes
      there is an "anthropocentric" assumption in Aristotle generally. In fact this assumption
      belongs only within practical science.

(1094a3–5). Though the beasts also have activities, especially sense perception, probably they do not engage in them for their own sake, as do humans.[14] By distinguishing activities and products, Aristotle prepares for recognition that happiness is an *activity*, a type of life as an end in itself, rather than any product. And by suggesting that where there is a product, it is "better" than the human effort producing it, or where arts are subordinate to each other the ends of the higher arts are preferred, he establishes a practical hierarchy of ends (1094a5–6). "Better" (βελτίω) here means more choice-worthy or more end-like. Aristotle thus introduces an unobjectionable criterion of "value", ranking, or normativity: what is more end-like is better. And lesser ends are in turn for the sake of further and more end-like ends, which are thus even better. Now while from a theoretical standpoint humans and their actions as natural are surely better than any artifacts they make, such as houses, in the practical context the end is better than the efforts to bring it about. By giving priority in the practical context to the end in this way, and thereby having a straightforwardly factual scheme of appraisal without theoretical appeal, Aristotle avoids fact–value distinctions and has his definite practical basis for objectivity.[15]

Human projects and ends being various, Aristotle must show that this variety allows for an ultimate human end: happiness. Any project must have its own end, to avoid infinite regress of ends, for desire and planning would be empty if we do each thing for the sake of something further without termination (1094a18–22). But this only proves that any present project must have a final aim so as not to be vain, rather than that all projects undertaken at dif-

---

14   Though any and all activity as activity has its end in itself, the beasts do not choose to engage in the various activities for their own sake. Humans can desire to do any activity for its own sake and for the sake of happiness.

15   I suggest that the fact-value distinction really emerges with the sophists and their opposing nature and convention. When Plato and Aristotle strive to give what is conventional some basis in what is natural, they resist any easy fact-value or descriptive-prescriptive distinction (see the way that Socrates in Plato *Republic* I 338b–341a exposes Thrasymachus's descriptive and prescriptive distinction). Witt 2015 doubts that ethics as normative can be science because its subject domain is variable and too like what is conventional, such as money. She fails to note that Aristotle attributes a use to money, and so denies it is *purely* conventional (cf. her 282 with *Pol.* 1257a34–b5). "Use" (χρεία, χρῆσις) can be even wider than "function" (ἔργον), so, contrary to Witt 2015, 289, money and actions according to virtue can have a use and lend themselves to science. Aristotle rejects science of the *accidental* rather than the conventional (*Metaph.* VI 2), for the conventional, based on what is natural, may hold universally and so necessarily or for the most part. E.g., the standard measures of different communities differ, though wholesale measures are *always* everywhere greater than retail measures (*NE* V 7.1134b35–1135a5).

ferent times in the course of a life must or should have the same ultimate aim. Aristotle needs a further argument for establishing that all the projects of a person might have a *single* ultimate end.[16]

Surely we may often be somewhat indefinite about what our goal is, and especially about the ultimate human goal, if there is one. Yet we should allow that if there *is* an ultimate human goal, it would be quite significant to gain familiarity with what it is (1094a22–26). This is a practical argument: we are more likely to hit the target we see. And this is more compelling still if some persons do seem to lead superior lives through some care and attention. The decisive practical consideration Aristotle offers in favor of a highest human end is that in the hierarchy of the arts there is a highest art, political science, devoted to the human end (1094a26–b11). Since political science as Aristotle conceives it encompasses the ends of all the other arts and sciences, he ensures that there is no end beyond those he is considering for happiness. Putting the human end in the political context seems helpful because the political association has an end embracing all other ends, and the community strives to be a lasting association rather than a temporary enterprise. If there is a political art devoted to the ultimate human end, and presumably there is, then there must be such an end.

Aristotle thus argues practically that there is an ultimate good for humans. He thereby fulfills the methodological requirement for science of the *Posterior Analytics* II 1, first to establish *if* or *that* there is something to investigate, in this case the human end happiness, and only then inquire *what* or *on account of what* it is. He is establishing eudaemonism as the paradigm for practical science.[17] Usually one argues that there is some subject matter so that there can be a science of it, which to some extent he has, though here Aristotle also uses the apparent existence of the science, political science, to guarantee its subject matter and principle. Success in presenting such a science will secure that there is the human end.

Has Aristotle's practical argumentation clinched the view *that* there is some final end for humans? He has not given a demonstrative argument that we have a final end since we *cannot* demonstrate first principles.[18] Yet he has

---

16   The fullest discussion of infinite regresses is in *Metaph.* II 2, where Aristotle argues that infinite regress destroys the whole notion of cause, but in *NE* 1094a18–22 Aristotle merely expects appreciation that with no final answer to the "why are you doing this?" question, there does not really seem to be any goal at all, which eliminates acting purposively.

17   See Broadie and Rowe 2002, 261.

18   Eudaemonism cannot be demonstrated, and is not a necessary conception, for one can choose to live a non-eudaemonistic life. Living randomly is possible or seeking unlim-

made it very plausible, and if he depicts happiness convincingly, this might really ensure likelihood. Those who resist living as eudaemonists ignore the practical case made that we live better if we suppose there is such an end so that we can live in an organized fashion. Aristotle has indicated a hierarchy of ends in human projects, with the end better than what is for its sake. There cannot be an infinite regress of ends if action is to be purposive. Since there is a science devoted to considering the end, political communities and their citizens that compose them have a final, ultimate end. None of this argumentation for eudaemonism depends upon theoretical philosophy, and no theoretical development will put this practical argumentation on a firmer basis.

If we resist this sort of argumentation for the eudaemonistic approach to practical science, Aristotle cautions about the sort of precision to expect in practical science (*NE* I 3). Ethics lacks precision since its universal principles generally only hold for the most part.[19] Because practical affairs are so variable and particular, there is inevitably limited precision in the ability of ethics to guide us in action.[20] Variability and imprecision pertain to establishing ultimate principles in ethics, as we saw with the practical grounding of eudaemonism, and in the application of the principles to particular situations.[21] Is

ited pleasure or power, such lives having no definite end. Socrates seems to have hit upon eudaemonism as very practical in his elenctic conversations. Once he can get an interlocutor to agree that he seeks happiness and wishes to avoid being miserable, whatever way the interlocutor understands happiness, so long as it is a definite end, virtue inevitably becomes vital. By this strategy Socrates gets a reluctant conversation partner to concede the desirability of virtue.

19   Some commentators (see Broadie 1991, 18) suggest that there must be universal truths in ethics that are not merely for the most part so: such as that matters in ethics are only for the most part so, or that moral virtue lies in a mean, or that happiness involves activity according to virtue. Reeve 1995, 22–27 argues that there may be some unconditional scientific knowledge in ethics because the good person judges correctly and because the human mind is without matter. Yet we must doubt more than hypothetical necessity in ethics since *enmattered* humans are seeking a happy life and judging, and the previous note showed that the eudaemonistic approach will not necessarily apply for every person.

20   See Broadie and Rowe 2002, 265.

21   Scott 2015, 138 speaks of "practical and theoretical precision" as if they could apply to the same science, but the distinction is erroneous inasmuch as the subject matter of a science—which pertains to the aim of the science, the involvement with matter, the variability of the subject matter, and the need for additional assumptions—is the sole cause of levels of imprecision pertaining to principles and application. Practical science, due to its subject matter, appropriate human action and passion, will not gain further precision

practical science then genuinely science at all? Need science depend on mathematical precision? The productive sciences, which vary in precision—the more
mathematical arts such as surveying being more precise than medicine—still
are all arts and sciences since they have causes and achieve non-accidental success. So less precision does not have to destroy the very status of art or science.
And despite all the variations in practical matters, the principles hold "for the
most part" (ὡς ἐπὶ τὸ πολύ, see 1094b14–22), which according to *Posterior Analytics* I 30 and II 12.96a8–19 suffices for science.[22]

What sort of sophistication and training accords with the requirement for
practical science? Aristotle asserts:

---

by additional assistance from theoretical science. Precise theoretical mathematics is such
because it deals with intelligible entities from abstraction; application to sensible beings
changes the subject matter and reduces the precision. Scott 2015, 133 shows that he misses
the shift in subject matters: "This sounds more like a reference to the restriction on theoretical precision, where we are concerned not with what is possible given the nature of
the subject matter, but what is appropriate given our practical concerns". He erroneously
supposes that the subject matter remains invariant even when the aims of sciences differ, as if the fisherman and ichthyologist, both dealing with fish, have precisely the same
subject matter. But their very different interests regarding the fish mean different subject
matters, as pure and applied mathematics have different subject matters. And Henry 2015,
189 quotes Aristotle's 1098a20–31, "We must also remember what has been said before and
not look for precision in all things alike, but in each class of things only such precision as
is related to the subject matter at hand and only as much as is appropriate to the enquiry.
For a carpenter and a geometer look for right angles in different ways: the former does so
insofar as the right angle is useful for his work, while the latter enquires what it is (*ti estin*)
or what sort of thing it is, since he is an observer of truth. We must act in the same way,
then, in all other matters as well so that our main task may not be subordinated to minor
questions". Henry comments: "Since the ultimate aim of moral enquiry is action, the definitions and accounts the student of ethics formulates should be filled out only up to the
point where they will be useful for action. While those definitions and accounts *could be*
made more precise (just like the carpenter's account of the right angle), given the practical
aims of ethics the theoretical part of the enquiry should not get bogged down by 'minor
questions' (minor relative to the practical ends of ethics)". But Aristotle is indicating that
more precision about right angles gets us *outside* carpentry into geometry; in no way does
carpentry involve the precision of geometry. There is no "theoretical part of the enquiry"
into either carpentry or ethics.

22 Of course for Aristotle even natural philosophy deals with beings that generally have
perishable matter, which permits them to be or not be, as animals may lose a limb due
to injury. Therefore for him much natural science has principles holding only for the most
part in application to natural beings (cf. Henry 2015, 177–188).

Now each man judges well the things he knows, and of these he is a good judge. And so the man who has been educated in a subject is a good judge of that subject, and the man who has received an all-round education is a good judge in general. Hence a young man is not a proper hearer of lectures on political science; for he is inexperienced in the actions that occur in life, but its discussions (*logoi*) start from these and are about these; and, further, since he tends to follow his passions, his study will be vain and unprofitable, because the end aimed at is not knowledge but action. (τὸ τέλος ἐστὶν οὐ γνῶσις ἀλλὰ πρᾶξις)

1094b27–1095a6

Practical science is about action, so the sophistication expected is about this. The person suitably educated for this cannot be one who lives merely by passions or has undeveloped character, which accords with the point in *Metaphysics* VI 1 that practical science has its principles in us, i.e., in the choosing person. It does not detract from the scientific status of practical science that one's character impacts on one's scientific understanding. One has to be a good person to be good in this science, since this science is about action and passion, whereas theoretical sciences, having their principles in the things studied themselves, do not call for a special character of the student but affinity for those things studied. Requisite for practical science is a proper affinity with its own subject matter, actions, and passions. The end of this science is not just knowledge (γνῶσις), Aristotle says, but action (πρᾶξις). Ethical understanding is knowledge, but as concerned with action, it is not theoretical knowledge.[23] Though practical science pertains to every human as a human, similarly with other difficult arts and sciences, only some are prepared for it and good at it.[24]

---

23   Pat Macfarlane pointed out to me that 1095a5–6 is ambiguous so that Aristotle might also say that the young fail as students of ethics because the aim of the *students* is action rather than insight. If the ambiguity about the end being that of the students or of the science is deliberate, then Aristotle may say that the students are too little in search of insight through just wishing to do what their passions tell them, and this incapacitates them for improving their action by means of the science primarily directed toward action. The beasts act effectively by acting on their passions, but humans have to develop appropriate character and understanding to perfect their human passions and actions.

24   Burnyeat 1980, 81 comments: "He [*sc.* Aristotle] is not attempting the task so many moralists have undertaken of recommending virtue even to those who despise it: his lectures are not sermons, nor even protreptic argument, urging the wicked to mend their ways ... Rather, he is giving a course in practical thinking to enable someone who already wants to be virtuous to understand better what he should do and why".

When Aristotle gets to exploring the proposed candidates for what happiness is (*NE* I 4), such as the life of money-making, the pleasure-seeking life, the political life, and the theoretical or contemplative life, it is reassuring that there are but few real possibilities.[25] This may enable a comprehensive consideration of all the viable candidates, thus surpassing the narrowness of any particular culture since such lives are more or less available everywhere. In his treatment of these different lives, Aristotle uses the term *bios*, which also appears in the biological works for ways of life (e.g., 1095b15, b17, b23, b31, b33, 1097b9, b15, 1098a18). He will soon also use the term *zôê* for the life activity, such as perceiving or thinking, as he does in the *De Anima* and elsewhere (1097b9, b33, 1098a1, a13). Nonetheless, this selection of terms for life does not, appeal to or rely upon his natural scientific works.[26]

In arguing dialectically against the lives of seeking pleasure, honor, virtue, or money, Aristotle introduces considerations of serving as an end, i.e., being final, and serving as sufficiently encompassing, i.e., being self-sufficient. Both of these criteria he could find in Plato's *Philebus*. They will become his tests for a life adequate for the happy life.[27]

Nicomachean Ethics I 6 takes up another possible candidate for the goal of life, Plato's extraordinary proposal in *Republic* VI of the Idea of the Good. In fact, Plato's name is not mentioned at all, and it is not really essential that Aristotle get right what Plato meant, for Aristotle's crucial purpose here is just my present purpose, separating practical from theoretical science. Were the Idea of the Good the human end and also the ultimate principle of theoretical science, practical science would have no independence. There would be a grand unity of all science. Thus the Idea of the Good, understood in certain ways, introduces into practical science a principle that goes beyond its own proper field. In

---

25   We may wonder why Aristotle ignores power as a possible end for life, for power is not quite the same as honor or recognition. Those who think that the good is whatever anyone happens to want may suppose that power is most vital since power enables you to get what you want. But the life that seeks power turns a means into an end, for power allows us to use it for something further, and so in fact it is not a definite and eudaemonistic goal. Power is an endless and limitless pursuit, which does not fit with eudaemonism. The view of humans as insatiable, found in the *Gorgias*, *Republic* I, and in Hobbes, attacks eudaemonism.

26   Contrast Shields 2015, 238–239.

27   As the *Metaphysics* identifies criteria for substantial being, i.e., being "a this" and separate (τόδε τι ὂν καὶ χωριστόν, e.g., *Metaph.* V 8.1017b24–26), practical science has its own criteria for the happy life, being final and self-sufficient, which emerge from its own practical reflections.

attacking this incursion into practical science, therefore, Aristotle defends the division of the sciences, and he protects practical science practically against invasions from without.

Regarding this topic of "the universal better", Aristotle indicates that it should be considered, but it is arduous because it takes up the thought of friends who introduced the forms (1096a11–17). But as philosophers seeking to preserve the truth, dear (φίλοιν) as both friends and the truth are, it is pious (ὅσιον) to honor the truth (προτιμᾶν τὴν ἀλήθειαν) before friends. Why? Friends (*philoi*) and philosophy (*philosophia*) are both lovable. How do we decide on truth over friends? This seems to be a practical decision, and Aristotle goes with what is more pious. What is more pious is saving the truth rather than merely accepting a friend's wrong view, which most likely is better ultimately for the friend as well. This opening reflection on the opposition of goals, and the need to make a choice, already looks toward the relationship of theoretical and practical science. Aristotle practically puts the theoretical higher, as even dearer than practical science, so he now makes a decision based upon the practicality of piety regarding the truth. Only to the extent that a practical argument can be made for truth does it belong in practical science. This decision will serve both practical science and theoretical science, and of course it no more hurts science than Aristotle in fact hurts his friends. In seeming to attack Plato, Aristotle echoes passages in Plato's *Phaedo* 91c and *Republic* 595b–c and 607c, ironically showing further piety in relation to his friends. Broadie and Rowe suggest that emphasis upon friendship means Aristotle shares values with Platonists and his rejection of their Idea of the Good need not mean rejection of the contemplative life they espouse, and we also have the amusing further irony here that truth is what is most dear, while in this context at least practical science is the truth.[28] And if the Idea of the Good is a theoretical notion, by raising questions about this theoretical position, Aristotle exposes the danger of resting practical science on theoretical principles.

To eliminate the Idea of the Good as pertinent to practical science, Aristotle utilizes considerations from the logical works (applicable in practical as in theoretical works). He observes that good is used equivocally, and in fact it transcends the categorial division of beings inasmuch as there are good things in every category of being. There is, then, no single science that has the good for its subject. He questions whether the good itself as good, even were it eternal, differs in terms of goodness from other good things; yet the goodness of all the

28   See Broadie and Rowe 2002, 269.

different good things is explained in different ways and not dependent upon any Idea of the Good. Regarding whether there are Ideas such as the good, he states:

> But perhaps these subjects had better be dismissed for the present; for perfect precision about them would be more appropriate to another branch of philosophy. And similarly with regard to the Idea; even if there is some one good which is universally predicable of goods or is capable of separate and independent existence (χωριστὸν αὐτό τι καθ᾽ αὑτό), clearly it could not be achieved (πρακτόν) or attained (κτητόν) by man; but we are now seeking something attainable.
>
> 1096b30–35

He obviously declares that extended consideration of the theory of Ideas goes outside practical science (cf. 1096b5–8 where he similarly puts dealing with the views on the One and Good of Pythagoreans and Speusippus outside his present concerns). If further treatment of such a good does not belong to practical science, then what relevance can it have for ethics? None of the other arts studies it, and they succeed well without it. Aristotle clearly denounces the Idea of the Good as figuring in an account of human happiness. He thus seeks to secure practical science from inappropriately straying into theoretical terrain.

Following the dismissal of the Idea of the Good, a theoretical object, as relevant to practical science, Aristotle works out his own account of what happiness is. *Nicomachean Ethics* I 7, which offers the preliminary account of happiness, has often been supposed to rely on Aristotle's theoretical positions. Yet we may show that he instead builds upon what he has so far secured in the *Ethics*. On his way to determining *what* happiness is, he renews the case *that* there is a single end that is happiness. The various actions and arts have different ends or goods, he acknowledges (1097a15–28), but among these ends some are more ultimate since others are chosen for their sake. Anything instrumental toward further ends is not final or complete (τέλειον). This accords with his previous discussion that the best is something final (1097a28; cf. 1094a18–22, 1095b30–1096a2). What is final or complete should therefore be most choice-worthy:

> Now we call that which is in itself worthy of pursuit more complete (τελει-όΤερον) than that which is worthy of pursuit for the sake of something else, and that which is never desirable for the sake of something else more complete than the things that are desirable both in themselves and for

the sake of that other thing, and therefore we call complete without qualification that which is always desirable in itself and never for the sake of
something else (τὸ καθ' αὑτὸ αἱρετόν ἀεὶ καὶ μηδέποτε δι' ἄλλο). Now such
a thing happiness, above all else, is held to be; for this we choose always
for itself and never for the sake of something else, but honour, pleasure,
reason (*nous*), and every excellence we choose indeed for themselves (for
if nothing resulted from them we should still choose each of them), but
we choose them also for the sake of happiness, judging that through them
we shall be happy. Happiness, on the other hand, no one chooses for the
sake of these, nor, in general, for anything other than itself.

1097a30–b6

Happiness is the most final and choice-worthy goal since all other ends, though
ends, are also chosen for the sake of happiness, but happiness is never chosen
for the sake of any other end. Our pursuit of ends must have some final end,
call it happiness, if our deliberations are to make sense. As reflective beings, our
deliberations can take the end of our entire life into consideration; rationality
in action requires that we deliberate with some ultimate end in view, vague
as it may be, and we never in fact speak of seeking happiness for the sake
of something further. Such support for positing an ultimate end may only
ultimately certify *that* there is human happiness when he convincingly shows
what it is.

Is there a way he can fill in what happiness is, rather than keeping it vaguely
as the most final end? If happiness is a sort of *life*, it seems most promising as a
self-sufficient life needing nothing further. Since *teleion* is ambiguous, meaning
either final, as that for the sake of which all else is chosen, or complete, i.e., what
is missing nothing, Aristotle adds being self-sufficient to guarantee completeness and clear choice-worthiness. *Self*-sufficiency (*autarcheia*) might suggest
satisfying the self, but Aristotle has an expansive notion of the self that includes
the person's family and friends and fellow citizens since humans belong naturally in political association (1097b8–11).[29] This means that humans naturally
have inclinations and ends that can only be satisfied in human community.
"Self-sufficiency" has nice ambiguity: it can mean provision of basic needs *or*
the condition we deem worthy to be selected taken all by itself (here is where

---

29   Aristotle does not here refer to his discussion of naturally political animals in *Historia
      Animalium* I 1. The anti-eudaemonist rejects the view that humans are naturally political
      beings suited for just life since the rejection has each person insatiably seeking unlimited
      power, and hence humans are in conflict that subsides only through a conventional
      contract permitting political life.

it especially overlaps with "complete"). The happy life should be final and self-sufficient. While finality as the ultimate end may keep happiness quite vague as a requirement for rational action, in conjunction with self-sufficiency, which concentrates upon happiness as satisfying basic and higher human needs, Aristotle gets toward concreteness.

Do the criteria of finality and self-sufficiency seem indisputable, more so than any of the substantive candidates for happiness? Perhaps even skeptics might allow these as criteria for the human good, if anything could satisfy them.[30] This appears to be Aristotle's conviction, as fitting with his viewing the "better" as what is more end-like (1094a5–6). The question then remains whether anything can fulfill these criteria for happiness.

Aristotle tries to concretize his account of happiness through the "function argument", which commentators often suppose looks to and even depends upon his theoretical views.[31] I show that he instead continues his reflection upon what preceded. He early on spoke of works or products (*erga*, 1094a5), and he now goes further in considering whether there is a work or function (*ergon*) for a human being. A function argument appears in Plato's *Republic* I 352d–354a, where the function or work of something is what it alone can do or what it does better in comparison with other things that might also do it. The background assumption is that whatever has a function, the function is unique or peculiar to that thing since it alone does it well or does it best. Aristotle will be seen to avail himself of this assumption when he seeks what is peculiar to humans, but he also more definitely and emphatically than Plato uses the point about what something does best to sift among the possible human works to find that which is the best and in which the human good lies.[32] Now for Aristotle, things having a function seem to be tools, whatever humans use as means, and bodily organs and psychical capacities of living beings that a plant or animal employs. Tools and organs of plants and animals that can be used by the living being have functions, rather than the living being itself in its entirety.[33] Talk of

---

30   See Klein 1988 and Irwin 1988, 359.

31   Scott 2015, 117 says, "the very claim that human beings have a function is metaphysical, committing Aristotle to some form of teleology". But the argument that humans have a function is in fact a practical claim, and especially as it is treated in relation to human efforts.

32   Baker 2015, 231–236 and 242–243 compares Plato and Aristotle on *ergon*, and indicates that Aristotle goes further by making the comparison class not just other things that might achieve similar *erga* but also "other things that an x, *qua* x, can achieve". In this way Aristotle seeks the very good of the thing in its *ergon*.

33   Barney 2008, 299–300 misreads Plato as supposing that only instruments *we* use can

a function or work for a human, i.e., the being as a whole, is metaphorical, and a way of speaking found only in practical contexts. Aristotle first has to argue that the human function is significant, if there is one, and that there is such a function. And we can see the need for such argument since a function for humans is not a notion from the theoretical works but a novelty here. Having established that there is a function, he will determine what the human function is.

The good of a thing lies in the function when there is one (1097b22–33). This is no theoretical result but the recognition that, for example, the good for a shoemaker *as a shoemaker* consists in making shoes well, and the good of a knife as such an instrument is cutting well. The *function* of the function argument, what it can perhaps do well practically, is to assist locating what is the good for the human being. If the good for what has a function lies in the function and the function is peculiar to that kind of thing, the good becomes unique to what has the function. To argue that there is a human function, Aristotle appeals by analogy to various artisans as clearly having functions and to parts of the body as having functions. These might or might not be weak analogies or fallacies of composition, i.e., features of the narrower class or of the parts applied to the wider class or the whole. Perhaps from the practical perspective of the productive arts, the way all the arts have functions and enter into a hierarchy, as discussed previously, supports a function in human life

---

have a function. The notion of function extends beyond this, but she rightly sees that the notion does have limits. In fact we do not generally find Aristotle himself speaking in the natural treatises of the function of a whole living substantial being but merely of its parts (or its body as serving soul). So the function argument as found in the *Ethics* is not borrowing from theoretical contexts. In *PA* ii 2.648a15 Aristotle refers to τὰ ἔργα καὶ τὴν οὐσίαν ἑκάστῳ τῶν ζῴων, but the context is the parts of animals and the plural for *erga* conjoined with singular *ousia* tells against supposing he speaks of the *ergon* of a whole animal (cf. Lennox 2001, 189). *HA* 488a7–8 speaks of the *ergon* of diverse species of political animals, *GA* 731a24–26 speaks of the *ergon* of the whole genus of plants and living things, and *Cael.* 286a8–11 speaks as if of the *ergon* of the heavenly *bodies* as eternal motion, the motion serving the life of the divine being. So these passages do not really speak of the function of a whole individual substantial living being. Generally, functions for species are problematic if species are distinguished by having features "more or less" (see Henry 2015, 172 and Witt 2015, 280), for "more or less" sits poorly with the notion of function as what something alone can do or does best. Shields 2015, 240 admits, "Organisms, by contrast [to designed instruments], do not have easily recognisable functions," but none of the theoretical passages he points to—*Mete.* 390a10–15, *GA* 734b21–24, *PA* 640b18–23, *Metaph.* 1029b23–1030a17 (239)—in fact support the claim that Aristotle supposes a natural function for individual living beings.

generally, for the arts seem to cover all human needs. And the function of the human as a whole may call for the integrated functions of all the parts of the body. This argumentation, especially in conjunction with the possibility that human desires are in principle capable of being satisfied, as suggested by the criterion of self-sufficiency, suffices for practical purposes for establishing the possibility of a human function.[34] Having secured that function is a practical way to get at the good and that the human has a function, Aristotle must determine the human function.

His argument to specify the function works by continuing to reflect upon what he has been saying from the very start of this treatise. He began by declaring that all human efforts have purposes or ends and a multiplicity of these. Unlike plants and other mortal animals, we humans reflect upon these purposes and ends, as evidenced by deliberation and choice that allow for an ultimate end among the multiplicity of ends.[35] The condition for the possibility of all specifically *human* doing, and especially as enters into the ultimate project of happiness, is that we can think or reason about what we do. So the conclusion that the human function involves speech or reason (*logos*) is not the selection of one unique human capacity among others, such as laughing, praying, or telling jokes. Instead it is the designation of what makes *any* or all *human* action or activity (understood in the widest sense) possible. Human thought or reflection makes possible every effort that is unique to humans, including all the arts and all other human purposive practices.

Here is Aristotle's compressed formulation of the argument for what is the human function:

---

34 Leunissen 2015, 229 comments about this part of the argument: "The first section is very rhetorical in nature, and never actually establishes affirmatively that humans in fact have a function: it moves from the observation that (human) artists and body parts such as hands (which belong specifically to humans) have functions to the implicit *suggestion* that it would be strange if humans were 'by nature functionless'" (and Shields 2015, 241 denies that Aristotle "sets out to prove that human beings have a function"). These commentators overlook Aristotle's actual argument since they seek theoretical demonstration rather than the practical demonstration offered by Aristotle.

35 That humans do so many different things, as seen in the multiplicity of the arts and their oversight by the highest political art, contrasts with the way the beasts tend to a very narrow range of efforts, even in the case of the social animals. This supports that human action has a rather different basis, a much greater neediness than the beasts but a much higher-level capacity possibly to satisfy that neediness. The beasts operate largely by the impulse of their nature, while humans are led naturally to reflection and choice about their numerous possibilities.

> Life (ζῆν) seems to be common (*koinon*) even to plants, but we are seeking what is peculiar (*idion*) to man. Let us exclude, therefore, the life of nutrition and growth (θρεπτικὴν καὶ τὴν αὐξητικὴν ζωήν). Next there would be a life of perception, but *it* also seems to be common even to the horse, the ox, and every animal. There remains, then, an active life of the element that has a rational principle (πρακτική τις τοῦ λόγον ἔχοντος).
>
> 1097b33–1098a4

We notice that he looks to what dominates the sort of life: nutrition and growth, perception, or *logos*. Does this require theoretical background or just appreciation that *human* life is not simply nutritive or sense-perceptive life? The peculiarly human function or good of humans cannot consist in what the *genera* of plants and beasts also do because the human function and good must be unique and apply to *individuals* within the human species. He quickly dismisses lives that involve only such common functions and cannot explain human action and choice. Yet because nutritive life and perception are prominent in the *De Anima*, interpreters suppose theoretical works undergird the present argument. But does Aristotle appeal at all to such treatises? Must any notice that plants are alive and grow or that other animals perceive rely on theoretical science? As previously noted, the theoretical works do not generally speak this way of functions for whole natural living beings. And he here has *logos* distinctive of human practice, whereas were he really following the *De Anima* he should instead refer to mind (*nous*), as he does in book 10. And the mention of the horse, prominent in Plato's *Republic* I 352e (cf. *NE* II 6.1106a15–24), may alert us that horses have a function for humans who use them. Tame horses serve humans, but what otherwise is the function of the horse kind? I thus question whether the function argument as practically employed here fits into any strict theoretical context.

Logos as our fundamental capacity should be compelling since this is what he and those like us now engaging with him are utilizing. He locates the capacity that underlies *all* that he has been discussing so far in the *Ethics* in considering acting for ends and the arts. "Reason" need not be used here as the contrary of unreasonable, since then it would already include the notion of virtue or excellence, but reason here means a capacity that may be used well or poorly. The other animals lack it nearly completely, and so they cannot deliberate and choose projects toward an ultimate end.[36]

---

36   It might seem that the gods also have *logos*, since *Metaph.* XII has them thinking, and *logos* would not be peculiar to us. But the gods do not have reason or mind (*nous*) since mind

The human function turns out to be "activity of soul in accordance with, or not without, rational principle" (1098a7–8). Happiness is *activity* since this is an *end*, and he says "activity of *soul*" since *logos* somehow pertains to soul. This account shows, as suggested, that reason is the capacity that enters and enables *all* peculiarly human doing. According to reason or not without reason covers reasoning itself, activity deriving directly from it, or activity involving desire and character influenced by reason. The activity of the desiring part of the soul that can obey *logos* may be said to be not without *logos*.

The good for something that has a function lies in the function. Virtue or excellence at the function enables doing the function well. A lyre-player has the same function as a good lyre-player (1098a8–16). Comparison with the artisan, where art can be taken as virtue at the task, perhaps makes it unnecessary to argue *that there is* virtue relating to the human function. The addition of the excellence at the function makes the person a good person, and thus enabled the person may achieve the human good:

> Our agency is almost always embedded in some social role which we accept as normative, and which involves just the unity of doing well and faring well to which Aristotle draws our attention. The good doctor typically enters the consulting room aiming not to maximize utility, nor to obey the categorical imperative, nor for that matter to maximally serve her own interests, but simply *to do a good job*—that is, to act successfully as a good doctor, just as she might at other times of the day aim to act as a good friend, sister, dog-owner, party member, and so on for every description she takes as contributing to her identity.[37]

---

or *logos* is merely a capacity, and the gods are not simply in potentiality. They instead are always thinking (*noesis*) in actuality rather than being potentiality or power in any way (see Macfarlane and Polansky 2009). Aristotle does not get into this here, which would take him into his theoretical position. Our highest activity and highest happiness, contemplation, is not the human function, which is wider, i.e., to use reason or mind. We share the highest activity with the gods but not the function. Our function, utilization of reason, also makes our highest activity, contemplating, possible for us. If we accept the critique by Baker 2015, 253–254 of translating *ergon* as "function", then we may restate our point thus: the wide or generic notion of human *ergon* is activity of soul according to reason or not without reason, while the best specific human *ergon* is contemplation, which alone is shared with god.

37   See Barney 2008, 317.

There can be many human tasks all linking as human tasks in some way to our ability to reason and serving the ultimate human end. The peculiar human good is then performing the human function according to virtue. And if there are several kinds and levels of human virtues, the highest human good and happiness will be activity according to the best and most final of these and in a complete life (1098a16–18). It remains for Aristotle to clarify the kinds of virtue and to determine which might be best and most final.

What has the account of happiness accomplished? Though it is merely an outline and requires filling in subsequently (1098a20–26), it helpfully gets at the first principle of practical life. He has perhaps secured eudaemonism. Can we easily deny that the human good or happiness consists in activity deriving from using reason in accordance with virtue in a complete life? Some surely will resist this, but has Aristotle not provided a compelling practical reflection about human action, what enables such action, and what makes it good? Is his account not as precise as possible in general (1098a26–33)? In the case of his first principle, do we continue to seek *why* it is so, or must we accept *that* it is so (1098a33–b3)? Regarding how we arrive at first principles, Aristotle states:

> Now of first principles we see some by induction (ἐπαγωγῇ), some by perception (αἰσθήσει), some by a certain habituation (ἐθισμῷ τινί), and others too in other ways. But each set of principles we must try to investigate in the natural way (ᾗ πεφύκασιν), and we must take pains to determine them correctly, since they have a great influence on what follows. For the beginning is thought to be more than half of the whole, and many of the questions we ask are cleared up by it.
>
> 1098b3–8

This is intended to reassure us about his first principle arrived at the way it naturally should be in practical science. We cannot demonstrate first principles, but we get them adequately in other ways. How he arrived at the practical principle of happiness is probably by each of the ways here mentioned, and so as is natural. Practical principles come through a combination of perception, habituation, and induction. Perception enters when Aristotle has observed that some persons live better lives than others. Being well brought up, i.e., having good habituation, contributes to recognition of the role of virtue in the human good. Aristotle's frequent usage of proverbs and common sayings in this section, practical induction, confirms that we think practically in seeking principles. He hardly suggests that practical science goes outside its own realm to borrow principles from other sciences. His claim about the beginning being more than half the whole indicates confidence in what he has said about the practical principle and its significance. He celebrates his own success. When he proceeds in *NE* I 8–12 to verify that his account of happiness fits with common sayings, with the way people praise and blame, and much else, he discloses that he overcomes as many perplexities as have been raised about the human good, so his account provides as reliable a basis for practical science as we might attain.

The filling in of his outline account of the human good requires clarification about virtue. When Aristotle divides the soul to distinguish the types of virtue into character and intellectual virtue, he pertinently insists that the political scientist for this purpose needs only practical knowledge of the soul:

> The student of politics, then, must study the soul, and must study it with these objects in view, and do so just to the extent which is sufficient for the questions we are discussing; for further precision is perhaps something more laborious than our purposes require. Some things are said about it, adequately enough, even in the discussions outside our school, and we must use these; e.g. that one element in the soul is irrational and one has a rational principle.
>
> I 13.1102a23–28

This accords with my emphasis upon division of the sciences, that the aim of the science enters into determining its subject matter, and that for practical science Aristotle need not introduce what he does in the *De Anima*, even if he in effect here utilizes the nutritive, locomotive, and intellective faculties, leaving out the perceptive. In defending his present division of soul, into that which has *logos* and that which is *alogon*, as adequate for his purpose, he ignores theoretical questions about what it means to say the soul has parts, whether they are really distinct in being or just in account. Even if there is much more to say theoretically about the soul, it is questionable whether this impacts at all on practical science![38] He is content with this quite basic division.

Yet Leunissen and Shields contend that Aristotle expects students of political science to have considerable theoretical knowledge of the soul, though Leunissen admits, "whenever a 'more exact' account about human psychology is required, Aristotle often provides this in the immediate context within

---

38   Those in the twentieth century who looked for chronological development in Aristotle's thought contrasted the "psychology" here with that in the theoretical works, in line with their chronological hypotheses. But our emphasis upon Aristotle's scrupulous attention to the division of the sciences makes such trajectories in Aristotle's thought about soul misguided.

the *Nicomachean Ethics* itself",[39] which raises the issue that I now take up for both their positions. Shields holds that the function argument depends on a hierarchy of possible functions and a disjunctive syllogism, for he thinks, deriving from the account in the *De Anima*, the human function must sequentially be either nutritive life or perceptive life or rational life, so when not the first two, it must be the third. Shields then claims, "Neither the hierarchy nor the disjunctive syllogism employed in the function argument would be available to someone who had not studied the soul. It follows, then, that anyone in a position to develop and deploy anything at all like Aristotle's function argument will have engaged in some such study".[40] I have instead urged that rather than looking toward theoretical works about the soul, Aristotle's argumentation right from the start of the treatise relies upon the clear fact that all human doing depends upon thought and reflection. But my present objection has a quite different point. Shields and Leunissen expect dubiously that the "student of political science" is someone having the equivalent theoretical and practical insight of Aristotle as composer of the *Ethics*, and not merely someone *learning* from Aristotle's ethical work. Shields asserts, "the ethicist, whose mission it is to characterize the highest and finest human good ... will need to know these moorings, and so will not be able to conduct ethical theory, however practical a science ethics may be, without first understanding the theoretical science from which its terms immediately derive" (249). And he further says, "Aristotle's exhortation to the politician to study the soul is not lightly made: he is suggesting that the politician needs to know the soul and its workings in a detailed and intimate manner, in the manner, that is, of someone who is a scientist and not merely a practitioner" (252). Their case then amounts to demanding that the student of the *Ethics* have all, or nearly all, the ability and insight of Aristotle!

I acknowledged initially that Aristotle might not have written his practical treatises without previously working out his theoretical positions, but this is not to urge that *anyone* practically wise and engaging in politics needs to be on his level of practical and theoretical understanding. Once Aristotle has written the *Ethics*—which someone not equaling Aristotle's intellectual development just might have done somewhat comparably—I contend that those engaging with his text are spared the need to be theoretically sophisticated. It suffices for them to become successful students and practitioners of political science that they were properly reared and suitably comprehend what Aristotle offers in the *Ethics* (see 1094b27–1095a13 and *NE* X 9 about the sort of student expected).

---

39   See Leunissen 2015, 226.

40   See Shields 2015, 246.

Aristotle presents this, in conjunction with his *Politics*, as the complete political philosophy (1181b12–15). Were the student to have to be as, or nearly as, theoretically and practically adept as Aristotle, as Leunissen and Shields suggest, the *Ethics* might be in vain since all who worked on it adequately would become theoreticians leading the theoretical life. Thus the concern in Plato's *Republic* about philosophers returning to the cave might be an insurmountable and politically destructive difficulty for Aristotle.

II   The Rest of the *NE* is Free from Theoretical Assumptions

What intellectual capacity is Aristotle using to give his outline account of happiness in *NE* I and then to fill this in during the remainder of the work? Anagnostopoulos asks whether practical wisdom (*phronesis*) conceived as deliberating about means to ends could be what is enabling Aristotle to develop the *Ethics*.[41] He calls this the "narrow" view of *phronesis*, which seems inadequate for dealing with practical matters universally as undertaken in the *Ethics*. But does this then mean that being a student of political science or writing a treatise of practical science calls upon *sophia* or some theoretical capacity rather than *phronesis*? By analogy, if a person with a productive art writes about the art, for example a carpenter about carpentry, do we suppose that this requires a further intellectual capacity? We expect that someone genuinely possessing an art has the principles of the art and the ability to apply them, so the person can deal with the particulars of immediate production, and, if reflective and articulate, can speak generally about the universals involved. Thus an art may enable someone to make a product or to teach others the art (1180b13–34). Similarly, we should expect the person with *phronesis* to be able to deliberate about immediate means to concrete ends and also to reflect generally about ends and the entire practical life. Thus we can maintain that *phronesis*, the practical intellectual virtue, is what elaborates practical science as found in the *Ethics*, even if Aristotle as author knows more himself. *Phronesis* works out, in the context of practical science, the four sorts of causes identified in the *Physics*. Obviously happiness is the end, the passions are the matter given form by virtue and character, and choice is the moving cause, with *phronesis* also articulating the intellectual faculties and deliberating to generate choices in the service of happiness and to develop character. Yet Aristotle conscientiously avoids linking his eliciting of the four explanatory causes in the *Ethics* too closely with his

---

41   See Anagnostopoulos 1994, chapter 3.

accounts elsewhere, and his way of arriving at these principles is thoroughly practical. We have seen this already regarding the end happiness in the previous section. We continue to explore the way he keeps within practical science for the rest of the *Ethics*, including those sections that refer to theoretical science and the contemplative life.

In working out what is character or moral virtue, Aristotle says that he can only give an outline account since matters of conduct permit only limited precision (1103b34–1104a11). By comparisons to such arts as medicine and gymnastics training (1104a11–b3), he arrives at the view that appropriate action is neither excessive nor deficient, and that doing appropriate actions generates and sustains the suitable character virtue. In further clarifying what virtue is as a mean, he distinguishes passions, potentialities for these, and states (*hexeis*) of character that dispose us to experience them well or badly (*NE* II 5). While these three notions come into play in theoretical contexts, he makes no reference whatsoever to such contexts here, and he does not elsewhere speak of three things in the soul to set up the process of elimination such as developed here. Also when he frequently appeals here to nature and what is by nature (see start of *NE* II), such usage pertains to what is inborn in humans or the obvious motions of natural bodies such as earth and fire. In his working out his accounts of the particular moral virtues in books 3–5, he refers to what is praised and blamed, to lines of poetry, to historical events and figures, and to what is taken to be more difficult (in accord with the saying "fine things are difficult"), but never to his theoretical works. And his investigations of the voluntary and involuntary, as well as deliberation and choice, keep to points that those without theoretical sophistication could follow and accept (III 1–5). His treatment of justice in book 5 uses only basic mathematics, and when he must turn to mathematics he carefully explains his terms (see, e.g., 1131b12–13). So the first half of the *Nicomachean Ethics* keeps to practical arguments and considerations.

In book 6 that distinguishes the virtues and capacities of the intellect, Aristotle is still employing *phronesis*, even if with the assistance of the *Posterior Analytics* (see 1139b27 and b32–33). The book begins with the indication that it will finally speak about the capacity to locate the intermediate (*meson*) and not the excess or deficiency (1138b18–34). This capacity is definitely *phronesis*, and we expect that the faculty thus disclosing *phronesis*, which is *phronesis* itself, will similarly be dealing with all the intellectual faculties. Nowhere other than this practical context does Aristotle set out all these intellectual faculties and virtues in quite this way. This is because other contexts do not require this sort of investigation in which *phronesis* is demarcated along with its place in relation to the other intellectual capacities in human life. Here the practical distinction of intellectual faculties focuses primarily on their aims in correspondence with their subject matters, whereas different approaches tend to be taken in theoretical contexts. For example, *Metaphysics* VI 1 distinguishes the kinds of science based on where the principles are, and *Physics* II 2 distinguishes the physicist and mathematician by the way they investigate. Being practically wise, of key significance for ethics, requires that practical wisdom recognize its relationship with the productive and theoretical sciences. *Phronesis* appreciates that it should oversee the productive sciences, and though the action according to virtue that is its primary focus is good in itself, this good action is further in service to the contemplative or theoretical life. It is a fundamental practical insight of Aristotle, in line with Plato's, that without some notion of a philosophical life beyond the life of actions according to virtues of character, individuals and communities are likely to lose their way.

This need for a life beyond politics and the arts can be observed in Plato and Aristotle's ambivalence toward Sparta and Athens. While in their heyday Spartans especially pursued virtue and Athenians culture, the Spartans could not well endure peacetime, for their virtue was too narrowly about war, and the Athenians following the Persian War pursued culture and the various arts so avidly and indiscriminately that they succumbed to sophistical cultivation. Political life, optimally having its end in itself, yet often without discernable further results, may tend to go astray. Citizens are in danger of seeking something more, such as money, honor, and conquest (see 1177b1–26). A way to keep proper order in political life is to see politics subordinated to a higher life, a life of the highest culture, theoretical science, which does not conflict with justice. This is for the good of the political life itself, which benefits from serving something higher. Human intellect, which makes action possible, also threatens to undermine action by luring it, along with the passions, to the grandeur seemingly offered by the external goods. The philosophers alternatively urge the practical insight that the human being is not the highest being and that human life needs to be devoted to something beyond it. Aristotle says:

> Therefore, wisdom (*sophia*) must be comprehension (*nous*) combined with knowledge (*episteme*)—knowledge of the highest objects (ὥσπερ κεφαλὴν ἔχουσα ἐπιστήμη τῶν τιμιωτάτων) which has received as it were its proper completion. For it would be strange to think that the art of politics, or practical wisdom, is the best knowledge (σπουδαιοτάτην), since man is not the best thing in the world.

1141a18–22

As much as humans may care for themselves, unless there is some higher concern, there may be too limited a view of the self. Yet, it does not require theoretical science to appreciate things beyond the human:

> But if the argument be that man is the best of the animals, this makes no difference; for there are other things much more divine in their nature even than man, e.g., most conspicuously, the bodies of which the heavens are framed.
>
> 1141a33–b2

The appeal here is not to theoretical arguments but to what is conspicuous in agrarian communities looking to the heavens as governing the agricultural cycle and having divine dignity surpassing the human.

The end of *NE* VI guides *phronesis* to keep each of the intellectual virtues to its own domain:

> But again it [*phronesis*] is not *supreme* (*kuria*) over wisdom (*sophia*), i.e. over the superior part of us, any more than the art of medicine is over health; for it does not use it but provides for its coming into being; it issues orders, then, for its sake, but not to it. Further, to maintain its supremacy would be like saying that the art of politics rules the gods because it issues orders about all the affairs of the state.
>
> 1145a6–11

Phronesis arranges things for the sake of *sophia* rather than ordering it around, and the political community is ultimately for the sake of philosophizing. Aristotle urges practically that *sophia*, and its exercise as *theoria*, surpasses the practical life. This is not an appeal to let philosophers or theoreticians rule, but to let them think, i.e., it is a cultural aim. But this clearly implies that for humans the theoretical life has some dependence on the practical life. Theoreticians lack practical astuteness if they fail to recognize their political vulnerability and practical incapacity. Theoretical activity does not think about practical things, or there would be no need for practical wisdom. But this means that the *Ethics* cannot be developed by theoretical wisdom.

NE VI 2 divides the intellect into a part dealing with things the principles of which are incapable of being otherwise and another part dealing with things the principles of which could be otherwise (1138b35–1139a17). Each part of the intellect pursues truth, but the scientific part (ἐπιστημονικόν) seeks truth in theoretical science, while the calculative part (λογιστικόν) seeks truth about means to ends in practical or productive sciences (1139a26–31 and b12–13). The

way *NE* VI is arranged, Aristotle takes up *episteme* quickly to guide and set up
the rest of the treatment of the intellectual capacities (1139b18–26). *Episteme*
can be used widely for knowing, especially suggesting know-how, but it here
gets a narrower sense.[42] The initial grasp of principles by induction differs from
episteme in the strict sense. If induction (ἐπαγωγή) and syllogism (συλλογισμός)
are the ways the *Analytics* proposes for gaining understanding, it is induction
that delivers understanding of principles and *episteme* must be the ability
to make demonstrative syllogisms from the grasp of principles. In the *Ethics*
Aristotle speaks of the capacity involved in induction as *nous*. The complete
intellectual virtue for theoretical science, *sophia*, will then be *nous* for grasping
principles that cannot be otherwise and *episteme* for providing demonstrations
based on such principles (*NE* VI 6–7).[43]

Clarity about *episteme* in relation to *nous* and *sophia* allows for viewing the
practical and productive intellectual capacities in analogy to the theoretical
ones, as they are all ways of being in the truth. Whereas he explicitly names
three intellectual capacities involved in the theoretical sciences, it may seem
that he only has *techne* for production and *phronesis* for action. Yet in the
case of productive science, one must have the form of the product as the
starting point of making. This principle, the form of the product, develops
in the maker by practicing making things, especially under the guidance of
someone already expert. The person gaining this form as the end or principle
can then calculate the means to the end. So art (*techne*) requires having both
the form (end or principle) of the product and being able to calculate how to
bring the product into reality. This combination of having the end and being
able to calculate the productive steps or means to the end is the art itself, the
art comprises universal principles and particular applications. Similarly, with
practical wisdom, we must gain principles, which in this case we do through
habituation of character. Moral or character virtue directs us to the end, i.e.,
the most ultimate or more particular ends. For example, the brave person is
disposed toward brave actions and the good person generally seeks *eupraxia*.
This direction toward ends through the shaping of desire by character virtue,
combined with deliberative cleverness (*deinotes*) that is the calculative ability

---

42   Similarly *nous* can be used widely or narrowly (see 1168b28–1169a3). And *sophia*, Aristotle
      indicates, is equivocal (see 1141a9–20).

43   The distinction of getting to principles and then making demonstrations connects with
      Aristotle's comment that Plato asked whether we are on the way to or from the principles
      (see 1095a30–b1), and with the upper two divisions of the divided line in Plato's *Republic*
      VI, *dianoia* demonstrating from assumed principles and dialectic seeking to secure the
      principles.

to determine how to achieve the ends, constitutes practical wisdom (VI 12). *Phronesis* can be the narrow sort equipped to calculate about particular actions, or the sort to reflect more generally since it combines moral virtue that has the end and principle with cleverness for calculation particularly or universally. Though we can analyze art and *phronesis* as indicated, Aristotle's treatment emphasizes the unity of the capacity.

The faculty that can work out particulars from universal principles, must also have some insight into the universal principles. So we have a capacity providing us more and less general principles along with a capacity to reason from them; and this integrated ability forms the intellectual virtue *phronesis*. Thus Aristotle has utilized material from the *Analytics* in conjunction with practical experience of the aims of intellectual faculties to develop analogous accounts of the capacities involved in theoretical, productive, and practical science. To determine generally and particularly what we should do, *phronesis* must have a practical understanding of the different sorts of intellectual capacities that enter into human life, and the sciences they support. This understanding of the relation of *phronesis* to the rest of the intellect Aristotle has provided by employing *phronesis*. He uses *phronesis* in book 6 as he does throughout the *Ethics*.

In dealing with pleasure, Aristotle considers Eudoxus's argument that all beasts and humans pursue pleasure as evidence that it is good and the best (1153b25–1154a1). Clearly all pursue pleasure but not apparently the same pleasures. Hedonism may fit with or oppose eudaemonism. Pleasure might be a determinate end, but if everyone merely pursues whatever pleasures he or she supposes best and to the extreme, this goes against eudaemonism. Aristotle acknowledges that pleasure leads to much confusion; still there may be a better view of pleasure:

> But since no one nature or state either is or is thought the best for all, neither do all pursue the same pleasure; yet all pursue pleasure. And perhaps they actually pursue not the pleasure they think they pursue nor that which they would say they pursue, but the same pleasure; for all things have by nature something divine in them (πάντα γὰρ φύσει ἔχει τι θεῖον). But the bodily pleasures have appropriated the name both because we oftenest steer our course for them and because all men share in them; thus because they alone are familiar, men think there are no others.
>
> 1153b29–1154a1

Aristotle suggests that we really all pursue the same pleasure, the natural pleasures, though we get confused. We mistakenly suppose that "pleasure" has to mean primarily the obvious bodily pleasures, which tend to excess, rather than the truly natural pleasures that for humans go beyond the body. Little is said to clarify this here, though it may look toward the natural human function of thoughtful action and forward to the view that learning and then contemplating are the greatest human pleasures. This sort of appeal to nature and what is by nature resembles the earlier section regarding natural political justice (*NE* V 7, esp. 1135a3–5). Aristotle offers no theoretical considerations in the section on natural political justice since he makes his case with arguments based on analogy (e.g. right-handedness as prevalent though ambidextrousness can be developed, retail and wholesale measures in markets, and constitutions), and neither does he make any theoretical appeal in dealing with natural pleasures, which will presumably be those of the good person and accompany the better and higher activities.

In the discussions of pleasure and friendship, Aristotle uses the distinction of activity (*energeia*) from becoming (*genesis*), which recalls the distinction of *energeia* from *kinesis* (motion) in *Metaphysics* IX 6.1048b18–35. This might seem a difficult distinction to attribute to practical thinking inasmuch as Aristotle demarcates actuality and potentiality and the further distinction of activity and motion in his theoretical work, *Metaphysics* IX.[44] The distinction, however, is crucial for practical science. When happiness is called an activity in *NE* I, this is in contrast with mere disposition, e.g., virtue, but also with processes that have some external end and must consequently terminate when they reach that end. Life, as an activity filled with further activities, such as perceiving, enjoying, doing deeds, and so on, can be both complete at each moment and continuable, or it would have a necessary termination, as do all but celestial

---

44   Burnyeat 2008 argues that in fact the passage *Metaph.* 1048b18–35 only appears in some inferior manuscripts and should not even be there. If this is correct, no further argument is needed that the distinction of *energeia* and *genesis* belongs in practical contexts. Yet Burnyeat seems incorrect that first philosophy does not require the distinction, whether or not the passage 1048b18–35 belongs to the text, since the distinction appears in *Metaph.* IX 8, as Burnyeat (232) acknowledges, and the unmoved movers of book 12 are pure activities of thinking. So whether or not the passage belongs in the *Metaphysics*, as the distinction surely does, since the *Ethics* does not appeal to the passage, and as Burnyeat also points out, Aristotle does not in the *Ethics* distinguish activity and motion as he does in the passage, he may employ in the *Ethics* something like the distinction. My claim that the *NE* does not appeal to the theoretical works allows that in 1074b2–3 when he says that he has given a more precise account of *kinesis* elsewhere, and this may surely refer to the *Physics*, this is hardly dependence upon theoretical principles. Practical science definitely requires the distinction of activity from becoming to elucidate happiness, action (*praxis*), and pleasure as activities having their ends in themselves.

motions. The contrasting of *praxis* (action) and *poiesis* (production), vital for practical science, requires the distinction of activity complete at every moment yet continuable from motion that is incomplete until its end (see, e.g., *NE* VI 4). In those contexts in the *Ethics* in which Aristotle applies the notion of *activity*, he does so without appeal to theoretical works, but he gives enough clarification so that his concept can serve the practical purpose.

In *NE* VIII and IX Aristotle develops a rich account of friendship. Now do we usually find out about friendship by reading philosophers, or do we consider common sayings, poetry, and songs (1155a32–b16)? Even philosophical reflection upon love and friendship looks to *endoxa* from such sources (cf. Plato's *Lysis*). Common sayings have it that friendship is between similar people, "like is friend to like" and "birds of a feather flock together", but other common sayings have opposites as friends, "potter against potter". Euripides, Heraclitus, and Empedocles seem to incorporate one or the other of these sayings into their thought when they try to explain the natural world through some sorts of cosmic love (1155a32–b8). Aristotle appropriately dismisses cosmic love and love in the natural world as his topic, for it merely seems anthropocentric extension of human love, and he is not trying to link his ethics and politics with theoretical philosophy:

> The scientific problems we may leave alone (for they do not belong to the present inquiry); let us examine those which are human and involve character and feeling, e.g., whether friendship can arise between any two people or people cannot be friends if they are wicked, and whether there is one species of friendship or more than one.
>
> 1155b8–13

Here, and in several similar passages in which Aristotle turns aside from a topic that would get him outside his practical reflections (cf. 1096b7–8, 1159b23–24, 1178a22–23), we see clear cognizance of the definite distinction of practical and theoretical science. When in 1155a18–20 Aristotle does refer to other animals as loving each other, this is only in defense of his initial evidence that humans have love for each other rather than some independent theoretical appeal.

In arguing for the importance of friendship in a happy life, Aristotle puts considerable emphasis upon self-awareness of activity (1170a29–b8). Such self-awareness is explained in theoretical contexts by the view that cognition takes place through reception of and assimilation to form, when the sense or mind takes on the cognizable form of its object and thus in a way becomes its object. Hence in perceiving or thinking the object, the animal or person is also perceiving or thinking the very activity itself since the activity now is formally its object (see esp. *De Anima* III 2). Yet in the practical context in the *Ethics* Aristotle gives no such explanation but merely assumes that there is the awareness and perception of activity, for cognition would not do much good for animals, and humans in particular, if they were not aware of their own cognition. And since living is naturally good and awareness of good things as ours is pleasant, the awareness of our perceiving or thinking, i.e., our living, is itself pleasant. Living is especially choice-worthy to the good, and the good person relates to the friend as another self, or almost so, such that he can often contemplate the friend better than himself (1169b30–1170a4). Aristotle claims that as we are pleasantly aware of our own living, so we are aware of the living of our friends. In interacting we become co-aware of our own living and the friend's. If our own living is choice-worthy, then so will be the friend's. Aristotle in defending friendship plays on the possibility of *con-sciousness*, or in Greek *syn-aisthanesthai*, which can mean to know (perceive) together with oneself and/or together with one's friend (1170b8–19).

In book 10 Aristotle comes around to defending the theoretical or contemplative life as the very best for humans, even if he defends it only in outline (1176a31). It may seem that this gets him out of the domain of practical science, for how should practical science be able to evaluate theorizing? Yet we suggested that in book 6 *phronesis* ranked practical science in relation to theoretical, and when we look at Aristotle's arguments in *NE* X 6–8, we find that they are all practical arguments favoring the theoretical life. In fact they are all basically developments of arguments that he has already utilized.[45]

Aristotle starts the consideration of the ultimate happiness by restating earlier positions and reaffirming them (1176a32–b9). Happiness is an activity rather than a *hexis*. Of activities some are for the sake of further things whereas

---

45 In 1179a33–35 Aristotle indicates that even the treatments of virtue, friendship, and pleasure have been in outline (τοῖς τύποις). Should we not then appreciate that he is offering an explanation why his practical science takes the form that it does and not holding out any possibility of fuller theoretical additions? Though he aims for practical science to be comprehensive and consider things from all sides, he sticks to the appropriate sort of argumentation. In practical science this can only be outline treatment, for its universal principles hold only for the most part, and practice most concerns particulars to which the universal accounts of science apply in a rough way requiring interpretation. Also, since he assumes he speaks to those well brought up, he does not usually elaborate extensively or engage in much of the rhetorical effort that might enter into a more protreptic approach to virtue. Yet when he argues for the contemplative life, Aristotle employs protreptic arguments because the superiority of the contemplative life cannot be taken for granted, even with a well-reared audience.

others are choice-worthy in virtue of themselves. Happiness, as self-sufficient, would have to be among the activities choice-worthy in virtue of themselves. In effect Aristotle reviews the three sorts of freely chosen lives from book 1 (1095b17–19), the life of pleasant amusements that may seem especially choice-worthy and end-like (1176b9–1177a11), followed by consideration of the political and contemplative lives. That the human is most importantly mind has become a theme since book 6 (see esp. IX 4). The redirection from *logos* to *nous* as most importantly human prepares for the celebration of the theoretical life. Mind can be applied to both political action and theoretical activity. Happiness is the activity of soul in accordance with virtue and particularly the highest virtue. This turns out to be *sophia*, so the highest activity will be theoretical activity.

Aristotle first offers a series of arguments based on the features of happiness and theorizing that give theorizing the highest ranking in the happy life (1177a19–b15). Happiness, he shows, has such and such features, and contemplating best possesses these features: contemplating deals with the best things in us and beyond us, it is most continuous, most pleasant, most self-sufficient, most loved for itself, and most leisurely. The desirable features presented as belonging to happiness are those he has offered through the whole of the *Ethics*, and now he locates them most plainly in contemplative activity. The argument has this structure:

> Happiness is a, b, c, d, e, f.
> Contemplative life best possesses a, b, c, d, e, f (or is most a, b, c, d, e, and f).
> ———————————————————————————————
> Therefore, happiness is especially contemplative life. (1177a19–b26)

The argument here cannot be demonstrative, and is not even a valid syllogism, since it is in the second figure with the middle term undistributed.[46] This is no real syllogism unless the premises are in fact treated as bi-conditionals. Despite failing as a syllogism, since happiness and contemplative life share so many features, the argument still can be fairly compelling, and this is all clearly practical argumentation.[47]

---

46 See Burnyeat 2005, 159–162.

47 It is practical methodologically, and it serves the practical life, as previously argued, by subordinating it to some higher life (see esp. 1177b4–15 where Aristotle links political life with war in possibly seeking ends outside itself). Since practical life tends to go outside itself for its end, the best end outside itself to serve is the contemplative life, which is arguably the happiest and most orderly life.

The next argument, the main argument favoring the contemplative life, also goes over previous ground. Aristotle contends that the contemplative life is most our own inasmuch as mind (*nous*) is best in us and most what we are (though the *activity* of mind most raises us to the divine, 1177b31–1178a8). This further explicates the first feature: contemplation deals with the best things. Why should what is best in us, i.e., mind, be most what we are (see 1168b31–33)? Starting in book 6 Aristotle frequently connects humans with mind, whereas in book 1 he instead connected us with *logos*. Mind makes *logos* possible, and *logos* is what generates all peculiarly human doing, as previously argued, hence mind must be most us. So the best life of the mind must be most of all our life. This argumentation in support of the previous argument about features, actually about the first feature (contemplating is the activity of what is best in us and concerning the best things), should be viewed as the principal argument for the theoretical life. The human being is primarily mind, and each living being will be most itself and pursue its own activity when it does what is the best of which it is capable. Hence the human should lead its own life, which is that of the mind. This sort of argument is not theoretical since it follows out the practical thought in *NE* I 7 that something that has a function will have its good in that function, and its work is best when done in accordance with virtue, especially the best and most complete virtue. The main argument in book 10 is then the refinement of the argument going back to book 1.

Aristotle started with the arguments about features, I believe, to contrast the philosophical and political lives. Without these initial arguments it might be unclear whether the activity of mind is meant to be the practical or theoretical life. Thus the argumentative line here is to begin with the six features arguments that establish that the theoretical life is the most complete happiness, and then to argue that such a life is most our own, and we should engage in what is most our own life, the main argument ultimately being this:

> (P1) Living well is living according to one's own life (doing one's own work or function well).
> (P2) The human's own work is the contemplative life.
> _____
> (C) Living well (happiness) is the contemplative life.

The contemplative or theoretical life is most happy (εὐδαιμονέστατος) because it is the activity of what is most naturally our own and best in us (1178a4–8). This is a practical argument based on the practical assumption that individual living beings have a function.

The contemplative life being a divine life, Aristotle introduces the gods to reinforce the main argument that the theoretical life is most our own and best

(1177b26–1178a8 and 1178b7–23). Gods, assumed especially blessed and happy, are not so due to just actions, brave actions, or any practical action, but the worthy activity left to them is then theoretical activity. This loose elimination argument is hardly a theoretical determination about what the gods are (as in *Metaphysics* XII), but a practical argument about what the gods are like and how we are happiest by being most like them. Humans and gods can be happy, but the beasts perhaps not, so happiness, whether the practical or theoretical life, extends only to beings capable of contemplation (*theoria*, 1178b24–32). Humans approach the deity closest by theorizing (and such approach is not impractical, as might be the case were the gods envious). Once there is mind, the possibility of *theoria* opens up, and happiness consists principally in this, with even practical reflection a kind of consideration and *theoria*.[48]

The life of the mind is separate (1178a22–23), yet humans have needs. The life of good actions requires some external equipment (1178a28–b3), while theoretical activity makes lesser demands for equipment and opportunity:

> But the man who is contemplating the truth needs no such thing, at least with a view to the exercise of his activity; indeed, they are, one may say, even hindrances, at all events to his contemplation; but insofar as he is a man and lives with a number of people, he chooses to do excellent acts (τὰ κατὰ τὴν ἀρετὴν πράττειν); he will therefore need such aids to living a human life. (πρὸς τὸ ἀνθρωπεύεσθαι)
>
> 1178b3–7

Little additional is needed by those having acquired leisure for contemplation, and many material possessions can encumber them. Yet as living with others the theoretician will have occasions for action, with some consequent requirement for equipment. This seems the strongest acknowledgment that the person living the separate theoretical life also has to engage in practical actions since the person is not completely separate.

Left somewhat unclear is whether theoreticians have also to be truly good persons, or practically competent to engage in actions. It seems likely that any theoretician will hopefully be kept from wickedness and any vice by the direc-

---

48   When Aristotle says that "Happiness must be some form of contemplation" (θεωρία τις, 1178b32), he may mean that the highest sort of contemplation, theorizing, is happiness. But he might also be speaking more widely since *theoria* is ambiguous. It can mean that sort pertaining to theoretical science, but Aristotle has also throughout the *Ethics* been using the term broadly to mean something like consideration or using verbal forms of it to mean "to consider" (see, e.g., 1122b17, 1140a11–12, b9–10, 1169b33).

tion of their major efforts toward theoretical objects. Yet there are no guarantees for highly developed moral virtue in theoreticians. Aristotle is not advocating a "mixed life" that combines theorizing with political activity. Rather his arguments support the theoretical life as the highest; and we may hope that the theoretician will also have practical wisdom. So he advocates "mixed *capacities*", that is, being theoretically and practically adept, but living by preference the theoretical life. If the *Ethics* has done its job, the theoretician will have seen value in being, as well as helped to be, practically wise. So combining being practically and theoretically wise need not mean the theoretician also leads a political life, but the theoretical life with the additional capacity to legislate.

Regarding the modest external prosperity needed, Aristotle points to Solon and Anaxagoras (1179a9–17). These men are perhaps examples of those happy in their involvements in politics and theorizing, Solon representing the practical and Anaxagoras the theoretical life. Aristotle insists that truth in practical matters is judged based on the facts and life (ἐκ τῶν ἔργων καὶ τοῦ βίου κρίνεται), and arguments must be in accord with these (1179a17–20):

> We must therefore survey what we have already said, bringing it to the test of the facts of life (τὰ ἔργα καὶ τὸν βίον φέροντας), and if it harmonizes with the facts we must accept it, but if it clashes with them we must suppose it to be mere theory (λόγους ὑποληπτέον). Now he who exercises his intellect and cultivates it seems to be both in the best state and most dear to the gods (θεοφιλέστατος). For if the gods have any care for human affairs, as they are thought to have (ὥσπερ δοκεῖ), it would be reasonable both that they should delight in that which was best and most akin to them (i.e., intellect) and that they should reward those who love and honor this most, as caring for the things that are dear to them and acting both rightly and nobly (καὶ ὀρθῶς τε καὶ καλῶς πράττοντας). And that all these attributes belong most of all to the wise man (τῷ σοφῷ) is manifest. He, therefore, is the dearest to the gods. And he who is that will presumably be also the happiest; so that in this way too the wise man will more than any other be happy.
>
> 1179a20–32

Aristotle rather ironically presents this reflection upon the gods and what they esteem right after saying that we need to be careful about arguments and stick to the facts. The "facts" (*erga*) should be the very observable works (*erga*) of the best life, but some of these turn out to be about the presumably unobservable gods. Does Aristotle really hold that the gods have friends, and we should expect them to reward their friends? Or does he merely say that it seems so? This argumentation is surely practical. He uses the gods to support our most divine life. Most god-beloved are those most living the life of the mind closest to the gods' lives ("god-beloved" recalls Plato's *Euthyphro*). Would it really give more support to such argumentation to look toward *Metaphysics* XII? Does he deliberately end his defense of *theoria* with this argument about what the gods love since it tends to stick with us, whether or not it is a precise argument? May it be the most practical argument of all, which can be usefully employed by practically wise persons?

Happiness, we have seen, extends as far as *theoria* and is our own life. The practical life also uses mind, but needs to be in service to something higher. Yet the political life of practical actions according to virtue is also happy, if less blessed than the theoretician's. The theoretical life is even more exalted because it is most our own, directed at higher things, more continuous activity, more self-sufficient, more for its own sake, most pleasant, and most leisurely. Those engaged in the theoretical life are most like the gods, and they are most loved by the gods.

Are these arguments directed toward philosophers, or are they arguments directed toward non-philosophers? They pertain to philosophers, to prospective philosophers, and to the practically wise or those seeking to be so.[49] Aristotle's scrupulous methodological avoidance of theoretical principles, and the argument for the interdependence of theoretical and practical lives fits the treatise for these audiences. For those aspiring to be practically wise, it offers guidance regarding character development and serves the practical purpose of recognition of something higher than practice. And the treatise provides arguments politicians can use when needed in political life. For the philosophers or prospective philosophers, it entices them to their proper life and reassures them about its worth, for perhaps even philosophers sometimes doubt their choice when they seem to themselves rather powerless and without honor. Aristotle has bolstered the philosophers; he also alerts them to their situation. Their life is highest but somewhat practically precarious. Whatever the practical needs involved—requisite external goods and a political community organized to accept philosophers—these are *not* the job of theoretical wisdom to supply. So the theoretical life has some unavoidable dependence upon a practical life other than its own. The dependence is most likely greater of theoretical on practical science, the reverse of the dependence that I have been resisting.

---

49   Tessitore 1996, 15–20 usefully considers the audience for the *Ethics* and suggests that it is those well brought up, some of which are limited to the political life while others of these might be won to a theoretical life.

I have endeavored to demonstrate that Aristotle offers compelling arguments in the *Nicomachean Ethics* that secure practical science while never depending upon theoretical positions. Practical science is too important for human life to rest upon sciences that are in dispute or threaten to get us in dispute or hold the interest of too few individuals. Aristotle astutely and scrupulously builds his accounts in practical science independently of his work in the theoretical sciences. Also, as genuine science having its own subject matter, practical science should have its own principles. Pertinently he insists in *Posterior Analytics* I 7.75b14–17: "nor can one prove by any other science the theorems of a different one, except such as are so related to one another that the one is under the other—e.g. optics to geometry and harmonics to arithmetic" (cf. *Rhetoric* 1358a1–26). Since practical science does not have this sort of subordination to theoretical science, one cannot prove its results from those of theoretical sciences, and Aristotle does not try to do this. In reading the *Ethics* and construing its arguments, it should be taken to be a genuine and independent science hardly standing to benefit from any "longer route" through theoretical science. What is more, this Aristotelian insight about practical science should hold ever after. So long as humans remain humans, ethics cannot wait on and does not require support from theoretical science.

CHAPTER 11

Aristotle on the (Alleged) Inferiority of History to Poetry[*]

Thornton C. Lockwood

Abstract

Aristotle's claim that poetry is "a more philosophic and better thing" than history (*Poet.* 9.1451b5–6) and his description of the "poetic universal" have been the source of much scholarly discussion. Although many scholars have mined *Poetics* 9 as a source of Aristotle's views toward history, in my contribution I caution against doing so. Critics of Aristotle's remarks have often failed to appreciate the expository principle that governs *Poetics* 6–12, which begins with a definition of tragedy and then elucidates the terms of that definition by means of a series of juxtapositions. The juxtaposition between poetry and history is one such instance that seeks to elucidate what sort of plot exemplifies a causal unity such that the events of a play unfold with likelihood or necessity. Within that context, Aristotle compares history and poetry in order to elucidate the object of poetic mimesis rather than to criticize history as a discipline. Viewing Aristotle as antagonistic toward history fails to appreciate the expository structure of the *Poetics* and obscures the resource that history provides to the poet, a point that I explore by considering what Aristotle would have thought of an "historical" tragedy like Aeschylus's *Persians*.

[*] An early version of this paper was presented at a conference on "History, Philosophy, and Tragedy" at the University of Southern Florida in February 2012, at which time I received thoughtful, helpful comments from Joanne Waugh, Ippokratis Kanztios, Christos Evange-liou, and Dana Munteanu (who also offered comments on later drafts of the paper). Pierre Destrée has offered very perceptive criticisms that spoke directly to the weakest points in my argument. I am especially grateful for the invitation to contribute this chapter to *Reading Aristotle*; Bill Wians and Ron Polansky have challenged me to improve my chapter in response to their probing questions. Finally, I would like to thank Allen Speight, who first introduced me to the philosophical (and non-philosophical) sides of Aristotle's *Poetics* many years ago (and for whom I wrote a much, much earlier draft of this paper in graduate school).

In *Poetics* 9 and 23, Aristotle infamously contrasts history and poetry in a fashion that often offends modern readers—perhaps especially modern historians. As *Poetics* 9 puts it: "poetry is a more philosophical and better thing than history, since poetry states more universal things whereas history states particular things" (9.1451b5–7).[1] Modern historians such as de Ste. Croix have dismissed Aristotle's remarks as an instance of an inconsistent application of his own principles or, in the words of Martin Ostwald, "a deplorable blindness to historiography"; others, such as Collingwood and Finley, have claimed that Aristotle's remarks reflect a dearth of archive material or a "Greek" sense of timelessness.[2] Although Gomme seems correct to say that Aristotle's characterization of Herodotus—an explicit target in *Poetics* 9—is hardly adequate and that perhaps Aristotle would have emended "I did not mean this to be my last word about history", one is still left wondering what would have been Aristotle's thoughts about history (if indeed it crossed his mind at all).[3] Indeed, *Poetics* 9 appears to be what Heath in his chapter in this volume characterizes as "Aristotelian polemic at its most robust" (475 in this volume).

Although *Poetics* 9 and 23 look like the place to answer the question of what he thinks about history, I think we should refrain from doing so, at least without attending to the larger contexts of which the chapters are a part. I would like to argue that viewing *Poetics* 9 (and the additional remarks in *Poetics* 23) as establishing an antagonism between the genres of history and poetry loses sight of the explanatory and expository principles that Aristotle follows in *Poetics* 6–12, unnecessarily maligns history as a form of investigation, and obscures the possibility of history as a storehouse for poetical material. No doubt, in *Poetics* 9 Aristotle identifies the ἔργον or work of a poet—that he or she is "more a maker of stories (μύθων) than a maker of metered verses" (9.1451b27–28)—by means of a juxtaposition with the ἱστορικός; but the main point of the chapter is to distinguish the right sort of plot unity from plots organized chronologically or episodically. Whether history (much less ἱστορία) is in any way unphilosophical or constrained to chronicling particular events

---

1 Unless otherwise indicated, all parenthetical references are to Aristotle's *De Arte Poetica*. Translations are my own, although they are indebted to those of Halliwell 1995 and Janko 1987; Greek text is Kassel 1966.

2 See de Ste. Croix 1992, 24; Ostwald 2002, 9; Collingwood 1946, 25–28, 42–43; Finley 1987, 15.

3 See Gomme 1954, 73. Armstrong 1998, 447 note 4 writes: "How could Aristotle seem to have got Herodotus, his sample historian so wrong (cf. 1451b2–4)? Herodotus tells stories, after all". By contrast, Heath 2009a, 70 implies that Aristotle gets the contrast right: "The poet's job description is more demanding than the historian's. Why? The historian reports a series of events, while the poet *constructs* a sequence of events".

are questions that are simply off the table—as they should be, since *Poetics* 9 is not intended as a critique of ἱστορία.[4] What seems more interesting is that *Poetics* 9 opens the door for "historical" or even "contemporary" plots along the lines of Aeschylus's *Persians*. Rather than criticize or disparage history, when understood within its larger context *Poetics* 9 incorporates history into the repertoire of the poet.

To explore these claims, I first look at how *Poetics* 9 fits within the broader analysis of *Poetics* 6–12 and more specifically that of plot unity in *Poetics* 7–9. Within that context, it is clear that Aristotle's juxtaposition of history and poetry grounds a contrast between different approaches to plot unity more so than any sort of critique of the discipline of history. In the second part of my paper, I show that Aristotle's remarks in *Poetics* 9 about the "philosophical" nature of poetry explain by contrast with history how a dramatic plot should be organized, specifically that its poetic universal should be "in accord with what is likely or necessary" (κατὰ τὸ εἰκὸς ἢ τὸ ἀναγκαῖον [9.1451b9]). In the third part of my paper I argue that reading poetry and history as antagonistic ignores the resources that Aristotle thinks history offers to the poet. To illustrate the point, I conclude my paper with speculation about how Aristotle would view an "historical" tragedy like Aeschylus's *Persians*.

I   "Likely or Necessary" Plots and the Context of *Poetics* 9

Although the *Poetics* as a whole is fragmentary in places, *Poetics* 4–12 is guided by and organized around a very clear expository principle, namely the stipulation of a definition and then the elucidation of that definition through the determination of its terms. Although my focus is on Aristotle's elucidation of his definition of tragedy in *Poetics* 9, the definition of tragedy "arises out of what has so far been said" (ἐκ τῶν εἰρημένων [6.1449b23]), which refers to the developmental or perhaps even teleological account in *Poetics* 4–5 of the emergence of tragedy as a distinct form of enacted mimesis separate from comedy,

---

4   Carli 2011 conclusively shows that when Aristotle wishes to evaluate the epistemic pedigree of ἱστορία (for instance, in the biological writings, the *Constitution of Athens*, and the *Ars Rhetorica*), he has far more to say than what misinterpretations of *Poetics* 9 would suggest. As Ron Polansky has suggested to me, that ἱστορία includes rudimentary factual observation does not entail that it is limited only to "particulars" (a point also shown by Carli's work). Powell 1987 argues that Aristotle has in mind the "logographic" parts of Herodotus more so than the ἔργα μεγάλα τε καὶ θωμαστά or the αἰτίη that Herodotus initially announces as the object of his investigation (Hdt. 1 1).

epic, and other forms of narrative representation. Aristotle first identifies the natural causes (αἰτίαι [4.1448b4–5]) responsible for the generation of the art of poetry—that humans by nature are "mimetic" and take pleasure in imitation—and then chronicles the development and differentiation of comedy, epic, and tragedy from mere improvisations. The broader explanatory principle of *Poetics* 4–12 is thus the establishment of a distinct natural kind, its definition, and then the elucidation of that definition. As Heath shows in his own chapter in this volume, *Poetics* 4–12 also clearly builds up to the evaluation of the best kind of tragic plot in *Poetics* 13–14.

Poetics 6 begins by offering a promissory note—deferring discussion of epic and comedy (the former is taken up in *Poetics* 23–26 and the latter, apparently, in the lost second book of the *Poetics*)—and then defines tragedy in part as "the mimesis of an action (πράξεως) that is good, complete, and of magnitude" (1449b24–25). *Poetics* 7–9 subsequently explore the notion of "action" in the definition by means of articulating what I will call the "practical unity" of a plot, namely that a plot derives its unity from imitating a single πρᾶξις or action.[5] *Poetics* 7 first unpacks the definition of tragedy with respect to the "wholeness" and "magnitude" of plot (7.1450b23–25). To say that tragedy imitates an action that is "whole" means that the action has a beginning, middle, and end—and the end is that which occurs "necessarily or usually" (ἐξ ἀνάγκης ἢ ὡς ἐπὶ τὸ πολύ [7.1450b29–30]). To say that the action imitated has a certain magnitude is to say that its length is sufficient to allow a transformation—from prosperity to adversity or from adversity to prosperity—again, to occur "in accord with a probable or necessary sequence of events" (κατὰ τὸ εἰκὸς ἢ τὸ ἀναγκαῖον ἐφεξῆς [7.1451a12–13]).[6] Both claims taken together reiterate Aristotle's commitment

---

5   Both chapters 7 and 9 commence with transitional phrases (διωρισμένων δὲ τούτων [7.1450b21] and φανερὸν δὲ ἐκ τῶν εἰρημένων [9.1451a36]) that suggest an interconnected textual unit. Else 1967, 302 notes that *Poetics* 9 presents itself as "a direct inference from what has gone before". Halliwell 1987, 98 claims that *Poetics* 7–9 comprise a section of argument devoted to plot unity; Halliwell 1998, 99–106 sees the focus as the "necessity-and-probability principle".

6   Aristotle's sustained analysis of "the likely or the necessary" culminates in *Poetics* 9, although it is invoked repeatedly throughout the *Poetics*; see 7.1450b29–30, 7.1451a13–14, 8.1451a27–28, 10.1452a20, 11.1452a24, 15.1454a34, 17.1455a16–20, 18.1456a23–25, 19.1456b4, and 24.1460a23–24. As commentators generally note, "necessity" (ἀνάγκη) in Aristotle's phrase is simply what happens without exception rather than a more dramatic sense of "fate" or "inevitability"; by "likely" (τὸ εἰκός), he means "what happens for the most part" (a term explored at greater length in the *Rhetoric*, see for instance *Rhet.* I 2.1357a22–b25). See further Halliwell 1998, 99–106 and Frede 1992, 197–219.

to what I will call his "poetic realism", namely the doctrine that the parts or events in a tragedy should unfold in a causally interrelated sequence that is in accord with what is likely or necessary within the "logic" of the overall drama.[7] Whereas the discussions of "wholeness" and "magnitude" in *Poetics* 7 introduce necessity and likelihood as central characteristics of good plots, *Poetics* 8 and 9 elucidate such "poetic realism" by means of juxtaposition with plots that lack such causal determination.

One could imagine a plot deriving its unified structure by "imitating" the acts of a specific individual—for instance, the biographical chronicle of all the actions of a heroic person. *Poetics* 8 contemplates but rejects such an organizing principle for plot on the grounds that "an individual person performs many actions that yield no unitary action" (8.1451a18–19). Homer could have, of course, written the *Odyssey* as a chronicle of the life of Odysseus—beginning, perhaps, with his feigned madness to avoid fighting at Troy and continuing beyond his return home to Penelope. But such a chronicle has no "practical unity", and since no such single action unifies the biographical chronicle, its events would also lack "a necessary or probable connection" (8.1451a27–28); by contrast, the *Odyssey*'s greatness lies in the fact that it—like the *Iliad*—is unified around a single action the unfolding of which in time exhibits an internal structure, namely, it has a beginning, middle, and end, that are organically connected and causally interrelated (cf. 23.1459a37–b1).[8] *Poetics* 8 illuminates the notion of causally determinate plot structure—that events arise through what is necessary or probable—by means of a negative contrast with a sort of biographical tragedy unified by having an individual person as its object of imitation. But it does not follow that *Poetics* 8 thereby disparages biography or

---

7 "Realism" is a loaded term. Minimally, I take the term to convey what is plausible or believable (i.e., τὸ πιθανόν [9.1451b16]). What is possible is plausible (9.1451b15, 24.1460a25–27, 5.1460b23), but as Aristotle quotes Agathon, "it is probable (εἰκός) that many things occur contrary to what is likely (παρὰ τὸ εἰκός)" (19.1456a23–25, 25.1461b15; cf. *Rhet.* II 24.1402a9–13). Halliwell 1998, 103 notes that Aristotle's "realism" is not the same as verisimilitude or *vraisemblance*, since Aristotle is explicit that tragedy represents characters as better than they are in real life and comedy represents them as worse (2.1448a16–18, 5.1449b10, 15.1454b9–11). By contrast, Carli 2010, 320 goes too far when she claims that Aristotle "believes that there should be an essential homology between the arrangements of the incidents of a poem (that is, the plot) and the order of the world of human affairs".

8 MacIntyre 1984, 204–220 proposes to ground Aristotle's normative philosophy in a notion of "narrative order" as an alternative to his outdated teleological biology. According to *Poetics* 8, human lives do not exhibit such an order. For further reflection on the point, see Halliwell 2012.

character sketches.[9] Rather, *Poetics* 8 clearly follows the explanatory principle implied by the investigation of the definition of tragedy two chapters earlier; it compares biographical unity as a principle for organizing a plot with the notion of practical unity in order to elucidate the latter.

The place of *Poetics* 9 within the overall discussion of plot, I believe, exhibits a parallel comparison between chronological unity and practical unity, following the explanatory model of the two previous chapters. As Heath puts it in his own chapter in this volume, Aristotle's explanatory model "exhibits the process of thinking one's way to a conclusion as more instructive than one which simply states or proves the conclusion" (337, below). One could imagine a plot deriving its unified structure by imitating the acts of a specific time period—one that exhibited both a beginning and an end and a chronological succession of events. *Poetics* 9 (and 23) are devoted to showing the error of unifying a plot in such a fashion, just like *Poetics* 8 was devoted to showing the error of unifying a plot around a biography.[10] Homer could have, of course, written the *Iliad* as the chronicle of the events during the Trojan War—from say the seduction of Helen through the story of the Trojan horse or the murder of Priam (23.1459a30–32). But according to Aristotle, such an account fails to exhibit an internal unity according to which events follow "in accord with what is likely or necessary". Put succinctly, chronological succession does not entail necessary or likely succession: *post hoc ergo propter hoc* is both a logical fallacy and a poor principle for plot construction. As Aristotle puts it in the sequel of *Poetics* 10, with respect to the parts of a plot it makes a great difference whether things happen *because* of their antecedents (διὰ τάδε) or only *after* their antecedents (μετὰ τάδε [10.1452a20–21]).

---

9   Theophrastus composed precisely such a work, *Characters*, which identifies the sorts of things that specific character types (e.g., the boor, the grouch, the fraud) are likely to do.

10   As noted above, *Poetics* 6 (1449b21–22) offers a promissory note about the examination of epic that builds upon the differentiation of forms of mimesis in *Poetics* 4–5; *Poetics* 23–26 fulfills that promise and indeed presupposes the earlier differentiation, especially in its contrasts between tragedy and epic. Although *Poetics* 23 is devoted to the analysis of epic, rather than tragedy, and is structurally distinct from the analysis of plot in *Poetics* 7–9, Aristotle's description of epic plot mirrors that of tragic plot, viz. it should concern "a single, whole, and complete action, with beginning, middle, and end" (23.1459a18–20). Else 1967, 571 notes that "most epics are simply histories-in-verse. They relate what happened to happen to one man or a number of men during a given period, instead of presenting a single, unified action with a beginning, middle, and end ... But this natural assumption is corrected by Aristotle. Epic is to follow the pattern of tragedy, not history, in its structure".

Poetics 23 takes up the point by means of a contrast between epic and history. Aristotle writes that the internal structure of epic

> should not be like histories, which require an exposition not of a single action (μιᾶς πράξεως) but of a single period (ἑνὸς χρόνου), with all the events (in their contingent relationships)[11] that happened to one person or more during it. For just as there was a chronological coincidence between the sea battle at Salamis and the battle against the Carthaginians in Sicily, though they in no way converged on the same goal, so in a continuous stretch of time event sometimes follows event without yielding any single goal.[12]
>
> 23.1459a21–29

Aristotle's explicit point is that whereas history takes chronological unity as an organizing principle of its account, a principle that lacks a *telos* or aim that necessarily or logically connects events,[13] poetry ought to compose plots in which "the component events should be so structured that if any is displaced or removed, the sense of the whole is disturbed and dislocated" (8.1451a32–34). Apparently drawing upon a metaphor from Plato's *Phaedrus*, Aristotle likens the parts of both tragedy and epic to a living animal whose organic parts

---

11   "In their contingent relationships" is the Halliwell 1995 translation of ὧν ἕκαστον ὡς ἔτυχεν ἔχει πρὸς ἄλληλα (1459a24). Although Carli 2011, 328–331 is correct to stand behind the more literal rendering of the Greek (she provides "each of which events relates to the others as the case may be"), she appears to miss the force of Aristotle's example of the battles of Salamis and Sicily.

12   It is unclear what stories Aristotle is familiar with concerning the battles of Salamis and Himera, which apparently took place on the same day in 480 BCE. Herodotus reports a Sicilian tradition about the coincidence of the two battles (VII 166), within an extended narrative about the initial actions of the Hellenic League, which included sending messengers to Argos, Sicily, Corcyra, and Crete (VII 145–171). Gomme 1954, 72–74 takes Aristotle to task for falsely presenting the example as if it were one that Herodotus presents as chronological ordering. But Aristotle may be alluding to a different tradition, written by the historian Ephorus and preserved in Diodorus Siculus (XI 1.4), which claimed that Xerxes sought to open a "second front" in his war on Greece and proposed to Carthage an alliance that would coordinate their attacks on both the Greek mainland and Greek western colonies. See further, Else 1967, 575–577.

13   Carli 2011, 328–329 is correct to point out that Aristotle's "sometimes" (ἐνίοτε [23.1459a28]) implies that there are instances in which historical events do aim toward some *telos*. But I think she is wrong to suggest that it is the historian's job to make his or her object the search for such a *telos* in chronological events.

consist in an interrelated whole (7.1450b34, 23.1459a20–21; cf. *Phdr.* 264b–c). Chronological succession can never provide such organic interconnection, and Aristotle's main point consists in drawing the contrast and cautioning poets from forgetting the difference between their art and the art of history.[14]

If my understanding of the explanatory principle that guides the inquiry of *Poetics* 6–9 is correct, then Aristotle's remarks about history in *Poetics* 9 need to be understood as one of several comparisons he makes to elucidate the notion of plot unity.[15] The contrasts between practical unity and both biographical and chronological unity exhibit less a criticism or devaluation of biography and history and more a clarification of the proper principle for unifying dramatic plots. *Poetics* 8–9 elucidates the poet's ἔργον, that he is "more a maker of plots than of verses" (9.1451b27–28), by contrasting different principles for unifying plots. But that the poet is not an historian or a biographer is by no means a criticism of history or biography. Elsewhere, Aristotle points out that the poet is also not a natural scientist (even if a natural scientist like Empedocles can put his works into verse [1.1447b17–19]), but such an observation in no way disparages natural science. Focusing on how to read Aristotle's argument in *Poetics* 6–12 guards an interpretation from taking Aristotle's remarks about history out of its explanatory context (which his critics seem prone to do). Let me now turn to the arguments of *Poetics* 9 to support the claim that even though Aristotle states that poetry is a "more philosophical and better" thing than history, he does not therein mean to criticize history.

---

14   Would the converse hold, viz. that Aristotle would caution the historian to refrain from storytelling? Although Aristotle never explicitly quotes Thucydides (*Athenian Constitution* 33.2 appears to refer to *History of the Peloponnesian Wars* VIII 97.2), I suspect he would be sympathetic to the claim in Cornford 1907 that Thucydides's *History* retains a narrative arc like a tragedy. De Ste. Croix 1992, 51 argues that Thucydides has "lessons … that are implicit in the narrative and do not need to be spelt out in the *History* in general terms"; but as Heath 2009a, 70 note 43 notes, spelling out a point in terms of universality is precisely what is at issue.

15   Aristotle's contrast between different kinds of unity—"biographical" unity, "chronological" unity, "tragic" (or praxis-focused) unity—invites the question of whether Aristotle has in mind a "focal" sense of unity that either tragedy represents or that is an approximation of the unity of natural substances. Certainly Aristotle's discussion of the parts of tragedy makes one wonder whether he envisions the unity of tragedy as an organic whole that imitates the mereology of natural substances.

II   Chronological, Practical, and Episodic Unity in *Poetics* 9

Although the allegedly polemical contrast of history and poetry at first glance
seems to be the subject matter of *Poetics* 9, in fact the chapter continues the
inquiry begun in the two previous chapters concerning the claim that plots
must be "in accord with what is likely or necessary". Aristotle contrasts history
and poetry to elucidate his doctrine of "poetic realism", but it is misleading
to read *Poetics* 9 as a critique of history rather than a comparison between
poetry and history (a point also made in Carli 2010, 317–318). Rather, *Poetics*
9 as a whole contrasts three kinds of unity for the organizations of plots—
that of chronological unity or temporal succession, practical unity (namely, one
organized around a single πρᾶξις or action), and episodic unity—in order to
determine which sort of plot is most in accord with what is "likely or necessary".
The claim that poetry is "a more philosophical and better thing" (φιλοσοφώτερον
καὶ σπουδαιότερον [9.1451a6–7]) than history is minimally an evaluative claim
about the architectonic status of literary genres, but it serves primarily as part
of Aristotle's explanation of "poetic universals".

Poetics 9 begins by drawing an inference from the discussion of its preceding
chapters, viz. that it is the function (ἔργον) of the poet to relate not what has
happened but what may happen in accord with what is possible or necessary
(9.1451a36–38). To amplify the point, Aristotle invokes a contrast: some think
that the defining mark of the poet is that he or she puts his words into verse,
whereas others use prose. But the work of Herodotus could be put into verse
and he would still not be a poet, since his work articulates a chronological
unity or succession of events (9.1451b2–4; cf. 2.1447b13–20).[16] Thus Aristotle's
contrast: to elucidate poetic unity, he contrasts it with chronological unity. The
difference between the poet, who aims at practical unity, and the historian, who
aims at chronological unity, is that:

---

16   Such is the point of disagreement for more sympathetic readers of Herodotus. Sicking
      1998, 153 quite plausibly points out that although parts of the *History* (e.g., book 2's record
      of customs in Egypt) seem to lack narrative force, *History* I and VII–IX present an extended
      narrative—beginning with Croesus, but continuing through the account of Xerxes, and
      cumulating in the early stages of Athenian expansionism (a problem that Aristotle himself
      seems to allude to in *Politics* V 4.1304a22)—about the dangers of accumulated wealth and
      power. Aristotle in general is not especially appreciative of Herodotus and at one point
      even calls him ὁ μυθολόγος (*GA* III 5.756b5, discussing Hdt. II 93). See also *GA* II 2.736a10
      and *HA* III 22.523a15 with Hdt. III 101; *EE* VII 2.1236b9 with Hdt. II 68; *Rhet.* III 16.1417a7
      with Hdt. II 30; and *HA* VI 31.579b2 with Hdt. III 108.

One states what has happened (τὰ γενόμενα) whereas the other states the kinds of things that could happen (οἷα ἂν γένοιτο). On account of this (διό), poetry is a more philosophical and better thing than history, since poetry states more universal things whereas history states particular things. Universal means the kinds of things that it suits a certain kind of person to say or do in terms of what is likely or necessary: poetry aims for this, even though attaching names to the agents. A particular means what Alcibiades did or experienced.

9.1451b4–11

To explicate Aristotle's contrast between chronological and practical unity, let me state first what he means by the so-called "poetic universal" he invokes in this passage and then explain his claim that poetry is "a more philosophical and better thing" than history.

Poetics 9 has generated significant discussion on the meaning of the "poetic universal".[17] On the one hand, there appears to be a consensus that when Aristotle says that "universal (καθόλου) means the kinds of things that it suits a certain kind of person to say or do in terms of what is likely or necessary" (9.1451b8–9), he is using the term "universal" in a sense different from the way that it is used elsewhere in his writings, viz. as an attribute that is predicated of numerous individuals.[18] Rather, a "poetic universal" specifies the necessary or likely causal connection between a type of person and what he or she might do or say, whereas an "historic particular" concerns the contingent connection between a specific person and what he or she in fact did.[19] Aristotle seems to have in mind a "particular" along the lines of "Alcibiades mutilated the Herms on the eve of the Sicilian invasion". By contrast, a "poetic universal" is something like "Powerful hubristic men often disregard religious sensibilities".[20] In both

17   See, for instance, Heath 1991, 389–402; Armstrong 1998, 451–452; Heath 2009a, 68–72; Carli 2010, 333–336.

18   For the notion of καθόλου as an attribute predicated of numerous individuals, see *Int.* 7.17a38–b1. Armstrong 1998, 450–451 criticizes the claim that the "poetic universal" is such a predicate.

19   For consensus on this claim, see Halliwell 1998, 106–107; Heath 1991, 389–390; Armstrong 1998, 454; and Carli 2010, 304–305. Both Armstrong and Carli stress the novelty of their positions against others, but in doing so I think they overstate the extent of disagreement between commentators on this point.

20   The clearest expression of this view is Armstrong 1998, 451–454, which claims that the poetic universal is an "event-token", viz. a general rather than specific articulation of the relationship between a character and the actions that he or she is likely to do. What

instances, an action—saying or doing something—is predicated of a subject; but in the case of the universal, that subject is a general type whereas in the case of the particular, that subject is an actual person or token. In both instances, there is a relationship between the subject and the predicate; but in the case of the universal, that relationship (if it is truly a well-crafted poetic universal) is likely or necessary whereas in the case of the particular, that relationship is a contingent matter of fact.

Yet disagreement emerges over the epistemic significance of the poet's use of "poetic universals". At one end of the spectrum, Carli has argued that the poet's use of universals establishes "a profound kinship with philosophy, because of the intrinsic connection between mimesis and form ... Like the lover of wisdom, the maker of plots has the capacity to see the determinate formal structures that make our world and its transformations intelligible".[21] For Carli, although poetry remains epistemically distinct from and inferior to philosophy, nonetheless the poet is a seeker of truth in the world, one who makes the fundamental structure of human action accessible for cognition. At the other end of the spectrum, Heath claims that "when Aristotle says that poetry is more philosophical than history, there is no implication that poets are particularly philosophical ... [Aristotle] takes a consistently permissive attitude toward irrationalities and impossibilities in poetry, provided that the poet can prevent them *seeming* irrational or impossible".[22] Aristotle incorporates into "poetic license"[23] a repertoire of illusory techniques that aim at the production of tragic pleasure in an audience, including the use of the paradoxical to astonish (9.1452a3–11), the representation of untruths such as lies about the gods (25.1460b35–1461a1), the use of fallacious reasoning to bring about a recognition (16.1455a12–16, 24.1460a18–26), and even the representation of the impossible, if in doing so it attains the aim (*telos*) of the poetic art itself (25.1460b23–26).[24] It seems hard to reconcile the illusions produced by the poetic art with the claim that it produces proto-philosophical universals that approximate reality.

---

is obscured in Armstrong's analysis (or at least in his term "event") is the relationship between the nature of a kind of character and what he or she is likely to do (which is the main focus of Aristotle's poetic universal).

21   See Carli 2010, 333.

22   See Heath 2009a, 71.

23   As Heath 2009a correctly notes.

24   By "impossible", Aristotle means something like Achilles's pursuit of Hector in the *Iliad* (XXII 131 ff.), which seems to imply an entire army of Greeks standing still and not pursuing Hector while Achilles forbids them to do so (24.1460a14–18).

I submit that the source of the disagreement stems from an ambiguity in Aristotle's use of the term καθόλου in the *Poetics*. As noted above, in *Poetics* 9 Aristotle intends by universal the representation of the likely or necessary causal connections between a character type and that character's actions. But elsewhere in the *Poetics*, Aristotle appears to use the term καθόλου in its more literal sense, namely something said "with respect to the whole" where the "whole" is the overall structure of a drama.[25] Thus, Aristotle notes that the Athenian comedian Crates was the first to abandon iambics (i.e., particularized comedies that made light of specific individuals) and compose "generalized speeches, that is plots" (καθόλου ποιεῖν λόγους καὶ μύθους [5.1449b7–9]). By "plot", Aristotle means the structure of a drama that gives it a sense of a whole with a beginning, middle, and end. One might more literally translate "καθόλου λόγος" (in this context) as "an account of the whole of the play". Aristotle uses the term καθόλου in a similar sense when he advises a poet in composing plots "to set them out as universal, and only then introduce episodes"; as he further clarifies:

> I mean that he might investigate what is universal in them in the following way, e.g., that of Iphigeneia: a girl has been sacrificed and disappears in a way unclear to the people who sacrificed her. She is set down in another country, where there is a law that foreigners must be sacrificed to the goddess; this is the priesthood she is given. Some time later it turns out that the priestess's brother arrives ... after he arrives, he is captured. When he is about to be sacrificed, he makes himself known to [his sister].[26]
>
> 17.1455a34–b9

The "universal of Iphigenia" lacks a specification of logical connectives between actions (a detail emphasized in *Poetics* 9)[27] but it provides the notion

25 Commentators are split on whether these are two different senses of the term καθόλου: Heath 1991, 390–391 claims they are distinct; Armstrong 1998, 453–454 argues that they are not. Carli 2010, 329 notes 125–126 leans toward Armstrong but notes differences between the use of the term in *Poetics* 9 and 17. The one other use of the term καθόλου in the *Poetics* does not resolve the issue: Aristotle notes in his discussion of the part of "thought" (διάνοια) in drama that a speech in a play may say something "universal", but καθόλου here means a "general truth" (6.1450b12).

26 Several lines later in the chapter, Aristotle offers a similar account of the *Odyssey* (17.1455b16–23), which is presumably another καθόλου (although Aristotle now calls it τῆς Ὀδυσσείας ... ὁ λόγος [17.1455b16–17]).

27 The "poetic universal" in *Poetics* 17 also lacks names, episodes, and even crucial plot determinations: Aristotle is clear that such a universal is present in the different plays that Euripides and Polydius composed based on the same poetic universal (17.1455b9–10).

of an action unfolding sequentially as a plot, namely as a sense of a whole with a beginning, middle, and end (a detail lacking in the account of poetic universals in *Poetics* 9). But both of those aspects—likely or necessary causal connections and a sense of sequence within a narrative whole—distinguish the practical unity of a poet's plot from the chronological unity of an historian's account. Chronological unity, at least on Aristotle's account, can provide neither.

In what sense, then, is poetry "more philosophic" than history? The poet's use of universals that specify the likely or necessary causal structure of a play displays, without stating explicitly, the "why" (τὸ διότι) of an action; by contrast, the historian only shows a series of events, namely an account of the "that" (τὸ ὅτι) of a temporal sequence. Although displaying the "why" of an action is not the same thing as explaining that "why" (which is what philosophy itself does), the poet's role in providing such a display is the basis for Aristotle's use of the comparative form of "philosophical".[28] At the same time, saying that poetry deals with poetic universals that enact the "why" of an action does not by itself elevate poetry to the level of philosophy or even truth claims about the world.[29] The "why" that the poet discloses is true of the whole that a drama displays, but that drama may be entirely fictitious or even "untruthful" in the sense that it holds no corresponding relationship to the actual world. What I have entitled "poetic realism" throughout my paper concerns the plausibility that arises through the logical or causal connectives within a play—namely, that its events seem to unfold because of one another (9.1452a1–4, 10.1452a20–21). I see nothing in Aristotle's *Poetics* that commits him to the claim that what the poet discloses in a well-composed play is "true" in some sort of sense of corresponding to the "real world". Indeed, as Aristotle repeatedly reminds his reader, tragedy represents its characters as "better" than people are in real life

---

28   For Aristotle's juxtaposition of the "why" and the "that", see *Metaphysics* 1 1.981a15–16, a24–31. See further Carli 2010, 309–312; cf. Heath 2009a, 60–61, 68–70. My explanation is consistent with Armstrong 1998, 448, which claims that poetry is more philosophic because "grasp of the universal enables the person with knowledge or skill to understand, with respect to her field, the reasons why things are the way they are or why tasks ought to be done in a certain way".

29   "Cognitivist" interpretations of catharsis—which identify the pleasure experienced in viewing tragedy solely with its cognitive understanding—sometimes seize upon the claim in *Poetics* 9 that tragedy is "more philosophical" in support of its position, but, as Lear 1992, 325 notes "if we look to what Aristotle means by 'universal' [in *Poetics* 9], it is clear that he does not mean 'universal which expresses the essence of the human condition', but something much less grandiose: that poetry should refrain from describing the particular events of particular people and instead portray the sorts of things a given type of person might say or do". Halliwell 1998, 110 concurs.

and comedy represents them as "worse".[30] For Aristotle, it is the essence of both comedy and tragedy to in some profound sense misrepresent reality rather than truthfully document it.

In what sense, then, is poetry "better" (σπουδαιότερον) than history? The root of Aristotle's comparative—σπουδαῖος—admits of several different meanings, none of which seems immediately relevant to the contrast between poetry and history. The term can mean "good" in an ethical sense, a sense that Aristotle uses when he claims that tragedy as a genre represents people who are good or better than they are in everyday life; by contrast, comedy represents people as bad (φαῦλος) or worse than they are in everyday life.[31] When Aristotle defines tragedy as the mimesis of an action that is σπουδαῖος, presumably he is again using the ethical sense of the term since tragedy represents the actions of good persons (6.1449b24). Since what is bad is in some sense laughable or unserious, Aristotle also sometimes uses the term σπουδαῖος in contrast as what is "serious" or "elevated"; thus,[32] he notes that comedy μὴ σπουδάζεσθαι or was not taken seriously (5.1449b1, cf. 19.1456b14–15). Some have thought to connect Aristotle's use of the comparative form of σπουδαῖος to his assertions about tragedy representing σπουδαῖος persons or actions, but such a claim fails because poetry in *Poetics* 9 explicitly includes comedy (e.g., 9.1451b11–15).[33] For the same reason, it is unclear why poetry—including comedy—is a more serious (as opposed to ridiculous) thing than history; surely comedy is far less serious (and represents people who are less good) than history, which presumably represents people such as they are (2.1448a4–5). Someone might argue that poetry is better insofar as grasping a universal is a higher cognitive achievement; but such a reading of σπουδαιότερον seems to make the term redundant after the claim that poetry is more philosophic.

Aristotle concludes his comparison of poetry and history by noting that "even should his poetry concern actual events (τὰ γενόμενα), he is no less a poet for that, as there is nothing to prevent some actual events being probable as well as possible, and it is through probability that the poet makes his material from them" (9.1451b29–32). Earlier in *Poetics* 9, τὰ γενόμενα or "the things that have happened" were identified as the domain of history (9.1451b4), but now

---

30   2.1448a16–18, 3.1448a27, 5.1449b10, 15.1454b9. Aristotle reports that Sophocles represents people as they ought (δεῖ) to be whereas Euripides represents them as they are (25.1460b32–34).

31   2.1448a1–5, 1448a16–18, 3.1448a27, 5.1449b9–10. In this sense of the term, Aristotle also refers to specific tragedies and actions as being either good or bad (5.1449b17, 25.1461a6).

32   Perhaps anticipating Rodney Dangerfield.

33   See Heath 2009a, 399 note 37.

Aristotle points out that they are also the domain of the poet. I submit that Aristotle claims that poetry is a "better" thing than history because although by contrast history and poetry simply have different jobs or tasks, there is a sense in which poetry can operate in the domain of history in a way that history is incapable of reciprocating.[34] That art that has a more inclusive domain than another art is a more comprehensive and thus a better (σπουδαιότερον) art (cf. *NE* I 2.1094b4–5). Although *Poetics* 9 remains primarily a contrast between poetry and history, to this extent the text minimally offers an evaluative claim about the architectonic status of different literary genres.

Although I have focused on the discussion of poetry and history (which takes up the majority of *Poetics* 9), the remainder of *Poetics* 9 contrasts the "likelihood or necessity" found in plots organized by practical unity with that found (or more accurately, not found) in what Aristotle characterizes as "episodic plots", namely a play that strings together a series of episodes and thus lacks overall unity, rather like a series of unrelated skits.[35] Such episodic plots are those "in which the episodes follow one another with neither probability nor necessity" (1452b35) and appear to lack either the biographical unity described in *Poetics* 8 or the chronological unity described in the first part of *Poetics* 9.

Aristotle's characterization of episodic plots as being "worst" (χείρισται 9.1451b34) seems to imply the completion of the comparisons in *Poetics* 8–9. Aristotle's best plot connects a universal character type to his or her actions according to the principle of practical unity. Biographical plots connect likely actions to a character (either a universal type or an historical person), but are constrained to include all the details of that character's actions unfolding in time. Historical "plots" possess a chronological unity, but such unity is particular or contingent. Episodic plays appear to be more like skits of artlessly com-

---

34   My argument is thus a variant of the claim found in Armstrong 1998, 448–449 that σπουδαιότερον should be rendered as something like "superior" or "better".

35   Aristotle suggests that poets construct episodic plots either due to incompetence or (in the case of good poets) because they wish to showcase the skills of a particular actor (9.1451b35–37). What Aristotle seems to have in mind is the development of what Hall 2002, 12–15 describes as "virtuoso *tragoidoí*", namely "superstar" thespians whose performances resembled more concerts or recitals than theatrical productions. The Aristotelian *Problemata* XIX 15 appears to document the emergence of such professionals and the effects of competitive performance upon musical practices; the *Rhetoric* disapprovingly notes that actors have become more important than poets (III 1.1403b31–35). Lockwood, forthcoming, addresses Aristotle's critical attitude toward the problem of competitive performances.

bined incidents that lack any sort of unity. Within the context of these comparisons, Aristotle contrasts poetry with history since historical plots (especially
those found in epic) exhibit a notion of chronological unity, namely succession in time. But such a contrast does not imply that history is in some sense
unphilosophical or that the discipline fails to possess knowledge and it is a misinterpretation to elevate that contrast to the level of a disciplinary criticism.[36]
Such a misinterpretation both misconstrues Aristotle's text and obscures the
way that history is a sort of handmaiden to poetry, a topic to which I turn in the
third part of my paper.

III   "Historical" Tragedy in The *Poetics* and Aeschylus's *Persians*

Although the poet is a maker of stories, Aristotle claims that "even should his
poetry concern actual events (τὰ γενόμενα), he is no less a poet for that, as
there is nothing to prevent some actual events being probable as well as possible, and it is through probability that the poet makes his material from them"
(9.1451b29–33). As noted above in the second part of my paper, when Aristotle
points out that historical events usually lack any likely or necessary causal connections or tend toward some end, his "sometimes" (ἐνίοτε) implies that sometimes they do exhibit such patterns (23.1459a28). Aristotle clearly endorses—at
least in principle—the genre of "historical" tragedies and viewing *Poetics* 9 as
a criticism of history impedes appreciation of the storehouse of examples that
history presents to the poet.[37] Such a play would need to be organized in accord

---

36   Finley 1987, 11–12 writes that *Poetics* 9 "has been explained away by clever exegesis, as if
      Aristotle were one of the pre-Socratic philosophers of whom only a few cryptic sentences
      survive, which can be made to fit a thousand different theories; or it has been politely
      dismissed as not dealing with history at all. This last argument has a dangerous element
      of truth in it. It is not only chapter nine which does not deal with history; Aristotle never
      does". Presumably Finley would characterize my position as one of the "clever exegetes";
      but even if the results of my article are largely negative, viz. that *Poetics* 9 should not
      be read as a criticism of history, Carli 2011 provides the "positive" response to Finley's
      argument.

37   Janko 1987, 93 claims that in his discussion of "historical" tragedy, Aristotle is thinking
      primarily of stories from the Trojan War. Even if Aristotle primarily has events from the
      heroic age in mind, his comments remain applicable to "actual" events, whether con-
      temporary or historical. Indeed, it is difficult to distinguish "historical" from "mytho-
      logical" plots because it is unclear that Aristotle distinguishes myth from history (our
      word for "myth" of course is Aristotle's own term for plot, i.e., μῦθος). Nonetheless, he
      does distinguish between plays that use completely fictitious names (such as Agathon's

with practical rather than chronological unity and the composition of its poetic universal would incorporate the poetic license Aristotle affords to tragedy in general, which would delimit criticism of its historical facticity. But if a poet discerned the basis for such a poetic universal within the particulars of historical experience, then he or she has clear license on Aristotelian grounds for producing such a non-traditional plot.

Although Aristotle never discusses Aeschylus's *Persians*, which was produced in 472 BCE and is the retelling of the battle of Salamis (480 BCE) from the perspective of the Persian royal court, I submit that the play is a good example of what Aristotle would praise as an historical tragedy.[38] Although it goes beyond the purpose of my paper to consider whether Aristotle would have agreed with the Athenian judges who awarded *Persians* first prize in 472, the drama illustrates the mix of history and poetic license that I think is characteristic of Aristotle's brief description of "historical" tragedy.[39] By means of conclusion to my paper, I would like to speculate about how Aristotle would view such a play.

In choosing to write a tragedy based on an historical event, Aeschylus followed his predecessor Phrynichus, whose *Phoenician Women* (produced in 476) also dramatized the naval defeat at Salamis and that Aeschylus alludes to in the opening lines of the *Persians*.[40] More infamously, in approximately 492 Phrynichus produced the *Capture of Miletus*, which depicted the siege and destruction of the Ionian city of Miletus. According to Herodotus (VI 21), the play's production caused the audience to burst into tears; Athens fined Phrynichus 1,000 drachmas "for reminding them of their own evils" and ordered that the play never be performed again. Although "historical" tragedies are unusual in the surviving corpus of tragedy, it is wrong to treat them as quasi-historical documentaries rather than literary productions.[41]

Antheus [9.1451b21–22]) and those that use "well-known" (γνώριμα) names or incidents; see also his discussion of "inherited" or "traditional" plots (τοῖς παραδεδομένοις [14.1453b22–26]).

38   Unless otherwise noted, line references within the text are to the Greek line numbers of Hall 2007. I have generally followed the translations of Sommerstein 2008.

39   Pelling 1997, 16–18 and Munteanu 2012, 151–163 argue that *Persians* could have produced something like Aristotelian fear and pity in an Athenian audience; Harrison 2000, 51 argues the contrary.

40   The Hypothesis for *Persians* claims that "In his treatise on Aeschylus's plots Glaucus says that the *Persians* was modeled on the *Phoenician Women* of Phrynichus".

41   Podlecki 1966 and Lattimore 1943 argue that the historical nature of *Persians* required verisimilitude in a way totally absent in tragedies based on mythological stories. By

Although Aeschylus interjects moments of verisimilitude into the play, for instance in the messenger's account of the battle of Salamis (353 ff.) or the three catalogs he provides of Persian combatants (21–55, 302–330, 958–1001),[42] neither his audience nor the City Dionysia judges (who awarded the play first place) apparently had any problem with the exercise of poetic license and the recasting of events to suit narrative purposes. For example, Aeschylus depicts Darius as the voice of Greek wisdom and uses his character as a foil to Xerxes.[43] Aeschylus has Darius criticize his son for bridging the continents of Asia and Europe and conducting military campaigns on the Greek mainland (745–751), but as an Athenian audience would know full well, Darius did the same during his own expedition into Scythia in 513 (which included the bridging of the Bosporus) and his invasion of Attica in 490 (Hdt. IV 89, VI 102–104). A second instance of poetic license is Aeschylus's depiction of the battle as including two equal parts, a naval component in the bay of Salamis and a land component on the island of Psyttaleia.[44] The parallels between land and sea components serve a number of dramatic purposes, such as the humiliation of Persian nobles and the praise of Athenian forces (441 ff.); but Aeschylus's depiction of the land battle on Psyttaleia drastically exaggerates its importance and strays from Herodotus's treatment of it.[45] Finally, the messenger's depiction of an ill-fated retreat and destruction of the Persian remnant at the River Strymon allows Aeschylus to show the cosmic or divine reversal of Xerxes's bridging of the Hellespont (495 ff.): whereas Xerxes's invasion began with the shackling and bridging of natural forces, it ends with natural forces destroying his retreating army. But the destruction of the Persian army at the River Strymon

---

contrast, Pelling 1997, 2 argues that the literary motifs present in the play (for instance, its use of light and darkness or sea and land), "fit too well" to be historical.

42   Hall 2007, 108–109 notes that although the historicity of Aeschylus's lists of names from the Persian forces is uncertain, a possible source is Herodotus's predecessor, Hecataeus, whose *Periegesis* purportedly enumerates "all the tribes under Darius and showing how great the king's power was" (Hdt. V 36).

43   Kennedy 2013, 79–81 provides numerous instances within the play that illustrate Aeschylus's literary juxtaposition of Darius and Xerxes independent of historical fact.

44   The messenger's depiction of the battle to the Persian queen repeatedly emphasizes the two-part nature of the battle at 433–434, 568, 676, 720, and 728. Pelling 1997, 9 notes that the motif of "land and sea" predominates throughout the play and it is "evocative … to have the Persians so outclassed at their own game—but only at the end, and only because the sea battle has gone the way it has".

45   See Herodotus VIII 95 (which devotes only a paragraph to the incident). Strauss 2005, 193–195 presents a modern historian's perspective.

apparently was entirely Aeschylus's invention.[46] Aeschylus is no stranger to poetic license: we know from his *Agamemnon* that he could enthrall an audience by even altering the identity of the king's murderer.[47] Aeschylus exercises the same poetic license in his "historical" tragedy, and it is a misunderstanding of dramatic verisimilitude to claim that such poetic license is precluded on "historical" grounds.

Although the existence of *Persians* does not by itself prove the claim that Aristotle has a place for history in his *Poetics*, at the least it presents an actual example of a poet working from τὰ γενόμενα to construct a poetic universal, one which is oriented by the poet's rather than the historian's function. But even if *Persians* appears repeatedly to recast particular details of the naval battle at Salamis, plausibility has its limits (albeit flexible ones). In addition to the historical liberties I note above, one is reminded that the play brings the dead king Darius back to life—on stage—in what must have been one of the most visually thrilling moments in the play (680 ff.). However "historical", Aeschylus's *Persians* remains a poetic tragedy, which I think Aristotle would have applauded.

---

46   See Lincoln 2000.

47   *Agamemnon* (1370 ff.) casts Clytemnestra as the killer; Homer, by contrast, in the *Odyssey*
      (1 40 ff.), identifies Aegisthus as Agamemnon's killer. By contrast, Aristotle claims that
      some details from traditional plots cannot be "undone" (he gives the example of Orestes
      killing his mother [14.1453b22–26]).

CHAPTER 12

Aristotle on the Best Kind of Tragic Plot: Re-reading *Poetics* 13–14

Malcolm Heath

Abstract

It is widely held that Aristotle presents two contradictory accounts of the best kind of tragic plot in chapters 13 and 14 of the *Poetics*. But an explicit cross-reference between the two chapters puts it beyond doubt that Aristotle regarded their conclusions as mutually supporting. Since Aristotle often expects readers to be willing to follow a prolonged and circuitous argument without drawing premature conclusions about his final conclusion, the first part of chapter 13 must be viewed as an interim stage in a complex exposition. The first part of chapter 13 contains lexical and logical anomalies, often overlooked, which provide pointers to Aristotle's strategy in making a case against those who advocate double plots, and against those who reject plots that end in misfortune. Against these opponents Aristotle insists that plots that end in misfortune are not faulty, but not that such plots are required. The careful formulation of his initial conclusion, using grammatical forms that specify a trajectory of change rather than its end-point, leaves both possibilities in play. There is therefore no contradiction when, on emerging from the polemical context of chapter 13, he adopts an inclusive, rather than a narrowly exclusive, conception of the best kind of tragic plot and develops a graded hierarchy of the sub-types it contains.

I   Introduction

At the beginning of *Poetics* 13, Aristotle introduces the question of what things poets should aim at, and what things they should avoid, in constructing tragic plots (*Poet.* 13.1452b28–30). Constraints established in the preceding chapters (1453b30–33) provide the point of departure for an argument that leads to what I shall call the Familiar Conclusion: Aristotle recommends plots in which "the sort of person who is not outstanding in moral excellence or justice" undergoes a change from good fortune to bad fortune "not due to any moral defect or depravity, but to an error (*hamartia*) of some kind" (1453a7–

12).[1] In this paper I shall argue that the Familiar Conclusion cannot be, in any straightforward sense, a conclusion; and if it is not a conclusion, its apparent familiarity must be illusory. Dispelling that illusion will teach us something about Aristotle's understanding of tragedy, and also (I hope) something about reading Aristotle.

Why can the Familiar Conclusion not be a conclusion? One obvious point: Aristotle continues the discussion for another eighty lines. It makes no sense to suppose that he has spoken his last word on a subject when he has so many words left to say. That is not in itself decisive. Aristotle might have established his conclusion, and then devoted his remaining words to elaborating it or drawing out its further implications. But, on a standard interpretation, that is not what he does. On the contrary, in chapter 14 a new formulation of the original question introduces an argument that reaches a *different* conclusion: chapter 13, it is supposed, awards first place to plots that end in misfortune, but chapter 14 ranks plots in which something terrible happens less favorably than plots in which the terrible event is averted (1454a4–9). Most interpreters have concluded that the two chapters are inconsistent.[2]

Yet Aristotle apparently saw no inconsistency. When he elaborates on his statement of the Familiar Conclusion in chapter 13 (1453a12–17), he adduces the practice of tragedians as supporting evidence: a "sign" (1453a17–22). His conclusion about the optimal tragic plot in chapter 14 (1454a4–9) is supported by the fact that it explains (1454a9, διὰ γὰρ τοῦτο) the phenomenon that constituted that sign. This explicit cross-reference puts it beyond reasonable doubt that Aristotle regarded the conclusions of the two chapters as mutually supporting.[3] There is a presumption, therefore, that the chapters were written to be read as a single extended exposition, coherent and consistent, though complex. If so, then it is a mistake to suppose that the first part of chapter 13 formulates Aristotle's final conclusion, or that the two chapters formulate inconsistent conclusions. The Familiar Conclusion in chapter 13 must be a staging-point on the way to a Final Conclusion in chapter 14.

---

1 Translations from the *Poetics* are adapted from Heath 1996.
2 Moles 1979 has a useful discussion, though in the end he is unable to escape the conclusion that there is a "flat contradiction" (91). Compare, e.g., the perplexity expressed at Heath 1996, xxxi.
3 Contrast the interpretation of those who explain the apparent inconsistency by suggesting that Aristotle changed his mind: e.g., Stinton 1975, 252–253 (= 1990, 183); Glanville 1949.

II   A Circuitous Enquiry

There is nothing intrinsically implausible in that suggestion. Aristotle often
expects his readers to be willing to follow a prolonged and even circuitous
enquiry before drawing a final conclusion. Two examples will illustrate this on
a large scale. In *Generation of Animals* the account of reproduction in the first
two books leaves many phenomena unexplained, including the inheritance
of traits in the maternal line. In book 4 the theory as initially formulated is
extended and enriched so that it can account for those phenomena. Readers
who suppose that Aristotle's views are adequately encapsulated by formulae
derived from the first two books alone, such as the allocation of form to the
male parent and matter to the female (*GA* I 20.729a9–12; II 1.732a6–11), are likely
to misunderstand his theory of reproduction. In the *Nicomachean Ethics* Aristotle gives an answer to the question about the best human life (*eudaimonia*) half
way through the first book (*NE* I 7.1098a16–18). That initial formula, explicitly
an outline that needs to be filled in (1098a20–22), provides the starting point
for an investigation that is not completed until book 10. There he awards primacy to the contemplative life (X 7.1177a16–18, 1178a7–8), with the practical life
ranked as *eudaimonia* in a secondary (though still genuine) way (X 8.1178a9, δευ-
τέρως). Aristotle places the contemplative life on his agenda in book 1, with a
promise to return to it later (I 5.1095b19, 1096a4–5); but this is done so unob-
trusively that readers who have conscientiously worked their way through the
detailed examination of the practical virtues in the intervening books may be
surprised, and even bewildered, by the conclusion that Aristotle finally draws.[4]

On a smaller scale, consider the discussion of what produces animal movement in *On the Soul* III 9–10. The first stage (*An.* III 9.432b14–433a8) takes
the form of an elimination argument: Aristotle works through four candidates (nutrition, perception, thought, desire), and eliminates those that cannot
account for all cases of movement. Since all the candidates fail the test, this
leads to an apparent impasse. In the second stage (433a8–21), Aristotle breaks
the impasse by redefining one of the candidates from the first stage and sus-
pending the implicit assumption that there must be a *single* cause of movement: if "thought" is limited to practical thought, but also extended beyond reasoning to include *phantasia*, then movement may be produced by thought and
desire *acting together*. The final stage of the argument (433a21–26) reformulates
this conclusion, reinstating in a more sophisticated form the original assump-

---

4 The literature is huge: see, e.g., Dahl 2011. Books 1 and 10 are designed to frame a unified
   argument: Natali 2007, 374–375; Lockwood 2014.

tion of a single cause: movement is not produced by thought (broadly defined) *and* desire, but by desire *informed by* thought (or misinformed: 433a26–29).

It seems unlikely that Aristotle was blindly groping his way toward a conclusion as he wrote this passage. More probably, he regarded an exposition that exhibits the process of thinking one's way to a conclusion as more instructive than one that simply states or proves the conclusion. In this exhibition he engineers an impasse, escapes from it by modifying the original assumptions, and thereby reaches an interim conclusion that, though not correct as stated, has sufficient validity to point the way to a more satisfactory solution in the final stage. As a pedagogical demonstration of how to think about a problem, this seems admirable. It also provides *us* with an important lesson in reading Aristotle: patience is a necessary virtue.

If chapter 13 is, as I have suggested, a staging point on the way to the Final Conclusion in chapter 14, then we have been misreading it. My attempt to re-read it begins by highlighting two details of the text that interpreters have not found sufficiently puzzling: a Lexical Anomaly, and a Logical Flaw.[5] Paying attention to these details, I shall argue, will help us understand what Aristotle was doing in chapter 13.

III   A Lexical Anomaly

The Familiar Conclusion is reached by means of an argument that, like the first stage of the example from *On the Soul*, proceeds by elimination. The first step in this Elimination Argument is as follows: "So it is clear first of all that decent men (τοὺς ἐπιεικεῖς ἄνδρας) should not be seen undergoing a change from good fortune to bad fortune: this does not evoke fear or pity, but disgust" (*Poet.* 13.1452b34–36). Is that clear? Far from it. Aristotle's analysis of pity in the *Rhetoric* makes the existence of decent (*epieikēs*) people a precondition of pity: if we thought there were no such people, we would regard everyone as deserving their misfortunes (*Rhet.* II 8.1385b34–35).[6] How, then, can it be true that

---

5   This paper is a re-reading also in the sense that it revisits, and substantially revises, a line of interpretation tentatively sketched out in Heath 2008. The present paper largely supersedes that earlier version: but some details have not been repeated here (they will be revisited elsewhere).

6   In *NE* IX 8.1169a15–18, as elsewhere (Vahlen 1914, 267–268), ἐπιεικής is not clearly distinct from σπουδαῖος, which describes the kind of person that tragedy imitates (*Poet.* 2.1448a1–2; 3.1448a26–27; 5.1449b9–10), and whose undeserved sufferings evoke pity (*Rhet.* II 8.1386b4–7).

misfortune befalling a decent person evokes disgust and not pity? The Elimination Argument therefore begins with an extraordinary claim. I am not the first to have reached that conclusion.[7] Scholars puzzled by Aristotle's choice of the word *epieikēs* have generally reassured themselves with the thought that its meaning is fixed by the Familiar Conclusion. Though the semantic difficulty is often frankly acknowledged,[8] no explanation is given of how readers are supposed to foresee what lies twelve lines ahead. Janko's blunt rejection of this evasion is entirely justified.[9] Janko still maintains that "to be consistent he [i.e., Aristotle] *ought* to have written 'perfectly good men' here". But if that is what, for consistency, Aristotle ought to have written, why did he not write it? Carelessness is one possibility; another is that consistency was not in this context his primary concern. If that suggestion seems surprising, recall that in the example from *On the Soul* demonstrating the process of thinking one's way to a conclusion took priority over maintaining consistency in the definition of "thought" between the preliminary elimination argument and its constructive sequel.

Aristotle most commonly uses "decent" in binary opposition with terms of moral and social disparagement.[10] In this usage, it must apply to the full range

---

7   E.g., Lucas 1968, 140: "nothing could be less 'manifest' than the truth of this extraordinary statement"; Stinton 1975, 237 (= 1990, 164): "The first situation ruled out by Aristotle in chapter 13 as untragic is that morally good men, ἐπιεικεῖς ἄνδρες, should be represented as changing from good fortune to bad. This is in itself surprising and far from evident ...; for ἐπιεικής is a word of moderate commendation, and overlaps in sense with χρηστός and σπουδαῖος, words designating qualities which Aristotle elsewhere prescribes for the stage-figures of tragedy".

8   E.g., Lucas 1968, 140: "It appears from 53a7–9 τοὺς ἐπιεικεῖς ἄνδρας is here to be understood as ἀρετῇ διαφέρων καὶ δικαιοσύνῃ, 'outstanding in goodness and righteousness'. This is not the normal meaning of the word, nor indeed one easily paralleled". Stinton 1975, 237 (= 1990, 164): "This difficulty is partly resolved by the context: ἐπιεικεῖς, being opposed to ὁ μήτε ἀρετῇ διαφέρων καὶ δικαιοσύνῃ, must stand here for σφόδρα ἐπιεικής, morally faultless ... though this is hard to get out of the Greek".

9   Janko 1987, 100: "'Decent' is a synonym for 'good', and cannot mean 'perfect': to suppose that it does is an illegitimate solution to this problematic statement".

10   E.g., opposed to φαῦλος: *Topics* I 7.113a13–14; *NE* III 5.1113b14; IV 9.1128b21–27; V 4.1132a2–4; IX 8.1168a31–33; 12.1172a8–11; X 6.1176b24; 9.1180a8–10; *Eudemian Ethics* VII 2.1238b1–2; *Politics* II 7.1267b6–8; 12.1274a14–15; III 11.1282a25–26; *Rhet.* II 11.1388a35–36; 19.1392a23–24; to πονηρός: *NE* IX 2.1165a8–10; to μοχθηρός: *NE* VIII 10.1160b16; IX 4.1166b27–28; 8.1169a15–18; *Pol.* VI 8.1322a23–24; to social categories (δῆμος, πλῆθος): *NE* IX 6.1167a35–b1; *Pol.* V 8.1308b27–28; VI 4.1318b34–35. Some particular cases: (i) at *NE* IX 6.1167a35–b1 the ἐπιεικής is clearly distinguished from "the best" (οἱ ἄριστοι); (ii) *NE* V 4.1132a2–4 envisages an ἐπιεικής committing fraud or adultery: no inference should be drawn from this, since the point of the passage is the law's indifference to person, not the personal characteristics

of morally good people, and cannot be limited to those who are outstandingly good. But in that case, it includes people whose misfortunes (as we have seen from the *Rhetoric*) Aristotle regards as pitiable, and cannot sustain the first step in the Elimination Argument. On the other hand, the binary opposition is inconsistent with Aristotle's account of the plot-type that survives the Elimination Argument. At that point, Aristotle makes room for the intermediate character, and the virtuous antithesis to the depraved (1452b36–37, 1453a9) is no longer merely "decent": at *this* point it becomes "outstanding in moral excellence or justice" (1453a7–8). The move from a binary to a ternary division of ethical character is not an *ad hoc* novelty: Aristotle has done this already in chapter 2 (1448a1–5). Nor does it involve any inconsistency. The subsequent refinement that the person who undergoes a change from good fortune to bad fortune should be "better ... rather than worse" than the intermediate character (1453a16–17) shows that in Aristotle's view ethical character is not neatly compartmentalized, but distributed along a continuum. Since there is no uniquely correct way of dividing a continuum, different divisions may be appropriate for different analytical tasks. In chapter 4, for example, the binary division gives structure to Aristotle's very schematic history of poetry (1448b22–26); here, however, the analysis and comparison of tragic plots requires a more nuanced framework.

As in the example from *On the Soul*, therefore, an elimination argument is used to produce an impasse, the solution to which involves a change in the initial terms of the debate. In this case, the initial terminology produces a premise that is implausible if taken in its normal sense; removing the implausibility by taking the terminology in a non-standard sense leaves an undistributed middle—which Aristotle exploits in the Familiar Conclusion. We shall return later to the question of what expository advantage is gained by this maneuver. Before that, there is a second puzzling feature to consider.

---

of the ἐπιεικής; (iii) at *NE* IX 9.1170a27 τοὺς ἐπιεικεῖς καὶ μακαρίους does imply exceptional virtue: but that is because exceptional happiness requires exceptional virtue, not because exceptional virtue is implied by ἐπιεικής; (iv) in *NE* VIII 4.1157a16–18, the only instance I have found of a neutral character, neither ἐπιεικής nor bad, the ternary scheme is explicit; (v) of the other two occurrences of ἐπιεικής in the *Poetics*, one (15.1454b8–15) is concerned with characters who have ethical shortcomings, and is thus inconsistent with exceptional virtue, while the other (26.1462a2) places it in binary opposition to φαῦλος, in accordance with Aristotle's common usage. Aristotle has another, more specialized use of ἐπιεικής, describing a form of justice that does not insist on the letter of the law when that is inappropriate, so is willing to take less than its legal entitlement out of fairness (*NE* V 10; cf. *Rhet.* I 13.1374a26–b23); but this does not seem relevant to *Poetics* 13.

IV   A Logical Flaw

The Lexical Anomaly in the Elimination Argument is less significant than the Logical Flaw in the transition from the Elimination Argument to the Familiar Conclusion: "we are left, therefore (ἄρα), with the person intermediate between these" (1453a7). Aristotle thus presents the Familiar Conclusion as an *inference* from the Elimination Argument. But this inference is, in fact, invalid. For the inference to be valid, the plot in which the intermediate character undergoes a change to bad fortune must be the only remaining possibility. But there is at least one alternative plot-type that has not as yet been eliminated: the "double" plot.

This logical error is easily overlooked, because Aristotle has not yet drawn our attention to the existence of double plots. It is only *after* the faulty inference about the best kind of tragic plot has been stated that double plots are mentioned (though still not explained): "Necessarily, therefore (ἄρα), a well-formed plot will be simple rather than (as some people say) double ..." (1453a12–13). The rejection of the double plot therefore purports to be a necessary inference from what has just been said about the plot based on the intermediate character. But that simply compounds the logical error. The conclusion that "we are left ... with the person intermediate between these" only follows if there is no alternative. A conclusion that *presupposes* that no other kind of plot is available cannot then be used to *exclude* other kinds of plot.[11]

There is no way to repair the Logical Flaw. Aristotle reviews a variety of single plots, and shows which of them is best. But showing that one kind of single plot is superior to other single plots cannot possibly prove that the best single plot is superior to the double plot. The argument that leads to the Familiar Conclusion is therefore flawed in its underlying conception. Aristotle was very good at arguing:[12] why, then, has he presented us with such a bad argument here?

---

11   This will be obvious if one considers how the argument would have progressed if the existence of the double plot had been recognized before the "necessary" inference is drawn: "We are left, therefore, with *two alternatives*: the person intermediate between these *and the double plot*. Necessarily, therefore, a well-formed plot will be simple rather than double".

12   And he was alert to the possibility of a statement being presented as if it were the conclusion of a valid syllogism when it is not: *Rhet.* II 24.1401a1–8; *Soph. El.* 15.174b8–11.

v   The Agonistic Context

The Familiar Conclusion leads up to the rejection of the double plot, which is what "some people say" is the best kind. So Aristotle is engaged in debate with a current rival to his own view. The importance of this agonistic context is clear from the fact that he returns to the rival theory in the last part of chapter 13 (just under a fifth of the chapter). It is only at this late stage that he reveals what the double plot is. Previously he mentioned and rejected the double plot without explaining it (1453a13); now we learn that it is a plot in which the outcome is opposite for better and worse characters, as in the *Odyssey* (1453a30–33). Aristotle rejects the rival theory's claim that a plot such as that of the *Odyssey* is the *best* kind of tragic plot. But he does not deny that it is tragic: he rates it as the *second* best kind of tragic plot (δευτέρα 1450a30). That is not surprising: Aristotle elsewhere treats both the *Iliad* and the *Odyssey* as analogous with tragedy (4.1448b38–1449a2; 23.1459b7–15, cross-referring to 18.1455b32–1456a3).[13] What is surprising is that he apparently goes on to deny what he has just asserted. He now says that the pleasure that the double plot affords is *not* the pleasure of tragedy, but more akin to the pleasure of comedy (1453a35–36). To illustrate this claim, he refers to a plot in which Orestes is reconciled with his father's murderer "and no one gets killed by anybody" (1453a36–39). That is certainly comic, according to Aristotle's characterization of comedy: it is disgraceful and does not involve pain or destruction (5.1449a32–37). But it is completely unlike the *Odyssey*: Odysseus is not reconciled with the suitors, and the suitors do get killed. If the *Odyssey* provides a paradigm of the double plot, therefore, the transformation of a tragic plot of second rank into a comic burlesque is a caricature of the rival theory.

Aristotle's treatment of his opponents here is not underhand, however. In the strategically delayed explanation of the double plot, and in the pointer to its Odyssean prototype, he has provided all that we need to know about the opposing position to recognize that the burlesque plot is not really what the rival theory recommends. And the opponents are treated gently by the standards of Aristotelian polemic at its most robust. Contrast, for example, the comparison of the theory of Forms to meaningless "tum-ti-tums" (τερετίσματα, *Posterior Analytics* I 22.83a32–34), or of the opponents of non-contradiction to vegetables (*Metaphysics* IV 4.1006a14–15). The fun he pokes at his opponents

---

13   The clear statement in *Poet.* 23.1459b7–9 that epic and tragedy have the *same* kinds of plots is often, and perversely, neglected by scholars attempting to solve the difficulties of text and interpretation in 18.1455b32–1456a3. See Tarán-Gutas 2012, 280 (*ad* 1456a2).

here might be compared to the satirical image of Pythagoreans getting in a tizzy (θορυβεῖσθαι) about the universe and posting a guard (*On the Heavens* II 13.293b1–8).[14] Such cases do, at any rate, confirm that Aristotle is not always engaged in dispassionate analytical reasoning: he can be wickedly playful. If we are to make sense of chapter 13, therefore, we need to attend, not only to the logical and (as the passage from *On the Soul* reminded us) pedagogical structure of Aristotle's arguments, but also to his debating tactics.

The last part of the chapter shows how important the rejection of the double plot is to Aristotle. We might therefore wonder whether the double plot is implicitly present in the first part of the chapter, which leads up to its first explicit rejection at the head of the restatement of the Familiar Conclusion (1453a12–13). Since we do not have direct access to the position that Aristotle is opposing, we cannot be sure. But the indirect access provided by Aristotle's critique provides some grounds for conjecture. To have explanatory value, a conjecture should furnish Aristotle's opponents with an argument in favor of their preferred outcome, and also make sense of Aristotle's response. One thought presents itself immediately: to secure the primacy of the double plot, all possible single plots must be shown to be in some respect unsatisfactory. Two points follow. First, it would make sense if the advocate of the double plot deployed something like Aristotle's Elimination Argument. Since the successful elimination of every single plot really would succeed in showing that the double plot is superior to all single plots, the double plot theorist's version of the argument would not suffer from the flaw identified in Aristotle's version. Secondly, an elimination argument for the double plot will be easier to formulate if the ethical world is divided in two, so that the faultiness of every single plot can be displayed in the course of a brief but systematic review of a maximum of four possible variants. The binary division of the ethical landscape is a useful device in the hands of advocates of the double plot, since it creates a trap from which the advocate of single plots at first sight has no escape. It is, of course, also intrinsic to the concept of a double plot, which is defined by opposite outcomes for better and worse characters. Aristotle is therefore not only escaping from the apparent trap when he rejects the binary division: he is also exposing a fundamental weakness in his opponent's position.

How might an advocate of the double plot have gone on to exhibit the positive merits of the plot-type that Aristotle ranks as second best? Taking the *Odyssey* as the paradigm of the double plot, it would be possible to argue that elements that cannot produce a satisfactory plot on their own may be

---

14   Aristotle's humor: Quandt 1981; Touloumakos 1996.

satisfactory when combined. Plato's evocation of a recitation of the scene in which Odysseus is about to attack the suitors (*Ion* 535b) shows that it has a powerful emotional impact of the kind we expect from tragedy: Ion's comment suggests that the scene inspires pity (perhaps) and (certainly) fear (535c). The hero is in a pitiable position, and the risks that he runs evoke the possibility of failure and a terrible ending, but his victory avoids this morally disgusting (*miaron*: 13.1452b36) outcome and the downfall of his wicked enemies secures an agreeable effect (*to philanthrōpon*: 1452b38, 1453a2).[15] Aristotle's version of the Elimination Argument omitted the plot in which a good person undergoes a change from bad to good fortune: this, though agreeable, is self-evidently lacking in fear and pity. An advocate of the double plot, however, might argue that turning this defective single plot into a double plot preserves the agreeable outcome in a way that allows the introduction of fear and pity, while still avoiding the disgust that disqualifies the plot in which a decent person moves from good fortune to bad.

What is puzzling in Aristotle's Elimination Argument, therefore, makes sense in his opponent's version of the argument. For an advocate of the double plot the ethical dichotomy maps the space of possibilities in a way that produces an apparent impasse, from which the double plot provides an escape. Conversely, in Aristotle's response, temporary acquiescence in the dichotomy facilitates a demonstration of the flaw in his opponent's argument: when the original terms of the debate are rejected, the apparent impasse is exposed as an artifact of his rival's ethical over-simplification. In this perspective, the Lexical Anomaly constituted by the use of "decent" in the Elimination Argument

---

15 *To philanthrōpon* is a quality absent from plots in which a morally bad person enjoys a change from bad to good fortune (13.1452b36–1453a1), but present in plots in which a morally bad person undergoes a change from good to bad fortune; plots of the latter kind lack the pity and fear that are required for tragedy (1453a1–7). The most plausible interpretation, in my view, is that "a plot or incident would ... be φιλάνθρωπος in that it has an agreeable effect; it would be agreeable, pleasing, gratifying, satisfying" (Carey 1988, 133). Carey provides references to alternative interpretations: the main candidates are (i) satisfaction at justly deserved suffering; and (ii) humane feeling (sympathy for human suffering, detached from any assessment of desert). See further Heath 2008, 9–10 note 31. Since there has been no previous indication in the *Poetics* that *to philanthrōpon* is something that tragedy aims at, its prominence in the Elimination Argument may reflect the tastes of those who prefer double plots: see Lamberton 1983, 99. I understand the cryptically expressed reference to *to philanthrōpon* at 18.1456a19–23 as follows: this (i.e. surprise) achieves the tragic effect (i.e., fear/pity), and (in addition, the agreeable effect of) *to philanthrōpon*; and *this* (i.e., *to philanthrōpon*) happens when someone who is clever but bad is deceived, or someone who is courageous but unjust is defeated.

is no longer puzzling. A word that can be used in binary opposition with terms of moral and social disparagement is just what an advocate of the double plot requires: his argument would collapse if only those "outstanding in moral excellence or justice" were eliminated. In Aristotle's version, those troubled by a sense that decent people are recipients of pity *par excellence* will soon discover that they had cleverly anticipated the objection to his opponent's argument that subsequently motivates Aristotle's substitution of a more adequate mapping of the ethical landscape. Those who were not troubled will soon learn that they should have been.

We saw earlier that the Elimination Argument fails to establish Aristotle's Familiar Conclusion. We have now seen what it succeeds in doing: it shows that the double plot theorist has failed to establish *his* conclusion. A plausible inference is that this is what it was designed to do. If so, it performs its task in a striking and instructive way. That is consistent with the suggestion that the point of the first part of chapter 13 does not lie exclusively in argument: polemical and pedagogical considerations must also be taken into account.

VI   A Not-So-Familiar Conclusion

Showing that an opponent's argument fails to support their conclusion is not enough to show that the conclusion is incorrect; nor does it show that one's own conclusion is correct. So valid arguments in favor of the Familiar Conclusion are still needed. Aristotle goes on to provide them, and it is in these further arguments that his positive case for the Familiar Conclusion is to be found.[16] Before we examine them, however, we need to be clear about precisely what commitments Aristotle has incurred in formulating the Familiar Conclusion. Again, careful attention to the text is needed.

Both in the first formulation of the Familiar Conclusion (1453a9) and in its restatement (1453a13–14) Aristotle speaks about the change from good to bad fortune using the present tense of the participle (μεταβάλλων) and infinitive (μεταβάλλειν). In Greek, the present tense of the infinitive and participle is used to speak of process, by contrast with the aorist tense, which connotes completion. This distinction, and Aristotle's sensitivity to its philosophical significance, can be illustrated by a sentence from the *Physics*: "nor is that which

---

16   If my interpretation is incorrect, these further arguments are still necessary to make a valid case for the Familiar Conclusion, because of the Logical Flaw. My interpretation acquits Aristotle of an oversight.

cannot change capable of changing into that into which it cannot change"
(*Phys.* VI 10.241b7–8: οὐδὲ τὸ μεταβαλεῖν ἀδύνατον ἐνδέχοιτ᾽ ἂν μεταβάλλειν εἰς
ὃ ἀδύνατον μεταβαλεῖν). What may seem tautological in English translation
becomes meaningful when we pay attention to the oscillation in the Greek
between aorist (μεταβαλεῖν) and present (μεταβάλλειν) infinitives: "that which
cannot *complete a change* [aorist] is not capable of *being in the process of
changing* [present] into that into which it cannot *complete a change* [aorist]".[17]
Elsewhere in the *Poetics* Aristotle uses aorists to describe completed changes in
the history of tragedy's development;[18] in chapter 14, when describing the plot-
type in which an intended act of violence toward unrecognized kin is averted
by recognition, he uses the aorist when speaking of its averted accomplishment
(πρὶν ποιῆσαι), but a present infinitive when speaking of the act as imminent but
as yet unfulfilled (τὸ μέλλοντα ποιεῖν). So the persistent use of present participles
and infinitives when speaking of the change of fortune must be significant.[19]
Aristotle is commenting on the process of change, not its completion: the
trajectory of the change, rather than its outcome.

In formulating the Familiar Conclusion, therefore, Aristotle commits himself to a change of fortune with a certain trajectory without specifying either
the completion of that change or its non-completion. If that neutrality is sustained through the rest of chapter 13, the way would lie open to a resolution of
the alleged inconsistency with chapter 14. Is it sustained?

VII The Positive Case

Having affirmed the superiority of his preferred single plot to the double plot
(1453a12–17), Aristotle advances two substantive arguments in support of his
position. First, he notes a trend in the practice of tragedians toward a limited
range of suitable plots (1453a17–22). This is a "sign" (1453a17) supporting his
view of the best kind of plot: in fact, as we saw in the Introduction, it is *the*

---

17   More concretely: since a kitten cannot *change* (aorist, signaling completion) into a carrot,
      it makes no sense to say that the kitten *is changing* (present, signaling process) into a
      carrot.

18   4.1449a14 μεταβολὰς μεταβαλοῦσα; a20 ἐκ σατυρικοῦ μεταβαλεῖν. He also uses the noun
      μετάβασις at 5.1449a37.

19   Present participle/infinitive of μεταβάλλω: 7.1451a14; 13.1452b34–35, 1453a9, 1453a13–14; of
      μεταπίπτω: 13.1453a2; of μεταβαίνω: 18.1455b27. He also uses the noun μετάβασις for the
      change of fortune in chapters 10–11 (reserving μεταβολή for the transitions in reversal and
      recognition) and 18.1455b29.

sign to which chapter 14 cross-refers. Secondly, he rejects criticisms of Euripides (1453a23–30). He introduces this second point by saying: "this is why those who criticize Euripides ... are making the same mistake". So at this point he is drawing an *inference from* his own theory, not providing *evidence for* it. But he goes on to provide that evidence. The audience reception of the Euripidean plays that have been criticized is the "greatest sign" (1453a26–27) that the critics are wrong and his own view is correct: in (successful) performances, such plays appear extremely tragic, and Euripides appears the most tragic of poets. To understand the significance of these arguments, we need to take account of two background assumptions and a fundamental methodological principle.

The first background assumption is that people will tend, over time, to find better ways to do things. Arts generally develop by a process of incremental improvement,[20] and poetry is no exception: it has advanced by gradual innovation and enhancement (4.1448b22–24; cf. 1449a13–14). The process is not infallible: epic poets failed to learn from Homer's discovery of the way that plots should be unified (8.1451a16–22; 23.1459a37–38); a poetic or musical culture can be corrupted if the demands of self-promoting performers or vulgar audiences become dominant (9.1451b36–1452a1; *Pol.* VIII 6.1341a11–13; 7.1341b10–18). But, in general, the evolved practice of practitioners of a mature art can be regarded as *prima facie* evidence for the way the art *should* be practiced.[21]

The second background assumption is that what people think has evidential value. The empirical data (*phainomena*) include observational data, but also people's opinions. Especial weight attaches to opinions that have some claim to good standing (*endoxa*): for example, those that are held universally, or widely, or by those most qualified to judge (*Top.* I 1.100a29–b23; cf. 10.104a8–11; *Divination in Sleep* 1.462a14–16). But "*every* individual has some contribution to make to the truth" (*EE* I 6.1216b30–31);[22] no one attains the complete truth, but no one misses it entirely (*Metaph.* II 1.993a30–b7). Since we have an imperfect grasp of the truth, opinions are likely to conflict; *endoxa* may be false (*Top.* VIII 12.162b27). A theory will be most in harmony with the empirical data if it shows that conflicting opinions all have some element of truth—or, if not all of them, at least the "the greater number and the most authoritative" (*NE* VII 1.1145b2–7; cf. *EE* VII 2.1235b13–18). So when Aristotle approaches a question in ethics, for example, he insists on the importance of taking account of what

---

20   *Soph. El.* 34.183b17–34 (Aristotle sees his own transformational contribution to logic as exceptional: 183b34–36, 184b1–8). Cf. *NE* I 7.1098a22–26.

21   On this, and the social factors that may influence the development of a poetic tradition positively or negatively, see Heath 2009b, 474–480; 2013, 75–83.

22   An overstatement: for exceptions see *EE* I 3.1214b28–1215a3; cf. *Rhet.* I 1.1355a15–18.

people say (e.g., *NE* I 8.1098b9–12), and sets out to identify the elements of truth in those opinions and to explain the errors.[23]

Given these background assumptions, the two arguments that constitute Aristotle's positive case for the Familiar Conclusion are both empirically based. Consequently, they make the case more effectively than the abstract theoretical reasoning of the Elimination Argument. Aristotle repeatedly insists on the need to start from observation (e.g. *History of Animals* I 6.491a7–14; *GA* III 10.760b27–33) and criticizes theories based on abstract assumptions and arguments, rather than on observed facts (e.g. *Cael.* III 7.306a5–17). This is the fundamental methodological principle. The importance that Aristotle attaches to it can be illustrated from his discussion of the sterility of mules in *Generation of Animals*. Having demolished explanations proposed by Empedocles and Democritus (II 8.747a23–b27), he introduces an alternative account of his own, which "perhaps would seem to be more plausible" (747b27–28). But after he has expounded this theory (747b30–748a7) he immediately dismisses it as "empty" theorizing, not grounded in empirical evidence, with which it is in fact in conflict (748a7–14). Aristotle's pedagogical concerns are again in evidence: concocting a dummy theory in order to expose its vacuity is an imaginative way to draw attention to the crucial methodological lesson to be learned from the critique of Empedocles and Democritus.

It is clear from this passage in *Generation of Animals* that what Aristotle says is not always to be understood as a straightforward statement of his own considered opinion: context is crucial. In one respect Aristotle's procedure here is more cautious than in the first part of *Poetics* 13 as I have interpreted it. The dummy theory is introduced tentatively, and the description of the theory as abstract (λογική), in the sense that it operates at a level of generality that makes it relatively remote from explanatory principles specific to the phenomenon in question (747b28–30), would have put those already familiar with the methodological point on their guard (cf. e.g., *EE* I 8.1217b22–23; *GC* I 2.316a5–14; *APr.* I 30.46a17–27). There is no such hint in the confident opening of the Elimination Argument ("So it is clear first of all ...", 1452b34). In another respect, however, Aristotle's procedure in the Elimination Argument is less radical. The dummy theory about the sterility of mules is invented in order to suffer unqualified rejection; in *Poetics* 13 the Elimination Argument (which,

---

23   The advocates of the double plot might appeal to the preference that some people have
      for such plots in support of their thesis: Aristotle suggests that this misguided preference
      results from a defect of character, "weakness" (1452a33–35). To the extent that we find this
      explanation plausible, we have additional reason to conclude that the double plot cannot
      be the best kind of tragic plot.

I have argued, Aristotle did not invent, but borrowed from an opponent) is not rejected in its entirety. Aristotle agrees with his opponent that the key variables are ethical status and the direction of the change of fortune; he agrees that plots that evoke disgust rather than pity and fear must be rejected; and he agrees that a change to bad fortune may evoke disgust, depending on the ethical status of the character who undergoes that change. The crucial feature of the argument that he rejects is the binary division of ethical character. His procedure is to correct this error, and to follow the modified argument to its legitimate conclusion. The correction is, admittedly, a far-reaching one: when he goes on to speak of "someone of the kind specified, or better than that, rather than worse" (1453a16–17), Aristotle approves plots that intrude significantly into the ethical space that the double plot theorist had tried to fence off.

We may now return to the question of whether the neutrality with regard to outcome preserved in the first part of chapter 13 is sustained when Aristotle develops his positive case for the Familiar Conclusion. Two points may give rise to doubt. In the first sign, when he expresses emphatic approval for tragedies about characters who suffer or do terrible things Aristotle uses aorist infinitives, signaling completion (1453a20–22, ἢ παθεῖν δεινὰ ἢ ποιῆσαι); in the second sign, he rejects criticisms of Euripidean plays that end in bad fortune (1453a25–26, τελευτῶσιν).[24] Here, then, he explicitly commits himself to the completion of a change to bad fortune being "correct" (ὀρθόν, 1453a26). But that is still a limited commitment. If such plots are correct, the advocates of the double plot and the critics of Euripides are wrong to exclude them; it does not follow that they are *required* by the best kind of plot. To reach that stronger conclusion an additional premise would be needed: that the best kind of tragic plot must be narrowly defined, so as to admit of no variants. Aristotle does not supply that premise, and there is no evidence that he tacitly assumed it. On the contrary: as I mentioned at the outset, in chapter 14 he refers back (1454a9–13) to the first "sign" in chapter 13 (1453a17–22) in support of the claim that plots in which the unfortunate outcome is averted are superior. So he cannot

---

24   White 1992, 231 (cf. 233) notes that 1453a24–26 is the first mention of endings in chapter 13. This term is carried on into the subsequent discussion of double plots (1453a32 τελευτῶσα, a38 ἐπὶ τελευτῆς). The ending (τελευτή) is also important in chapter 7, but there the point is structural: plots must have closure. The conditions for closure (7.1450b29–30) are satisfied equally by a change to bad fortune that is completed in accordance with necessity or probability, and by a change to bad fortune that is pre-empted unexpectedly but in accordance with necessity or probability (for this combination see 9.1452a3–4), provided in each case that there is nothing else that necessarily or probably happens next. Chapter 7 is therefore neutral with regard to the question addressed in chapter 13.

have understood that sign as evidence that the best kind of plot requires an unfortunate ending.[25]

Aristotle's conception of the best kind of plot therefore specifies a trajectory but is neutral as to outcome. That is not a bland neutrality.[26] The crux of Aristotle's dispute with the advocate of the double plot is not the double plot in itself: Aristotle rates it less highly than its advocate does, but does not eliminate it. The crux is the *exclusion* of plots in which the change to bad fortune is completed. The critics of Euripides make the same error (1453a24). Since they are distinguished from the advocate of the double plot, they must have a different positive preference: a plausible hypothesis is that they prefer single plots in which the outcome is averted. At the end of chapter 14, Aristotle himself declares that such plots are optimal. In his dispute with the critics of Euripides, therefore, even more than in his dispute with the advocates of the double plot, Aristotle's objection is not so much to the opponents' positive preference, but to their *exclusion* of something that he regards as genuinely tragic.

Conclusion

In the first part of chapter 13, I have argued, Aristotle stages a demonstration that an argument designed to establish the primacy of the double plot by the elimination of all alternatives is faulty. In the second part he shows that this argument's intended conclusion is false by providing two empirically grounded signs that his own preferred category of single plots is superior. That category is introduced in terms that specify the trajectory of the change of fortune, but not its outcome. The following shift in focus to plots in which the change to bad fortune is completed cannot mean that such plots are required or preferred: that would be inconsistent with the conclusion of chapter 14, which gives first place to plots in which the change is not completed. If the advocate of the double plot were Aristotle's only opponent, we might understand the focus

---

25   In 1453a23 "this plot-structure" must refer back to the trajectory-specific but outcome-neutral position formulated in 1453a7–17, and not restrictively to the plots with unhappy endings of 1453a17–22. Since 1453a17–22 is introduced in support of 1453a7–17, and retrospectively invoked in support of 1454a4–9, there is nothing to recommend an interpretation of 1453a23 that makes 1453a17–22 modify the outcome-neutral formulation of 1453a7–17 in a way that brings it into conflict with 1454a4–9.

26   Bouchard 2012, 192 understands Heath 2008 as "lessening the importance of the conclusion of the play": I hope it will become clearer from what follows why I do not accept that interpretation of my argument.

on plots in which the change to bad fortune is completed as purely tactical: establishing the correctness of these plots establishes *a fortiori* the correctness of plots in which the change is not completed. But the opening of a second front against the critics of Euripides shows that more is at stake. Even though Aristotle shares their (inferred) preference for plots in which the change to bad fortune is not completed, he insists that the rejection of plots that end in bad fortune is an error. He is therefore committed to defending the whole of the category that is defined in outcome-neutral terms in 1453a7–17.

As we observed in the large-scale architecture of the *Nicomachean Ethics* and the *Generation of Animals*, an interim formulation that serves as a starting point for further enquiry is not uncharacteristic of Aristotle. In the *Poetics*, likewise, chapter 13 reaches interim conclusions and chapter 14 pursues the investigation further, assessing the relative merits of different variants within the best kind of tragic plot inclusively defined in chapter 13. The implication in chapter 13 that these plots should be based on interactions within a family (1453a18–19) is taken up in chapter 14 (1453b14–22), and provides the starting point for an analysis that reaches the conclusion that it is best if someone interacts with a family member in ignorance in a way that creates a trajectory from good fortune to bad fortune (the intended harm), but this outcome is averted by recognition (1454a4–9). We may assume, from chapter 13, that the agent is not morally outstanding, and is set on a trajectory to misfortune by "an error of some kind" (1453a7–10). Ignorance is one kind of error,[27] and the recognition by which the error is revealed and corrected automatically entails that the plot has the advantages of the complex plot. So there is clear cohesion between the conclusions of chapter 14 and the premises stated at the start of chapter 13.[28]

We might say that, having defined the best kind of tragic plot in inclusive terms in chapter 13, in chapter 14 Aristotle determines what is the *best* of the best. But if we do say that, we must be careful. Though he is willing to eliminate some plot-types as untragic, Aristotle's objection to the error of Euripides's critics shows that his goal is not to insist on the best of the best to the exclusion of all else, but to resist the exclusion of any genuinely tragic option. Far from insisting that tragedies should conform to a narrowly defined ideal, he argues against such narrowness on more than one front, and constructs a diverse, graded hierarchy of tragic plots. This should not surprise us. Aristotle's ultimate aim is to understand tragedy as a genre. If tragedy comprises a field of

---

27   Not, I suspect, the only kind: but this is not the place to discuss the scope of *hamartia*.

28   There is more to be said about the argument of chapter 14, but this will need to be done elsewhere: Heath 2008, 14–16 has some tentative preliminary suggestions.

diverse possibilities, simply awarding a prize to one pre-eminent variant will contribute less to our understanding of tragedy than a ranking that reveals the structure of that diversity.

Reflecting on the consequences of a more exclusive policy will confirm that Aristotle had good reason to resist the exclusion of genuinely tragic options other than the best of the best. Aristotle regards the *Iliad* as an outstanding poem: the epic corpus would be impoverished if it were discarded. It would therefore be absurd to maintain that the *Iliad* should be discarded on the grounds that it has a simple plot (24.1459b14), and that plots should be complex rather than simple (13.1452b31–32). Aristotle also regards Sophocles's *Oedipus* as an outstanding tragedy: the tragic corpus would be impoverished if it were discarded. But its plot-type is ranked second best in chapter 14 (1453b29–31, 1454a2–4). The abundant evidence for the play's exceptional status elsewhere in the *Poetics* relates to other features, such as the handling of the recognition and the combination of recognition with reversal.[29] Sophocles's *Oedipus* is an outstanding tragedy, therefore, not simply because of its plot-type, which is not in the last analysis the best of the best (and that, in any case, it shares with many inferior tragedies), but because of its distinctive combination of other technical excellences. Despite the importance of plot, therefore, the quality of a tragedy cannot be deduced from its plot-type alone. The superiority of tragedy over epic, for which Aristotle argues in chapter 26, obviously does not mean that every individual tragedy is superior to the *Iliad*. Similarly, it is possible for one play (e.g. *Oedipus*) to be superior to another (e.g. *Ion*), even if its plot-type is inferior. Other things being equal, the superior plot-type will yield a superior play. But if a particular body of material affords exceptional opportunities, and a dramatist of exceptional talent is able to exploit them, other things will not be equal. Aristotle was right to resist the exclusion of any genuinely tragic option.

---

29   *Oedipus* illustrates reversal (11.1452a22–26, alongside Theodectes's *Lynceus*); the recognition is excellent because it coincides with reversal (11.1452a32–33), and because it "arises out of the actual course of events" (16.1455a16–18, alongside *Iphigeneia in Tauris*). The terrible act against a family member is "outside the play" (14.1453b31–32). The plot's irrationalities are also kept outside the play (15.1454b6–8; 24.1460a28–30). Sophocles has not made the mistake of composing a tragedy "out of a body of material which would serve for an epic" (18.1456a10–19 with 26.1462a18–b7).

Bibliography

Ackrill, J.L. 1981. *Aristotle the Philosopher*. Oxford: Clarendon Press.

Alexander of Aphrodisias. 1989. *On Aristotle's Metaphysics 1*. W.E. Dooley, S.J. trans. Ithaca: Cornell University Press.

Altman, W.H.F. 2010. "The Reading Order of Plato's Dialogues." *Phoenix* 64: 18–51.

Anagnostopoulos, G. 1994. *Aristotle on the Goals and Exactness of Ethics*. Berkeley: University of California Press.

Aquinas, St. Thomas. 1970. *Commentary on the Posterior Analytics of Aristotle*. F.R. Larcher trans. Albany NY: Magi Books.

Armstrong, J.M. 1998. "Aristotle on the Philosophical Nature of Poetry." *Classical Quarterly* 48: 447–455.

Asper, M. 2003. "Peripatetische 'Schulskripte'." Unpublished chapter of Habilitationsschrift Freiburg.

Asper, M. 2007. *Griechische Wissenschaftstexte*. Stuttgart: Franz Steiner Verlag.

Asper, M. 2015. "Peripatetic Forms of Writing: A Systems-Theory Approach." 407–432 in O. Hellmann and D. Mirhady eds. 2015. *Phaenias of Eresus*. New Brunswick and London: Transaction Publishers.

Bäck, A. 2000. *Aristotle's Theory of Predication*. Leiden: Brill.

Bagnall, R.S. 1995. *Reading Papyri, Writing Ancient History*. New York: Routledge.

Baker, S. 2015. "The Concept of *Ergon*: Towards an Achievement Interpretation of Aristotle's 'Function Argument'." *Oxford Studies in Ancient Philosophy* 48: 227–266.

Balme, D.M. 1987. "Aristotle's Biology was not Essentialist." 291–312 in Gotthelf and Lennox eds. 1987.

Balme, D.M. and A. Gotthelf. 1992. *Aristotle: De Partibus Animalium 1 and De Generatione Animalium 1*. Oxford: Clarendon Press.

Baltussen, H. 2008. "Dialectic in Dialogue: The Message of Plato's *Protagoras* and Aristotle's *Topics*." 203–226 in E. Anne Mackay ed. 2008. *Orality, Literacy, Memory in the Ancient Greek and Roman World. Orality and Literacy in Ancient Greece*. vol. 7. Leiden and Boston: Brill.

Barnes, J. 1970. "Property in Aristotle's *Topics*." *Archiv für Geschichte der Philosophie* 52: 136–155.

Barnes, J. 1975a. *Aristotle's Posterior Analytics*. Translated with a Commentary. 2nd edn. 1994. Oxford: Clarendon Press.

Barnes, J. 1975b. "Aristotle's Theory of Demonstration." 65–87 in Barnes, Schofield, and Sorabji eds. 1975.

Barnes, J. 1980. "Review of Martha Nussbaum, *Aristotle's* De motu animalium." *Classical Review* 30: 222–226.

Barnes, J. 1981. "Proof and the Syllogism." 17–59 in Berti ed. 1981.

Barnes, J. 1995. "Metaphysics." 66–108 in J. Barnes ed. 1995. *The Cambridge Companion to Aristotle*. Cambridge: Cambridge University Press.

Barnes, J. ed. 1984. *The Complete Works of Aristotle: The Revised Oxford Translation*. 2 vols. Princeton: Princeton University Press.

Barnes, J., M. Schofield, and R. Sorabji eds. 1975. *Articles on Aristotle. vol. 1: Science*. London: Duckworth.

Barnes, J., M. Schofield, and R. Sorabji eds. 1979. *Articles on Aristotle. vol. 4: Psychology and Aesthetics*. London: Duckworth.

Barney, R. 2008. "Aristotle's Argument for a Human Function." *Oxford Studies in Ancient Philosophy* 34: 293–322.

Beriger, A. 1989. *Die aristotelische Dialektik. Ihre Darstellung in der* Topik *und in den* Sophistischen Widerlegungen *und ihre Anwendung in der* Metaphysik *M 1–3*. Heidelberg: Carl Winter.

Berti, E. 1996. "Does Aristotle's Conception of Dialectic Develop." 105–130 in Wians ed. 1996.

Berti, E. ed. 1981. *Aristotle on Science. The "Posterior Analytics." Proceedings of the Eighth Symposium Aristotelicum held in Padua from September 7 to 15, 1978*. Padova: Editrice Antenore.

Bodéüs, R. 1993. *The Political Dimensions of Aristotle's Ethics*. Albany: State University of New York Press.

Bodnár, I. 2015. "The *Problemata physica*. An Introduction." 1–9 in Mayhew ed. 2015.

Bolotin, D. 1998. *An Approach to Aristotle's Physics with Particular Attention to the Role of His Manner of Writing*. Albany: State University of New York Press.

Bolton, R. 1987. "Definition and Scientific Method in Aristotle's *Posterior Analytics* and *Generation of Animals*." 120–166 in Gotthelf and Lennox eds. 1987.

Bolton, R. 1991. "Aristotle's Method in Natural Science: *Physics* I." 1–29 in L. Judson ed. 1991. *Aristotle's Physics: A Collection of Essays*. Oxford: Clarendon Press.

Bonitz, H. 1955. *Index Aristotelicus*. 2nd edn. Graz: Akademische Druck-U. Verlagsanstalt.

Bostock. D. 1994. *Aristotle*: Metaphysics *Books Z and H*. Oxford: Clarendon Press.

Bostock, D. 2000. *Aristotle's Ethics*. Oxford: Oxford University Press.

Bouchard, E. 2012. "Audience, Poetic Justice, and Aesthetic Value in Aristotle's *Poetics*." 183–213 in I. Sluiter and R.M. Rosen eds. 2012. *Aesthetic Value in Classical Antiquity*. Leiden: Brill.

Bowen, A.C. and C. Wildberg eds. 2009. *New Perspectives on Aristotle's* de Caelo. Leiden and Boston: Brill.

Bowman, A.K. and G. Woolf. 1994. "Literacy and Power in the Ancient World." 1–16 in Bowman and Woolf eds. 1994.

Bowman, A.K. and G. Woolf eds. 1994. *Literacy and Power in the Ancient World*. Cambridge: Cambridge University Press.

Brandis, C.A. 1835–1866. *Handbuch der Geschichte der griechisch-römischen Philosophic*. Berlin: Reimer.

Brentano, F. 1862/1975. *Von der mannigfachen Bedeutung des Seienden nach Aristoteles*. Freiburg: Herder; *On the Several Senses of Being in Aristotle*. G. Rolf trans. Berkeley: University of California Press.

Brink, C. 1932. *Stil und Form der pseudoaristotelischen Magna Moralia*. Eschenhagen: Ohlau Verlag.

Broadie, S. 1991. *Ethics with Aristotle*. Oxford: Oxford University Press.

Broadie, S. 2009. "The Possibilities of Being and Not-Being in *De caelo* I.11–12." 29–50 in Bowen and Wildberg eds. 2009.

Broadie, S. and C. Rowe. 2002. *Aristotle Nicomachean Ethics: Translation, Introduction, and Commentary*. Oxford: Oxford University Press.

Brunschwig, J. 2007. *Aristote: Topiques livres v–viii*. Paris: Les Belles Lettres.

Buckley, M.J. 1971. *Motion and Motion's God: Thematic Variations in Aristotle, Cicero, Newton, and Hegel*. Princeton: Princeton University Press.

Burnyeat, M.F. 1980. "Aristotle on Learning to Be Good." 69–92 in Rorty ed. 1980.

Burnyeat, M.F. 1981. "Aristotle on Understanding Knowledge." 97–139 in Berti ed. 1981. *Aristotle on Science: The Posterior Analytics*. Padua: Antenore.

Burnyeat, M.F. 2001. *A Map of Metaphysics Zeta*. Pittsburgh: Mathesis Publications.

Burnyeat, M.F. 2004. "Introduction: Aristotle on the Foundations of Sublunary Physics." 7–24 in J. Mansfeld and F.A.J. de Haas eds. 2004. *Aristotle's On Generation and Corruption I. Proceedings of the 15th Symposium Aristotelicum*. Oxford: Oxford University Press.

Burnyeat, M.F. 2005. "ΕΙΚΩΣ ΜΥΘΟΣ." *Rhizai* 2: 143–165.

Burnyeat, M.F. 2008. "*Kinesis vs. Energeia*: A Much Misread Passage in (but not of) Aristotle's *Metaphysics*." *Oxford Studies in Ancient Philosophy* 34: 219–292.

Carey, C. 1988. "'Philanthropy' in Aristotle's *Poetics*." *Eranos* 86: 131–139.

Carli, S. 2010. "Poetry is More Philosophical than History: Aristotle on Mimesis and Form." *Review of Metaphysics* 64: 303–336.

Carli, S. 2011. "Aristotle on the Philosophical Elements of *Historia*." *Review of Metaphysics* 65: 321–349.

Carteron, H. 1926. *Physique*. Paris: Les Belles Lettres.

Casson, L. 2001. *Libraries in the Ancient World*. New Haven: Yale University Press.

Cavalli, F. 1490–1495. *De numero et ordine partium ac librorum physicae doctrine*. Venice: Capcasas.

Charles, D. 2000. *Aristotle on Meaning and Essence*. Oxford: Clarendon Press.

Charlton, W. 1970. *Aristotle's Physics 1 and 2*. Translation with introduction and notes. 2nd edn. 1983. Oxford: Clarendon Press.

Chiba, K. 2010. "Aristotle on Essence and Defining-Phrase in his Dialectic." 203–252 in D. Charles ed. 2010. *Definition in Greek Philosophy*. Oxford: Oxford University Press.

Chroust, A.-H. 1996. "The First Thirty Years of Modern Aristotelian Scholarship (1912–1942)." 41–65 in Wians ed. 1996.

Chroust, A.-H. 1962. "The Miraculous Disappearance and Recovery of the Corpus Aristotelicum." *Classica et Mediaevalia* 23: 50–67.

Coles, A. 1995. "Biomedical Models of Reproduction in the Fifth Century B.C. and Aristotle's *Generation of Animals*." *Phronesis* 40: 48–88.

Collingwood, R.G. 1946. *The Idea of History*. Oxford: Oxford University Press.

Cook, K. 1996. "Sexual Inequality in Aristotle's Theories of Reproduction and Inheritance." 51–67 in Ward ed. 1996.

Cooper, J. 1990. "Metaphysics in Aristotle's Embryology." 55–84 in Devereux and Pellegrin eds. 1990. Rpt. 174–203 in J. Cooper. 2004. *Knowledge, Nature, and the Good*. Princeton: Princeton University Press.

Cooper, J.M. 2012. "Conclusion—and Retrospect. *Metaphysics* A 10." 335–364 in C. Steel and O. Primavesi eds. 2012. *Aristotle's Metaphysics Alpha. Symposium Aristotelicum*. Oxford: Oxford University Press.

Cope, E. 1877. *The Rhetoric of Aristotle*. 3 vols. Cambridge: Cambridge University Press.

Corcilius, K. 2008. *Streben und Bewegen. Aristoteles' Theorie der animalischen Ortsbewegung*. Berlin and New York: Walter De Gruyter.

Cornford, F. 1907. *Thucydides Mythistoricus*. London: E. Arnold.

Cribiore, R. 1996. *Writing, Teachers and Students in Greco-Roman Egypt*. Atlanta: Scholars Press.

Dahl, N.O. 2011. "Contemplation and *Eudaimonia* in the *Nicomachean Ethics*." 66–91 in J. Miller ed. 2011. *Aristotle's Nicomachean Ethics: A Critical Guide*. Cambridge: Cambridge University Press.

Davidson, D. 1984. *Inquiries into Truth and Interpretation*. Oxford: Clarendon Press.

De Leemans, P. 2001. Aristoteles Latinus XVII 2: II–III. *De progressu animalium, De motu animalium. Translatio Guillelmi de Moerbeka*. Bruxelles: Brepols.

de Ste. Croix, G.E.M. 1992. "Aristotle on History and Poetry." 23–32 in Rorty ed. 1992.

Derrenbacker, R.A. Jr. 2005. *Ancient Compositional Practices and The Synoptic Problem*. Leuven and Paris: Leuven University Press.

Devereux, D. and P. Pellegrin eds. 1990. *Biologie, Logique, et Metaphysique chez Aristote*. Paris: Editions du CNRS.

Dirlmeier, F. 1962. *Merkwürdige Zitate in der* Eudemischen Ethik *des Aristoteles*. Sitzungsberichte der Heidelberger Akademie der Wissenschaften, Philosophische-Historische Klasse. 2. Heidelberg: Akademie der Wissenschaften.

Dorandi, T. 1999. "Organisation and structure of the philosophical schools." 54–62 in J. Barnes, J. Mansfeld, and M. Schofield eds. 1999. *The Cambridge History of Hellenistic Philosophy*. Cambridge: Cambridge University Press.

Drossaart Lulof, H.J. 1965. *Nicolaus Damascenus on the Philosophy of Aristotle*. Leiden: Brill.

Dupont, F. 2009. "The Corrupted Boy and the Crowned Poet: or, The Material Reality and the Symbolic Status of the Literary Book at Rome." 143–163 in W.A. Johnson and J.N. Parker eds. 2009. *Ancient Literacies: The Culture of Reading in Greece and Rome.* Oxford: Oxford University Press.

Düring, I. 1943. *Aristotle's De Partibus Animalium: Critical and Literary Commentaries.* Goetborg: Elanders Boktryckeri Aktiebolag.

Düring, I. and G.E.L. Owen eds. 1960. *Aristotle and Plato in the Mid-fourth Century: Papers of the Symposium Aristotelicum Held at Oxford in August, 1957.* Göteborg: Elanders Boktrycheri Aktiebolag.

Eigler, G., T. Jechle, G. Merziger, and A. Winter eds. 1990. *Wissen und Textproduzieren.* Tübingen: Narr Francke Attempto.

Else, G.F. 1967. *Aristotle's Poetics: The Argument.* Cambridge MA: Harvard University Press.

Falcon, A. 2005. *Aristotle and the Science of Nature: Unity without Uniformity.* Cambridge: Cambridge University Press.

Falcon, A. 2010. "The Scope and Unity of Aristotle's Study of the Soul." 167–181 in Van Riel and Destrée eds. 2010.

Falcon, A. 2012. "The Reception of Aristotle's Study of Animals in the Latin World." *Documenti e Studi sulla tradizione filosofica medievale* 23: 521–539.

Falcon, A. 2015a. "Aristotle and the Study of Animals and Plants." 75–91 in K.B. Holmes and K.D. Fisher eds. 2015. *Frontiers of Ancient Science. Essays in Honor of Heinrich von Staden.* Berlin and New York: Walter de Gruyter.

Falcon, A. 2015b. "The Argument of *Physics* 8." 265–283 in M. Leunissen ed. 2015. *Aristotle's Physics: A Critical Guide.* Cambridge: Cambridge University Press.

Ferejohn, M. 1994. "The Definition of Generated Composites in Aristotle's *Metaphysics*." 291–318 in T. Scaltsas, D. Charles, and M.L. Gill eds. 1994. *Unity, Identity and Explanation in Aristotle's Metaphysics.* Oxford: Oxford University Press.

Ferejohn, M.T. 2009. "Empiricism and First Principles in Aristotle." 66–88 in G. Anagnostopoulos ed. 2009. *A Companion to Aristotle.* Malden MA and Oxford: Wiley-Blackwell.

Finley, M. 1987. "Myth, Memory, and History." 11–33 in *Use and Abuse of History.* New York: Penguin.

Flashar, H. 1983. *Aristoteles. Problemata Physica.* "Aristoteles Werke in deutscher Übersetzung" 19. Berlin and Darmstadt: Wissenschaftliche Buchgesellschaft.

Fögen, T. 2009. *Wissen, Kommunikation und Selbstdarstellung. Zur Struktur und Charakteristik römischer Fachtexte der frühen Kaiserzeit.* Munich: Verlag C.H. Beck.

Fögen, T. ed. 2005. *Antike Fachtexte—Ancient Technical Texts.* Berlin: Walter de Gruyter.

Föllinger, S. 1993. "Mündlichkeit in der Schriftlichkeit als Ausdruck wissenschaftlicher Methode bei Aristoteles." 263–280 in W. Kullmann and J. Althoff eds. 1993. *Vermit-*

tlung und Tradierung von Wissen in der griechischen Kultur. Tübingen: Gunter Narr Verlag.

Föllinger, S. 2005. "Dialogische Elemente in der antiken Fachliteratur." 221–234 in Fögen ed. 2005.

Föllinger, S. 2012. "Aristotle's Biological Works as Scientific Literature." *Studies in History and Philosophy of Science* 43: 237–244.

Frede, D. 1992. "Necessity, Chance, and 'What Happens for the Most Part' in Aristotle's *Poetics*." 197–219 in Rorty ed. 1992.

Frede, M. and G. Patzig. 1988. *Aristoteles Metaphysik z*. München: Verlag C.H. Beck.

Furth, M. 1988. *Substance, Form and Psyche: An Aristotelian Metaphysics*. Cambridge: Cambridge University Press.

Gill, M.L. 1980. "Aristotle's Theory of Causal Action in *Physics* III, 3." *Phronesis* 25: 129–147.

Glanville, L. 1949. "Tragic Error." *Classical Quarterly* 43: 47–56.

Goldin, O. 1996. *Explaining an Eclipse: Aristotle's* Posterior Analytics *2.1–10*. Ann Arbor: University of Michigan Press.

Gomme, A.W. 1954. *The Greek Attitude to Poetry and History*. Berkeley: University of California Press.

Gotthelf, A. 1987. "First Principles in Aristotle's *Parts of Animals*." 167–198 in Gotthelf and Lennox eds. 1987.

Gotthelf, A. 2008. Review of C.C.W. Taylor. *Aristotle*, Nicomachean Ethics*, Books II–IV*. *Notre Dame Philosophical Review* 2008.10.05 [http://ndpr.nd.edu/news/29816 -nicomachean-ethics-books-ii-iv-3/].

Gotthelf, A. and J. Lennox eds. 1987. *Philosophical Issues in Aristotle's Biology*. Cambridge: Cambridge University Press.

Gotthelf, A. and M. Leunissen. 2010. "'What's Teleology Got to do with It?' A Reinterpretation of Aristotle's *Generation of Animals* V." *Phronesis* 55: 325–356.

Graham, D. 1987. *Aristotle's Two Systems*. Oxford: Clarendon Press.

Grene, M. 1963. *Portrait of Aristotle*. Chicago: University of Chicago Press.

Hagel, S. 2015. "Sound Reasoning in *Problemata* 11? Disentangling the Components of Voices." 151–171 in Mayhew ed. 2015.

Hall, E. 2002. "Singing Actors of Antiquity." 3–38 in P. Easterling and E. Hall eds. 2002. *Greek and Roman Actors*. Cambridge: Cambridge University Press.

Hall, E. 2007. *Aeschylus Persians*. Oxford: Aris and Phillips.

Halliwell, S. 1987. *Poetics of Aristotle: Translation and Commentary*. Chapel Hill: University of North Carolina Press.

Halliwell, S. 1995. *Aristotle Poetics*. Loeb Classical Library. Cambridge MA: Harvard University Press.

Halliwell, S. 1998. *Aristotle's Poetics*. Chicago: University of Chicago Press.

Halliwell, S. 2012. "Unity of Art without Unity of Life? A Question about Aristotle's Theory of Tragedy." *Atti Accademia Pontaniana, Napoli* 61: 25–40.

Halper, E.C. 1993a. "Aristotle on Knowledge of Nature." 93–116 in *Form and Reason: Essays in Metaphysics*. Albany: State University of New York Press.

Halper, E.C. 1993b. "Aristotle's Accidental Causes." 155–184 in *Form and Reason: Essays in Metaphysics*. Albany: State University of New York Press.

Halper, E.C. 2005. *One and Many in Aristotle's* Metaphysics: *The Central Books*. 2nd edn. Las Vegas: Parmenides Press.

Halper, E.C. 2009. *One and Many in Aristotle's* Metaphysics: *Books A-Δ*. Las Vegas: Parmenides Press.

Hankinson, R.J. 2009. "Natural, Unnatural, and Preternatural Motions: Contrariety and the Argument for the Elements in *de Caelo* 1.2–4." 83–118 in Bowen and Wildberg eds. 2009.

Harari, O. 2004. *Knowledge and Demonstration: Aristotle's* Posterior Analytics. Dordrecht: Kluwer Academic Publishers.

Harris, W.V. 1994. *Ancient Literacy*. Cambridge: Cambridge University Press.

Harrison, T. 2000. *Emptiness of Asia: Aeschylus' Persians and the History of the Fifth Century*. London: Duckworth.

Heath, M. 1991. "The Universality of Poetry in Aristotle's *Poetics*." *Classical Quarterly* 41: 389–402.

Heath, M. 1996. *Aristotle: Poetics*. Harmondsworth: Penguin.

Heath, M. 2008. "The Best Kind of Tragic Plot: Aristotle's Argument in *Poetics* 13–14." *Anais de Filosofia Clássica* 2.3: 1–18.

Heath, M. 2009a. "Cognition in Aristotle's *Poetics*." *Mnemosyne* 62: 51–75.

Heath, M. 2009b. "Should There Have Been a *Polis* in Aristotle's *Poetics*?" *Classical Quarterly* 59: 468–485.

Heath, M. 2013. *Ancient Philosophical Poetics*. Cambridge: Cambridge University Press.

Henry, D. 2006. "Understanding Aristotle's Reproductive Hylomorphism." *Apeiron* 39: 257–287.

Henry, D. 2007. "How Sexist is Aristotle's Developmental Biology?" *Phronesis* 52: 251–269.

Henry, D. 2015. "Holding for the Most Part: The Demonstrability of Moral Facts." 169–189 in Henry and Nielsen eds. 2015.

Henry, D. and K.M. Nielsen eds. 2015. *Bridging the Gap between Aristotle's Science and Ethics*. Cambridge: Cambridge University Press.

Hintikka, J. 1996. "The Development of Aristotle's Ideas of Scientific Method." 83–104 in Wians ed. 1996.

Horster, M. and C. Reitz eds. 2003. *Antike Fachschriftsteller: Literarischer Diskurs und sozialer Kontext*. Stuttgart: Franz Steiner Verlag.

Hussey, E. 1983. *Aristotle Physics: Books III and IV*. Translation with introduction and notes. Oxford: Clarendon Press.

Irwin, T. 1980. "The Metaphysical and Psychological Basis of Aristotle's Ethics." 35–53 in Rorty ed. 1980.

Irwin, T. 1988. *Aristotle's First Principles*. Oxford: Clarendon Press.

Jaeger, W. 1912. *Studien zur Entstehungsgeschichte der* Metaphysik *des Aristoteles*. Berlin: Weidmannsche.

Jaeger, W. 1913. "Das Pneuma im Lykeion." *Hermes* 48: 30–73.

Jaeger, W. 1934. *Aristotle: Fundamentals of the History of His Development*. Translated with the author's corrections and additions by R. Robinson. Oxford: Clarendon Press.

Janko, R. 1987. *Aristotle: Poetics*. Indianapolis: Hackett.

Johnson, M.R. 2005. *Teleology in Aristotle*. Oxford: Oxford University Press.

Judson, L. 2005. "Aristotelian Teleology." *Oxford Studies in Ancient Philosophy* 29: 341–366.

Kahn, C.H. 1966. "Sensation and Consciousness in Aristotle's Psychology." *Archiv für Geschichte der Philosophie* 48: 43–81. Rpt. 1–31 in Barnes, Schofield, and Sorabji eds. 1979.

Kanthak, A.M. 2013. "Obscuritas—eine Strategie griechischer Wissenschaftsliteratur." 157–185 in U. Schmitzer ed. *Enzyklopädie der Philologie*. Göttingen: Edition Ruprecht.

Kassel, R. 1966. *Aristotelis de arte poetica liber*. Oxford: Oxford University Press.

Kennedy, R.F. 2013. "A Tale of Two Kings: Competing Aspects of Power in Aeschylus' *Persians*." *Ramus* 42: 64–88.

Kinneavy, J.L. 1971. *A Theory of Discourse*. Englewood Cliffs: Prentice Hall.

Kirwan, C. 1971. *Aristotle's Metaphysics Books* Γ, Δ, Ε, *Translated with Notes*. Oxford: Clarendon Press.

Kirwan, C. 1993. *Aristotle*—Metaphysics *Books* Γ, Δ, *and* Ε. Oxford: Clarendon Press.

Klein, S. 1988. "An Analysis and Defense of Aristotle's Method in *Nicomachean Ethics* i and x." *Ancient Philosophy* 8: 63–72.

Koch, P. and W. Oesterreicher. 1985. "Sprache der Nähe—Sprache der Distanz. Mündlichkeit im Spannungsfeld von Sprachtheorie und Sprachgeschichte." *Romanistisches Jahrbuch* 36: 15–43.

Kosman, L.A. 1969. "Aristotle's Definition of Motion." *Phronesis* 14: 40–62.

Kraut, R. 1989. *Aristotle on the Human Good*. Princeton: Princeton University Press.

Kraut, R. 2014. "Aristotle's Ethics." in *Stanford Encyclopedia of Philosophy*. E.N. Zalta ed. [http://plato.stanford.edu/archives/sum2014/entries/aristotle-ethics/]

Kraut, R. ed. 2006. *The Blackwell Guide to Aristotle's Nicomachean Ethics*. Malden MA: Blackwell.

Kullmann, W. 1974. *Wissenschaft und Methode*. Berlin: De Gruyter.

Laks, A. 2009. "Aporia Zero (*Metaphysics* Β 1, 995a24–995b4)." 25–46 in M. Crubellier and A. Laks eds. 2009. *Aristotle: Metaphysics Beta. Symposium Aristotelicum*. Oxford: Oxford Univeristy Press.

Laks, A. and M. Rashed eds. 2004. *Aristote et le movement des animaux*. Villeneuve d'Ascq Cedex: Presses Universitaires du Septentrion.

Lamberton, R.D. 1983. "*Philanthropia* and the Evolution of Dramatic Taste." *Phoenix* 37: 95–103.

Landor, B. 1985. "Aristotle on Demonstrating Essence." *Apeiron* 19: 116–132.

Lang, H. 1983. "The Structure and Subject of *Metaphysics* Λ." *Phronesis* 28: 257–280.

Lang, H. 2009. *The Order of Nature in Aristotle's* Physics*: Place and the Elements*. Cambridge: Cambridge University Press.

Laspia, P. 1997. *L'articolazione linguistica. Origini biologiche di una metafora*. Roma: La Nuova Italia Scientifica.

Laspia, P. 2008. "Metaphysica Z 17, 1041b11–33. Perché la sillaba non è gli elementi?" 219–228 in E. De Bellis ed. 2008. *Aristotele e le tradizione aristotelica*. Soveria Mannelli CZ: Rubettino.

Lattimore, R. 1943. "Aeschylus on the Defeat of Xerxes." 82–93 in *Classical Studies in Honor of William Abbott Oldfather*. Urbana IL: University of Illinois Press.

Lawrence, G. 2006. "Human Good and Human Function." 37–75 in R. Kraut ed. 2006.

Lear, J. 1992. "Katharsis." 315–340 in Rorty ed. 1992.

Leggatt, S. 1995. *Aristotle On the Heavens 1 and 2, with an Introduction, Translation and Commentary*. Warminster: Aris and Phillips.

Lemaire, J. 2016. "L'Argument Λογικός est-il Dialectique? Logique et Dialectique chez Aristote." 203–221 in J.-B. Gourinat and J. Lemaire eds. 2016. *Logique et Dialectique dans l'Antiquité*. Paris: Vrin.

Lengen, R. 2002. *Form und Funktion der aristotelischen Pragmatie*. Stuttgart: Franz Steiner Verlag.

Lennox, J.G. 1994. "Aristotelian Problems." *Ancient Philosophy* 14: 53–77.

Lennox, J.G. 1999. "The Place of Mankind in Aristotle's Zoology." *Philosophical Topics* 27: 1–16.

Lennox, J.G. 2001a. *Aristotle's Philosophy of Biology, Studies in the Origins of Life Science*. Cambridge: Cambridge University Press.

Lennox, J.G. 2001b. *Aristotle on the Parts of Animals I–IV, Translated with an Introduction and Commentary*. Oxford: Clarendon Press.

Lennox, J.G. 2005. "The Place of Zoology in Aristotle's Natural Philosophy." 58–70 in R.W. Sharples ed. 2005. *Philosophy and the Sciences in Antiquity*. London: Ashgate.

Lennox, J.G. 2006. "Aristotle's Biology and Aristotle's Philosophy." 292–315 in M.L. Gill and P. Pellegrin eds. 2006. *A Companion to Ancient Philosophy*. London: Blackwell.

Lennox, J.G. 2009. "*De caelo* II 2 and its Debt to the *De incessu animalium*." 187–214 in Bowen and Wildberg eds. 2009.

Lennox, J.G. 2010. "Aristotle's Natural Science: The Many and the One." 1–23 in Lesher ed. 2010.

Lennox, J.G. 2015. "Aristotle's *Posterior Analytics* and the Aristotelian *Problemata*." 36–60 in Mayhew ed. 2015.

Lesher, J. ed. 2010. "From Inquiry to Demonstrative Knowledge: Essays on Aristotle's *Posterior Analytics*." *Apeiron* 43.2–3.

Lesky, E. 1950. *Der Zeugungs- und Verbungslehren drs Antike und ihr Nachwirken*. Wiesbaden: Franz Steiner Verlag.

Leunissen, M. 2010a. *Explanation and Teleology in Aristotle's Science of Nature*. Cambridge: Cambridge University Press.

Leunissen, M. 2010b. "Aristotle's Syllogistic Model of Knowledge and the Biological Sciences: Demonstrating Natural Processes." 31–60 in Lesher ed. 2010.

Leunissen, M. 2015. "Aristotle on Knowing Natural Science for the Sake of Living Well." 214–231 in Henry and Nielsen eds. 2015.

Lewis, F. 2013. *How Aristotle gets by in Metaphysics Zeta*. Oxford: Oxford University Press.

Lincoln, B. 2000. "Death by Water: Strange Events at the Strymon (*Persae* 492–507) and the Categorical Opposition of East and West." *Classical Philology* 95: 12–20.

Lloyd, G.E.R. 1983. *Science, Folklore, and Ideology*. Cambridge: Cambridge University Press.

Lloyd, G.E.R. 1987. "Dogmatism and Uncertainty in Early Greek Speculative Thought." 297–312 in M. Détienne ed. *Poikilia. Etudes offerts à J.P. Vernant*. Paris: Editions de l'EHESS.

Lloyd, G.E.R. 1990. "Aristotle's Zoology and his Metaphysics: The *Status Questionis*." 7–35 in Devereux and Pellegrin eds. 1990.

Lockwood, T. 2014. "Competing Ways of Life and Ring Composition (*NE* x 6–8)." 350–369 in R. Polansky ed. *Cambridge Companion to Aristotle's Nicomachean Ethics*. Cambridge: Cambridge University Press.

Lockwood, T. Forthcoming. "Is there a *Poetics* in Aristotle's *Politics*?" In D. Munteanu, M. Heath, and P. Destrée eds. *The Poetics in its Aristotelian Context*. Cambridge: Cambridge University Press.

Louis, P. 2002. *Aristote. Problèmes*. Texte établi et traduit par P. Louis. Tome I. Paris: Les Belles Lettres.

Lucas, D.W. 1968. *Aristotle's Poetics*. Oxford: Clarendon Press.

Lynch, J.P. 1972. *Aristotle's School*. Berkeley: University of California Press.

Macfarlane, P. and R. Polansky. 2009. "God, the Divine, and *Nous* in Relation to the *De anima*." 107–123 in G. van Riel and P. Destrée eds. 2009. *Ancient Perspectives on Aristotle's De Anima*. Leuven: Leuven University Press.

MacIntyre, A. 1984. *After Virtue*. 3rd edn. 2007. South Bend IN: University of Notre Dame Press.

Madigan, A. 1999. *Aristotle, Metaphysics: Books B and K 1–2*. Oxford: Clarendon Press.

Matthews, G. 1986. "Gender and Essence in Aristotle." *Australasian Journal of Philosophy* 64 supplement: 16–25.

Mayhew, R. 2004. *The Female in Aristotle's Biology*. Chicago: University of Chicago Press.

Mayhew, R. 2011. *Aristotle: Problems*. 2 vols. Cambridge MA: Harvard University Press.

Mayhew, R. ed. 2015. *The Aristotelian* Problemata physica*: Philosophical and Scientific Investigation*. Leiden and Boston: Brill.

McKirahan, R.D. 1992. *Principles and Proofs: Aristotle's Theory of Demonstrative Science*. Princeton: Princeton University Press.

Meissner, B. 1999. *Die technologische Fachliteratur der Antike*. Berlin: Walter de Gruyter.

Menn, S. 1995. "The Editors of the *Metaphysics*." *Phronesis* 40: 202–208.

Menn, S. 2002. "Aristotle's Definition of the Soul and the Programme of the *De Anima*." *Oxford Studies in Ancient Philosophy* 22: 83–139.

Menn, S. 2015a. *The Aim and Argument of Aristotle's* Metaphysics. Retrieved January 28, 2015 [from https://www.philosophie.huberlin.de/institut/lehrbereiche/antike/mitarbeiter/menn/contents].

Menn, S. 2015b. "Democritus, Aristotle, and the *Problemata*." 10–35 in Mayhew ed. 2015.

Mill, J.S. 1843. *A System of Logic Ratiocinative and Inductive*. London: John W. Parker.

Moles, J. 1979. "Notes on Aristotle, *Poetics* 13 and 14." *Classical Quarterly* 29: 77–94.

Moraux, P. 1951. *Les listes anciennes des ouvrages d'Aristote*. Louvain: Éditions universitaires de Louvain.

Morison, B. 2004. "Self-Motion in *Physics* VIII." 67–80 in Laks and Rashed eds. 2004.

Morsink, J. 1982. *Aristotle on the Generation of Animals*. Washington: University Press of America.

Mosquera, G. 1998. "L'interprétation de l'argument λογικῶς chez Aristote." *Les Etudes Classiques* 66: 32–52.

Munteanu, D. 2012. *Tragic Pathos: Pity and Fear in Greek Philosophy and Tragedy*. Cambridge: Cambridge University Press.

Mure, G.R.G. trans. 1928. *Analytica Posteriora*. In Ross ed. 1928 and in Barnes ed. 1984.

Natali, C. 2007. "Rhetorical and scientific aspects of the *Nicomachean Ethics*." *Phronesis* 52: 364–381.

Natali, C. 2013. *Aristotle: His Life and School*. Edited by D.S. Hutchinson. Princeton: Princeton University Press.

Neschke, A.B. 1980. *Die Poetik des Aristoteles*. Frankfurt: Verlag Vittorio Klostermann.

Netz, R. 2001. "On the Aristotelian Paragraph." *Proceedings of the Cambridge Philological Society* 47: 211–232.

Nielsen, K. 2008. "The Private Parts of Animals: Aristotle on the Teleology of Sexual Difference." *Phronesis* 53: 373–405.

Nussbaum, M. 1978. *Aristotle's* De motu animalium. Princeton: Princeton University Press.

Nussbaum, M.C. 1982. "Saving Aristotle's Appearances." 267–293 in M. Schofield and M.C. Nussbaum ed. 1982. *Language and Logos: Studies in Ancient Greek Philosophy Presented to G.E.L. Owen*. Cambridge: Cambridge University Press.

Ong, W.J. 1967. *The Presence of the Word: Some Prolegomena for Cultural and Religious History*. New Haven: Yale University Press.

Ostwald, M. 2002. "Tragedians and Historians." *Scripta Classica Israelica* 21: 9–25.

Owen, G.E.L. 1960. "Logic and Metaphysics in Some Earlier Works of Aristotle." 163–190 in Düring and Owen eds. 1960.

Owen, G.E.L. 1961. "Tithenai ta Phainomena." 83–103 in S. Mansion ed. *Aristote et les problèmes de method*. Louvain and Paris: Publications Universitaires de Louvain and Éditions Béatrice Nauwelaerts. 167–190 in J.M.E. Moravcsik ed. 1968. *Aristotle: A Collection of Critical Essays*. Notre Dame: University of Notre Dame Press. 113–126 in Barnes, Schofield, and Sorabji eds. 1975. 239–251 in G.E.L. Owen. 1986. *Logic, Science, and Dialectic. Collected Papers in Greek Philosophy*. Ithaca: Cornell University Press.

Owen, G.E.L. 1965. "The Platonism of Aristotle." 14–34 in Barnes, Schofield, and Sorabji eds. 1975.

Owens, J. 1966. "Aquinas and the Proof from the 'Physics'." *Mediaeval Studies* 28: 119–150.

Owens, J. 1978. *The Doctrine of Being in the Aristotelian Metaphysics*. 3rd edn. Toronto: Pontifical Institute of Mediaeval Studies.

Paulus, J. 1933. "La Théorie du premier moteur chez Aristote." *Revue de philosophie* 33: 259–294 and 394–424.

Peck, A.L. 1942. *Aristotle: Generation of Animals*. Loeb Classical Library XIII. Cambridge: Harvard University Press.

Pegis, A.C. 1973. "St. Thomas and the Coherence of the Aristotelian Theology." *Mediaeval Studies* 35: 67–117.

Pellegrin, P. 2009. "The Argument for the Sphericity of the Universe in Aristotle's *de Caelo*: Astronomy and Physics." 163–185 in Bowen and Wildberg eds. 2009.

Pelling, C. 1997. "Aeschylus' *Persae* and History." 1–19 in C. Pelling ed. 1997. *Greek Tragedy and the Historian*. Oxford: Oxford University Press.

Pelling, C. 2000. *Literary Texts and the Greek Historian*. London and New York: Routledge.

Peramatzis, M. 2010. "Essence and *Per Se* Predication in Aristotle's *Metaphysics* z.4." *Oxford Studies in Ancient Philosophy* 39: 121–182.

Pfeiffer, R. 1968. *History of Classical Scholarship: From the Beginnings to the End of the Hellenistic Age*. Oxford: Clarendon Press.

Podlecki, A.J. 1966. *The Political Background of Aeschylean Tragedy*. Ann Arbor: University of Michigan Press.

Polansky, R. 2007. *Aristotle's De Anima*. Cambridge: Cambridge University Press.

Polansky, R. 2014. "Giving Justice its Due." 151–179 in R. Polansky ed. 2014. *The Cambridge Companion to Aristotle's Nicomachean Ethics*. Cambridge: Cambridge University Press.

Politis, V. and P. Steinkrueger. 2017. "Aristotle's Second Problem about the Possibility of A Science of Being *qua* Being: A Reconsideration of *Metaphysics* Γ 2." *Ancient Philosophy*. 37.

Powell, C.T. 1987. "Why Aristotle has no Philosophy of History." *History of Philosophy Quarterly* 4: 343–357.

Prantl, C. 1843. *De Aristotelis librorum ad historiam animalium pertinentium ordine atque dispositione*. Munich: Cotta.

Prantl, C. 1851. "Über die Probleme des Aristoteles." *Abh. Bayr. Akad. D. Wiss* 6: 339–377.

Quandt, K. 1981. "Some Puns in Aristotle." *TAPA* 111: 179–196.

Quarantotto, D. 2011. "Il dialogo dell'anima di Aristotele con se stessa. 1 *Problemata*: l'indagine e l'opera." 23–57 in B. Centrone ed. 2011. *Studi sui* Problemata Physica *Aristotelici*. Napoli: Bibliopolis.

Quarantotto, D. 2016. "Aristotle's Way away from Parmenides's Way. A Case of Scientific Controversy and Ancient Humor." *Elenchos* 37: 209–228.

Rapp, C. 2002. *Aristoteles—Rhetorik*. 2 vols. Berlin: Akademie Verlag.

Rapp, C. 2013. "Sprachliche Gestaltung und philosophische Klarheit bei Aristoteles." 283–303 in M. Erler and J. Hessler eds. *Argument und literarische Form in der antiken Philosophie*. Berlin-Boston: Walter de Gruyter.

Rashed, M. 2004. "Agrégat de parties ou vinculum substantiale?" 185–202 in Laks and Rashed eds. 2004.

Reeve, C.D.C. 1992. *Practices of Reason: Aristotle's* Nicomachean Ethics. New York: Oxford University Press.

Robb, K. 1994. *Literacy and Paideia in Ancient Greece*. New York and Oxford: Oxford University Press.

Rorty, A.O. ed. 1980. *Essays on Aristotle's Ethics*. Berkeley: University of California Press.

Rorty, A.O. ed. 1992. *Essays on Aristotle's Poetics*. Princeton: Princeton University Press.

Rose, V. 1854. *De Aristotelis librorum ordine et auctoritate commentatio*. Berlin: Reimer.

Ross, G.R.T. 1973. *Aristotle*, de Sensu *and* de Memoria. Text and translation with introduction and commentary. New York: Arno Press.

Ross, W.D. 1923. *Aristotle*. London: Methuen.

Ross, W.D. 1924. *Aristotle's Metaphysics. A Revised Text with Introduction and Commentary*. 2 vols. Oxford: Clarendon Press.

Ross, W. 1936. *Aristotle's Physics*. Oxford: Clarendon Press.

Ross, W.D. 1950. "Introduction." in W.D. Ross ed. *Aristotelis Physica*. Scriptorum Classicorum Bibliotheca Oxoniensis. Oxford: Clarendon Press.

Ross, W.D. 1965. *Aristotle's Prior and Posterior Analytics. A Revised Text with Introduction and Commentary*. Oxford: Clarendon Press.

Ross, W.D. ed. 1928. *The Works of Aristotle*. Oxford: Clarendon Press.

Rossi, L.E. 1979. "I poemi omerici come testimonianza di poesia orale." 73–147 in R. Bianchi Bandinelli ed. 1979. *Storia e Civiltà dei Greci. Origini e sviluppo della Città. Il medioevo greco* (1). Milano: Bompiani.

Sachs, J. 1995. *Aristotle's* Physics: *A Guided Study*. New Brunswick NJ: Rutgers University Press.

Schickert, K. 1977. *Die Form der Widerlegung beim frühen Aristoteles*. Munich: Verlag C.H. Beck.

Schütrumpf, E. 1989. "Form und Stil aristotelischer Pragmatien." *Philologus* 133: 177–191.

Scott, D. 2015. *Levels of Argument: A Comparative Study of Plato's* Republic *and Aristotle's* Nicomachean Ethics. Oxford: Oxford University Press.

Sedley, D. 1991. "Is Aristotle's Teleology Anthropocentric?" *Phronesis* 36: 179–196.

Shields, C. 2007. *Aristotle*. Abingdon and New York: Routledge.

Shields, C. 2015. "The Science of Soul in Aristotle's *Ethics*." 232–253 in Henry and Nielsen eds. 2015.

Sicking, C.M.J. 1998. "Aristotle and Herodotus." 147–157 in *Distant Companions: Selected Papers*. Leiden: Brill.

Siwek, P. 1963. *Aristotelis Parva naturalia graece et latine*. Rome: Romae.

Slomkowski, P. 1997. *Aristotle's* Topics. ("Philosophia antiqua", 74). Leiden, New York, Köln: Brill.

Smith, R. 1997. *Aristotle: Topics i and viii*. Oxford: Clarendon Press.

Smith, R. 1999. "Dialectic and Method in Aristotle." 39–56 in M. Sim ed. 1999. *From Puzzles to Principles? Essays on Aristotle's Dialectic*. Lanham MD: Lexington Books.

Solmsen, F. 1960a. *Aristotle's System of the Physical World: A Comparison with His Predecessors*. Ithaca: Cornell University Press.

Solmsen, F. 1960b. "Platonic Influences in the Formation of Aristotle's Physical System." 213–235 in Düring and Owen eds. 1960.

Sommerstein, A. 2008. *Aeschylus: Persians, Seven against Thebes, Suppliants, Prometheus Bound*. Cambridge MA: Harvard University Press.

Sorabji, R. 1981. "Definitions: Why Necessary and in What Way?" 205–244 E. Berti ed. 1981.

Spengel, L. 1848. "Über die Reihenfolge der naturwissenschaftlichen Schriften des Aristoteles." *Bayerische Akademie der Wissenschaften, Abhandlungen der Philosophisch-Philologische Klasse* 5.2: 143–167.

Stinton, T.C.W. 1975. "*Hamartia* in Aristotle and Greek Tragedy." *Classical Quarterly* 25: 221–254.

Stinton, T.C.W. 1990. *Collected Papers on Greek Tragedy*. Oxford: Clarendon Press.

Strauss, B. 2005. *The Battle of Salamis*. New York: Simon and Schuster.

Strauss, L. 1978. *City and Man*. Chicago: University of Chicago Press.

Striker, G. 2009. *Aristotle Prior Analytics* I. Translation with an introduction and commentary. Oxford: Clarendon Press.

Tarán, L. and D. Gutas. 2012. *Aristotle's Poetics. Editio Maior of the Greek Text with Historical Introductions and Philological Commentaries*. Leiden: Brill

Taub, L. 2015. "'Problematising' the *Problemata*: The *Problemata* in Relation to Other Question-and-Answer Texts." 413–435 in Mayhew ed. 2015.

Tessitore, A. 1996. *Reading Aristotle's Ethics*. Albany: State University of New York Press.

Thomas, R. 1994. "Literacy and The City-state in Archaic and Classical Greece." 33–50 in Bowman and Woolf eds. 1994.

Touloumakos, J. 1996. "Witz und Humor bei Aristoteles." *Tekmeria* 2: 120–134.

Tress, D. 1996. "The Metaphysical Science of Aristotle's *Generation of Animals*." 31–50 in Ward ed. 1996.

Ugaglia, M. 2004. *Modelli idrostatici del moto da Aristotele a Galielo*. Rome: Lateran University Press.

Vahlen, J. 1914. *Beiträge zu Aristoteles' Poetik*. Leipzig: Teubner.

van der Eijk, P.J. 1994. *Aristoteles. De insomniis, De divinatione per somnum*. Berlin: Akademie Verlag.

van der Eijk, P.J. 1997. "Towards a Rhetoric of Ancient Scientific Discourse: Some Formal Characteristics of Greek Medical and Philosophical Texts (Hippocratic Corpus, Aristotle)." 77–129 in E.J. Bakker ed. *Grammar as Interpretation. Greek Literature in its Linguistic Contexts*. Leiden and New York: Brill.

van der Eijk, P.J. 2005. *Medicine and Philosophy in Classical Antiquity*. Cambridge: Cambridge University Press.

van der Eijk, P.J. 2005a. "Theoretical and Empirical Elements in Aristotle's Treatment of Sleep, Dreams and Divination in Sleep." 169–205 in van der Eijk 2005.

van der Eijk, P.J. 2005b. "Divine Movement and Human Nature in *Eudemian Ethics* 8,2." 238–258 in van der Eijk 2005.

van der Eijk, P.J. 2013. "Galen and the Scientific Treatise: A Case Study of *Mixtures*." 145–175 in M. Asper ed. *Writing Science*. Berlin and New York: Walter de Gruyter.

van Riel, G. and P. Destrée eds. 2010. *Ancient Perspectives on Aristotle's* De Anima. Leuven: Leuven University Press.

Verbeke, G. 1969. "L'Argument du livre VII de la *Physique*: Une Impasse philosophique." 250–267 in I. Düring ed. 1969. *Naturphilosophie bei Aristoteles und Theophrast: Verhandlungen des 4. Symposium Aristotelicum veranstaltet in Göteborg, August, 1966*. Heidelberg: Lothar Stiehm Verlag.

Verdenius, W.J. 1985. "The Nature of Aristotle's Scholarly Writings." 12–21 in J. Wiesner ed. *Aristoteles. Werk und Wirkung*. vol. 1. Berlin: Walter de Gruyter.

Vlastos, G. 1991. *Socrates: Ironist and Moral Philosopher*. Cornell: Cornell University Press.

von Fritz, K. 1960. *Mathematiker und Akusmatiker bei den alten Pythagoreern*. München: Verlag der Bayerischen Akademie der Wissenschaften.

Waitz, T. 1844–1846. *Organon*. 2 vols. Leipzig: Hahn.

Ward, J. ed. 1996. *Feminism and Ancient Philosophy*. New York and London: Routledge.

Waterlow, S. [Broadie]. 1988. *Nature, Change, and Agency in Aristotle's* Physics: *A Philosophical Study*. Oxford: Clarendon Press.

White, S.A. 1992. "Aristotle's Favourite Tragedies." 221–240 in Rorty ed. 1992.

Whiting, J. 1988. "Aristotle's Function Argument: A Defense." *Ancient Philosophy* 8: 33–48.

Wians, W. 1989. "Aristotle, Demonstration, and Teaching." *Ancient Philosophy* 9: 245–253.

Wians, W. 1996. "Scientific Examples in the *Posterior Analytics*." 131–150 in Wians ed. 1996.

Wians, W. 2005. Review of Mayhew 2004. *Aestimatio* 2: 42–48.

Wians, W. 2012. "The Beginnings of the *Metaphysics*." 30–46 in J. Oldfield ed. *Sources of Desire: Essays on Aristotle's Theoretical Works*. Newcastle-upon-Tyne: Cambridge Scholars.

Wians, W. ed. 1996. *Aristotle's Philosophical Development: Problems and Prospects*. Lanham MD: Rowman and Littlefield.

Wieland, W. 1975. "Aristotle's Physics and Problem of Inquiry into Principles." 127–140 in Barnes, Schofield, and Sorabji eds. 1975.

Williams, B. 1985. *Ethics and the Limits of Philosophy*. Cambridge: Harvard University Press.

Williams, B. 1993. *Shame and Necessity*. Berkeley: University of California Press.

Williams, C. 1982. *Aristotle's* De Generatione et Corruptione. Oxford: Clarendon Press.

Wilson, M. 2000. *Aristotle's Theory of the Unity of Science*. Toronto: Toronto University Press.

Witt, C. 1985. "Form, Reproduction, and Inherited Characteristics in Aristotle's Generation of Animals." *Phronesis* 30: 46–57.

Witt, C. 1996. "The Evolution of Developmental Interpretations of Aristotle." 67–82 in Wians ed. 1996.

Witt, C. 2015. "'As if by Convention Alone': The Unstable Ontology of Aristotle's *Ethics*." 276–292 in Henry and Nielsen eds. 2015.

Woods, M. 1982. *Aristotle's Eudemian Ethics i, ii, and viii*. Oxford: Clarendon Press.

Zeller, E. 1862. *Die Philosophie bei den Griechen*. II.2. 2nd edn. Tübingen: L. Fr. Fues.

Zeller, E. 1962. *Aristotle and the Earlier Peripatetics: Being a Translation from Zeller's 'Philosophy of the Greeks'*. vol. 1. B.F.C. Costelloe and J.H. Muirhead trans. New York: Russell & Russell.

Zingano, M. 2005. "L'*ousia* dans le livre z de la *Métaphysique*." 99–130 in M. Narcy and A. Tordesillas eds. 2005. *La* Métaphysique *d'Aristote—perspectives contemporaines*. Paris: Vrin.

Index of Aristotle Citations

Metaphysics (*cont.*)

V 2.1013a27	157n71
V 3.1014b9–14	13
V 3.1014b16–17	90
V 6.1016b35–1017a3	95
V 7.1017a19–30	58
V 8.1017b24–26	288n27
V 9.1017b27–1018a4	156n64, 156n67
V 11.1018b33	156n64
V 26.1023b29–32	72
V 29.1024a29	157n71
VI 1	138n37, 287, 302
VI 1.1025b2–3	162
VI 1.1025b7–18	58, 60, 61
VI 1.1025b29	157n71
VI 1.1026a10–31	138n36
VI 2	283n15
VII	31–42
VII 1.1028b2	258n1
VII 2.1028b16–27	12
VII 3.1028b36–37	41
VII 3.1029a30–32	139n40
VII 3.1029a33–b3	72
VII 4	10n8, 36
VII 4.1029b13	9n5
VII 4.1029b23–1030a17	
	292n33
VII 4.1030a27–28	37
VII 4.1030a35	17n13
VII 7–9	10n8
VII 10.1035b34	157n72
VII 11.1037a10–17	138n36
VII 13	12n10
VII 13.1038b9–12	156n63
VII 15.1039b26–27	40n27
VII 15.1040a27–b2	59
VII 16.1040b5–9	254n45
VII 16.1040b21	13
VII 16.1040b23–26	157n70
VII 17	36, 57–58, 105n29
VII 17.1041b11–33	126
VIII	36
VIII 3.1043b16	40n27
IX 2.1046b8–9	83n28
IX 2.1046b15–22	85
IX 6.1048b18–35	306
IX 7.1049a13–18	90
IX 8	306n44
IX 8.1049b27–28	40n27

X 2.1053b16–21	13
X 4.1055a29–33	78
X 7	94
X 7.1057b23–34	78
XI 1.1059b26–27	157n72
XI 2.1060b20	156n64
XI 3.1061a29–b1	138n36
XI 4.1061b18–32	138n36
XI 10.1066b26	34
XII	311, 313
XII 1.1069a17–18	141n44, 155n60
XII 1.1069a25–30	12
XII 1.1069a30–b2	91n35
XII 2–5	74n24, 95
XII 3.1070a4–9	87
XII 5.1071a29	157n72
XII 6–7	58
XII 8.1074b2–3	306n44
XII 10	282n13
XIII 4.1078b17–19	281
XIII 6	33
XIII 8.1084b5	156n64
XIV 4.1091a19	34

Meteorology   6n13, 162

I 1.338a20–23	162
I 1.338a20–339a10	173, 215–216, 240
I 1.338b20	162
I 1.339a7–10	162, 242n22
I 9	89n34
II 1.353a34–b6	179
II 6.363a30–31	168n5
III 2.111b6–10	282n12
III 2–6	110n37
IV 12.390a10–15	292n33
IV 12.390b15–23	240

Nicomachean Ethics   235n46, 277–314,
                                         350

I	310
I 1.1094a1–2	134, 282
I 1.1094a3–5	283
I 1.1094a5–6	292
I 2.1094a18–22	284n16, 290
I 2.1094a22–26	284
I 2.1094a26–b11	284
I 2.1094b4–5	329
I 3	285
I 3.1094b14–22	286

18.1455b27	345n19
18.1455b29	345n19
18.1455b32–1456a3	341
18.1456a2	341n13
18.1456a10–19	351n29
18.1456a19–23	343n15
18.1456a23–25	318n6, 319n7
19.1456b4	318n6
19.1456b14–15	328
20	125n50
23	316, 320–321
23–26	318, 320n10
23.1459a18–20	320n10
23.1459a20–21	322
23.1459a21–29	321, 330
23.1459a30–32	320
23.1459a37–b1	319, 346
23.1459b7–15	341
24.1459b14	351
24.1460a14–18	325n24
24.1460a18–26	325
24.1460a23–24	318n6
24.1460a25–27	319n7
24.1460a28–30	351n29
25.1460b6	123n44
25.1460b23	319n7
25.1460b23–26	325
25.1460b32–34	328n30
25.1460b35–1461a1	325
25.1461a6	328n31
25.1461b15	319n7
26	351
26.1462a2	338n10
26.1462a18–b7	351n29

Politics 300

I 8.1256b15–32	282n13
I 9.1257a34–b5	283n15
II 7.1267b6–8	338n10
II 12.1274a14–15	338n10
III 11.1282a25–26	338n10
V 4.1304a22	323n16
V 8.1308b27–28	338n10
VI 4.1318b34–35	338n10
VI 8.1322a23–24	338n10
VII 1.1323b40–1324a4	168n7
VIII 3.1337b22–27	131
VIII 6.1341a11–13	346
VIII 7.1341b10–18	346

Posterior Analytics 56–71

I	62
I 2	4
I 2.71b19–22	62
I 2.71b20–22	16
I 2.71b22–25	62
I 2.72a6–16	91, 166n2
I 2.72a14–24	62, 166n1
I 3	68n18
I 3.72b18–22	166n2
I 4	19
I 4–5	109n36, 110, 232–233
I 4.73a37–b3	68
I 4.73b25–74a3	107, 156n64
I 4.73b26–27	61
I 5.74a35–b4	108
I 6.74b5–6	91
I 6.74b21–23	16
I 6.75a18–20	156n67
I 7	21, 278n3
I 7.75b14–17	314
I 9	30
I 9.76a17–25	166n2
I 10.76a31–32	166n2
I 10.76a32–41	158, 166n1
I 10.76a39	157n69
I 10.76b2–11	158
I 11	30
I 13.78a22–23	63
I 13.78a28–30	63
I 13.78a31–38	80
I 13.78b4–11	63
I 13.78b32–34	63
I 14.79a17–32	62n12
I 19.81b18–23	16
I 21.82b35	10n8, 18
I 21.82b37–83a1	159
I 22	18, 21
I 22.83a5–20	158
I 22.83a32–34	341
I 22.83a33	12
I 27–30	110
I 28.87a38–39	62
I 30	286
I 30.87b19–27	156n67
I 31.87b29–39	156b64
I 32	20, 21
I 32.88a37–b	157n69

General Index

Averroes 221n16, 222
axioms; *see also* principles 30, 71, 160, 166,
218, 226
axiomatic system 71

Bäck, A. 156n67
Bagnall, R.S. 131n15
Baker, S. 292n32, 295n36
Balme, D.M. 238, 240n13, 240n17, 241n18,
247n30, 254n45
Baltussen, H. 132n23
Barnes, J. 3, 4n4, 9n4, 10n8, 47n33, 56n7,
58n8, 67n17, 97n1, 128n3, 129n5, 140n43,
156n62, 157n69, 158n74, 159, 160n77,
160n78, 160n79, 161n83, 228n34, 240n17,
258n1, 282n11
Barney, R. 292n33, 296n37
Beare, J.L. 198n27
Beriger, A. 117n43
Berti, E. 128n3
Bible 197
biological works 193n21, 217, 219, 220–221,
240, 244, 282n12, 317n4
biology; *see also* physics 179, 218, 220–221,
225, 235, 239–240, 278, 288, 319n8
Bloch, D. 194n22
blood 176n16, 177, 248, 249–250, 253
Bodéüs, R. 183n6, 187n13
Bodnár, I. 103n19
body 136, 148–164, 244, 249, 269, 272, 306
human 174–176, 255n48
in relation to soul 222, 234
in *Physics* 140–142, 146, 154
indivisible 13–14
movable 150, 154
perfect magnitude 149, 152, 154
Bolotin, D. 88n33
Bolton, R. 54n6, 65n16, 167n4, 244n26,
247n31
Bonitz, H. 32n21, 157n70, 222n17
Bostock, D. 9n3, 278n2
Bouchard, E. 349n26
Bowen, A.C. 244n25
Bowman, A.K. 132n21
Brandis, C.A. 145n53
Brentano, F. 258n1
Broadie, S. (Waterlow) 85n31, 89n34, 151n57,
284n17, 285n19, 285n20, 289
Brunschwig, J. 47n34

Buckley, M.J. 56n7
Burnyeat, M.F. 4n4, 10n7, 41, 42n28, 166,
169n8, 240n14, 277, 287n24, 306n44,
309n46

Carey, C. 343n15
Carli, S. 317n4, 319n7, 321n11, 321n13, 323,
324n17, 324n19, 325, 326, 327n28,
330n36
Carteron, H. 48
Casson, L. 130, 131n17
categories 93–94, 149, 289
catharsis 327n29
cause (*aitia*); *see also* four causes; efficient
cause; final cause; formal cause; material
cause 36, 57, 61, 64–65, 67, 74, 88, 138–
139, 199, 203, 206, 232, 242, 250–251, 255,
258, 262, 266, 268, 271, 315, 318–319, 327,
336
Cavalli, F. 221n16
certainty 52
chance (*tuche*) 86–87, 138–139
change; *see also* motion
accidental vs. substantial 79, 86–89, 137–
138
Charles, D. 10n8, 54n6, 64n13
Charlton, W. 73n22, 137n33
Chiba, K. 10n7
choice (*prohairesis*) 99, 216, 282, 287, 289,
290–291, 294, 300, 301, 309, 313
choice-worthy 283, 290–291, 308–309
Chroust, A.-H. 128n3, 129n6
Cicero 182
cleverness (*deinotes*) 304–305
coincidence 199–200, 202, 203–204, 206,
321n12
Coles, A. 237n2, 251n38, 255n48
Collingwood, R.G. 316
common, universal 136, 137–145, 147–148,
154, 155, 157–161, 162–164, 232, 240–241,
242, 247n30
condensation, rarefaction 77
consistency 52, 53, 69n21
and inconsistency 237–239, 245, 248, 253,
316, 335, 338, 339, 345, 349
contemplation (*theoria*) 288, 289, 295n36,
301, 302, 303, 306, 308–313, 336
continuous 139, 140, 144, 167, 339
contrary 24, 77–78, 144, 151, 171

Printed in the United States
By Bookmasters